Physical Educat
19

Sport, History and Culture

Edited by

Professor Richard Holt
Professor Matthew Taylor

International Centre for Sports History and Culture
De Montfort University, Leicester

Vol. 11

PETER LANG
Oxford · Bern · Berlin · Bruxelles · New York · Wien

Physical Education in Irish Schools, 1900–2000: A History

Conor Curran

PETER LANG

Oxford · Bern · Berlin · Bruxelles · New York · Wien

Bibliographic information published by Die Deutsche Nationalbibliothek
Die Deutsche Nationalbibliothek lists this publication in the Deutsche
Nationalbibliografie; detailed bibliographic data is available on the Internet at
http://dnb.d-nb.de.

A catalogue record for this book is available from the British Library.

Library of Congress Cataloging-in-Publication Data

Names: Curran, Conor, author.
Title: Physical education in Irish schools, 1900–2000 : a history / Conor
    Curran.
Description: Oxford ; New York : Peter Lang, [2022] | Series: Sport, History and
    Culture, 1664-1906 ; volume 11 | Includes bibliographical references and
    index.
Identifiers: LCCN 2021032760 (print) | LCCN 2021032761 (ebook) | ISBN
    9781789978421 (Paperback) | ISBN 9781789978438 (eBook) | ISBN
    9781789978445 (ePub)
Subjects: LCSH: Physical education and training—Ireland—History—20th
    century. | Physical education and training—Curricula—Ireland. |
    Physical education teachers—Training of. |
    Education—Curricula—Ireland. | Education and
    state—Ireland—History—20th century. | Education and state—Northern
    Ireland—History—20th century. | Sports—Ireland—History—20th
    century. | Sports and state—Ireland—History—20th century.
Classification: LCC GV246.5 .C87 2022 (print) | LCC GV246.5 (ebook) | DDC
    796.071—dc23
LC record available at https://lccn.loc.gov/2021032760
LC ebook record available at https://lccn.loc.gov/2021032761

Cover image: Staff and some pupils in the gymnasium at the Royal School Portora,
Enniskillen, during the 1907-8 school year. Courtesy of Robert Northridge.

Cover design by Peter Lang Ltd.

ISSN 1664-1906
ISBN 978-1-78997-842-1 (print)
ISBN 978-1-78997-843-8 (ePDF)
ISBN 978-1-78997-844-5 (eBook)

© Peter Lang Group AG 2022

Published by Peter Lang Ltd, International Academic Publishers,
52 St Giles, Oxford, OX1 3LU, United Kingdom
oxford@peterlang.com, www.peterlang.com

This publication has been peer reviewed.

Contents

Figures

Acknowledgements

This book could not have been written without the support of the Irish Research Council. In 2017, I was awarded a two-year Government of Ireland Postdoctoral research fellowship to conduct a study of the history of physical education in Ireland. This was undertaken through the School of Education at Trinity College Dublin. I would like to express my thanks to my supervisor, Dr John Walsh, who agreed to take on the project and assisted me with the application process. Dr Walsh's advice was highly significant in my undertaking of the Fellowship and without his guidance, this study would not have been completed. I would also like to acknowledge the support of the staff of the School of Education during my time researching and teaching there, particularly Fiona McKibbin, Dr Michelle Share, Dr Andrew Loxley, Linda McHugh and Dr Andrew Gibson.

My wife Joanne and my family have also been very supportive throughout the writing of this book. Yet again, I am thankful to them for their encouragement of my passion for history and sport. I am also grateful to Professor Mike Cronin, who initially suggested that I undertake a study of the history of physical education in Ireland, and to Dr Seamus Kelly, Dr Conor Heffernan, Dr Tom Hunt, Dr Kristian Naglo, Professor Dilwyn Porter, Shane Supple, Aaron Ó Maonaigh, Seán McGourty, Mervyn Elder, Sheelagh Watford and Dr Julia Brennen for their support and advice.

Undertaking the research for this book meant numerous trips to archives. I am grateful to the staff of the National Library of Ireland in Dublin for their assistance, particularly to Berni Metcalfe and Glenn Dunne for granting me permission to publish a number of pictures from their collections. In Belfast, the staff of the Public Record Office of Northern Ireland were as always very helpful, especially the Head of Public Services there, Stephen Scarth, who has assisted me in the organisation of a number of sports history-related conferences there over the past three years. In addition, I would like to thank Avril Loughlin and the Deputy Keeper of Records there for granting me permission to reproduce a number of PRONI's photographs in this book. I also owe my thanks to William Lynn of Foyle College Archive, Sharon Casement of the Royal Belfast Academical Institution, Laura McKinney of Methodist College, Robert Northridge of Portora Royal School, Blackrock College archivist Clare Foley, Declan O'Keeffe of Clongowes Wood College and Paddy O'Reilly of Trinity Comprehensive who were all very helpful in providing me with a large selection of pictures. I am also very grateful to Seán McGeown of the Department of Education of Northern Ireland, and to the staff of Belfast Central Library.

I would also like to express my thanks to the staff of a number of educational bodies in the Republic of Ireland, particularly the Department of Education, the Secretariat of Secondary Schools and the Irish National Teachers' Organisation. I am also grateful to the Gaelic Athletic Association, the Football Association of Ireland and the Irish Football Association for allowing me to access their archives. I am also thankful to the thirty-five teachers who took part in the interviews which feature in this book. I would also like to thank Professor Tom O'Donoghue for granting me access to his postgraduate thesis. Finally, I wish to express my gratitude to Professor Richard Holt and Professor Matthew Taylor for accepting my proposal for their sports history and culture book series and to Lucy Melville and the staff of Peter Lang.

Abbreviations

ASTI	Association of Secondary Teachers of Ireland
BSA	Birmingham Small Arms (Company)
BTEC	Business and Technology Education Council
CBS	Christian Brothers' School
CPE	Curricular Physical Education
CYMS	Catholic Young Men's Society
FAI	Football Association of Ireland
GAA	Gaelic Athletic Association
GCSE	General Certificate of Secondary Education
HODS	Heads of Department
ICHPER	International Council on Health, Physical Education and Recreation
IFA	Irish Football Association
INTO	Irish National Teachers' Organisation
IRA	Irish Republican Army
IRFU	Irish Rugby Football Union
JBM	Joint Managerial Body
JP	Justice of the Peace
MOH	Medical Officer of Health
NACA	National Athletic and Cycling Association
NCCA	National Council for Curriculum and Assessment

NCPE	National College of Physical Education
NICER	Northern Ireland Council for Educational Research
NIHE	National Institute of Higher Education
NIPEA	Northern Ireland Physical Education Association
NS	National School
NUI	National University of Ireland
PE	Physical Education
PEAI	Physical Education Association of Ireland
PRO	Public Relations Officer
PRONI	Public Record Office of Northern Ireland
PT	Physical Training
PTI	Physical Training Instructor
RIC	Royal Irish Constabulary
RUC	Royal Ulster Constabulary
SCNI	Sports Council for Northern Ireland
TD	Teachta Dála
UCPE	Ulster College of Physical Education
VEC	Vocational Educational Committee

Introduction

On the eve of the twenty-first century, physical education was a subject which still remained on the periphery of the curriculum in both primary and second level schools in the Republic of Ireland. In November 1988, Fine Gael politician Jimmy Deenihan, a man who had achieved sporting success as part of the Kerry senior men's Gaelic football team in a career that spanned from 1973 until 1983, winning five All-Ireland medals amongst numerous other honours, described the subject's treatment by the Irish government as 'a national scandal'.[1] Deputy Deenihan was a man with sport close to his heart and was a qualified physical education teacher. He had come through a new system which had been established in the early 1970s for those seeking qualifications in the subject.[2] The foundation of the National College of Physical Education in Limerick in 1973, the first co-educational centre for training physical education teachers in the Republic of Ireland, had offered much promise.[3] In addition, in a frenzy of enthusiasm which had largely dissipated within Irish political circles by the late 1980s, the Irish government had introduced a revised curriculum for primary schools which included a new system of physical education in 1971.[4] While there were some curricular improvements in the early part of that decade, physical education continued to be neglected and this was laid bare in a number of European surveys carried out in the latter decade of the twentieth

---

1   'Dáil Éireann Debate – Tuesday, 8 Nov 1988. Vol. 383, No. 8. Private Members' Business. – National Lottery (Amendment) Bill, 1988: Second Stage.' Retrieved from <https://www.oireachtas.ie/en/debates/debate/dail/1988-11-08/21/> [Accessed 2 November 2020].

2   *Irish Examiner*, 3 December 1973.

3   *Belfast Telegraph*, 26 February 1973.

4   *Irish Examiner*, 24 November 1971 and *INTO Primary School Curriculum Survey* (Dublin: INTO, 1974), 17 and 23.

century as Ireland was regularly shown to be at the bottom of tables related to time allocated to the subject.[5] Many Irish second level schools
did place an emphasis on sporting success, with strong traditions of
codes such as rugby, soccer, hurling and Gaelic football developing in
numerous schools, but the place of PE in the curriculum was often neglected at the expense of sporting glory.[6] It also developed an unfortunate
reputation as one which was frowned upon by non-specialist teachers
and was open to abuse in terms of pupil participation, particularly by
students taking final examinations in subjects considered more worthy
of academic prowess and more valuable for a future career path. It was
not until 2017 that the Department of Education announced that physical education would be piloted as a Leaving Certificate examination
subject in a number of secondary schools.[7]

Deputy Deenihan was not the only politician to win All-Ireland
medals, but he was one of the few to push for the development of an adequate system of physical education in Irish schools. This reluctance on the
government's part to take physical education seriously contrasted to most
other countries in Western Europe. The development of sport in Ireland
followed patterns elsewhere to a certain extent, but there were also distinct
differences. Christopher Young has noted the unique way in which codified
sport grew in Ireland.[8] In looking at how it developed differently there, he
points to the arguments of Richard Holt. Writing in 2009, Holt stated that

> British sport claimed proudly to be above politics, but it was permeated with im-
> perial values and class distinctions. French sport was based on the British model but
> explicitly designed to strengthen France after her defeat at the hands of Prussia in
> 1870. In Germany and more widely in continental Europe more attention was given

5   *Irish Independent*, 6 August 1996 and 26 August 1997.
6   See, for example, *Irish Independent*, 3 November 1980.
7   'Curriculum and Syllabus: Phase 1 Physical Education in Senior Cycle' Retrieved
     from <https://www.education.ie/en/Schools-Colleges/Information/Curriculum-
     and-Syllabus/leaving-certificate-physical-education.html> [Accessed 25 March
     2018].
8   Christopher Young, 'Sport in West and North Europe' in Robert Edelman and
     Wayne Wilson, *The Oxford Handbook of Sports History* (Oxford: Oxford University
     Press, 2017), 331–45, 333.

to collective forms of gymnastic exercise than to modern sports. America invented a new national sport [baseball] and turned it into a business.[9]

As Holt has also noted, 'Ireland picked its way through this maze, rejecting the monotony of mass gymnastics but also refusing to follow the dominant forms of British sport. It adopted amateur values but rejected the social distinctions that went with them.'[10] The Irish public 'embraced spectator sport but refused the American model of sport as commercial entertainment' and 'in doing so Ireland created a unique blend of the traditional and the modern', with the Gaelic Athletic Association [GAA] emerging, after a rocky start, as the most successfully organised sporting organisation in Ireland by the early twenty-first century.[11] Efforts to develop a satisfactory system of physical education ebbed and flowed over the course of the twentieth century, with the Irish government generally reluctant to invest heavily in sport for much of that period following partition in 1921.[12]

This book explores a major aspect of the daily school lives of children and teenagers who grew up in twentieth-century Ireland which has not yet received a full academic assessment.[13] Set within the period from 1900 until

9   Richard Holt, 'Ireland and the Birth of Modern Sport' in Mike Cronin, William Murphy and Paul Rouse (eds), *The Gaelic Athletic Association 1884–2009* (Dublin: Irish Academic Press, 2009), 33–45, 45.
10   Ibid.
11   Ibid.
12   For an assessment of the effects of partition on Irish society see in particular Cormac Moore, *Birth of the Border: The Impact of Partition in Ireland* (Kildare: Merrion Press, 2019). Following the Government of Ireland Act of 1920 and the Anglo-Irish War, which led to a truce and partition in 1921, the Irish Free State, consisting of twenty-six counties, eventually established its own government in Dublin while Northern Ireland, consisting of six counties, developed its own government in Belfast.
13   Although 'Physical Education' was generally not the term used by the Department of Education for this modern day subject in the early years of the Irish Free State with 'drill', 'physical drill' and 'physical training' more commonplace, it has been used as an umbrella term for this book's central topic at various stages throughout. In 1932 the *Revised Notes for Teachers: Drill* was amended to *Revised Notes for Teachers: Physical Training* following a suggestion from Inspector Morris who was involved in their drafting. He noted that 'Physical Training', 'Drill' and 'Physical Education' had been utilised in the draft text. By the late 1930s the term 'Physical

2000, it is the first detailed study of the history of physical education across Ireland and examines why Independent Ireland's governments neglected its place within primary and secondary schools for the greater part of the twentieth century. The state of PE in Ireland in the early twentieth century is assessed, and the factors which fostered, or discouraged, the implementation of this subject within Irish schools are examined. The reasons why Irish governments failed to establish PE as a compulsory subject within Irish schools until the 1970s are investigated, and a comparison of wider international trends, and more closer to home, with Northern Ireland, which is examined through separate chapters, is given. How PE became integrated into Irish schools and became accepted as a genuine subject worthy of teaching is established through an investigation of the role of the government, teacher-training bodies and educationalists in its development. This book also examines some of the educational experiences of retired and active primary and second level school teachers from the late 1940s until the early 2000s.

This monograph makes a significant contribution to the historiography of education while adding to the increasing range of academic writing on the development of sport in Ireland. It is also highly significant in terms of contemporary European Commission debates about obesity, health care, socio-economic accessibility and state-saving and whether or not sufficient time is being devoted to physical education within schools.[14] While naturally there is some overlap with school sports and games, and these have been assessed at various stages throughout, it is important to state that this is not a history of school competitions. As the main focus is on mainstream primary and second level schools, it is also not intended to examine PE within Reformatory or Industrial Schools in this monograph. A dearth of space also means that the development of PE in Special schools is similarly not given the analysis merited, but it is intended to return to research this more fully at a later stage.

Education' had become more common. See NAI ED/12/31032. 'Revised Notes for Teachers' Drill. Physical Training in National Schools, Preparatory Colleges and in Training Colleges. Memo of 9.9.32 of Chief Inspector' and TAOIS/S11053. 'Physical Education. The Report of the Committee, 1938', 8.

14   See, for example, *Irish Examiner*, 7 May 2015.

The Historiography of Physical Education in Ireland

Despite a growing awareness of the value of health, fitness and recreation within modern society, government policies towards physical education in Ireland in the twentieth century have not yet received a comprehensive historical examination.[15] Mainstream texts on modern Irish history have generally failed to assess the development of physical education within Irish schools. Specialist works on education in Ireland fail to provide an in-depth analysis of the evolution of physical education.[16] Most specialised studies of the history of Irish teacher-training colleges have also neglected to examine how the training of PE was dealt with in their assessments.[17] An exception is David Fleming's study of the University of Limerick, in which the author, in a detailed chapter on the early development of the National College of Physical Education [NCPE], which was later replaced by Thomond College of Education, notes that by the 1960s, 'physical education was among the new subjects that the department wished to promote' in schools.[18] This decade is generally associated

---

15 *Irish Times*, 6 May 2015.
16 See in particular, Séamus Ó Buachalla, *Education Policy in Twentieth Century Ireland* (Dublin: Wolfhound Press, 1988), 66 and 266; John Coolahan, *Irish Education: History and Structure* (Dublin: Institute of Public Administration, 1981), 40 and *Towards the Era of Lifelong Learning: A History of Irish Education 1800–2016* (Dublin: Institute of Public Administration, 2017), 28; Donald Harman Akenson, *A Mirror to Kathleen's Face: Education in Independent Ireland 1922–1960* (Montreal and London: McGill-Queen's University Press, 1975); *Education and Enmity: The Control of Schooling in Northern Ireland 1920–1950* (New York: David & Charles (Holdings) Limited, Newton Abbot/Barnes & Noble Books, 1973) and Seán Farren, *The Politics of Irish Education 1920–65* (Belfast: The Institute of Irish Studies, 1995), 16.
17 See, for example, James Kelly (ed.), *St Patrick's College Drumcondra: A History* (Dublin: Four Courts Press, 2006), 151.
18 David A. Fleming, *The University of Limerick: A History* (Dublin: Four Courts Press, 2012), 83–102.

with the expansion of education in the Republic of Ireland.[19] In particular, Fleming sees the Physical Education Association of Ireland [PEAI], established in 1967, and Captain Michael McDonough of the Irish Army, as key to the development of the subject in post-primary education.[20] The work of John O'Callaghan on the GAA is also valuable in his examination of structures for the training of PE teachers immediately prior to and after the founding of the NCPE in Limerick in 1973.[21]

This book draws largely on research carried out for an Irish Research Council postdoctoral fellowship on the history of physical education in Ireland which was undertaken by the author and builds on a small number of related studies of the subject previously published.[22] The initial work of Thomas O'Donoghue is an important starting point for any examination of physical education's history in Ireland. A chapter by Judith Harford and O'Donoghue on secondary school education prior to 1967 briefly re-emphasises the latter author's earlier findings on physical education, noting that 'from the 1930s, army and ex-army gymnastics instructors taught Swedish drill and put on drill displays for the public at annual school

19   See John Walsh, *The Politics of Expansion: The Transformation of Educational Policy in the Republic of Ireland, 1957–72* (Manchester: Manchester University Press, 2009).

20   Fleming, *The University of Limerick*, 83.

21   John O'Callaghan, *Plassey's Gaels: A History of the GAA at NIHE, NCPE, Thomond College and the University of Limerick, 1972–2012* (Cork: The Collins Press, 2013), 7–11. The NCPE was replaced by Thomond College in 1975 and this became part of the University of Limerick in 1991.

22   This has developed from a number of the author's research outputs including, Conor Curran, 'Physical Education in Ireland, 1922–1973.' Trinity College Dublin Contemporary Irish History Lecture, 2019; Conor Curran, 'The Irish Government and Physical Education in Primary Schools, 1922–37' in *Irish Historical Studies*, vol. 45, no. 167, (May 2021), 43–60, 47–8; Conor Heffernan and Conor Curran, 'Much Ado about Nothing? The Problems of Irish Physical Education, 1820–1920' in *Sporting Traditions*, vol. 37, no. 1 (May 2020), 65–86 and Conor Curran, 'The Development of Physical Education in Northern Ireland, 1922–1953 and the Role of Joan Burnett-Knight' in Conor Curran and Dilwyn Porter (eds), Sport and Education in Ireland: Special edition of *Sport in Society*, vol. 23, no. 8 (2020), 1299–319.

sports days'.[23] Drawing on his M.Ed. thesis, O'Donoghue had examined the attempt by the Department of Defence to introduce the Sokol system of physical education into Irish schools in the 1930s in an article published in *Irish Educational Studies* in 1985.[24] He has also looked at the Department of Education's policies towards sport in the period from 1926 until 1948 in the *International Journal of the History of Sport*.[25] He also sees the appointment of Captain Michael McDonough as inspector of PE in 1965 as key to its later growth in the Republic of Ireland, stating that it was not until then that 'physical education re-established itself' there.[26]

A number of unpublished postgraduate and doctoral studies have also shed some light on physical education's development in Ireland in the twentieth century. Written in 1939, Ellen Cooney's Masters dissertation is important in that it provides a contemporary account of the Sokol system of physical training and its impact on Irish schools.[27] Joseph Moran's 2013 postgraduate thesis is of note in that it mainly utilises interviews with a number of physical training instructors while also assessing a number of

23 Judith Harford and Tom O'Donoghue, 'Exploring the Experience of Secondary-School Education in Ireland Prior to 1967' in James Kelly and Susan Hegarty (eds), *Schools and Schooling, 1650–2000: New Perspectives on the History of Education* (Dublin: Four Courts Press, 2017), 159–77, 164.

24 Thomas A. O'Donoghue, 'The Policy of the State on the Promotion of Physical Education in Irish Secondary Schools 1924–73' (unpublished M.Ed. thesis, Trinity College Dublin, 1985) and 'The Attempt by the Department of Defence to Introduce the Sokol System of Physical Education into Irish Schools in the 1930s' in *Irish Educational Studies*, vol. 5, no. 2 (1985), 329–42.

25 Thomas A. O'Donoghue, 'Sport, Recreation and Physical Education: The Evolution of a National Policy of Regeneration in Éire, 1926–48' in *The International Journal of the History of Sport*, vol. 3, no. 2 (1986), 216–33.

26 O'Donoghue, 'The Attempt by the Department of Defence', 340. See also Paul Rouse, *Sport and Ireland: A History* (Oxford: Oxford University Press, 2015), 316–17.

27 Ellen Cooney, 'The Tendency towards Physical Training in the Sokol Way' (unpublished Minor Dissertation for Degree of M.A. in Educational Science, University College Dublin, 1939).

government files.[28] Captain Michael McDonough, in his M.Ed. thesis, drew
on an earlier analysis of the development of the subject in Ireland that he
had conducted for the Irish government in 1965, which is useful given that
this report does not now appear to be publicly available.[29] While this is
an important study, his thesis was written in 1980 and lacks a full examination of the archives now available to the researcher.[30] Similarly, Michael
Anthony Cotter's 1978 study of physical education in primary schools after
the introduction of the Revised Primary School Curriculum is important
in highlighting that despite the subject being compulsory at that level by
the late 1970s, issues remained, particularly regarding its full implementation and identity as a serious element of a school's weekly structure.[31]

Patrick Duffy, in his 1997 doctoral study of government policies towards PE, focuses mainly on the years from 1960 until 1996. He notes that
PE was largely ignored by the Department of Education until the 1960s
due to 'the strong academic and examination orientation of the school
system' while the Constitution of Ireland 'specifically excluded the State
from playing a mandatory role in the provision of physical education.'[32] Seán
McGourty's 1987 Masters thesis, entitled 'The Boys' Physical Education
Curriculum in Secondary Schools in Northern Ireland' is an important
work in understanding how PE developed there, but as yet no one has
undertaken a study of how its implementation differed historically within

28 Joseph Moran, 'The Role of the Military in the Development of Physical Education
    in Irish Schools from 1922 to 1973' (unpublished M. Science [Sports Studies] thesis,
    University College Dublin, 2013).
29 Captain Michael McDonough, 'Physical Education and the Sports Complex in the
    Community School' (unpublished M.Ed. thesis, Trinity College Dublin 1980).
30 Ibid.
31 Michael Anthony Cotter, 'An Investigation into the Teaching of Physical Education
    in National Schools (Public Primary Schools) in the Republic of Ireland' (unpub-
    lished M.Ed. thesis, Trinity College Dublin, 1978), 184–8.
32 Patrick Duffy, 'State Policy on School Physical Education with Specific Reference to
    the Period 1960–1996' (unpublished Ph.D. thesis, St Patrick's College Maynooth,
    1997), 1.

the contrasting education systems in the Republic of Ireland and Northern Ireland in the years after 1921 until the end of the twentieth century.[33]

In an article published in the *Irish Journal of Education* in 1978, Mike Sleap has noted what he calls 'the piecemeal development of the subject' and has stated that 'up till the 1960s, it was rarely taught in secondary schools and then only because of the keen interest of a principal and where facilities allowed'.[34] Denis O'Boyle has stated that 'up to 1965, there existed little or no financial commitment by the Department of Education towards the subject'.[35] As will be shown, both Sleap and O'Boyle's comments are in need of some revision, as the matter was not as straightforward as has been portrayed.

PE's development in Ireland has rarely featured in international publications examining the subject's history. Allen Guttmann has discussed the political and physical motivations behind the development of PE in a number of European countries and in the United States of America in the 1800s, while also assessing State control of sport in Communist, Nazi and Fascist countries in Europe in the following century.[36] He notes how these regimes 'programmatically instrumentalized sports as a means to demonstrate national revitalization and to symbolize ideological superiority', but says less about governments which were somewhat apathetic towards the development of sport within the educational system, as was the case in Independent Ireland for most of the twentieth century.[37] J. G. Dixon, P. C. McIntosh, A. D. Munrow and R. F. Willets focus mainly on major developments in Ancient Greece, Imperial Rome, Renaissance Italy, Tudor England and its more modern growth in Scandinavia, Prussia, the

---

33　Seán McGourty, 'The Boys' Physical Education Curriculum in Secondary Schools in Northern Ireland' (unpublished M.A. in Education thesis, Queen's University, Belfast, 1987).

34　Mike Sleap, 'A Survey of Physical Education in Irish Post-Primary Schools' in *The Irish Journal of Education*, vol. xii, no. 2 (1978), 107–18, 107.

35　Denis O'Boyle, 'Examinations in Physical Education: An Irish perspective' in *Irish Educational Studies*, vol. 6, no. 2 (1986), 176–91, 177.

36　Allan Guttmann, *Sports: The First Five Millennia* (Amherst and Boston: University of Massachusetts Press, 2000), 273–84 and 293–306.

37　Ibid., 293.

United States of America and England in their 1957 edited collection, *Landmarks in the History of Physical Education*.[38] John Welshman has noted key themes in physical culture and sport in England and Wales in the years from 1900 until 1940 but says little on how Northern Ireland was affected by changes in policy and teaching in the period.[39] He has written that 'the history of physical education has been generally neglected, and the few existing accounts tend to define it in relatively narrow terms'.[40] This, he believes, was possibly because the majority of initial work on the subject was carried out by those involved in PE teacher training.[41] He feels that the work of McIntosh, WD Smith and Sheila Fletcher generally can be placed in this category.[42] Steve Bailey and Wray Vamplew's *100 Years of Physical Education 1899–1999*, despite its title, focuses heavily on the Physical Education Association of the United Kingdom and offers nothing of note on Northern Ireland.[43] Similarly, Malcolm Tozer's *Edward Thring's Theory, Practice and Legacy: Physical Education in Britain since 1800* says little of developments in Northern Ireland, but this monograph is of value in examining how the subject took hold across the Irish Sea.[44] The combined work of Richard Holt and Tony Mason, *Sport in Britain 1945–2000*, through its examination of sport in schools in mainland Britain, is also of importance in that it provides an important framework for how physical education developed in Northern Ireland, despite the pronounced religious divides

38   J. G. Dixon, P. C. McIntosh, A. D. Munrow and R. F. Willets (eds), *Landmarks in the History of Physical Education* (London: Routledge, 1957).
39   John Welshman, 'Physical Culture and Sport in Schools in England and Wales, 1900–40' in *The International Journal of the History of Sport*, vol. 15, no. 1 (1998), 54–75.
40   Ibid., 54.
41   Ibid.
42   Ibid., and P. C. McIntosh, *Physical Education in England since 1800* (London, 1952); W. D. Smith, *Stretching Their Bodies: A History of Physical Education* (London, 1974) and Sheila Fletcher, *Women First: The Female Tradition in English Physical Education 1880–1980* (London, 1984).
43   Steve Bailey and Wray Vamplew, *100 Years of Physical Education 1899–1999* (Warwick: Warwick Printing, 1999).
44   Malcolm Tozer, *Edward Thring's Theory, Practice and Legacy: Physical Education in Britain since 1800* (Cambridge: Cambridge Scholars Publishing, 2019).

within the area.[45] Despite these assessments, much less has been published on the status of physical education itself within Irish schools throughout the twentieth century. Therefore, this new monograph aims to fill this gap within the historiography of both Irish education and sports history.

Methodology

A thematic approach is used within this book, which contains eleven chapters. These are generally set out on a chronological basis, with two of these focused on primary and second level schools in pre-partition Ireland, while six are based on its development in what is now the Republic of Ireland and three on Northern Ireland. This book utilises a number of sources which have not been fully assessed in previous studies of the history of physical education in Ireland. It makes extensive use of numerous national and provincial newspapers which have recently become more accessible through the Irish Newspaper Archives and the British Newspaper Archives.[46] Specialist newspapers, such as the *Irish Teachers' Journal*, available in the National Library of Ireland, have also been used as a source, while the *Reports of the Commissioners on National Education*, which contain valuable inspectors' reports from schools around Ireland, have also been utilised to assess the development of physical drill in the period from 1900 until 1920. Similarly, Intermediate Education Inspectors' reports from 1909 to 1910 are highly significant in providing a clearer picture of the state of physical exercise and the various forms provided in Irish second level schools at that time. Following partition, the system of primary and second level education in Ireland was amended in the early

---

45   Richard Holt and Tony Mason, *Sport in Britain 1945–2000* (Oxford: Blackwell Publishers, 2000).

46   The term 'Ulster' has been used to cover Northern Ireland in some newspaper reports included in this book. Geographically and politically, however, this terminology is incorrect as Donegal, Monaghan and Cavan are also part of the province of Ulster, yet lie within the Republic of Ireland.

1920s. The online availability of Dáil debates means that a clearer picture of how the Irish government treated the development of PE emerges through this study. Files on PE in the National Archives of Ireland in Dublin, such as that related to the National Programme Conference of 1925–6, where physical drill's status in the Irish Free State was reduced from a compulsory subject to an optional one, have also been examined. Three important reports on plans to develop PE in Independent Ireland in the period from 1938 to 1943, which are also located there, have also been assessed. Similarly, the use of military files at Cathal Brugha Barracks allow for a more in-depth look at military interaction with schools and training colleges, and the attempts to develop what was then the Czechoslovakian system of Sokol in a number of Irish schools in the 1930s.

An examination of the files of the Department of Education was also undertaken. These included departmental circulars, papers and progress reports. Reports from a number of teaching unions including the Irish National Teachers' Organisation [INTO] were also assessed, along with those from the Secretariat of Secondary Schools. The archives of Blackrock College were also used to assess their policies on sport and how this fitted into governmental policy on the teaching of physical education. The files of a number of national governing bodies for sport were also utilised, including the GAA and the Football Association of Ireland.

In Northern Ireland, the availability of Ministry of Education reports and files at the Public Record Office of Northern Ireland in Belfast have allowed the researcher to examine key developments which had previously not been assessed, such as the 1938 Physical Training and Recreation Bill and the rationale behind the government's decision to open the first specialist training college for PE in Belfast in 1953. Similarly, Cabinet, Finance and Local Authorities' files were also utilised as part of this study. The Department of Education of Northern Ireland's annual reports have also been included here for the first time in the context of developments in PE. Educational material in Belfast Central Library, such as that on the Ulster College of Physical Education, has also been accessed. The provision by Sheelagh Watford of the private papers of her aunt, Joan Burnett-Knight, who was PE organiser in Northern Ireland from 1944 until 1950, was also beneficial to this study in that they shed light on Miss Burnett-Knight's role in England, Northern Ireland and Germany in the mid-twentieth century. The files of the Irish Football Association are also of value in terms of resistance to the playing of soccer in grammar schools, and the organisation of schools' competitions.

An important and relatively novel part of this study involved teacher interviews. The views of fifteen primary and ten secondary school teachers who taught in the Republic of Ireland at various stages from the late 1950s onwards were explored. A mixture of serving and retired teachers from a variety of schools located in urban and rural locations were interviewed. Teachers were chosen from a range of schools including denominational, multi-denominational and non-state funded private schools. The views of teachers in co-educational and gender-specific schools were also explored, while the socio-economic status of schools was also taken into account. As this study also includes developments in Northern Ireland, interviews with ten post-primary teachers of PE were undertaken. An emphasis was placed on teacher-training experiences – how PE has been taught, the level of teacher training available, government policies towards the subject's implementation, staff and students' attitudes towards PE, and access to resources and facilities. Their inclusion means that an oral primary source can be used to gain Irish primary and secondary school teachers' personal experiences and allows for a more comprehensive analysis of how government policies were viewed.

The Development of Physical Drill in Primary Schools in Pre-partition Ireland

Introduction

This chapter examines the nineteenth and early twentieth century development of what is now referred to as physical education in Europe. It assesses the origins and growth of systems of physical training there, with particular emphasis on the work of Friedrich Ludwig Jahn and Per Henrik Ling. It will set these developments within the context of the sporting 'revolution' and discusses how drill was more favoured in British schools. In tracing the origins of modern school systems in Ireland, it illustrates how political connections with Britain, cemented through the Act of Union of 1800, meant that physical drill was initially the first form of physical training adopted on a compulsory basis within the Irish primary education system in the early 1900s. While a nationwide formal system for national schools had been established through the Stanley Letter in 1831, it was not until the 1900s that physical education began to gain more attention with the Second Boer War of 1899–1902 a factor in this.[1] The *Revised Programme for National Schools* of 1900 led to drill being more formally introduced and by the following year almost all of Ireland's primary schools had a physical drill programme.[2] Despite this initial surge of interest, resistance to its implementation temporarily came in some areas such as Munster with fears that the new subject was being

---

1   Coolahan, *Towards the Era of Lifelong Learning*, 9–10 and O'Donoghue, 'Sport, Recreation and Physical Education', 216–17.
2   *The Sixty-Eighth Report of the Commissioners of National Education in Ireland. Year 1901.* (Dublin: Alexander Thom, 1902), Section I. 38–9.

utilised as preparation for military recruitment.[3] However, it was initially quite well received and classes were organised to provide instruction for teachers in the subject with military men involved while private instructors also advertised their services in the national and local press.[4] The place of physical drill within teacher-training colleges such as St Patrick's College Drumcondra will also be examined as it was in these that trainee teachers received instruction in it, but many of those already qualified as teachers clearly struggled to master the new subject.[5] By the second decade of the twentieth century, inspectors' reports were indicating that issues with facilities and equipment were clearly hindering progress, while the introduction of Swedish Drill after 1909 meant that two systems of physical education were in use in Irish primary schools. The results of governmental attempts to develop a universal system in schools varied throughout the country.[6]

Physical Education's Growth and Spread in Europe

While forms of organised physical education have a history which stretches back to ancient civilisations, as Allen Guttmann has written, the roots of modern PE, as we know it today, can be traced back to the *Turnen* movement which originated in Germany in the early 1800s.[7] Friedrich Ludwig Jahn, known to his peers as *Turnvater* Jahn, felt that physical exercises for pupils should take place in the countryside rather than the

---

3   *The Cork Examiner*, 31 October, 21 and 29 November 1900.
4   Conor Curran, 'The Implementation of Physical Education in Primary Schools in the Irish Free State, 1922–1932.' Sport and Education in Ireland: History, Policy and Contemporary Issues Conference, Trinity College Dublin, 2018.
5   Curran, 'The Irish Government and Physical Education in Irish Primary Schools, 1922–37' in *Irish Historical Studies*, vol. 45, no. 167 (May 2021), 43–60, 47–8.
6   Ibid.
7   Guttmann, *Sports: The First Five Millennia*, 273. For an examination of practices in Ancient Greece and Rome, see Dixon, McIntosh, Munrow and Willets (eds), *Landmarks in the History of Physical Education*, 5–59.

classroom, and developed a *Turnplatz* which consisted of rings, ropes, platforms and towers.[8] As Mike Cronin has noted, *Turnen* was a type of gymnastics 'which was centred in ideals of exercise and bodily control'.[9] It later became institutionalised in private clubs across Germany and gymnastics there underwent a process of *Verschulung* or scholastification whereby 'German educators transformed Jahn's boisterous open-air activity into an indoor routine closely akin to military drill'.[10] Adolf Spiess had taught PE in Basel having moved there in 1844 and it was there that he established the methods of *Schulturnen* or educational gymnastics which later swept through the system of education in Germany.[11]

Although many modern sports placed an emphasis on the struggle against time, in *Turnen* and other types of gymnastic movement the focus was on control of space.[12] Gradually, however there was a decline in support for *Turnen*, but *Schulturnen* had a strong impact in a number of other countries. Jahn's friend Carl Euler, who took up residence in Brussels in 1860, modified the German system there and in 1865 a Belgian gymnastics federation was established by native Nicolaas Jan Cupérus.[13] A Dutch national association for PE was set up in the Netherlands in 1862 by a number of teachers inspired by Euler, while a Swiss migrant, Rodolfo Obermann, established a course in military gymnastics in 1833 in Turin. He later trained teachers in 1861 through the support of the Minister of Education, and in 1878 PE became compulsory in all Italy's schools. Despite this, a lack of funding meant that this law was difficult to implement at that time.[14]

In Scandinavia, cultural links with Germany meant that *Turnen* would find a presence there, with a *Turnverein* founded in Oslo by a German, Joseph Stockinger, in 1855.[15] However, Swedish physical educators were

---

8   Ibid.
9   Mike Cronin, *Sport: A Very Short Introduction* (Oxford: Oxford University Press, 2014), 41.
10   Guttmann, *Sports*, 274.
11   Ibid., 276–7.
12   Ibid., 276.
13   Ibid.
14   Ibid., 276–7.
15   Ibid., 280.

eager to develop their own methods of gymnastic training. The founder of Swedish gymnastics, Per Henrik Ling, drew on the teachings of Johann Christoph GutMuths rather than those of Jahn. He established his own system by rejecting the ropes, bars, rings and beams that were commonplace within the *Turnen* movement, and set up the Royal Central Gymnastic Institute in Stockholm in 1813, which is the oldest teacher-training institute for sport and gymnastics.[16] In Denmark, NFS Grundtvig was instrumental in the development of gymnastics there and as Hans Bonde notes, 'became a key exponent for continental Europe's attempt to maintain gymnastics' precedence over British competitive sport'.[17]

Richard Holt has shown that in France, gym was made compulsory in state schools by Minister of Education, Victor Duroy, in 1869, but a scarcity of space and equipment, and the unwillingness of teachers to supervise these lessons, meant that this initiative was not a great success.[18] By the late nineteenth century the military threat of their largest eastern neighbour saw the French adopt 'German style exercises which were designed solely to increase strength' rather than 'the Swedish type of gymnastics which placed greater emphasis on agility, grace and good posture'.[19] Despite this, in France, 'school gymnastics were relatively unimportant and most schools, even *lycées*, lacked the basic equipment'.[20]

In England, Ling's methods gained greater popularity than in France. Martina Bergman-Osterberg had a strong impact on British females' physical education and had trained in the Central Institute of Physical Education in Stockholm.[21] She was appointed Superintendent of Physical Education for London's schools in 1881 and went on to found the Hampstead Physical

16   Michael Krüger and Annette R. Hofmann, 'The Development of Physical-Education Institutions in Europe: A Short Introduction' in *International Journal of the History of Sport*, vol. 32, no. 6 (2015), 737–9, 738.

17   Hans Bonde, *Gymnastics and Politics. Nils Bukh and Male Aesthetics* (Gylling: Narayana Press, 2006), 12.

18   Richard Holt, *Sport and Society in Modern France* (London and Basingstoke, The MacMillan Press Ltd., 1981), 42.

19   Ibid., 48–9.

20   Ibid., 49.

21   Guttmann, *Sports*, 277 and 280.

Training College four years later.[22] In 1895, she set up a college at Dartford (Kent), with the Ling system favoured in her teaching, although the value of games was also recognised and a number of her female students devised rules for the sport of netball in 1900.[23]

As Guttmann states, 'the variants of European gymnastics seem only marginally different from one another when one compares all of them with the modern sports that all of them opposed'.[24] The Czechoslovakian Sokol movement developed initially from the *Turnen* although ironically, 'the Slavs resorted to a product of German culture in their efforts to liberate themselves from the political shackles of German and Austrian rule'.[25] However, they did not oppose modern sports to the same extent that the *Turnen* did, but placed a focus on their own language, literature, music and costume rather than German culture.[26] Miroslav Tyrs, a middle-class Czech student, established the first *Sokol* (Falkon) early in 1862, while Jindrich Fügner, an insurance salesman, became the movement's first president. Both were on the executive council of the Young Czechs, who were part of the Czech national Party. They were not the only men to develop German gymnastics into a vehicle for Slavic nationalism, with clubs also founded in Slovenia and in West Poland.[27] In 1937, the Sokol movement in Czechoslovakia had more than 800,000 members, just before it was put down by the Nazis.[28] In Russia, '*fizkul'tura* represented a third variation of the pre-1914 movement in Central and Eastern Europe' along with the aforementioned Turnen and Sokol in Germany and Czechoslovakia respectively.[29]

---

22 Ibid., 280.

23 P. C. McIntosh, 'Games and Gymnastics for Two Nations in One' in Dixon, McIntosh, Munrow and Willetts (eds), *Landmarks in the History of Physical Education*, 196–7.

24 Guttmann, *Sports*, 280.

25 Ibid.

26 Ibid., 282.

27 Ibid., 281.

28 Ibid.

29 Neil Carter, *Medicine, Sport and the Body: A Historical Perspective* [Paperback Edition] (Bloomsbury Academic: London and New York, 2014), 26.

As Cronin has written, 'across Europe physical education through gymnastics primarily was a far more powerful force than it was in Britain'.[30] The British system of teaching PE naturally had more influence in Ireland than those in other European countries. Holt has stated that 'drill' or 'gym' did not initially have a huge impact on the broader growth of British sport as 'a key element in the distinctiveness of the British tradition in British sport lies precisely in the lack of strong official backing for formal physical training and scientific measurement of average performance'.[31] In contrast to the developments in physical training in Central and Northern Europe, 'gym was for Germans. Britons *played* rather than exercised.'[32] Elementary schoolchildren in Britain could be taught drill through the implementation of the 1870 Education Act, although this was not compulsory. With the initiation of the 1902 Education Act, a broader programme of Physical Education was recommended although trainee teachers only began to receive instruction in the subject in 1908.[33] Neil Carter has noted that 'with the appointment of the first Chief Medical Officer, George Newman, in 1907, physical education was given a higher priority'.[34] As will be shown, this differed in some ways to Ireland, where wide-scale efforts to implement physical drill in primary schools were underway in 1900 through the *Revised Programme for National Schools*, but physical training in Intermediate schools did not become compulsory at that time and the systems in place varied from school to school.[35]

Holt states that in Britain, the way working class children learned to play took place in a different way to fee-paying pupils as 'military drill fleshed out with some general exercise was considered to be all that the ranks required'.[36] In some cities, such as Liverpool, elementary school children received instruction in drill from the 1860s, although by the middle of the

30 Cronin, *Sport*, 42.
31 Richard Holt, *Sport and the British: A Modern History* (Oxford: Oxford University Press, 1989), 11.
32 Ibid.
33 Ibid., 139.
34 Carter, *Medicine, Sport and the Body*, 21.
35 *The Irish News and Belfast Morning News*, 7 September 1900.
36 Holt, *Sport and the British*, 139.

1880s more attempts were being made to give boys the opportunity to play sport with the organisation of local competitions.[37] Drill was relatively easy for masters to teach while the emphasis on military style commands was perceived to assist discipline and offered rudimentary military training.[38]

As Lawton and Gordon have written, drill was rooted in the Imperialism of the nineteenth century and the improvement of the physique of children as well as the installing of cooperation and obedience in preparation for military activity within the British Empire.[39] The Second Boer War of 1899–1902 raised questions about the level of physical education in British schools.[40] Military training of children re-emerged with the Interdepartmental Committee on Physical Deterioration, established in 1904, seeking to encourage this.[41] Despite pressure for military training for youths and some senior army officials pushing to have rifle training implemented in elementary schools around that time, the Board of Education opposed this while legislation on the subject was prevented by the Labour Party.[42] However, the Officer Training Corps, supported by the War Office, was set up in 1910 for the development of a national cadet force. Lawton and Gordon also note that 'this vestige of militarism survived until well after the Second World War in British secondary grammar and public schools' but 'gradually, alternatives, such as social service work, were introduced as the ethos of militarism in schools diminished'.[43]

Despite the lack of focus on the *Turnen* system, educational institutions such as private schools and universities therefore did had a significant role in the growth of modern sport in Britain.[44] Although many private schools had become undisciplined with students often undermining their teachers by the late eighteenth century, the work of headmasters eager to

---

37   Ibid., 142.
38   Ibid.
39   Denis Lawton and Peter Gordon, *A History of Western Educational Ideas* (London: Routledge, 2002), 125–6.
40   *Kerry Weekly Reporter*, 9 June 1900.
41   Lawton and Gordon, *A History of Western Educational Ideas*, 126.
42   Ibid.
43   Ibid., 126–7.
44   Cronin, *Sport*, 30.

see reform, such as Thomas Arnold, helped them to regain control and improve learning while sport was used as a vehicle to control the students and teach them life lessons.[45] While rugby was the code that developed in the school bearing that sport's name, with laws set down by the pupils in 1845, an emphasis was placed on more kicking and less handling of the ball at Eton College, while a number of Cambridge University students decided upon a set of rules for association rather than rugby football.[46] As David Goldblatt has written, 'starting in the mid-nineteenth century through to the early twentieth century, in Northern Europe and the United States, the majority of the sports that we now play were codified from older games and recent experiments, or – like basketball and [Olympic] handball – invented completely anew'.[47] While this sporting 'revolution' was less noticeable in Ireland than its more industrialised and richer neighbour, Britain, by the late 1800s national associations were in place for a number of sports such as soccer, Gaelic games and rugby and competitive structures were also being developed at a provincial and local level.[48]

The Belmore Commission and Physical Drill in Irish Primary Schools

It was the primary school sector which received the majority of government attention in regard to the compulsory development of physical training in Irish schools in the early twentieth century. The formal system of National Schools in Ireland had been established through the Stanley Letter of 1831 following Catholic discontent about the proselytising

45   Ibid., 31.
46   Ibid., 31–2.
47   David Goldblatt, *The Games: A Global History of the Olympics* [Revised edition] (London: Pan Macmillan, 2018), 1–2.
48   For a discussion of the failure of the sporting 'revolution' in Donegal, for example, see Conor Curran, *The Development of Sport in Donegal 1880–1935* (Cork: Cork University Press, 2015).

nature of the Kildare Place Society, which had been founded in 1811.[49]
The British Government's motives for amending the system included
the view that literacy was 'regarded as the great channel to wider knowledge, while most children did not benefit from any formal schooling'.[50]
Although intended to be a non-denominational system of education, by
the middle of the nineteenth century it was evident that the Presbyterian
Church, the Roman Catholic Church and the Church of Ireland were
all opposed to secular instruction and the provision of religious lessons
outside the usual classroom hours.[51] Despite this, by 1900 the number
of state-supported national schools in Ireland had risen to 8,684 from
1,106 in 1835, although it must be noted that primary schools run by the
Church Education Society and the Irish Christian Brothers also existed
outside the national system.[52] By the early 1900s, most educated children
brought up in Ireland had come through a system in which, as Diarmaid
Ferriter states, 'parochial organisation, denominational segregation and
clerical management was the norm'.[53] Teachers' pay was based on results
of pupils, with attendance rates at national school level around 65 per
cent, while 'few were educated to secondary level' as 'much depended on
local circumstances, and, indeed, the degree of regional opulence'.[54]

The Belmore Commission, also known as the *Commission on Manual
and Practical Instruction in Primary Schools under the Board of National
Education in Ireland* was initiated in 1897 to assess the possibility of making
changes to the primary curriculum in Ireland. Thomas Walsh has stated
that 'it sought to replace the rigidity in the teaching and learning experience that had been introduced by the Payments by Results scheme and to
broaden the curriculum'.[55] As Coolahan has noted, this move was influenced

---

49   Coolahan, *Towards the Era of Lifelong Learning*, 9–10.
50   Ibid., 8–9.
51   Ibid., 12–15.
52   Ibid., 7.
53   Diarmaid Ferriter, *The Transformation of Ireland 1900–2000* (London: Profile
     Books, 2004), 88.
54   Ibid.
55   Thomas Walsh, 'Concepts of Children and Childhood from an Educational
     Perspective 1900–1940: Context, Curriculum and Experiences' in Ciara Boylan

by both child-centred and practical educationalists who challenged traditional ways of viewing the curriculum in elementary schools.[56]

According to the *Commission on Manual and Practical Instruction*, published in 1898, drill and physical exercises were 'recognised as subjects of instruction under the Board of National Education, in connection with Kindergarten'.[57] However, the Kindergarten system was only in use in 357 of the 8,606 national schools which were operational in 1896.[58] This meant that in most schools, with the exception of 'a few instances' where managers encouraged it, there was 'no official recognition of any kind of physical training'.[59] Some national schools did participate in competitions, with St Jude's of Ballynafeigh in County Antrim winning the National Physical Recreation Society's shield and medals in April 1901 for the fifth year in a row under the instruction of W. J. Ervine.[60] A few Irish newspapers advertised the sale of literature and equipment for physical drill, with KM Allen's School Stores in Arthur Street in Belfast apparently having Ireland's 'largest stock' of kindergarten goods and physical drill equipment in 1895, which also suggests some activity in the north-eastern city.[61]

This would indicate that physical drill did take place in some primary schools before 1900, but in the majority it did not. This contrasted to England and Scotland, where 'considerable attention' was given to physical training in primary schools.[62] At this point, Ireland lagged behind many other European nations in the development of physical education in primary schools. It was also reported by the Commission that 'almost

---

and Ciara Gallagher (eds), *Constructions of the Irish Child in the Independence Period* (Basingstoke: Palgrave Macmillan, 2018), 279–305, 28.

56 Coolahan, *Towards the Era of Lifelong Learning*, 27.

57 *Commission on Manual and Practical Instruction in Primary Schools under the Board of National Education in Ireland. Final Report of Commissioners* (Dublin: Alexander Thom, 1898), 50.

58 Ibid., 51.

59 Ibid.

60 *Belfast Newsletter*, 21 December 1901.

61 See, for example, *The National Teacher and Irish Educational Journal*, 22 September 1893 and 28 June 1895.

62 *Commission on Manual and Practical Instruction in Primary Schools under the Board of National Education*, 51.

every European country has its own system of school Drill, and the subject is considered so beneficial that it is compulsory in most elementary schools'.[63] They also outlined the value in adding physical training to national schools, stating that it was 'of great importance' to children. In particular, they noted that

> It makes them alert and orderly, trains them to hold themselves erect and to walk properly. It is specially desirable in towns, where bodily training in games, garden-work, and out-door occupations can rarely be obtained by the children of the working classes. For girls, both in town and country schools, it is particularly needed. Such training is no additional burden on school life. On the contrary, it is found from experience that it increases the attractiveness of the schools, and provides a welcome variety of occupation. Besides this, it develops physical strength, and the children return from it to their literary work with renewed zeal and energy.[64]

They recommended that 'it is most desirable that some simple form of Drill and Physical Exercises should be encouraged in all schools under the Board of National Education' and that 'such encouragement might be most fittingly given in the form of a grant for discipline and organisation, one condition of awarding the grant being that some approved and systematic instruction in Drill and Physical Exercises is regularly and efficiently given'.[65]

Medical reports also alluded to its neglect. A report entitled *The Sanitary Condition of our National Schools* was compiled in 1900, by Dr Anthony Roche, Professor on Medical Jurisprudence and Public Health in the Catholic University, following correspondence with inspectors.[66] The subject of hygiene was taught in only one training college, and only three trainee teachers had passed exams in it.[67] The idea that physical drill would help improve the physical appearance of children was also circulated in the press. One correspondent writing to the *Belfast Newsletter* in the early 1900s was critical of the physical state of many children, stating

---

63 Ibid.
64 Ibid.
65 Ibid., 52.
66 *The Freeman's Journal*, 21 February 1900.
67 Ibid.

that he was 'alarmed to see so many children displaying defects of carriage or slovenhness (sic) of attitude, which might be removed by a course of drilling and dumb-bell exercises'.[68]

The Belmore Commission's investigation resulted in the publication of the Commission of National Education's *Revised Programme for National Schools*, released in September 1900.[69] It was stated that 'kindergarten methods, manual instruction, drawing, object lessons and elementary sciences, singing, school discipline and physical drill' were 'compulsory in schools in which there are teachers holding certificates of competency to give instruction in them'.[70] These subjects were to be 'introduced into all schools as soon as possible'.[71]

Following the implementation of the *Revised Programme for National Schools*, the advancement of physical drill appears to have been swift. *The Report of the Commissioners of National Education in Ireland for the year 1900* deemed that out of a total of 8,684 national schools, by 31 December of that year progress had been made in the implementation of 'School Discipline and Physical Drill' in 6,494 or 74.8 per cent of these.[72] Thomas O'Donoghue has noted that the publication of *A Model Course of Physical Training* by the Board of Education in 1902, following consultation with the War Office, was important in the spread of information about the subject.[73] This development was linked to the rejection of many potential British army recruits in the Second Boer War, and the appointment of military instructors by schools was therefore encouraged by the Board of Education.[74]

68 *Belfast Newsletter*, 15 August 1903.
69 *The Irish News and Belfast Morning News*, 7 September 1900.
70 Ibid.
71 Ibid.
72 *The Sixty-Seventh Report of the Commissioners of National Education in Ireland. Year 1900* (Dublin: Alexander Thom, 1901), Section I. 38–9.
73 O'Donoghue, 'Sport, Recreation and Physical Education: The Evolution of a National Policy of Regeneration in Éire, 1926–48', 216–17.
74 Ibid.

Training Teachers in Physical Drill in Colleges

Efforts were most formally made in Ireland's teacher-training colleges to spread knowledge of the teaching of physical drill. By the early 1900s, nearly half of all primary school teachers had received teacher training.[75] With the implementation of the Revised Programme, traditional subjects were to take up four-sevenths of teacher-training time in training colleges, while the new subjects were given the remainder.[76] At that point, there were seven teacher-training colleges in Ireland, with the first of these founded in Marlborough Street in 1833.[77] Three others were also located in Dublin, including St Patrick's College, Drumcondra, Our Lady of Mercy College (Baggot Street) and the Church of Ireland College at Kildare Place, while De La Salle (Waterford), St Mary's College (Belfast) and Mary Immaculate College (Limerick) were also operational.[78] By 1901, drill was taught in the majority of these. Robert R. Clarke was in charge of instruction at Marlborough Street Training College, which catered for both male and female trainee teachers.[79] In January 1902, Clarke, the secretary of Loreto Physical Education Society, 'the largest association of the kind in Ireland', was awarded the National Society of Physical Education's Distinguished Service Medal.[80] This society was said to consist of 'the most eminent teachers of physical training in the [United] Kingdom'.[81] Clarke had been instrumental in encouraging the early development of physical education in Ireland and had trained the King's Scholars at Marlborough Street Training College.[82] More than 100

---

75 Coolahan, *Towards the Era of Lifelong Learning*, 26.

76 Thomas Walsh, 'The Revised Programme of Instruction, 1900–1922' in *Irish Educational Studies*, vol. 26, no. 2 (2007), 127–43, 133.

77 *The Sixty-Eighth Report of the Commissioners of National Education in Ireland. Year 1901* (Dublin: Alexander Thom, 1902), Section I. 38–9.

78 Ibid., Section II, 76.

79 Ibid.

80 *Weekly Irish Times*, 18 January, 1902.

81 Ibid.

82 Ibid.

of his students had been awarded teachers' National Physical Society of London certificates in drill having passed 'very severe examinations'.[83] The Loreto Physical Education Society had been established in January 1898 in order to promote physical education amongst Loreto schools pupils.[84] Although founded after the National Physical Recreation Society, mentioned above, it claimed to be 'the first body of educationalists to organise a graduated system of national physical education for their children', which predated that introduced by the Commissioners of National Education in Ireland.[85]

While St Patrick's College had no listed drill instructor in 1901, at Our Lady of Mercy Training College in Baggot Street, which provided instruction for female teachers, the subject was taught by Miss Mary Daly.[86] The Church of Ireland Training College at Kildare Place, which was co-educational, had a gymnastic instructor named Herbert L. Harte.[87] De La Salle College in Waterford, an all-male college, had a drill instructor in Sergeant Major Hibbert, while at St Mary's Training College in Belfast, a female institution, drill instruction was provided by Sergeant G. Croft.[88] However, by 1903, Chief Inspector Purser reported that drill at St Patrick's College was receiving 'due attention' while similar comments were made about the subject at the recently opened Mary Immaculate Training College in Limerick.[89] Hurling was popular amongst students at both St Patrick's College and De La Salle (see Figure 1) in the opening years of the twentieth century with the Gaelic Revival well underway, although other non-GAA

83   Ibid. and *Portadown News*, 4 January, 1902.
84   *Wicklow People*, 26 October 1901.
85   Ibid.
86   *The Sixty-Eight Report of the Commissioners of National Education in Ireland*, Section II, 3.
87   Ibid., 5.
88   Ibid., 6.
89   *The Seventieth Report of the Commissioners of National Education in Ireland. Year 1903*. (Dublin: Alexander Thom, 1905), Section II, 10 and 14.

Figure 1. De La Salle Training College Waterford hurling team, 1910. Courtesy of the National Library of Ireland.

codes maintained a presence in the former and the choice of sport was often contested there, as in other areas in Ireland at that time.[90]

By 1911, Swedish drill was preferred by the Commissioners of National Education, although it was not taught to all students as the teaching of physical drill lingered, particularly in St Patrick's College.[91] Some instructors travelled abroad to develop their skills in Swedish drill. In a report on Marlborough Street Training College, it was noted that

90 Dónal McAnallen, *The Cups that Cheered: A History of the Sigerson, Fitzgibbon and Higher Education Gaelic Games* (Cork: Collins Press, 2012), 21–3 and Curran, *The Development of Sport in Donegal, 1880–1935*, 205–10.

91 *The Seventy-Seventh Report of the Commissioners of National Education in Ireland. Year 1910–11* (Dublin: Alexander Thom, 1911), Section I, 11.

> The two Drill instructors (Miss Millar and Mr Warnock) have attended recently one of the holiday classes held at Silkeborg, Denmark, by Mr Junker, State Superintendent of Physical Training in Danish Schools. Good results may be expected from their visit, as it will enable them to introduce into their college a better knowledge of the so called Swedish drill exercises, which are based on sound hygienic principles, and are well suited for adoption in the National Schools of this country.[92]

By 1912, Swedish Drill had 'been taken up in all of the Colleges, though with varying results. In most of the Colleges the work in this department was good, and in some excellent'.[93] Difficulties remained, however. It was also reported that 'progress was retarded in two by exceptional circumstances – in one by want of adequate accommodation for physical exercises, and in the other by the want of a properly trained instructor'.[94] These issues illustrate mixed attitudes regarding the teaching of Swedish drill in the training colleges themselves.

Efforts to Instruct Existing Teachers in Physical Drill

With the implementation of the new curriculum, some schools and teachers saw it as necessary to organise external instruction themselves to learn physical drill. This came despite the fact that organisers were employed to provide guidance in a number of subjects in which some teachers were not well versed.[95] In October 1900, the Bandon branch of the National Teachers' Association agreed to establish a class in physical drill in order to enable them to undertake the National Board's new programme.[96] By the end of the month, Cork City and County Teachers' Association had set up classes in physical drill, 'under the care of a

---

92 Ibid., 10.
93 *The Seventy-Eighth Report of the Commissioners of National Education in Ireland. Year 1911–12* (Dublin: Alexander Thom, 1912). Section I, 6.
94 Ibid.
95 Walsh, 'The Revised Programme of Instruction, 1900–1922', 135.
96 *The Cork Examiner*, 26 October 1900.

competent instructor'.[97] By mid-March 1901 these classes in physical drill for national school teachers, which had taken place on Saturday mornings over a five week period in the Cork Model Schools, had concluded.[98] Around 100 male and female teachers from Cork city and county participated under the instruction of an ex-staff Sergeant Bonner.[99] He had experience of teaching children as 'for some years' as he had taught physical training in the city's convents and other educational institutions.[100] Dr Alexander, head inspector of national schools, had secured the use of the Model Schools for these classes through gaining the Commissioners' permission.[101] Interest was high as a number of teachers' requests to participate had to be turned down as the classes were too large.[102]

Some institutions also provided instruction for active teachers who were no longer in training college. Although Ireland's first military gymnasium was opened at the Curragh in the 1860s, civilian buildings of this nature were slower to be developed but were operational by the 1890s.[103] Naturally, a number of those involved in physical culture and gymnasia propagated the idea that theirs were the first in the country to open. In September 1900, the Dublin Gymnasium, located at Earlsfort Terrace, was described as an 'excellent institution' and as 'the pioneer, it might be fairly stated, of physical culture not alone in Dublin but in Ireland', with its popularity said to be growing every year.[104] Classes for children were held on Monday, Wednesday and Friday afternoons.[105] By October 1902, a physical drill class was being held there every Saturday for national school teachers.[106] As will be shown in chapter two, a number of intermediate schools had already developed their own gymnasiums by then.

---

97   Ibid., 30 October 1900.
98   *Irish Examiner*, 28 March 1901.
99   Ibid.
100   Ibid.
101   Ibid.
102   *The Irish Teachers' Journal*, 6 April 1901.
103   Heffernan and Curran, 'Much ado about Nothing', 75 and *Sport*, 4 January 1890.
104   *Irish Daily Independent*, 25 September 1900.
105   Ibid.
106   *Dublin Daily Express*, 6 October 1902.

By the early 1900s, regulated forms of physical culture associations which offered structured versions of drill were being developed in Britain and Ireland, with the latter home to a variety of related associations which saw physical fitness, hygiene and carriage as an important part of daily life. The editor of *The Irish Times*, in reviewing the state of physical culture in Ireland and England in July 1901 noted that

> There can be no doubt that, at all events until recent years, physical culture played too small a part in the training of Irish boys and girls …. there was no attempt at physical culture. In some schools the boys might play handball or football if they wished, but it was looked upon as an absurdity to take half an hour from Euclid or algebra or grammar in order to give it to the systematic development of the muscles. Fortunately, that condition of affairs has been gradually undergoing a radical change.[107]

This movement was said to have been led by Colonel Fox, the Inspector of Military Gymnasia in Britain and Ireland.[108] Conor Heffernan has noted that in the late nineteenth century there was 'an intensification in the number of gymnasiums, exercise classes and home training devices in Ireland and further afield' and this development became categorised 'under the umbrella term of "physical culture"' (see Figure 2).[109] He notes the appointment of a Monsieur Beaujeu by the Royal Hibernian Military School in Dublin in 1825 as the first attempt by an Irish school to teach physical drill to children.[110] Physical training was an important part of some associations for young people, with the Drogheda Catholic Boys Brigade, formed in 1900, promoting its value and rejecting 'intemperance and its concomitant evils'.[111]

In addition to those in Dublin, private instructors offered classes and demonstrations in physical culture in gymnasiums in Belfast.[112] Naturally,

---

107   *The Irish Times*, 5 July 1901.
108   *Weekly Irish Times*, 13 July 1901.
109   Conor Heffernan, 'The Irish Sandow School: Physical Culture Competitions in fin-de-siècle Ireland' in *Irish Studies Review*, Brian Griffin and John Strachan (eds), Special Edition: 'Sport in Ireland from the 1880s to the 1920s' vol. 27, no. 3 (2019), 402–21, 403.
110   Heffernan and Curran, 'Much ado about Nothing', 68.
111   *Drogheda Independent*, 22 December 1900.
112   See, for example, *Belfast Newsletter*, 1 April 1903.

Figure 2. A physical culture exhibition in south-east Ireland in the early twentieth century. Courtesy of the National Library of Ireland.

these instructors found employment in educational establishments. In September 1900, Miss Bertha Cotter, who had trained at Southport Physical Training College, was advertising the provision of classes for children and ladies in physical drill and gymnastics at the Royal Belfast Academical Institution.[113] Classes were not restricted to more urbanised areas and other venues were utilised. By the end of November 1900 plans were underway to host physical drill classes for national school teachers in the Lodge Hall in Bangor, County Down under the Misses Neill.[114] By September 1902 they had extended their practice to Ballyhackamore and Helen's Bay.[115] In

113   *Northern Whig*, 28 September 1900.
114   *North Down Herald and County Down Independent*, 30 November 1900 and 1 February 1901.
115   *Belfast Newsletter*, 12 September 1902.

December 1900, the Portadown Town Hall committee agreed that the venue could be used by local national school teachers for their drill class every Saturday for an hour.[116] By September 1901 Belfast was also home to the City School of Physical Culture, under the direction of P. Farrell, with private drill classes available for male and female teachers on Wednesday and Friday afternoons.[117]

The Board of Education also looked to private instructors for assistance in hosting examinations for qualifications in physical drill as teachers could also gain qualifications in the subject. In November 1900, *The Irish Teachers' Journal* noted that a large number of teachers in Dublin attended drill classes where most were awarded certificates confirming their ability to teach pupils in related exercises.[118] However, the publication also highlighted negative feelings towards inspectors, adding that despite these efforts, they would still struggle to satisfy their requirements when visiting schools.[119] This self-improvement appears to have been motivated by concerns over payment and the need to impress inspectors on their visits. As Séamus Ó Buachalla has stated, 'with the new programme of 1900, annual examinations by inspectors were abolished and an impressionist general verdict by an inspector during an unnotified visit became the sole determining factor on which the teacher's salary depended'.[120] Many teachers were unhappy with 'the lack of objectivity involved and the absence of a measurable recordable standard. Furthermore the classification and promotion scheme was treated as an official secret so that the teachers were not aware of the criteria on which they were officially classified.'[121]

At St Peter's schools in Camden Row (Dublin), physical drill theory and practice examinations were being held by December 1900, with the names of the thirty-seven successful candidates posted in *The Irish Teachers' Journal* that month.[122] This publication regularly included instructions for

116   *Portadown News*, 8 December 1900.
117   *Irish News and Belfast Morning News*, 21 September 1901.
118   *The Irish Teachers' Journal*, 3 November 1900.
119   Ibid.
120   Ó Buachalla, *Education Policy in Twentieth Century Ireland*, 90.
121   Ibid.
122   *The Irish Teachers' Journal*, 15 December 1900.

teaching physical drill and advertisements for related books in the years after it was introduced formally into the primary school curriculum.[123] In May 1901, a beginners' physical drill class was advertised to take place in the Young Men's Christian Association gymnasium in Wellington Place in Belfast, under the supervision of the aforementioned W. J. Ervine.[124] The class was scheduled to be held each Saturday during the months of May, June, August and September, with the intention to prepare them 'for the October Examination of the National School of Physical Education, whose certificates are recognised by the Irish Commissioners of Education'.[125] The same man had also produced modern physical drill charts for schools at that point and by autumn of 1901 was offering his own textbook *Modern Drill and Physical Exercises* for teachers of varying levels of proficiency in the subject.[126] In January 1902 he expressed his thanks in an advertisement in the *Belfast Telegraph* to teachers who had subscribed to his text on physical drill, and noted that it had been taken on by the Commissioners of National Education in Ireland and would thereafter only be available from their stores 'as per their authorised list'.[127]

Other reports highlight the success of these initiatives as they spread deeper into parts of rural Ireland and the enthusiasm of teachers was also noted. In 1902, it was stated in a government report that 'a class in Physical Drill was conducted in Athlone (Westmeath) by the gymnasium instructor, and the attendance of teachers amounted to forty'.[128] In addition, 'the same course' had been held for a class of teachers in Roscrea (Tipperary), while another was planned for Birr (King's County).[129] In Coleraine (Derry), 'the teachers formed, of themselves, a class for instruction in Drill, under

---

123 See, for example, *The Irish Teachers' Journal*, 6 October 1900, 2 and 23 February, 2 March 1901 and *The Irish School Weekly*, 13, 27 February and 19 March 1904. *The Irish Teachers' Journal* became known as *The Irish School Weekly* on 6 February 1904.
124 *Belfast Newsletter*, 10 May 1901.
125 Ibid.
126 *Northern Whig*, 24 May 1901 and 28 September 1901.
127 *Belfast Telegraph*, 13 January 1902.
128 *The Sixty-Eighth Report of the Commissioners of National Education in Ireland. Year 1901* (Dublin: Alexander Thom, 1902), Section I, 24.
129 Ibid., King's County is today commonly known as Offaly.

a competent man' while 'marked evidence of the desire to improve' could 'be found in the fact that the Meath teachers, at their own expense, started classes in Physical Drill' in Navan and Oldcastle.[130] There is less evidence that the Board of Education engaged in the widespread organisation of physical drill classes for those who were already qualified as teachers. Therefore it appears that in most cases, financial assistance in organising classes in physical drill was neglected by the Board of Education, and generally had to be undertaken outside of school hours and through local initiative.[131]

Opposition to Physical Drill in National Schools

Some teachers with an interest in sport and recreation, such as Galway-based Daniel Deeny, who had founded the County Donegal Football Association in 1894 before later moving to take up a teaching post in Salthill, inevitably saw the introduction of physical drill within the curriculum as a positive step. At a national school teachers' meeting in September 1900, Deeny stated that 'personally, I accord a hearty welcome to physical drill *(cheers)*, which I think will prove, not alone interesting, but be productive of very best results as far as the health, deportment and manners of children are concerned'.[132] By 31 December 1901, the subject was being taught in 8,439 or 97.1 per cent of 8,600 primary schools.[133] However, this masked local concerns about the motives behind the subject's introduction. In some parts of the province of Munster, some teachers were not as enthusiastic about teaching physical drill. At the half-yearly meeting of the Kerry National Teachers' Association in October 1900, concerns were expressed over the teaching of physical drill with its links to the army.[134] It was stated by the chairman that

130 Ibid., 25 and 28.
131 See also *Irish News and Belfast Morning News*, 15 April 1903.
132 *Irish Teachers' Journal*, 29 September 1900.
133 *The Sixty-Eighth Report of the Commissioners of National Education in Ireland. Year 1901* (Dublin: Alexander Thom, 1902), Section I, 38–9.
134 *The Cork Examiner*, 31 October 1900.

I think it would be very unwise to force it on the teachers, considering the present temper of our people. It is hard to blame the people when you take into account the stories that have reached them of so many of our brave soldiers - many of our former pupils - having been left to die of disease and neglect on the African veldt.[135]

David Fitzpatrick has noted that 'despite emphatic opposition to Irish involvement from almost every nationalist faction, about 30,000 Irishmen are thought to have served against the Boers, suffering 3,000 casualties'.[136] A letter from a Reverend McCann, in which he alleged that physical drill in schools was being used by the government to prepare young boys for army recruitment, was noted at a meeting of the Fermoy (Cork) Urban Council in November 1900.[137] Elsewhere in Cork, one Mitchelstown-based national school teacher, while happy to teach the subject, raised concerns in the press that a drop in school attendance, through parents' fears about the teaching of military drill, would impact on his salary.[138] News of these concerns quickly spread to other provinces. That same month, *The Northern Whig* described the school drop-out through parental fears of future army recruitment as 'an extraordinary scare' which was causing alarm in 'several districts in Munster'.[139]

Fears were also voiced in parts of Leinster. The Wexford-based *Enniscorthy Guardian* reported in December 1900 that one national school teacher's efforts to teach physical drill through his recruitment of a Royal Irish Constabulary [RIC] man had led to parents refusing to allow their children to attend the school, with the result that the physical drill class was withdrawn.[140] Not every school was against teaching the subject in that county, however. In January 1901 a motion at the Wexford National Teachers' Association meeting to hold a physical drill class on Saturdays prior to their Irish class, was 'met with the heartiest approval',

135 Ibid.
136 David Fitzpatrick, 'Militarism in Ireland, 1900–1922' in Thomas Bartlett and Keith Jeffery (eds), *A Military History of Ireland* (Cambridge: Cambridge University Press, 1996), 379–406, 379–80.
137 *The Cork Examiner*, 21 November 1900.
138 Ibid., 29 November 1900.
139 *Northern Whig*, 30 November 1900.
140 *Enniscorthy Guardian*, 1 December 1900.

with over thirty teachers stating they intended to participate.[141] As Raftery
and Delaney have shown, the intervention of the clergy was at times necessary to calm irate parents regarding misconceptions about the subject's
intended purpose.[142]

The *Report of the Commissioners for National Education* for 1903 indicated that in the Dublin Circuit, progress with physical drill was 'very good
in the schools' while in the Cork Circuit, it had also improved discipline
and 'all opposition to it' had 'long since ceased'.[143] However, while it was
'taught in nearly every school in the Castlebar Circuit' in Mayo, it was also
noted that some teachers did 'not take sufficient interest in it to render it
a valuable portion of the school course'.[144] Despite the initiatives organised above to spread knowledge of physical drill, putting this training into
practice and gaining experience in teaching the subject properly was clearly
a problem. Reporting on the Killarney Circuit, Mr Connelly noted that

> Of drill it is to be said that the teachers have not had an opportunity of being eye
> witnesses of proper Drill exercises. By seeing them they would learn more in five
> minutes than they would learn in five months by reading about them. It is chiefly to
> be praised because of the ingenuity they have displayed in translating into action the
> words of the text-books they possess. They have tried to make some sort of formal ex-
> hibition - the form without the substance. They do not realise its object and spirit.[145]

Teachers' opinions were clearly mixed in regard to physical drill's value. In
July 1902, at the annual meeting of the County Donegal National Teachers'
Association, the chairman, in his address, noted that some teachers felt
that too many subjects were being introduced and that Ireland's main
industry, agriculture, was being given less importance than 'weighing
sand, measuring water, physical drill or paper folding'.[146] In a letter to *The*

141   Ibid., 26 January 1901.
142   Deirdre Raftery and Catriona Delaney, '"Un-Irish and un-Catholic": Sports,
      Physical Education and Girls' Schooling' in *Irish Studies Review*, vol. 27, 325–43,
      330. See also *Northern Whig*, 18 January 1901.
143   *The Seventieth Report of the Commissioners of National Education in Ireland. Year
      1903* (Dublin: Alexander Thom, 1905), Section II, 24 and 33.
144   Ibid., 109.
145   Ibid., 172.
146   *Derry Journal*, 28 July 1902.

Irish Teachers' Journal, published in May 1903, John Cronin, a teacher at Scartaglin National School [NS], County Kerry, recommended that physical drill should be 'eliminated completely from the programme, as it is of no use, especially in country schools'.[147] In June 1903, the editor of *The Irish Teachers' Journal* was of the view that drill and singing should both be optional.[148] The INTO Central Executive Committee's report prepared for the organisation's annual congress in April 1904 illustrated that it was felt by many teachers that

> the new programme lowered the type of education imparted in the schools by prac-tically killing the teaching of mathematics; that the children wasted valuable time in employments, some of which were useless, such as tying knots, bending wire, 'measuring from fluid drachms to ounces', and others uncongenial and unsuitable, as military drilling, counter marching, running in step, etc.[149]

Some inspectors actually thought that farm work carried out by rurally located boys outside of school hours impacted on the value of Physical drill with a Mr Dewar noting in his 1904 report on the Sligo Circuit that he saw a difference in the subject's effects on males and females. He stated that 'the girls seem to have derived more benefit than the boys if one may judge from their bearing and carriage … the hard manual toil done by the boys, both before and after school hours, tends to nullify the influence of the drill exercises'.[150]

Attempts to Improve Perceptions of Physical Drill

The Board of Education did intervene in some ways to ensure it could be taught. In a circular issued to inspectors in November 1901, they were

---

147 *The Irish Teachers' Journal*, 16 May 1903.
148 Ibid., 13 June 1903.
149 *Dublin Evening Mail*, 1 and 2 April 1904.
150 *The Seventy-First Report of the Commissioners of National Education in Ireland. Year 1904* (Dublin: Alexander Thom, 1905), Section II, 26.

instructed to note that 'in schools in which Physical Drill cannot be conducted in full, according the *Revised Programme*, the pupils may at least
be trained to stand up straight and in graceful attitudes and to move from
one position to another during the day in an orderly manner'.[151] It was also
stated that it should take place outdoors and certainly not on an upper
floor of the school building.[152] Inspectors were also requested to make
teachers more aware that 'Physical Drill does not necessarily or generally
mean Military Drill, and that school games of a suitable character may
be substituted for drill'.[153] It was also noted that 'in the case of girls of the
higher standards suitable calisthenic exercises may be encouraged in place
of drill'.[154] However, these recommendations did not lead to any major
development of callisthenics or games in place of physical drill in Irish
primary schools at this time.

In January 1903, the Board of Education issued a memorandum which
gave 'some practical suggestions' in relation to 'the carrying out of physical
education, chiefly in rural schools'.[155] It was recommended that 'physical
training should be carried out by the teachers forming the ordinary staff
rather than by outside instructors'.[156] Drill was only to take place indoors
in adverse weather or when there was no available space outdoors. The use
of town halls, parish rooms, village institutes and barns 'or other suitable
buildings' was also advocated if bad weather was continuous and if the
school had no indoor space. However, it was felt that 'in a large number
of schools it would be possible to provide an open space for drill' while 'no
expensive apparatus' was needed. Wooden dumb-bells and staves were said
to be inexpensive while the use of dumb-bells and broomsticks was also
recommended. While games were thought to be 'valuable in themselves',
they were not a proper replacement for 'organised physical exercises even
in country schools'.[157] This was because, it was felt, that 'organised games,

151   *Circular to Inspectors. Revised Programme-New System of Inspection* (Dublin: Office
       of National Education), 28 November 1901, 2.
152   Ibid.
153   Ibid.
154   Ibid.
155   *Drogheda Independent*, 17 January 1903.
156   Ibid.
157   Ibid.

such as cricket and football, can generally be played only by a minority of the children, and almost necessarily exclude or fail to reach those most in need of development'.[158] The best way to reach all of the children was said to be 'by some form of regular combined exercise such as that proposed in the "model course" ', with exercises of the greatest benefit to physical appearance when each had a 'peculiar purpose and value in a complete system framed to develop duly all parts of the body'.[159] This appears to be a clear admittance that instructors, or resources, were not going to be universally supplied while encouraging teachers to improvise in their physical drill lessons. It also signifies that some official recognition was also given to the difficulties in drill's teaching in country areas. However, there was no major change to physical drill's existence on the curriculum in the following year when the curriculum was amended. Changes included 'specimen programmes' being 'devised as guidelines for different sizes of school' while manual instruction was removed. The allowance of bilingual programmes in Gaeltacht areas reflected a growth in strength of the Gaelic League, founded in 1893, in organising activities to promote the Irish language outside schools.[160]

Some journalists felt that the encouragement of competitions in physical drill by the Irish Amateur Gymnastic Association was necessary to motivate pupils to embrace it, with one writer of the view in December 1901 that 'the step taken by the Council in offering medals to the national schools has much to commend it' as it would encourage 'a spirit of rivalry between the classes'.[161] At times, these competitions were encouraged by the clergy. As Raftery and Delaney have illustrated, the Bishop of Canea, the Most Reverend Dr Donnelly, was fully in favour of the move to introduce compulsory physical drill in national schools.[162] In April 1901, following an exhibition of physical exercises at Loreto National School, Bray, he presented four medals to the school on behalf of the Loreto Physical Education Society and, speaking to the pupils, noted 'the great value of physical

158 Ibid.
159 Ibid.
160 Coolahan, *Towards the Era of Lifelong Learning*, 29.
161 *Weekly Irish Times*, 21 December 1901.
162 Raftery and Delaney, ' "Un-Irish and un-Catholic" ', 5–6.

education on their general health' and also offered his congratulations to the Commissioners of National Education for introducing physical drill within national schools.[163] In March 1902, the Loreto Physical Education Association held competitions in Loreto Colleges around Dublin city and county, with the examiner, Arthur C. Clague, stating that the results were better than in any other classes he had seen in the United Kingdom.[164] Exercises with a variety of resources including scarves, dumb-bells, barbells and Indian clubs took place.[165] In some areas attempts were made to encourage competitions in physical drill through non-religious patronage. In July 1912 Lady Garvagh, the patron of the Garvagh Industrial Association, announced she would present a challenge shield for physical drill amongst all the national schools in County Derry, with the event scheduled to take place at the organisation's first exhibition.[166] However, the 'small entry' was 'a rather disappointing feature' of the day's events.[167]

Displays of progress in physical drill were often given at school events. In October 1900, a school fundraising event was organised by Mrs Irwin, a Castledawson NS teacher.[168] This consisted of 'dumb-bell, wand, Indian club and ring exercises' and these were performed by the pupils in a way that reflected their teacher's precise training.[169] Dumb-bell exercises were recommended within the curriculum for pupils as young as those in third class.[170] Exhibitions of physical drill were at times given by school pupils at local community events, such as that by children attending Dunmurry School at the Dunmurry Bible Class annual entertainment in April 1903.[171] In May 1907, Empire Day was celebrated 'throughout a considerable part of the British dominions'.[172] While 'the celebration in Dublin was confined

163   *Wicklow People*, 6 April 1901.
164   *Freeman's Journal*, 27 March 1902.
165   Ibid.
166   *Northern Constitution*, 6 July 1912 and *Belfast Newsletter*, 7 August 1912.
167   *Northern Whig*, 20 September 1912.
168   *Tyrone Courier*, 1 November 1900.
169   Ibid.
170   *The Irish Teachers' Journal*, 29 December 1900.
171   *Belfast Newsletter*, 27 April 1903.
172   *Irish Independent*, 25 May 1907.

to the displays of flags from some of the public buildings, including Trinity College', at least one school was noted as giving a display of exercises and drill as children of Southwell NS in Downpatrick undertook these before being inspected by Captain and Adjutant Taylor, 5th Battalion Royal Irish Rifles.[173]

Despite efforts to improve how the subject was viewed, some nationalist organisations tried to negate its impact given its military connotations. At a meeting of the Education Committee of the Gaelic League in June 1907, 'it was stated that Irish dancing will now be sanctioned in lieu of physical drill on the curriculum of national schools'.[174] Official recognition of this appears to have been scarce, but the idea that physical drill could be ignored in order to implement aspects of Irish culture more fully received acknowledgement elsewhere, including in the *Sligo Champion*.[175]

Perseverance with Physical Drill

English Inspector of Schools, FH Dale, was clearly in favour of physical drill's value. In 1904 a report which he had undertaken on primary education in Ireland was published.[176] This was based on visits to eighty-seven national schools, eight convent schools and six model schools over a two month period.[177] While this was a relatively small number given that in 1901 there were 8,600 in operation, it does shed some light on conditions at the time. He stated that despite these schools being less fit for teaching than those in England, 'most of the Irish schools' were 'well supplied with the absolutely necessary equipment for school work'.[178] He added that

173   Ibid.
174   *Irish News and Belfast Morning News*, 14 June 1907.
175   Ibid.
176   *Report of Mr F.H. Dale, His Majesty's Inspector of Schools, Board of Education, on Primary Education in Ireland* (Dublin: Alexander Thom, 1904).
177   Ibid., 2.
178   Ibid., 86–7.

physical drill and drawing were 'practically universal, while object lessons and singing are rapidly approaching the same position'.[179] He also stated that in convent schools, where pupils were said to receive better instruction than that provided in primary schools, 'the physical exercises were also very well done'.[180] Dale felt that the introduction of physical drill, singing, drawing and object lessons to the curriculum had been 'most beneficial, and the State-grants for equipment, etc. in those subjects' had 'decidedly increased the efficiency of the instruction'.[181]

Thomas Walsh has noted that 'the proposed level of funding envisaged by the Commissioners never fully materialised' as 'the strain of the Boer War and the attempts of the British Treasury to devolve some level of financial responsibility of education to localities led to an actual reduction in funding for national education in Ireland'.[182] Dale's views were clearly at odds with general opinion espoused by the national union for primary teachers in Ireland, while it is not clear how widespread these State-grants actually were. In September 1906 the Central Executive of the INTO issued a statement again criticising the national schools' curriculum, as they felt 'much therein is vague and unidentified'.[183] In regards to physical drill in rural schools, it was felt that walking and agricultural labour were sufficient and that military drill needed to be avoided.[184]

Despite this, official instructions were strengthened to develop physical drill in Irish national schools following developments in Britain. The English Board of Education issued a syllabus of exercises in London in August 1909, with the recommendation in the preface that 'the physical health of the children lies at the root of education properly conceived' and 'Physical Education is essential to a sound intellectual training, and may be said to be fundamental in its effects on the individual'.[185]

179   Ibid., 70.
180   Ibid., 71 and 91.
181   Ibid., 91.
182   Walsh, 'The Revised Programme of Instruction, 1900–1922', 140.
183   *Freeman's Journal*, 26 September 1906.
184   Ibid.
185   *Irish Independent*, 26 August 1909.

As noted earlier, plans to amend the system to introduce Swedish drill in training colleges were slow to be implemented and naturally this overlapped with the schools themselves. The 1909 *Board of Education Syllabus of Physical Exercises for Schools* was based on Swedish educational gymnastics and had been taken on in the British navy and army.[186] The syllabus had been revised a number of times following initial publication in 1904, with the Board of Education noting that the period from 1906–9 'had been marked by the statutory recognition of the interest of the State in securing the physical well-being of the children in Public Elementary Schools'.[187] They added that 'the object of every system of education worthy of that name will be the concurrent development of a sound character, an active intelligence, and a healthy physique'.[188] By November 1909, the Swedish system of drill had also been made the RIC's official system.[189] That same month, the Right Hon. Mr Justice Ross, speaking at Rathmines College annual prize-giving ceremony, said that 'he was doing his very best to have the Swedish system of physical education introduced into every national school in Ireland'.[190] Some schools clearly did change their systems of physical training where expertise in the subject was available. By December 1910 the Swedish system of drill had been introduced in St Jude's School in County Antrim by W. J. Ervine, who was in charge of the running of the school's gymnasium.[191] In September 1912, a class in Swedish Drill and Physical Culture for teachers was being advertised in Belfast by W. Gilbert, the director of the City of Belfast Gymnasium.[192] That same month, the Central Presbyterian Association Gymnasium in Belfast was offering 'Special Swedish Drill Class for School Teachers'.[193] One of the female teachers there, Elsie L. Taylor, had been trained in Battersea

---

186 *Board of Education, The Syllabus of Physical Exercises for Schools. 1909* [Third Edition] (London: His Majesty's Stationery Office, 1911), vi.
187 Ibid.
188 Ibid., i.
189 *The Weekly Irish Times*, 20 November 1909.
190 *Dublin Daily Express*, 10 November 1909.
191 *Northern Whig*, 22 December 1910.
192 *Belfast Newsletter*, 11 September 1912.
193 *Belfast Telegraph*, 24 September 1912.

Polytechnic Training College, London, and, having taught in a number of schools, came to Belfast with 'an excellent reputation as a successful and popular teacher of physical training in all its branches, and in the various drill systems'.[194] However, given the difficulties in implementing physical drill in some schools, adapting to a different style was not straightforward, and it appears that many schools stuck to physical drill rather than the Swedish version, as will be shown.

The Failure to Improve Facilities and Resources for Physical Drill

While parental concerns may have eased, the provision of facilities did not significantly improve in many areas. These were a particular problem in Belfast, with one inspector's report noting that while sixty-nine city schools had playgrounds, thirty-two had none in 1905.[195] By the opening years of the next decade similar problems remained in many areas. In a report on the Northern Section of the Donegal Circuit for the 1910–11 school year it was noted that 'few schools have any appliances for physical culture'.[196] One inspector reporting on the Londonderry Circuit noted that 'the play-grounds are usually too cramped for games. I have not observed that the teachers, fresh from the Training Colleges, have put into practice anything that they have seen of the organisation of games in the practising schools connected with those institutions.'[197] It was also stated that 'a few of the schools are provided with dumb-bells and bar-bells; of other appliances for physical culture there are none'.[198] A lack

---

194   Ibid., 1 January 1910.
195   *The Seventy-Second Report of the Commissioners of National Education in Ireland. School Year 1905–6* (Dublin: Alexander Thom, 1906), Section II, 139.
196   *The Seventy-Seventh Report of the Commissioners of National Education in Ireland. Year 1910–11* (Dublin: Alexander Thom, 1911). Section I, 20.
197   Ibid., 34.
198   Ibid., 35.

of enthusiasm for physical drill was also noted in that region, with one inspector of the view that 'drill appears to have sustained a reaction, following the enthusiasm with which it was taken up on its first introduction. It finds a place on the timetable of practically all schools, but it is only in a minority of them that it is well taught'.[199] Further south, similar difficulties existed. In a report on the Kerry Circuit, Mr L. S. Daly stated that 'many of the playgrounds are too small. Some few schools are furnished libraries with more or less modest dimensions. In only a few are there appliances for physical culture, and these consist only of poles or dumb-bells'.[200] He also noted that 'except in Infant Departments there is a complete absence of organised games'.[201]

These reports highlight the inadequacies not illustrated in overall figures. By the end of 1910, it was noted that physical drill was being taught in 8,227 primary schools in Ireland.[202] This was a slight decrease from the figure of 8,439 noted for 1901 but it seemed to indicate the Board's initiatives had worked.[203] The publication of a teachers' instruction guide in Swedish drill was said to have had some benefits. Reporting on the Omagh Circuit in 1911, it was noted by Mr O'Reilly that 'until recently it was quite a general practice for pupils to carry their satchels suspended from the shoulders all day, but since the issue of the recent official pamphlet in Swedish drill this practice, I am glad to say, is being discontinued'.[204]

Despite this, teachers' methods of implementing the subject continued to be inadequate. Discussing the progress of physical drill in his report on the Athlone Circuit, Mr I. Craig was of the opinion that

---

199　Ibid., 42.

200　Ibid., 119.

201　Ibid.

202　W. J. M. Starkie, *The History of Irish Primary and Secondary Education during the Last Decade: An Inaugural Address Delivered on Monday 3rd July 1911 on the Occasion of the Inauguration of University Extension Lectures in the Queen's University, Belfast* (Belfast, 1911), 20.

203　*The Sixty-Eighth Report of the Commissioners of National Education in Ireland. Year 1901* (Dublin: Alexander Thom, 1902), Section I, 38–9.

204　*The Seventy-Eighth Report of the Commissioners of National Education in Ireland. Year 1911–12* (Dublin: Alexander Thom, 1912). Section I, 42.

Appliances for physical culture are seldom to be met except in the convent schools. Some drill exercises are, however, taught in every school, but in a listless and imperfect manner. Many teachers know little of the methods, the capabilities, and effects of physical education; and, the plea is often advanced that children in the country do not really stand in need of any form of bodily training, as they get plenty of exercise in walking to and from school and in work out of school hours.[205]

Pupils' attitudes towards games were also criticised. It was noted by Mr Fitzgerald in a report on the Cork Number Two Circuit that

Pupils play on the road in many cases, and sometimes a neighbouring field is available for football. There is however, not much disposition shown for play; pupils take their luncheon and trick about instead of taking part in any organised games. Save some football matches here and there, and some tug-of-war contests in connection with one school, I have seen no attempt at organised play. Some dumb-bells in a few schools, and poles for calisthenic exercises in the convent schools, are the only appliances for physical culture in the schools. Some provision is always made on the school time-tables for drill exercises, but interest in this branch does not seem to have been maintained. Up to the present I have seen Swedish drill in only one school.[206]

Attitudes regarding its value continued to be mixed and were often linked to the space required to teach the subject, and its benefits continued to be debated in the countryside. In July 1912, a proposal regarding making physical drill an optional subject was seconded and passed at the Navan Teachers' Association's quarterly meeting, the attendees having considered that its value was 'questionable' due to the lack of school space.[207] While this organisation lacked the power to implement any change in national policy, this is indicative of local attitudes towards the difficulty in providing for the subject where space was limited. *An Naosgach*, a writer in the nationalist newspaper *An Claidheamh Soluis* naturally welcomed a move away from military drill to what he saw as 'a more rational system' in April 1912, but this change to Swedish drill was difficult to implement everywhere.[208]

---

205   Ibid., 49.
206   Ibid., 125.
207   *Drogheda Independent*, 13 July 1912.
208   *An Claidheamh Soluis*, 13 April 1912.

The Dill Report and Physical Drill

In 1913, the Vice-Regal Committee of Inquiry into Primary Education in Ireland was held with sixty-five witnesses called between February and September of that year.[209] These were 'considered qualified by office and experience' and included Commissioners of the National Board, inspectors and teachers.[210] More commonly known as the Dill Report, it sought to investigate, under the chairmanship of Sir Samuel Dill, the running of the National Board and the system of inspection.[211] Following the inquiry, it was revealed that 'the Dill Report provided unassailable evidence that the national teachers had a just grievance' and that National Board Commissioner Dr W. J. M. Starkie 'had ruled the primary system with an iron hand'.[212] Despite this, Ó Buachalla has also stated that the INTO were unhappy with the report and that 'it had little effect on subsequent administrative policy; it did little to diminish the spirit of suspicion and hostility which existed continued even after the demise of Starkie in 1920 and the change of administration in 1922'.[213]

The inquiry also offers some evidence in relation to official views on the teaching of physical drill within the schools and illustrates that it remained favoured. Philip Ward, Commissioner of National Education, listed drill amongst the subjects that he felt were 'better taught' than they had been prior to the new system's introduction in 1900.[214] This was obvious given that it was not part of the pre-1900 curriculum, although W. J. Dilworth, the Secretary to the Board of National Education in Ireland, stated that

---

209   *Vice-Regal Committee of Inquiry into Primary Education (Ireland) 1913. Appendix to the Third Report of the Committee. Minutes of evidence 26ᵗʰ June–17ᵗʰ September 1913. with Appendices* (London: Alexander Thom, 1913). Final Report, 1.

210   Ibid.

211   Ó Buachalla, *Education Policy in Twentieth Century Ireland*, 90.

212   Ibid.

213   Ibid., and *Dublin Evening Telegraph*, 24 July 1920.

214   *Vice-Regal Committee of Inquiry into Primary Education (Ireland) 1913. Appendix to the Second Report of the Committee. Minutes of evidence 15ᵗʰ April–22ⁿᵈ May 1913. With Appendices* (London: Alexander Thom, 1913). 189.

he felt that 'very good work may be done in schools without drill' and that it was not essential to the school obtaining a 'highly efficient' grading.[215] Dr W. J. M. Starkie reiterated his view that since drill had been introduced in Irish schools in 1900, it had almost become a uniform development.[216] Former Chief Inspector James Joseph Hynes was of the opinion that drill was 'very important' when asked how significant it was 'in the up-bringing of the children', because, he stated, 'it was healthful' and conducive to the running of the school.[217] He also stated that it was 'very desirable' in schools and that the time given to it depended on the teacher and on the work being done by the pupils.[218] Chief Inspector T. P. O'Connor, when questioned if drill was necessary given that boys in country areas were said to receive plenty of physical exercise, stated that 'you must attend to their health or you cannot improve their minds'.[219] He also noted that some understanding should be shown to older teachers who were less capable of teaching it.[220] Another former Chief Inspector, Alfred Purser, felt that it 'ought to be taught in all the schools'.[221] These insights highlight a contrast between administrators and those teaching the subject, and the practicalities of its teaching appear to have been overlooked in some of these assessments.

The First World War and Primary Schools in Ireland

The outbreak of the First World War in July 1914 meant that the development of physical drill in Irish primary schools continued to falter as government energy was diverted elsewhere. However, it maintained a presence in many primary schools and even at some nationalist events.

215   Ibid., 31.
216   Ibid., 299.
217   Ibid.
218   Ibid., 105 and 106.
219   Ibid., 115.
220   Ibid., 103.
221   Ibid., 7.

At the Wexford Feis Carman, held in Enniscorthy on Whit Sunday and Monday, 1915, 'a grand display of physical drill and marching' was organised with 'hundreds of schoolchildren' participating.[222] Coolahan has stated that the war 'served to intensify the problems of Irish education in that any hopes of increased expenditure were dimmed and teachers were feeling the effects of rising prices and inadequate salaries'.[223] In one government report, published in 1917, it was naturally noted that war conditions had affected National Education's development.[224] School attendances fell in 1915 due to the movement overseas of military families and the need for older pupils to participate in agricultural work in rural areas, with a decline of nearly 2 per cent noted.[225] The reduction in male candidates enrolling in teaching colleges was also noted.[226] John Welshman has stated that while PE courses were set up in England, with scholarships for PE teachers and grants for organisers provided in some areas, 'in general, the First World War hampered progress as many male schoolteachers and PE instructors had been called up, and the war placed new financial limits on expansion'.[227]

The Report of the Commissioners also noted how an inquiry had been made following reports in some newspapers after the 1916 Rising that the events of Easter Week 'were to some extent to be attributed to the character of the teaching given in many of the national schools'.[228] Niamh Puirseil has written that this investigation was the result of comments from the Provost of Trinity College Dublin, J. P. Mahaffy, with six teachers having their teaching recognition withdrawn by the Board of National Education.

222   *An Claidheamh Soluis*, 15 May 1915.
223   Coolahan, *Towards the Era of Lifelong Learning*, 30.
224   *The Eighty-Second Report of the Commissioners of National Education in Ireland. School Year 1915–16* (Dublin: His Majesty's Stationery Office, 1917). Section I, 5.
225   Ibid.
226   Ibid.
227   John Welshman, 'Physical Education and the School Medical Service in England and Wales, 1907–1939' in *Social History of Medicine*, vol. 9, no. 1 (1996), 31–48, 36–7.
228   *The Eighty-Second Report of the Commissioners of National Education in Ireland. School Year 1915–16*. Section I, 7.

These included Thomas Ashe, who died on hunger strike in 1917.[229] Some history readers were withdrawn and a number of teachers apologised for wearing the badges, and as Puirseil also states, 'the 1916 Rising may not have in itself caused the partition of the INTO, whose members were not permitted to make political comments, but it was, arguably a catalyst nonetheless' as the Ulster Teachers' Union was formed in 1919 following INTO' members involvement in the Irish Trade Union Congress and Labour Party's anti-conscription campaign the previous year.[230] As Heffernan has shown, numerous Irish youths were exposed to nationalist ideology and physical training through St Enda's School in Rathfarnham, where one of the leaders of the Rising, Patrick Pearse, was headmaster, and through a number of organisations such as the Irish Volunteers, Na Fianna Éireann (see Figure 3), the Irish Citizen Army and Cumann na mBan.[231]

The war also hampered the development of school facilities as there had been 'a general suspension of work throughout the country' in relation to the development of school buildings.[232] School attendances were said to have declined again in 1918 due to 'the adverse circumstances arising from the War' and particularly 'during the autumn and winter of 1918, to a widely spread epidemic of influenza which was prevalent in all parts of the country and necessitated the closing of a large number of schools for several weeks at a time.'[233] Ida Milne has calculated that just over 20,000 people died of the Spanish Flu epidemic in Ireland during 1918–19, with schools closed 'for long periods' and sporting activity naturally affected as

229   Niamh Puirseil, 'The Schoolmasters' Rebellion: Teachers, the INTO and 1916' Published in Saothar 41 (2016) Retrieved from <http://www.niamhpuirseil.ie/the-schoolmasters-rebellion-teachers-the-into-and-1916> [Accessed 23 September 2020].

230   Ibid.

231   Conor Heffernan, 'Physical Culture in Ireland, 1893–1939', Unpublished Ph.D. thesis, University College Dublin, 2018, 60–96. I am grateful to Conor for sharing this chapter with me.

232   *The Eighty-Third Report of the Commissioners of National Education in Ireland. School Year 1916–17* (Dublin: His Majesty's Stationery Office, 1918). Section I, 5–6.

233   *The Eighty-Fourth Report of the Commissioners of National Education in Ireland. School Year 1917–18* (Dublin: His Majesty's Stationery Office, 1919). Section I, 5.

Figure 3. Na Fianna Éireann Physical Culture Class 1913. Courtesy of Matthew Potter.

a result, although some areas suffered more than others.[234] Sports teams at various levels were affected, and six members of a Tipperary team selected to play against Kerry in a GAA match were 'stricken down with the disease' in October 1918, while the following month the Monaghan GAA county board cancelled all 'important matches' as 'a large number of players' were 'unwell'.[235] Reports indicate that there was an improvement in 'health conditions' during 'the second quarter of 1919' with the result that attendance and school work both became more consistent for the rest of that year.[236]

The conclusion of the First World War in November 1918 meant that attention could again be given to school resources, although evidence for

234 Ida Milne, *Stacking the Coffins: Influenza, War and Revolution in Ireland, 1918–19* (Manchester: Manchester University Press, 2018), 60 and 156–61.

235 *Irish Examiner*, 28 October 1918 and *Nenagh Guardian*, 2 November 1918.

236 *The Eighty-Fifth Report of the Commissioners of National Education in Ireland. School Year 1918–19* (Dublin: His Majesty's Stationery Office, 1920). Section I, 5–6.

any major plans to improve playgrounds or the provision of equipment for physical drill is scarce. Coolahan has noted that 'one effect of the war as it drew to a close was a vision of a brighter and more egalitarian education system with some aspects of social legislation attached'.[237] He also states that 'the Fisher Education Act of 1918 in England was a good example of the new type of thinking which was making an impact'.[238] The establishment of two committees, the Killanin Committee, which focused on primary education, and the Molony Committee, to examine issues at intermediate level, led to a number of proposals to improve education in Ireland.[239] A number of these were later incorporated into the proposed MacPherson Education Bill in 1919, 'which sought a radical administrative reform of the Irish school system'. Despite this bill never being ratified, teacher salaries did improve but 'no co-ordinated reform package was implemented for Irish education' before the partition of the country.[240]

Overall school attendances in 1919 had shown 'a slight improvement over the previous year' but it was also noted that 'owing to disturbed conditions in the country and other causes' they were 'still lower than in the years immediately preceding the war'.[241] The Commissioners felt that it was 'a matter for satisfaction that speaking generally the working of the national schools, except in a few areas' had 'proceeded during the past year with much less disturbance than might have been expected'.[242] This was a reference to the War of Independence (1919–21), fought between the Irish Republican Army and British forces, which resulted in a truce with the Anglo-Irish treaty signed by British and Irish representatives in December 1921.[243]

237 Coolahan, *Towards the Era of Lifelong Learning*, 30.
238 Ibid.
239 Ibid.
240 Ibid.
241 *The Eighty-Fifth Report of the Commissioners of National Education in Ireland. School Year 1918–19.* Section I, 7.
242 Ibid.
243 Thomas Bartlett, *Ireland: A History* (Cambridge: Cambridge University Press, 2010), 406.

The Treaty was approved in the Dáil in January 1922, although by the middle of the summer of 1922 a civil war had broken out between those who were opposed to the Treaty and those who saw it as the only way at least some form of independence from Britain could be obtained.[244] With the victory of the pro-treaty forces apparent by the late spring of 1923, 'the way was open for a government led by WT Cosgrave to implement its vision of the Ireland, or at least twenty-six counties of it, that it had fought for'.[245] As Thomas Bartlett has written, 'there was almost no area of government, law, education or social policy that did not bear the stamp of the former rulers'.[246] There was, however, as he also notes, a strong attempt made to revive the Irish language in Free State schools, and this subject became compulsory in primary schools under the Cosgrave government. This also meant that 'subjects such as drawing and nature studies were to be elbowed off the curriculum in order to make way for it'.[247] As will be shown later, the policy of Gaelicisation also impacted on physical drill, but despite the subject's awkward nature, it remained compulsory for the first three years of the new Irish Free State after its inauguration in 1922.

Conclusion

By the early 1900s, an attempt had been made to revamp the primary school curriculum in Ireland and one of the impacts this had was that physical drill was included as a compulsory subject. This reflected trends in the provision of school exercises in other European nations but naturally physical drill was more favoured than gymnastics due to the British influence on Irish administration. However, there were a number of issues which meant that the subject was never fully embraced at a national level. In rural areas, a notion that children were already getting enough exercise

244 Ibid., 407.
245 Ibid., 419.
246 Ibid., 420.
247 Ibid., 427.

through walking to school or, particularly in the case of boys, working in agricultural labour, was prevalent, and this was an idea that remained extremely difficult to shake off for much of the twentieth century. Allied to this attitude was that some teachers were unhappy with having to teach 'new' subjects, and relationships between teachers and inspectors were certainly tense, with INTO meetings highlighting teachers' resistance to the teaching of physical drill. Resistance also came from some parents, with fears that the subject was being used as training for military service, although it must be noted that members of clergy, with their strong role and respect in the community, helped alleviate these worries. As shown above, some nationalists were beginning to float the idea that the Irish language should be allowed more time than physical exercise in schools. The state of physical drill was also problematic in England and Wales, with Welshman noting a lack of specialist staff, a scarcity of suitable playgrounds and unsuitable clothing and footwear hampering its early development.[248]

Despite the general lack of funding for its development at that time, physical drill was also embraced by numerous teachers throughout Ireland. While the subject was being taught in Ireland's training colleges by specialised instructors by the start of the twentieth century, upgrading the skills of those who already held teaching positions was clearly difficult to coordinate and it appears that teachers were mainly left to their own devices in this regard. Some local teaching organisations and groups set up classes outside of schools hours, and lessons in physical drill were also available from private instructors in gymnasia. However, the Board of Education were slow to provide in-service courses in the subject. Teachers' motivations to take up these classes, often at their own cost, were driven by a love of sport in some cases, the need to develop their own professional expertise and to improve their professional results with inspectors' visits in mind. While the Board of Education at times tweaked their instructions for teaching the subject through circulating guidance on this, their failure to invest significantly in developing facilities for teaching physical drill

---

248 Welshman, 'Physical Education and the School Medical Service in England and Wales', 35.

undoubtedly hindered its progress in Ireland's national schools. Admittedly, official figures illustrate that it was quickly being taught in most schools, but this masks the difficulty in its coordination, and as shown in inspectors' annual reports, there were vast inconsistencies in how the subject could be and was taught. Thomas Walsh has written that 'while conceptually well devised, the Revised Programme lacked a strategic implementation policy tempered to the societal and educational context of the day'.[249] By the eve of partition this state of affairs had not significantly improved, but it is important to note that, however badly physical drill was being taught, it was still a compulsory subject in the primary school curriculum before the primary education system was administratively divided along the lines of the new Free State and Northern Ireland after 1921. Chapter 2 examines the provision of physical training in Irish second level schools in the opening decades of the twentieth century.

---

249   Walsh, 'The Revised Programme of Instruction, 1900–1922', 141.

CHAPTER 2

Physical Training in Pre-partition Ireland's Second Level Schools

Introduction

This chapter begins with an assessment of structures for second level education in Ireland at the beginning of the twentieth century. A number of second level or intermediate schools were by the early 1900s already on their way to developing traditions of rugby and athletics with finance and prestige important factors in this. The growth of competitions was a notable development with trophies such as the Ulster Schools' Challenge Cup, which was initiated in 1876 for rugby, fostering interest in schools' sport.[1] Annual sports days and prize-giving ceremonies also strengthened the interest of pupils and the public. However, as will be seen, the systems of physical education used in Ireland's intermediate schools were varied and largely depended on the management, school ethos, finance and in turn the resources and facilities available. As O'Donoghue has stated, intermediate education in the early twentieth century 'had a strong sense of subservience to the dictates of external examinations and it catered almost exclusively for a university preparatory education to the neglect not only of physical education but of commercial, industrial, agricultural and other forms of education'.[2] Drill and the provision of games were by no means universally available to students in all of these schools. The involvement of the military within schools is also addressed in this chapter along with the impact of religious bodies, and it will be shown that while physical training and games were developing important roles in most

---

1   *Freeman's Journal*, 27 January 1876.
2   O'Donoghue, 'Sport, Recreation and Physical Education', 218.

intermediate schools, whether male, female or mixed, their development was often haphazard and attitudes towards their provision varied from school to school.

Physical Education and Games in Irish Second Level Schools in the Late Nineteenth and Early Twentieth Centuries

As Coolahan has written, 'secondary education was not subject to the high level of conflict and controversy that characterised national education in nineteenth century Ireland'.[3] He has added that 'it was the concern of a small minority of the population and, faithful to the canons of laissez-faire ideology, the state was slow to assume a direct responsibility for its provision'. More commonly known as 'intermediate education', it 'was provided through a wide range of institutions which varied enormously in quality' and lacked a 'co-ordinating agency to lay down standards'.[4] Religious involvement was overwhelming as 'the schools largely followed the denominational divisions of the community'.[5] By the early 1870s there were 574 'superior' schools, with this title generally afforded to those where the teaching of a foreign language was provided for pupils.[6] The curriculum generally focused on English and foreign languages including Latin, Greek and French while mathematics was also an important subject. The 1878 Education Act saw the setting up of a board of commissioners to administer public examinations with the power to give financial aid to school managers who had complied with their rules. Pupils who were successful in the exams were to be given certificates, exhibitions and prizes.[7] The board had £1 million at their disposal from the Disestablishment of the Irish Church in 1869 and as Coolahan has stated,

---

3   Coolahan, *Towards the Era of Lifelong Learning*, 46.
4   Ibid.
5   Ibid.
6   Ibid., 48.
7   Ibid., 50.

'the Act was a significant break in the laissez-faire ideology and preceded by a quarter century the formal acceptance of the principle of secondary education supported from public funds incorporated in the English Education Act of 1902'.[8] By the early twentieth century, the numbers of pupils attending superior schools had increased from 24,271 in 1891 to 35,306 in 1901.[9] However, weak students' education suffered as a result of the exceedingly competitive examination layout which existed.[10]

Mike Cronin and Roisin Higgins have noted in regard to the Irish education system and physical instruction, 'the choice of sport within any given school often came down to the interests of principals, individuals, priests or the favoured sports of any given order'.[11] In some schools, traditional games held sway prior to the growth of codified sports in the late nineteenth century. Julien Clenet has noted in his study of six fee-paying second level schools in Dublin in the late 1800s that although skittles and gravel football had been prominent in some schools, it was handball which was initially the most important of these traditional games with ball alleys common in many schools in the city.[12] Handball was one of the oldest sports in Ireland and was one of the first sports promoted by the GAA after it

---

8   Ibid.

9   Ibid., 52.

10   Ibid.

11   Mike Cronin and Roisín Higgins, *Places We Play: Ireland's Sporting Heritage* (Cork: Collins Press, 2011), 59. For a discussion of the dissemination of sports in nineteenth- and early twentieth-century Irish colleges and schools see Gerry T. Finn, 'Trinity Mysteries: University, Elite Schooling and Sport in Ireland' in *International Journal of the History of Sport*, vol. 27, no. 13 (2010), 2255–87; Mike Cronin, 'Trinity Mysteries': Responding to a Chaotic Reading of Irish History' in *International Journal of the History of Sport*, vol. 28, no. 18 (2011), 2753–60; Colm Hickey, 'The Evolution of Athleticism in Elite Irish Schools 1878–1914. Beyond the Finn/Cronin Debate' in *International Journal of the History of Sport*, vol. 30, no. 12 (2013), 1394–417.

12   Julien Clenet, 'Sport in Nineteenth Century Dublin Schools.' Paper given at Sport and Education in Ireland and Britain Conference, Public Record Office of Northern Ireland, Belfast, 27 September 2019. His analysis included Alexandra College, Blackrock College, High School, King's Hospital, St Columba's College and St Vincent's College,

was established by Michael Cusack and Maurice Davin in 1884.[13] Handball
alleys were at times the focal point of the parish and the game continued
in many areas into the twentieth century.[14] However, Clenet states that in
the late nineteenth century, the social pressure to adapt to more modern
games was felt by headmasters in schools such as Blackrock College, with
the French fathers there having to shift from an initial focus on drill and
callisthenics (Figure 4) to more modernised codes such as rugby and cricket,
while one clergyman there paid for an expensive bicycle track as cycling's
popularity grew.[15] Cricket was the first team game to be played by students
there (Figure 5), in 1865, five years after its foundation by a French priest,
Père Jules Leman and his friends, and rugby followed in the 1870s.[16]

In Tipperary, cricket's prominence in three schools run by religious
orders was instrumental to its growth in popularity in the nineteenth
century, although military involvement in the game was also highly significant.[17] Declan O'Keeffe has shown that a game known as 'gravel football', which had its origins at Stonyhurst in England, was initially popular
at the Jesuit colleges at Clongowes Wood (Kildare) and Tullabeg (King's
County).[18] Although the decisions to take on more modern sports such
as cricket, rugby (see Figures 6 and 7) and hockey were shaped by wider
changes in society as well as a love of play, it is important to remember that
schools had an academic rather than a sporting agenda.[19] In particular, drill
instructors were at times cut in order to save money and the organisation

13   Cronin and Higgins, *Places We Play*, 147.
14   Ibid., 146.
15   Clenet, 'Sport in Nineteenth Century Dublin Schools'.
16   Seán P. Farragher, *Blackrock College 1860–1995* (Dublin: Paraclete Press, 1995), 18
      and 'Blackrock College: History' Retrieved from <https://www.blackrockcollege.
      com/about/history-of-blackrock> [Accessed 14 November 2018].
17   Pat Bracken, *The Growth and Development of Sport in County Tipperary 1840–1880*
      (Cork: Cork University Press, 2018), 189.
18   Declan O'Keeffe, 'All the Other Boots and Legs Ran After': The Long Life and
      Slow Death of '*Gravel* Football'. Paper given at Sport and Education in Ireland
      and Britain Conference, Public Record Office of Northern Ireland, Belfast, 27
      September 2019. This game had become extinct at Clongowes Wood College by
      the eve of the First World War.
19   Clenet, 'Sport in Nineteenth Century Dublin Schools'.

Figure 4. Blackrock College callisthenics, archery and gymnastics in 1866.
Courtesy of Clare Foley.

of many sports was reliant on subscriptions, sympathetic masters and past pupils' donations.[20]

By the late nineteenth century, the use of specialised equipment was being developed in some of the more prestigious schools while gymnasiums and schools of physical culture had become more common in some cities and towns.[21] Referring to a new gymnasium opened in Dublin by January 1890, one journalist was surprised at 'the smallness of the number of boys attending the class' in drill, which was run by former army sergeant, Mr Clarke.[22] By the closing years of the decade, the notion of gymnasium drill for pupils had gained more credence. One reporter, writing in 1897, noted that 'less than five years ago a school gymnasium in this country was rather the exception than the rule, Ireland being very far behind England, where there is scarcely a school of any importance that has not a gymnasium'.[23]

20   Ibid.
21   See, for example, *The Coleraine Chronicle*, 21 March 1896.
22   *Sport*, 4 January 1890.
23   Ibid., 4 December 1897.

Figure 5. Blackrock College cricket team pictured in 1866. Courtesy of Clare Foley.

However, he stated that 'things took a turn in Dublin a few years ago, and since then many colleges have erected gymnasiums, the latest addition to the ranks being Belvedere College', where the theatre had been converted in a gymnasium. In addition, the college rector and his staff 'had the gymnasium fitted with the most up to date apparatus, dumbbells, clubs and barbells to no end, horizontal and parallel bars, [a] splendid pommel horse, and climbing ladders'.[24]

It appears that physical drill was not the school's preferred choice. They had also secured Sergeant Major Wright, 'the best teacher of gymnastics in this country' who was staff instructor at Dublin Garrison and who had trained members of the City of Dublin Gymnasium to the Irish

24   Ibid.

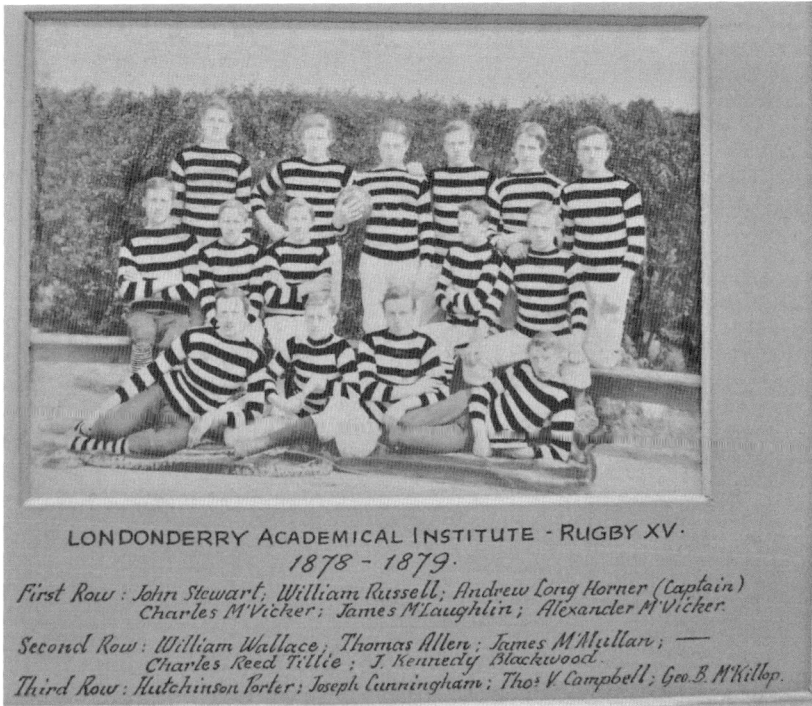

LONDONDERRY ACADEMICAL INSTITUTE - RUGBY XV·
1878 - 1879·

First Row : John Stewart; William Russell; Andrew Long Horner (Captain)
Charles M'Vicker; James M'Laughlin; Alexander M'Vicker·

Second Row: William Wallace; Thomas Allen; James M'Mullan; ——
Charles Reed Tillie ; J. Kennedy Blackwood.

Third Row : Hutchinson Porter; Joseph Cunningham; Thos V. Campbell; Geo. B. M'Killop.

Figure 6. Londonderry Academical Institute rugby team 1878–9.
Courtesy of William Lynn.

Championship. One reporter felt 'this system of teaching large classes such as in Belvedere College is perfect and has the most beneficial results'.[25] In 1900 a gymnastics club was present there.[26] By this time, regimented systems of physical training were also taking hold in many other Irish intermediate schools, although, as will be shown, this did not occur everywhere. In some schools, it was slower to develop than elsewhere. At St Columb's College in Derry, the teaching of drill was apparently first implemented in

25   Ibid.
26   Ibid., 28 April 1900.

LONDONDERRY ACADEMICAL INSTITUTION CRICKET XI. 1880.

Mr. Joseph Poole Ackley,   John Stewart, Mr. John C. Dick, M.A.,   James McLoughlin,   Charles McVicker,   Mr. Roberts
          (Art Master).   (Headmaster of Classical Department).   (Assistant Master).
          Thomas Reid,   Thomas Allen,   Andrew Long Horner,   Joseph Cunningham,   Alexander McVicker.
          James McMullen,   Charles Reed Tillie,   J. Kennedy Blackwood.

Figure 7.   Londonderry Academical Institution cricket team 1880.
Courtesy of William Lynn.

1898.[27] However, school sports had a much longer history. By the late nineteenth century these were well established at the Royal School at Portora
in Enniskillen, County Fermanagh, which was founded in 1618.[28] Prizes in
the 1870 sports day included 'opera glasses in the hundred yards ... a cigar
case for third prize, a walking stick for the mile, and a flask and breast pin
for the victors of the half-mile and high jump respectively'.[29]

27   *Intermediate Education Board for Ireland. Reports of Inspectors 1909–10. From No.
      82 to No. 168. Volume II* (Dublin: Intermediate Education Board for Ireland, 1910),
      Report Number 115.
28   *Belfast Newsletter*, 10 April 1929 and 17 March 1936.
29   Ibid., 17 March 1936.

The role of students and graduates in the development of sports clubs has been well noted elsewhere.[30] For example, by the early twentieth century, James Sproule Myles, an Irish rugby international who had attended Foyle College in Derry, had attempted to establish soccer and rugby teams in his native Ballyshannon, while he was also later involved in the local hockey team as honorary secretary.[31] As Neal Garnham has stated, while connections with Scotland and its migrant workers were highly significant in soccer's early development in Belfast, 'in Dublin, the sport's other main stronghold in Ireland, the role of the public schoolboy, who developed into the university student, was crucial'.[32] By the early 1880s, a number of Belfast schools had organised association football teams, with a team from Royal Academical Institution (Inst.) defeated by a Knock selection prior to Christmas 1880.[33] In Dublin, a team representing Terenure College was present in 1884 and in 1892 St Helen's School was a founder member of the Leinster Football Association.[34] Competitive schools' soccer initially faltered despite the establishment of a cup by the Irish Football Association in Belfast in 1883.[35] Four Belfast schools, namely Royal Academical Institution, St Malachy's College, Belfast Academy, Belfast Mercantile Academy, and a provincial team, representing Monaghan Protestant School, had initially entered.[36] By 1887, the competition was in decline with 'the paucity of entries' contributing largely to this.[37] Some early schoolboy players went on to form clubs, such as St Michael's Hall Celtic of Enniskillen, founded

---

30 See, for example, Neal Garnham, *Association Football and Society in Pre-partition Ireland* (Belfast: Ulster Historical Foundation, 2004), 25–6 and Tom Hunt, *Sport and Society in Victorian Ireland: The Case of Westmeath* (Cork, 2007), 174.

31 Curran, *The Development of Sport in Donegal*, 47–8 and 66–7 and Curran, *Sport in Donegal: A History* (Dublin: The History Press Ireland, 2010), 68–70.

32 Garnham, *Association Football and Society*, 27.

33 *Belfast Newsletter*, 25 December 1880.

34 *Sport*, 5 April 1884 and *Irish Times*, 27 October 1892.

35 *Belfast Newsletter*, 10 November 1883.

36 Ibid., 14 February 1884.

37 *Sport*, 17 May 1887.

in the 1901–2 season.[38] An attempt to establish a cup for schools was also made in Dublin, with matches in the *Sunday Independent* Cup, a trophy donated by the proprietors of that newspaper, taking place from 1907 until 1909, but the number of entries was similarly small and the trophy appears to have later been offered for another local soccer league.[39]

While the IFA initially failed to invest sufficient time in developing schools' soccer, schools' rugby was being played on a competitive provincial basis in post-primary schools in Ireland since the 1870s.[40] By the start of the autumn term in 1889, there were at least twenty-one intermediate schools affiliated with the Irish Rugby Football Union.[41] The two most significant competitions, the aforementioned Ulster Schools' Challenge Cup, and the Leinster Schools' Rugby Senior Cup, initiated in 1887, added greatly to the rivalry and prestige associated with rugby at that level.[42] The Ulster Schools' Challenge Cup Roll of Honour has been dominated by the Belfast-based Methodist College, the Royal Belfast Academical Institution and Campbell College.[43] However, some other schools at times have managed to at least temporarily break this stranglehold, and have also developed traditions of sporting prowess. By December 1907, the Royal School, Dungannon, who had just won the Ulster Schools' Cup for the first time, had in place 'a class for physical drill and gymnastics, conducted by Sergeant-Major Croft'.[44] It was noted by the headmaster, RF Dill, that the school valued the cup victory 'because of the prestige connected with the trophy, and because it was won after three hard games, all of them away

38   Conor Curran, 'The Social Background of Ireland's pre-World War I Association Football Clubs, Players and Administrators: The Case of South and West Ulster' in *International Journal of the History of Sport*, vol. 33, no. 16 (2016), 1982–2005, 1991.

39   *Sunday Independent*, 24 March 1907 and 3 May 1908 and *Irish Independent*, 9 December 1911 and 19 October 1912.

40   Garnham, *Association Football and Society*, 23.

41   *Sport*, 28 September 1889.

42   *Freeman's Journal*, 27 January and 29 February 1876 and Farragher, *Blackrock College 1860–1995*, 80.

43   'The Official Home of Ulster Rugby: Roll of Honour' Retrieved from <https://www.ulsterrugby.com/rugby-in-ulster/rugby-development/schools/roll-of-honour/> [Accessed 20 October 2019].

44   *Tyrone Courier*, 26 December 1907.

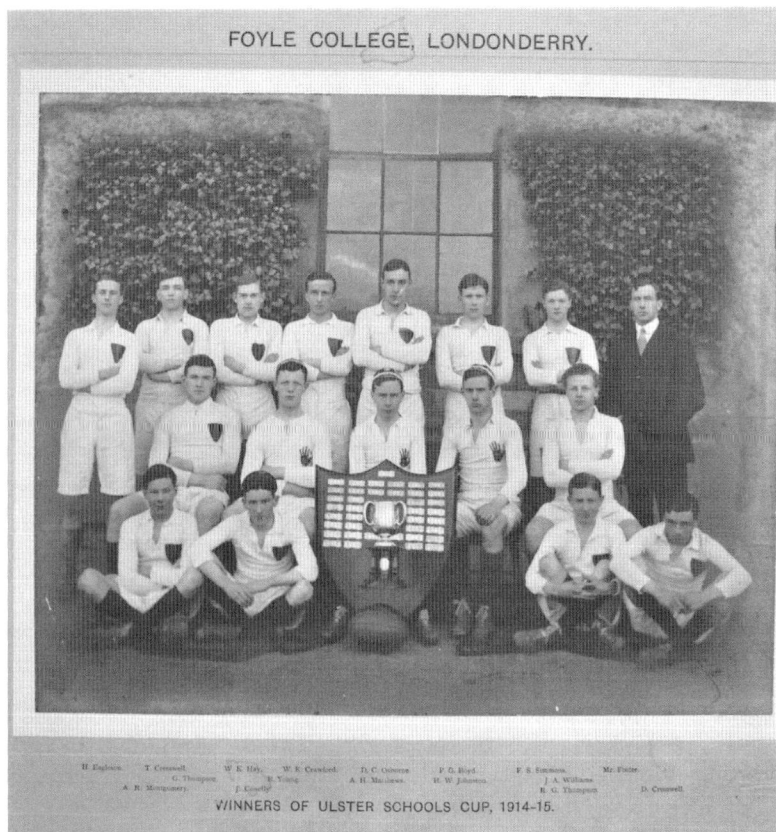

Figure 8. Foyle College, winners of the Ulster Schools' Cup in 1915.
Courtesy of William Lynn.

from home' while the 'high spirit and determination' of the boys was also mentioned.[45] The presence of Ireland international and British and Irish Lions player Alexander Foster, as head coach, was a significant factor in Foyle College's victory in the 1915 competition (see Figure 8), having also won the trophy in 1900.[46]

45   Ibid.
46   *Belfast Telegraph*, 8 January 1915.

Sports such as cricket and rugby became prominent in the Royal
Schools of Ulster, which had been established much earlier in the seven-
teenth century.[47] Despite the Protestant association with rugby in Ulster,
Cronin and Higgins have stated that sporting choices in schools 'do not necessarily follow a uniform religious pattern in which, for example, Catholic
schools all play Gaelic games; indeed Leinster schools rugby is dominated
by the top private Catholic schools'.[48] Blackrock, who later became the most
successful team in the Leinster Schools' Rugby Senior Cup, were apparently
so sure of victory in 1892 they allowed themselves to be photographed with
it before the competition began, only to be defeated in the first round.[49]
Competitive rugby structures for schools were somewhat slower to develop
in Ireland's two other provinces. The Munster Schools' Cup was first played
in 1909 while the Connacht Senior Cup was first held in 1913.[50]

Despite these sporting initiatives, physical training was not compulsory in Irish second level schools. As Coolahan has noted, 'the examination
structure introduced by the Act of 1878 copper-fastened the grammar-
school approach by allotting greater marks and rewards to the core subjects
of that tradition' and 'efforts made in 1902–3 to set up alternative courses
grouped under the headings classical, modern, mathematical and scientific failed to alter the prevailing trend'.[51] Although the Commission on
Intermediate Education had published a report in 1899 which highlighted
the imbalanced nature of the curriculum amongst other faults such as the
lack of public financial support, 'its recommendations amounted only to
modifications of the existing system, many of which turned out to be im-
practicable'.[52] This came despite comments on the value of physical training

---

47 See, for example, *The Londonderry Standard*, 31 May 1865 and *The Anglo-Celt*, 6
    October 1894.
48 Cronin and Higgins, *Places We Play*, 42.
49 Farragher, *Blackrock College 1860–1995*, 82.
50 Edmund Van Esbeck, 'Irish Game in Debt to Schools' Rugby' Retrieved from
    <https://www.independent.ie/sport/rugby/edmund-van-esbeck-irish-game-in-
    debt-to-schools-rugby-26014739.html> [Accessed 20 October 2019]. See also
    Liam O'Callaghan, *Rugby in Munster: A Social and Cultural History* (Cork: Cork
    University Press, 2011).
51 Coolahan, *Towards the Era of Lifelong Learning*, 43.
52 Ibid., 53.

from Oriel College principal, Elizabeth Miles, Junior Fellow at the Royal University of Ireland, Frederick G. Donnan, and the Director of the Science and Art Museum, Colonel G. T. Plunkett.[53] The *Intermediate Education Report*, completed in 1905 by F. H. Dale and T. A. Stephens, noted that physical training was being neglected amongst a number of 'serious defects'.[54] As Coolahan has stated, even recommended general changes were not adopted, mainly because 'there was a suspicion by school authorities of the extension of state involvement in intermediate education which the proposals implied'.[55] In addition, he notes that the biggest amendments in the intermediate education system in the period from 1909 until 1924 were the course's modification in 1908, the initiation of an inspectorate the following year and the elimination of the science course in 1910.[56] Preparatory grades were dropped in 1913 and in 1914 more emphasis was placed on commercial subjects. The following year, the written examination in science was re-introduced.[57]

Inspectors' Reviews of Physical Training in Irish Intermediate Schools, 1909–1910

Along with newspaper reports and other sources, inspectors' reports from school visits in 1909 and 1910 help illuminate the attention given to physical exercise in Ireland's intermediate schools in the early twentieth

---

53   O'Donoghue, 'Sport, Recreation and Physical Education', 217.

54   *Report of Mr F.H. Dale and Mr T.A. Stephens on Intermediate Education (Ireland)* (Dublin: Alexander Thom, 1905), 86.

55   Coolahan, *Towards the Era of Lifelong Learning*, 55. In particular, the report recommended the establishment of a central body to oversee education, a system of inspection to monitor which schools had attained the authority's required standard, 'block capitation grants' for schools of a satisfactory level, the removal of exam fees, the development of school curricula by schools themselves (under the authority's guidance) and the establishment of registration council for teachers.

56   Ibid.

57   Ibid.

century and illustrate how the system of games and drill was not universal in every school, as some schools placed more emphasis on sporting provision than others.[58] A total of 338 schools were visited by inspectors, with the general curriculum and facilitation of 'recreation' in 171 boys, 129 girls and 38 mixed schools reported upon. At this point, physical education was not an examination subject as opposed to more traditional subjects in the curriculum such as English and Latin and was often viewed as a subject that was encouraged as part of recreation and promoted to burn off excess energy and to develop character.[59] Therefore, the amount of time given to it in intermediate schools was not fixed nationally, and as will be seen, it varied throughout the country. In particular, drill was not supplied everywhere and, while some schools recruited military and RIC men, others catered for it internally.

Boys' Schools

Surprisingly, drill was not common in all intermediate boys' schools by 1910. For example, the Christian Brothers School [CBS], Armagh, St Patrick' College Armagh, St Joseph's Academy, Bagenalstown (Carlow) and St Muredach's College, Ballina (Mayo) were making no provision for it by the end of the opening decade of the twentieth century.[60] At

---

58   *Intermediate Education Board for Ireland. Reports of Inspectors 1909–10. From No. 1 to No. 81. Volume I* (Dublin: Intermediate Education Board for Ireland, 1910); *Intermediate Education Board for Ireland. Reports of Inspectors 1909–10. From No. 82 to No. 168. Volume II* (Dublin: Intermediate Education Board for Ireland, 1910); *Intermediate Education Board for Ireland. Reports of Inspectors 1909–10. From No. 201 to 332. Volume III* (Dublin: Intermediate Education Board for Ireland, 1910) and *Intermediate Education Board for Ireland. Reports of Inspectors 1909–10. From No. 401 to 436 Volume IV* (Dublin: Intermediate Education Board for Ireland, 1910).

59   *Thom's Official Directory of the United Kingdom of Great Britain and Ireland: For the Year 1911* (Dublin: Alexander Thom and Co., 1911), 753.

60   *Intermediate Education Board for Ireland. Reports of Inspectors 1909–10. From No. 1 to No. 81. Vol. I.* Reports Number 2, 4, 8, 10, 12, 13, 14, 16, 16a, 16b. See also CBS

Preston School, Abbeyleix (Queen's County), which was run by the Preston School Authority, drill was 'occasional' and was given by the local Head Constable of the RIC.[61] It was similarly described at the Diocesan College, Ballaghadeereen (Roscommon) and only took place when the recruiting sergeant was resident in town.[62] Having a military barracks nearby was beneficial. At Summerhill College in Sligo, drill was taught by a military man who was stationed in the town.[63]

Some schools provided more regular sessions of drill. An ex-Sergeant Major gave instruction in physical drill every Saturday morning at the Ranelagh School in Athlone (Westmeath) and two half-hour sessions were provided, twice a week, 'by a military man' at St Joseph's College, Ballinasloe (Galway).[64] Drill was taught twice weekly by Sergeant Major Wright at the Masonic Boys' School in Clonskeagh (Dublin) and an ex-army sergeant was responsible for instruction in drill at the Academy in Cookstown (Tyrone).[65] A gymnastic instructor of the 1st Battalion of the Hampshire Regiment taught drill and gymnastics at Foyle College Derry, and both were compulsory for students.[66] At Campbell College, it was included in the curriculum for the first four forms, with a cadet corps drill taking place every Wednesday afternoon for an hour.[67] In June 1911 the Cadet Corps associated with Campbell College were inspected by Colonel Hill after a physical drill display was given by them 'in the well-appointed gymnasium, under the direction of Sergeant Major Fallon'.[68] Along with Cork Grammar School, Campbell College had one of only

Ballinrobe, The Academy Ballymena, The Endowed School Bangor, the CBS at Oxford Street, CBS Divis Street and CBS Donegall Street in Belfast.

61　Ibid., Report Number 1. Queen's County is now known as Laois.

62　Ibid. Report Number 9.

63　*Intermediate Education Board for Ireland. Reports of Inspectors 1909–10. From No. 82 to No. 168. Volume II.* Report Number 151.

64　Ibid., Report Numbers 5 and 11.

65　Ibid., Report Numbers 44 and 46.

66　*Intermediate Education Board for Ireland. Reports of Inspectors 1909–10. From No. 82 to No. 168. Volume II.* Report Number 114.

67　*Intermediate Education Board for Ireland. Reports of Inspectors 1909–10. From No. 1 to No. 81. Vol. I.* Report Number 15.

68　*Belfast Newsletter*, 3 June 1911.

'two cadet corps of junior rank in Ireland'.[69] Preparation for the military or civil service was a common theme in Irish schools with a British-ethos at the turn of the century.[70] A few schools supplied artillery practice. The Academical Institute in Coleraine (Derry) provided weekly drill along with a rifle club.[71] At the High School in Dublin, a rifle club was operational along with rugby, cricket and athletics including cross-country running.[72] The Manor School Fermoy (Cork), which acted as 'preparatory for the public schools and Osborne', was also home to 'extensive grounds including Gymnasium, fitted with BSA Rifle range, Football and Cricket fields' and an 'isolated sanatorium'.[73]

There were numerous schools inspected where drill was simply taught internally. At the Christian Brothers' School in Fermoy it was taught by the Brothers themselves, 'every day for ten or five minutes'.[74] In some schools, Swedish drill was favoured. At the Royal School in Armagh, Swedish drill took place every morning before class.[75] At the Royal Academical Institute in Belfast, modified Swedish drill was compulsory for all pupils below middle grade, but it was voluntary for higher classes although it did have a place on the school curriculum.[76] An instructor taught Swedish drill at St Malachy's College Belfast twice a week, while at Chesterfield School in Birr (King's County), drill was taught for twenty minutes each morning by the headmaster and once a week by 'a military man'.[77] Some schools, such as St Vincent's College Castleknock (Dublin), provided both military and

---

69   Ibid.

70   Julien Clenet, 'Sport in Nineteenth Century Dublin Schools.'

71   *Intermediate Education Board for Ireland. Reports of Inspectors 1909–10. From No. 1 to No. 81. Vol. I*, Report Number 45.

72   Ibid. Report Number 70.

73   *Irish Times*, 30 August 1909. The Birmingham Small Arms Company Limited was generally known as the BSA.

74   *Intermediate Education Board for Ireland. Reports of Inspectors 1909–10. From No. 82 to No. 168. Volume II.* Report Number 88.

75   *Intermediate Education Board for Ireland. Reports of Inspectors 1909–10. From No. 1 to No. 81. Vol. I*, Report Number 3.

76   Ibid., Report Number 18.

77   Ibid., Report Numbers 20 and 21.

Swedish drill.[78] However, at the Christian Brothers' School, Our Lady's Mount in Cork, drill was 'for selected boys' only, on a twice weekly basis.[79]

In some other schools provision was scheduled only on a seasonal basis, with an hour every Saturday provided by a 'military expert' at Galway Grammar School during the winter and in CBS Kilrush (Clare) it was taught by 'one of the masters' in winter for a half hour every week on average.[80] 'Voluntary drill' was offered at the CBS in Kilkenny for 'two hours a week in the summer only' and was 'mainly for the bigger boys'.[81] At St Brendan's Seminary, Killarney (Kerry), drill was provided for one hour, two days a week from November to Easter.[82] Some schools taught drill with Indian clubs, such as St Ignatius College, Galway, while dumb-bells and barbells were used during lessons at the Presentation College, Glasthule (Dublin).[83] A few others left drill to local organisations, and the Board of Governors, who ran Omagh Academy in County Tyrone, ceased to organise its teaching as the majority of pupils were Brigade members.[84] Similarly, it was noted that at the Villiers' Endowed School in Limerick, a large proportion of boys belonged to the local Church Lads' Brigade and its inclusion was not necessary in the school.[85]

School authorities' attitudes towards the compulsory provision of games were varied. At the Preston School in Abbeyleix, cricket and hockey were mandatory, and all twenty-four boys there were required to take part in school games twice a week.[86] They also played by themselves 'practically every dry day'.[87] Cricket and [rugby] football was compulsory at the Royal School in Armagh, but at the Royal Academical Institute in Belfast, there

---

78 Ibid., Report Number 36.
79 Ibid., Report Number 48.
80 *Intermediate Education Board for Ireland. Reports of Inspectors 1909–10. From No. 82 to No. 168. Volume II*. Report Numbers 90 and 101.
81 Ibid., Report Number 97.
82 Ibid., Report Number 100.
83 Ibid., Report Numbers 91 and 93.
84 Ibid., Report Number 137.
85 Ibid., Report Number 111.
86 *Intermediate Education Board for Ireland. Reports of Inspectors 1909–10. From No. 1 to No. 81. Vol. I*. Report Number 1.
87 Ibid.

were 'no compulsory games' although 'all boys below middle grade' had
to undertake 'compulsory physical training (modified Swedish system)'.[88]
In a number of schools, boys were encouraged to play unless they were
physically unwell. This rule was in place at institutions such as St Patrick's
College Armagh, St Muredach's College, Ballina and at St Joseph's College,
Ballinasloe.[89] Similarly, at St Malachy's College in Belfast, games were 'not
compulsory, but every boy, physically fit' was 'induced' to take part while
at the Academical Institute in Coleraine, games were not compulsory but
every pupil was 'expected to engage in some of the school sports'.[90] In a
small number of schools, including the Christian Brothers College School
in Cork, boys who were deemed to be 'delicate' were given exemptions
from games.[91]

By the autumn of 1904, the GAA had organised a schools' league in
Dublin which later saw eighty teams, consisting of 12 to 17 year olds, encouraged to speak the Irish language while competing in Gaelic football
and hurling matches.[92] Some inspected schools naturally stuck to sports
which they felt suited their ethos, while others were less concerned about
nationalist or unionist perceptions. St Enda's in Rathfarnham, where Patrick
Pearse was headmaster, did not offer soccer, rugby, cricket or hockey and
instead Gaelic football, hurling and handball were compulsory and were
'organised by the boys with the cognisance of the masters'.[93] Gaelic football
took place in some schools such as St Muredach's College Ballina and at
the CBS in Cashel, Tipperary, and in the case of Lay College Knockbeg

---

88   Ibid., Report Numbers 3 and 18.
89   Ibid. Report Numbers 4, 10 and 11.
90   Ibid., Report Numbers 20 and 45.
91   Ibid., Report Number 47.
92   *Freeman's Journal*, 1 October 1904, *Irish Independent*, 4 February 1905 and Richard
     McElligott, ' "Boys Indifferent to the Manly Sports of Their Race" Nationalism
     and Children's Sport in Ireland, 1880–1920' in Brian Griffin and John Strachan
     (eds), Special edition of *Irish Studies Review*, 'Sport in Ireland from the 1880s to the
     1920s', vol. 27, no. 3 (2019), 344–61, 347.
93   *Intermediate Education Board for Ireland. Reports of Inspectors 1909–10. From No. 1
     to No. 81. Vol. I.* Report Numbers 15 and 17 and *Intermediate Education Board for
     Ireland. Reports of Inspectors 1909–10. From No. 82 to No. 168. Volume II.* Report
     Number 143.

Figure 9. Pupils at the CBS Waterpark, Waterford in 1908. Courtesy of the National Library of Ireland.

(Carlow) it was played along with rugby, hurling, cricket and a variety of indoor games which included billiards.[94] At the Christian Brothers' College School in Cork, rugby was the only game organised by staff, while at the Presentation College in Queenstown and at the CBS Waterpark in Waterford, soccer was the preferred football code, although cricket, hurling, rowing, billiards, athletics, nature rambles and cycling (see Figure 9) also took place at the latter.[95]

---

94 *Intermediate Education Board for Ireland. Reports of Inspectors 1909–10. From No. 1 to No. 81. Vol. I.* Report Numbers 10, 33 and 30.

95 Ibid., Report Number 47 and *Intermediate Education Board for Ireland. Reports of Inspectors 1909–10. From No. 82 to No. 168. Volume II.* Report Numbers 141 and 162. Queenstown is now known as Cobh.

Figure 10. St Patrick's College Armagh Association football team 1910–11. Courtesy of PRONI.

A nationalist agenda was prominent at St Augustine's Seminary, Dungarvan, where Irish dancing was compulsory, along with hurling, handball and [Gaelic] football.[96] Some schools offered a variety of football codes. At the Presentation Brothers' School in Boyle, County Roscommon, both soccer and Gaelic football were organised by staff.[97] As shown in Figure 10, soccer was played at St Patrick's College Armagh.[98]

Some school authorities felt that pupils' participation in local teams was sufficient in terms of the provision of physical exercise. At the CBS in Carlow, it was noted that it was unnecessary for the staff to organise

---

96   *Intermediate Education Board for Ireland. Reports of Inspectors 1909–10. From No. 1 to No. 81. Vol. I.* Report Number 80.

97   Ibid., Report Number 25.

98   Ibid., Report Number 4.

games for pupils as they belonged to locally based teams.[99] At the CBS in Drogheda, an unspecified form of football was played, but there were no organised school games although the boys there played with local teams.[100] Students organised their own games under the direction of the staff at Mount Melleray Seminary in Cappaquin, Waterford, while a boys' committee also organised games in conjunction with staff at the Masonic Boys' School in Clonskeagh.[101] Games were 'organised jointly by boys and masters' at the King's Hospital School in Dublin.[102] At the Grammar School in Galway, games were run by team captains with the assistance of 'one or more' of the schoolmasters.[103] At the Villiers' Endowed School in Limerick, games were organised by the staff 'in conjunction with boys' who selected their own officials for the hockey and cricket clubs there, which were run in winter and summer respectively.[104] Games were run by a committee of six boys and staff members at Kilkenny College.[105] The staff and 'captains of different divisions' were responsible for organising the games at Clongowes Wood College, where hockey, cricket, rugby and soccer were noted as being compulsory despite claims that Association football had been voted off the sports programme there a few years earlier.[106]

Each game had its own committee at Larne Grammar School in County Antrim, and rugby and cricket were played by almost every boy but were not compulsory.[107] At St Kieran's College, Kilkenny, games were not mandatory and were not organised by the staff; instead, pupils were encouraged to do this by themselves.[108] At St Brendan's Seminary, Killarney, 'some assistance' was given to pupils in the organisation of games by the President and Dean

---

99   Ibid., Report Number 29.
100 Ibid., Report Number 56.
101 Ibid., Report Numbers 28 and 44.
102 Ibid., Report Number 65.
103 *Intermediate Education Board for Ireland. Reports of Inspectors 1909–10. From No. 82 to No. 168. Volume II.* Report Number 90.
104 Ibid., Report Number 111.
105 Ibid., Report Number 98.
106 Ibid., Report Number 147 and Garnham, *Association football and Society*, 67.
107 *Intermediate Education Board for Ireland. Reports of Inspectors 1909–10. From No. 82 to No. 168. Volume II.* Report Number 104.
108 Ibid., Report Number 99.

there.[109] The Dean at St Thomas of Aquin College in Newbridge (Kildare) also assisted the boys there with games.[110] A prefect presided during recreation at Castletown De La Salle School in Mountrath in Queen's County, but the boys organised their own games.[111] At St Colman's College in Newry, County Down, the senior student, who was prefect for the year, organised the games, but the boys there formed their own committees and the priests were known to 'supervise and encourage a little'.[112] Some schools recruited external instructors for games. Pupils at the Endowed School in Bangor were coached in rugby by Mr MacIlwaine, who was a member of the Queen's College Belfast team.[113] Parental influence in the choice of codes was generally not noted in the inspectors' reports, but at the CBS in Wexford, the boys joined 'different teams according to parents' wishes' and no games were organised in the school.[114]

While Clongowes Wood College is reputed to be home to Ireland's oldest indoor pool, at a few other schools swimming was also available.[115] These included St Vincent's College Castleknock, which had its own swimming baths, while at Mountjoy School in Dublin, it was organised 'to some extent' along with football and cricket.[116] St Andrew's College, Dublin also offered swimming to pupils, along with cricket, football and tennis, and it was also taught at Wesley College, Dublin, with the same sports and handball.[117] At St Joseph's College, Mount Street, Roscrea, County Tipperary, pupils could avail of twenty acres of playing space around the college and

---

109   Ibid., Report Number 100.
110   Ibid., Report Number 132.
111   Ibid., Report Number 126.
112   Ibid., Report Number 135.
113   *Intermediate Education Board for Ireland. Reports of Inspectors 1909–10. From No. 1 to No. 81. Vol. I.* Report Number 14.
114   *Intermediate Education Board for Ireland. Reports of Inspectors 1909–10. From No. 82 to No. 168. Volume II.* Report Number 165.
115   Declan O'Keeffe, 'Clongowes Down through the Years' Retrieved from <https://www.jesuit.ie/blog/declan-okeeffe/clongowes-down-the-years/> [Accessed 28 November 2020].
116   *Intermediate Education Board for Ireland. Reports of Inspectors 1909–10. From No. 82 to No. 168. Volume II.* Report Numbers 36 and 66.
117   Ibid., Report Numbers 68 and 71.

(in good weather) an 'open-air swimming bath' in the college grounds.'[118] Campbell College owned a cricket ground of ten acres along with football pitches suitable for four matches.[119] At Kilkenny College, the school lawn was utilised for cricket practice, but matches were usually played on the 'county ground'.[120] However, most Irish intermediate schools did not offer cricket to pupils. At Bangor Endowed School in County Down, it was 'not successfully carried, owing to want of a good ground'.[121] With the game's popularity in Ireland in the late nineteenth and early twentieth centuries, it was not simply restricted to schools of a Protestant ethos. Some Christian Brothers Schools such as that in Oxford Street, Belfast, where it was played in a public park, provided it for pupils.[122] Similarly, it was part of the sport available at St Malachy's College Belfast, along with soccer, hurling, cycling, handball and tennis.[123] St Vincent's College Castleknock also provided cricket along with roller-skating, tennis, handball, rowing, swimming, football and billiards.[124] A few schools offered facilities for boxing, including the Academy, Omagh, where a punchbag and boxing gloves was available for those interested, and the Grammar School in Tipperary, which also had a range of other sports including football, cricket, handball, rackets, tennis and hockey on offer to pupils.[125]

The availability of space for physical education in intermediate Schools varied. St Patrick's College, Armagh was noted as possessing 'large playing fields in [the] school grounds'.[126] The Royal School, Armagh had 'ample

118 *Intermediate Education Board for Ireland. Reports of Inspectors 1909–10. From No. 82 to No. 168. Volume II.* Report Number 146.

119 *Intermediate Education Board for Ireland. Reports of Inspectors 1909–10. From No. 1 to No. 81. Vol. I.* Report Number 15.

120 *Intermediate Education Board for Ireland. Reports of Inspectors 1909–10. From No. 82 to No. 168. Volume II.* Report Number 98.

121 *Intermediate Education Board for Ireland. Reports of Inspectors 1909–10. From No. 1 to No. 81. Vol. I.* Report Number 14.

122 Ibid., Report Number 16.

123 Ibid., Report Number 20.

124 Ibid., Report Number 36.

125 *Intermediate Education Board for Ireland. Reports of Inspectors 1909–10. From No. 82 to No. 168. Volume II.* Report Numbers 138 and 154.

126 *Intermediate Education Board for Ireland. Reports of Inspectors 1909–10. From No. 1 to No. 81. Vol. I.* Report Number 4.

space' behind the school and a football field 'a short distance' away.[127] At the Academy in Ballymena, County Antrim, there was a play area near the school (which girls also attended), with junior and senior [rugby] football fields, while there was also 'an open ball-alley' and 'one tennis court and two outdoor badminton courts (for girls) of regulation size'.[128]

Some schools utilised nearby fields and sports grounds when they did not have sufficient space themselves. Pupils at the CBS in North Brunswick Street in Dublin availed of the hurling and 'football', organised for them in Phoenix Park by the Brothers.[129] At the CBS Kilkenny, hurling and 'football' were organised by the staff for pupils in St James's Park, 'about a quarter of a mile from the school'.[130] As well as the public park, mentioned above, CBS Oxford Street utilised 'an open space paved with cobbles adjacent to school, almost a quarter of an acre in extent' with permission given to the school by Belfast Corporation and 'private owners'.[131] Pupils at the CBS in Callan, County Kilkenny, had accessibility to 'a court yard of 150 square yards beside the school' and the town park, which was ten acres in size.[132] Kilkenny College rented a 'full-size' rugby field nearby, and they also had a ball-alley, which was availed of regularly.[133] Students at St Michael's College, Listowel, County Kerry, had the use of the public sports field which adjoined the college grounds.[134] Facilities for games at Midleton College, Cork included football and cricket grounds set in seventeen acres of grass, while students at the CBS, Mitchelstown had to make do with 'half an acre, with clay and gravel surface, beside the school'.[135]

127   Ibid., Report Number 3.
128   Ibid., Report Number 13.
129   Ibid., Report Number 61.
130   *Intermediate Education Board for Ireland. Reports of Inspectors 1909–10. From No. 82 to No. 168. Volume II.* Report Number 97.
131   *Intermediate Education Board for Ireland. Reports of Inspectors 1909–10. From No. 1 to No. 81. Vol. I.* Report Number 16.
132   Ibid., Report Number 27.
133   *Intermediate Education Board for Ireland. Reports of Inspectors 1909–10. From No. 82 to No. 168. Volume II.* Report Number 98.
134   Ibid., Report Number 113.
135   Ibid., Report Numbers 121 and 122.

In a few instances elsewhere, a lack of space had a serious impact on the provision of any kind of physical exercise. As well as CBS Mitchelstown (Cork), a few schools did not formally cater for it at all, such as the CBS in Monaghan, where the 'situation and size of playground' was listed as 'practically none' although a form of football and hurling were played in the street by the school.[136] At the Patrician Brothers' School, Carrickmacross, County Monaghan, the boys went home at the close of school each day and no games were arranged.[137] A lack of space appears to have curtailed serious development at the CBS Marino (Dublin), with only a 'small playground, concreted, [and] drained near the school' available and only half an hour given to playtime, from 12.30 p.m. to 1 p.m.[138] At the CBS in Gorey, County Wexford, which had 'a good ball-alley', handball was the only game organised by staff, with the school having only 'less than a quarter acre of concrete surface' for games.[139] Handball was still played in many boys' schools and ball alleys were quite common on their premises, such as at the CBS Kells in County Meath.[140]

While, as noted above, school competitions were underway since the late nineteenth century, inspectors generally failed to reflect on schools' activity in these. Participation in schools' sports competitions at both intra-school and inter-school levels were indirectly noted in some inspectors' reports, however, without naming specific competitions. Pupils at St Vincent's Orphanage Glasnevin (Dublin) had their own soccer league in the school, which was run by the Christian Brothers there.[141] Medals were given internally to 'football' teams at Summerhill College Sligo, which suggests an intra-school competition was operational.[142] An inspector's report

---

136   Ibid., Report Numbers 122 and 123.

137   *Intermediate Education Board for Ireland. Reports of Inspectors 1909–10. From No. 1 to No. 81. Vol. I.* Report Number 31.

138   *Intermediate Education Board for Ireland. Reports of Inspectors 1909–10. From No. 1 to No. 81. Vol. I.* Report Number 72.

139   *Intermediate Education Board for Ireland. Reports of Inspectors 1909–10. From No. 82 to No. 168. Volume II.* Report Number 94.

140   Ibid., Report Number 95.

141   *Intermediate Education Board for Ireland. Reports of Inspectors 1909–10. From No. 1 to No. 81. Vol. I.* Report Number 73.

142   *Intermediate Education Board for Ireland. Reports of Inspectors 1909–10. From No. 82 to No. 168. Volume II.* Report Number 151.

on St Flannan's College in Ennis (Clare) noted that along with playing 'football' and handball, they had been hurling champions of Munster for six years.[143] At the Catholic University School in Leeson Street, Dublin, 'football', tennis and cricket matches were played with other schools.[144] In St Kieran's College, Kilkenny, 'a number of matches were arranged with colleges and outside clubs' although as noted above, the students were urged to organise the games themselves.[145] It appears that matches took place outside of class-time and this may be why there was less noted of these by inspectors. The period of play available to male pupils was varied, and naturally this was extended for students who were Boarders as opposed to Day students who generally went home when school finished in the afternoon. Some Day pupils also went home for lunch and missed out on this opportunity for more informal playtime which would have been available if they were to remain eating on the school grounds. In a few schools, some games had been disbanded, such as at the CBS in Tralee (Kerry), where a form of football, probably Gaelic, had been played but by 1910 had 'been dropped owing to disputes which arose' from the previous year's matches.[146]

The amount of playtime allocated varied in many schools. Along with a half-hour period of Swedish drill in the morning, pupils at the Royal School in Armagh had 'about three hours after school' dedicated to play.[147] At the Christian Brothers' High School and St Peter and St Paul's High School in Clonmel (Tipperary), the period of play was from 2.30 p.m. to 3.30 p.m. on Thursday and 'on other evenings voluntary games' took place from 4 p.m. to 6 p.m.[148] At the Academical Institute, Coleraine, half an hour for play was given after breakfast, recess and after dinner from 3 p.m. until 7 p.m. in the summer, and to 6 p.m. in the winter.[149] The availability

143   Ibid., Report Number 83.
144   *Intermediate Education Board for Ireland. Reports of Inspectors 1909–10. From No. 1 to No. 81. Vol. I.* Report Number 59.
145   *Intermediate Education Board for Ireland. Reports of Inspectors 1909–10. From No. 82 to No. 168. Volume II.* Report Number 99.
146   Ibid., Report Number 155.
147   *Intermediate Education Board for Ireland. Reports of Inspectors 1909–10. From No. 1 to No. 81. Vol. I.* Report Number 3.
148   Ibid., Report Number 41.
149   Ibid., Report Number 45.

of a covered gymnasium at the school was undoubtedly a benefit there, particularly for usage in wet weather. The rugby-playing CBS College Cork, noted above, allocated one and a half hours three times a week for this code, while they also had the use of 'a covered ball-alley and gymnasium' with a total of four acres, which included 'a football ground about half a mile from the school'.[150]

At the CBS in James's Street in Dublin, 'only the recreation, 12.30 pm to 1 pm' was allocated as a play period, and on wet days the pupils had to remain in the building.[151] This contrasted to some others whose facilities meant that games and sport could still take place indoors when the weather was poor. At the Royal Academical Institute in Belfast, there were 'two covered courts and a gymnasium' while Blackrock College had indoor provisions in its corridors, a billiards room and a gymnasium.[152] As well as having 'about twenty acres' at the back of the college for cricket and football, Rockwell College in Cashel, County Tipperary had 'covered recreation halls' where 'parlour games' were held in bad weather.[153] St Vincent's College Castleknock was the site of a gymnasium, two billiard tables, a library, a skating rink and a swimming bath which was seventy-five feet by thirty-two feet.[154] Less fortunate were those at the CBS in Charleville and at CBS Sullivan's Quay in Cork, where it was reported that no provision was made for any games or physical activity of any sort.[155] Provision was also made for schools' sport at weekends in some schools such as CBS Callan (Kilkenny), where two hours were allocated on a Saturday afternoon.[156]

150   Ibid., Report Number 47.
151   Ibid., Report Number 60.
152   Ibid., Report Numbers 18 and 24.
153   Ibid., Report Number 34.
154   Ibid., Report Number 36.
155   Ibid., Report Numbers 39 and 49.
156   Ibid., Report Number 27.

Girls' Schools

In intermediate girls' schools, there were some similarities in the facilitation of physical education and other sport. Forms of drill were also
provided in girls' schools and some recruited military men to undertake
its teaching. At La Sainte Union Convent in Athlone, a military man
gave 'three quarters of an hour weekly to each section', while at the La
Sainte Union Convent in Banagher (King's County), Swedish drill was
preferred with a 'quarter hour each morning before nine' along with
'one hour weekly', given by a drill instructor.[157] A drill sergeant visited
Ursuline College in Blackrock, County Cork once a week, while at
the Loreto Convent in Clonmel, a drill master was employed 'for three
months in spring'.[158] A drill sergeant attended the Loreto Convent in
Youghal, County Cork, on a weekly basis during the Lenten term.[159]
'Anglo-Germanic and Swedish drill' was taught 'by highly qualified
instructors' at St Dominic's High School in Belfast.[160] At Alexandra
College, Dublin, Swedish drill was taught by 'the principal gymnastic instructor at Portobello Gymnasium' but it is clear that not every school
recruited drill instructors externally and, as in the case of Alexandra, it
was not always compulsory for students.[161] At the Seminary in Abbeyleix,
'at times fancy drill' was provided, while 'simple exercises with arms' and
techniques in the bending of the body were also taught.[162] At the Convent
Select School on the Crumlin Road, Belfast, musical drill was given for
one hour a week, while 'kindergarten' was the preferred style of drill at
the Ladies' Collegiate School, Bellavista, in Bangor.[163] Callisthenics was
provided for juniors at the Girls High School, Eglantine Avenue, Belfast,

---

157   *Intermediate Education Board for Ireland. Reports of Inspectors 1909–10. From No.
      201 to No. 332. Vol. III.* Report Number 205 and 212.
158   Ibid., Report Numbers 229 and 241.
159   Ibid., Report Number 332.
160   Ibid., Report Number 227.
161   Ibid., Report Number 252.
162   Ibid., Report Number 202.
163   Ibid., Report Numbers 215 and 218.

and some schools combined both military and Swedish drill, such as at Loreto Convent in Bray.[164] A sergeant attended the High School, Sydney Place, Cork, every Monday, for drill, and as there were also thirty-two pupils under the age of 10 enrolled along with sixty-one older students, younger pupils had ten minutes' drill on the other weekdays with a kindergarten mistress.[165]

In some convent schools, such as the Brigidine Convent in Mountrath, County Wexford, and at Loreto Convent, Mullingar (Westmeath), drill was taught by the Sisters themselves.[166] Like in the male schools, the type of drill taught was not the same everywhere. At the Diocesan Inter and Commercial School for Girls, Adelaide Road, Dublin, Sandow's drill was taught, twice a week, for half an hour each time.[167] Some pupils, such as the older girls at St Margaret's Hall School, on the Mespil Road, Dublin, attended nearby gymnasiums.[168] They went to Miss Studley's, while the small children were drilled by a teacher in the school.[169] She had opened Ling College in Dublin in 1900, where an emphasis was placed on Swedish drill.[170] However, O'Donoghue et al have stated that teaching under the Ling system was 'highly formalised and had a militaristic tone to it' and Ling College was more focused on facilitating clients rather than teacher training until the 1920s.[171] Miss Studley had previously attended Hampstead Physical Training College. Ling College was initially based in Harcourt Street but the premises were relocated at Upper Mount Street in 1923.[172] Senior pupils at the Waterside Ladies' School in Derry attended the nearby

---

164   Ibid., Report Numbers 219 and 231.
165   Ibid., Report Number 245.
166   Ibid., Report Numbers 302 and 303.
167   Ibid., Report Number 255.
168   Ibid., Report Number 262.
169   Ibid.
170   Thomas O'Donoghue, Judith Harford and Theresa O'Doherty, *Teacher Preparation in Ireland: History, Policy and Future Directions* (Bingley: Emerald Publishing, 2017), 42.
171   Ibid.
172   *Irish Press*, 27 February 1969.

barracks for drill twice a week.[173] As well as joining the Monkstown Hockey Club, girls at the Ladies College, Haddington House, Kingstown, Dublin, visited a YMCA gymnasium 'at certain times'.[174]

The time allocated to physical education and the provision of sport also varied in many girls' schools. At Russell Street School in Armagh, where there were only twelve pupils enrolled, drill was the only form of exercise provided, and took place in the winter.[175] At the Presentation Convent in Bagenalstown, one quarter hour per week of drill was provided, and it was felt by the management, which consisted of the local priest and a number of members of the community, that 'little exercise' was needed as the girls had 'to cycle many miles to school'.[176] At the Presentation Convent in Bandon, pupils received an unspecified form of drill for only 'a few minutes every day' and games were not organised by staff.[177] In contrast, around one and a half hours was given for exercise after school at St Dominic' High School in Belfast, while a half-day was also allocated to sport on Saturdays.[178]

While soccer, Gaelic football, rugby, hurling and cricket appear to be the most common sports in the boys' schools, as noted above, it was hockey, tennis, basketball, cricket and croquet which were more regularly found in girls' schools by 1910. Staff at the Seminary in Abbeyleix organised hockey in winter and cricket in summer, while cricket, hockey and tennis were organised by staff at La Sainte Union Convent in Athlone.[179] Hockey, tennis, rounders and an unspecified form of football were noted as being provided at La Sainte Union Convent in Banagher, while at Brookvale Collegiate School in Belfast, hockey was the preferred game of staff.[180] At Mount Prospect School on the Lisburn Road in Belfast, tennis, croquet and basketball were played, while tennis and rounders were offered

---

173 *Intermediate Education Board for Ireland. Reports of Inspectors 1909–10. From No. 201 to No. 332. Vol. III.* Report Number 298.

174 Ibid., Report Number 284. Kingstown is now known as Dún Laoghaire.

175 Ibid., Report Number 204.

176 Ibid., Report Number 207.

177 Ibid., Report Number 213.

178 Ibid., Report Number 227.

179 Ibid., Report Number 202 and 205.

180 Ibid., Report Number 212 and 217.

at Princess Gardens School in Belfast.[181] Pupils played hockey, rounders, cricket and tennis at St Dominic's High School in Belfast.[182] At Victoria High School in Derry, hockey (pictured in Figure 11) and tennis were played, while dancing also took place there.[183] Similarly, dancing was held in the Dominican Convent Blackrock, County Cork, along with hockey, cricket, tennis and rounders.[184] While rounders was clearly popular, a few schools offered baseball, including the Ursuline Convent, Coleraine.[185]

Figure 11. Victoria High School Derry hockey team, pictured in 1902 with the Ulster Ladies' Challenge Shield. Courtesy of William Lynn.

181   Ibid., Report Number 223 and 224.
182   Ibid., Report Number 227.
183   Ibid., Report Number 297.
184   Ibid., Report Number 230.
185   Ibid., Report Number 243.

As in the boys' schools, staff attitudes to the organisation of games in girls' schools varied. At St Mary's University School in Donnybrook, the governess organised the games although this was not the norm elsewhere and it was often the staff who were in charge of this.[186] However, at the Convent of Mercy in Athy, they did not organise any games.[187] Organisation of games was sometimes left to the students themselves, or took place through the staff and selected students. At Alexandra College in Dublin, a games' committee consisting of two staff members and students organised hockey and tennis.[188] At the Dominican Convent in Cabra (Dublin), it was noted that 'the girls divide themselves into various divisions for purposes of games'.[189] Some religious orders arranged physical training competitions for pupils, with 'upwards of two hundred pupils' joining 'some fifty teams' for 'the competitions comprising barbells, Indian clubs, dumbbells, figure marching and Swedish free exercises' which had been organised by the newly founded Holy Faith Physical Society by March 1912.[190] They were assisted by a number of men with experience of the subject, as events were to be supervised by the aforementioned Herbert L Harte, the society's physical education director, who was also the Glasgow School Board's Advisor of Physical Training, with Herbert Wright also involved in the judging.[191] Trophies and medals were to again to be presented by the Bishop of Canea, the Most Reverend Dr Donnelly.[192]

The space and facilities also at times dictated what was offered in the line of physical education in girls' schools. At the Convent of Mercy in Athy, which had only a small playground, games were not organised by staff, but pupils were sometimes allowed to walk around the Convent grounds and to play in a large field when the weather was suitable.[193] Reporting on the

186   Ibid., Report Number 251.
187   Ibid., Report Number 206.
188   Ibid., Report Number 252.
189   Ibid., Report Number 232.
190   *Freeman's Journal*, 28 March 1912.
191   Ibid.
192   Ibid.
193   *Intermediate Education Board for Ireland. Reports of Inspectors 1909–10. From No. 201 to No. 332. Vol. III.* Report Number 206.

Ladies Collegiate School, Bellavista, Bangor, the inspector noted the scarcity of facilities, including a 'very small garden' although there was also 'a special room' where drill was provided when the weather was wet.[194] There were many schools were games were not compulsory and were only 'encouraged', although in some, such as the Brigidine Convent in Abbeyleix and the Seminary in the same town, pupils had to participate.[195] 'Daily walks' were compulsory at the Convent of St Louis in Carrickmacross, while many other rural schools were eager to utilise the benefits of the fresh country air.[196] At St Mary's Intermediate School, Convent of Mercy, Arklow, pupils performed exercises in good weather in part of the large adjoining field which commanded a 'fine view' of the 'open sea'.[197] Students at St Rose's College, Taylor's Hill, Galway, had to opportunity to engage in 'sea-bathing' in summer.[198]

At the Ursuline Convent, Waterford, pupils had access to a gymnasium (pictured in Figure 12), playground and playing fields and participated in a game known as 'camp', along with hockey, cricket, croquet and tennis.[199] Students at the Princess Gardens School in Belfast had use of Ormeau Park, where they played rounders.[200] Some schools had their own hockey fields and tennis courts. Pupils at the Ursuline Convent in Blackrock, County Cork had 'a hockey field, playground and tennis ground' which they could access near the school, and 'grounds of about fifty acres' were also open for use.[201] At Victoria College in Belfast, there were one and a half acres 'divided between hockey and tennis, about one mile away, and two tennis courts in front of the college'.[202] There was also 'a very fine gymnasium'.[203] Girls at Loreto Convent in Bray had the 'run of the park, about forty

---

194   Ibid., Report Number 215.
195   Ibid., Report Numbers 201 and 202.
196   Ibid., Report Number 235.
197   Ibid., Report Number 203.
198   Ibid., Report Number 274.
199   Ibid., Report Number 300.
200   Ibid., Report Number 224.
201   Ibid., Report Number 229.
202   Ibid., Report Number 228.
203   Ibid.

Figure 12.   Ursuline Convent Waterford gymnasium and students, 1908.
Courtesy of the National Library of Ireland.

acres … and a special four-acre playing field'.[204] They also had access to an
asphalt tennis court.[205] The Rosetta High School in Belfast had a hockey
field measuring 'about an acre'. At the High School, Sydney Place, Cork,
the school had use of a full size hockey field and two tennis courts, while
their on-site recreation hall could accommodate 200.[206]

Pupils at Alexandra College Dublin had four acres of space for physical exercise at Milltown, and 'a large garden and tennis court in Earlsfort
Terrace.[207] A few years prior to the inspection, work had begun at the school
on developing a gymnasium which included a full range 'of Swedish drill

204   Ibid., Report Number 231.
205   Ibid.
206   Ibid., Report Number 245.
207   Ibid., Report Number 252.

apparatus'.[208] In what appears to be a novel development in Irish schools, a Physical Training Department was opened there in October 1914 with preparation for the Ling Association diploma examinations available as part of a two-year course.[209] It was overseen by Miss M. E. Tempest, the college's games' mistress, with Ling's Swedish system in place. Students undertook instruction in the theory and practice of gymnastics, with teaching practice under supervision also a requirement.[210] Accommodation was available to them at the college's hostel with the intention that when qualified, they would take up positions as gymnastics and games mistresses.[211]

Mixed Schools

Of the thirty-eight intermediate mixed schools reported upon by the in-spectors, less than a handful stipulated that games were compulsory. At the Ladies' School and Kindergarten in Duniris, Bangor, tennis was com-pulsory for all over 12 years of age, while hockey and rugby were compul-sory at the Royal School Raphoe in County Donegal.[212] With the absence of a national structure, amongst other factors such as the Irish weather and the slow nature of the game, cricket's importance in Ulster schools paled in significance to that afforded in many establishments there to competitive rugby.[213] Cricket had been played at Raphoe's Royal School since the 1860s at least with a match taking place between the school XI, made up of players of the local club, and Lifford Cricket club, to mark the birthday of Queen Victoria on 24 May 1865.[214] The smaller numbers

---

208   *Dublin Daily Express*, 17 August 1907.
209   *The Daily Express*, 4 July 1914.
210   *Irish Independent*, 29 May 1915.
211   Ibid., 27 May 1915.
212   *Intermediate Education Board for Ireland. Reports of Inspectors 1909–10. From No. 401 to 436 Volume IV.* Report Numbers 407 and 430.
213   For an assessment of the failure of cricket in Donegal see Curran, *The Development of Sport in Donegal*, 52–64.
214   *The Londonderry Standard*, 31 May 1865.

in mixed schools, ranging from only eleven pupils at the Preston School in Navan (Meath) to 167 at the Mercantile College in Belfast, meant that less emphasis was placed on team games in schools where numbers were low.[215] The figures for the latter school were exceptional, and the majority of mixed schools' figures came nowhere near this enrolment rate. At Gracehill Academy in Ballymena, which had a registration of just thirteen, 'owing to a small number of pupils' there were no games organised by staff.[216] Elsewhere in County Antrim, at the intermediate school in Ballymoney, the boys' committee organised games themselves, while at the Royal School, Raphoe, it was stated that the staff were on games committees and attended meetings and they also participated in practices.[217] At the Prior School in Lifford, games were organised by the head boy, but this power given to an individual pupil was generally not common in schools examined by the inspectors.[218]

In some schools which accepted male and female students, a balance of sports deemed suitable for both sexes was evident, with hockey played all year round at Methodist College while rugby and cricket (for boys) were seasonal.[219] At Ballymena Academy, rugby, tennis, badminton and handball were played.[220] However, at that point, rugby was generally a male sport while hockey, tennis and badminton would have been deemed as more socially acceptable for girls to play as opposed to forms of football and many female schools stuck to this view. Again, some school authorities felt that pupils' attachment to local clubs was sufficient exercise. At the Collegiate School in Limavady, it was noted that the staff did not organise games, as a large number of girls were members of the local Roebank Hockey team, and 'several, having to walk in four miles or so every day'

215 *Intermediate Education Board for Ireland. Reports of Inspectors 1909–10. From No. 401 to 436 Volume IV.* Report Numbers 410 and 426.
216 Ibid., Report Number 402.
217 Ibid., Report Numbers 403 and 430.
218 Ibid., Report Number 420.
219 *Intermediate Education Board for Ireland. Reports of Inspectors 1909–10. From No. 1 to No. 81. Vol. I.* Report Number 17.
220 Ibid., Report Number 13.

were satisfied with this arrangement.[221] Boys at the Intermediate School, Church Street, Tullamore (King's County) were members of 'local juvenile clubs' such as those of hockey and cricket while they also trained twice a week in a gymnasium 'under a competent instructor'.[222] Location again impacted on the provision of sports for some schools. At the Preston School in Navan, which was built in the centre of the town, there was 'no space available for a playground'.[223] The low number of pupils also affected the decision to seek a suitable area for exercise, as 'formerly, when the school was flourishing, a field outside the town was hired' but the school authorities remained hopeful of securing 'the use of a portion on the show field'.[224] Most of these schools did, however, have some space for playing games or exercise. Those at the Royal School in Raphoe had access to hockey and football fields measuring eleven acres, along with a ball court and tennis facilities, while they also had a second field, 1.25 acres in size.[225] Schools in more urban areas were naturally forced to adapt to the local environment, with pupils at the Mercantile School in Belfast having the use of the local ground at Cliftonville, where they could play a form of football, cricket and handball.[226]

As shown earlier, school authorities' attitudes to drill varied. At Methodist College, junior classes had musical drill along with marching three times weekly, but seniors had the option of taking gymnasium instead twice a week.[227] Only a few mixed schools hired instructors, with at least twenty schools not providing any drill. At Mount Oregon School in Whitehead, County Antrim, it was undertaken by Miss Haines and a military sergeant, while at the D'Israeli School in Rathvilly, County Carlow, it was given 'occasionally' by a drill sergeant for a forty minute

221 *Intermediate Education Board for Ireland. Reports of Inspectors 1909–10. From No. 401 to 436 Volume IV.* Report Number 421.

222 Ibid., Report Number 434.

223 Ibid., Report Number 426.

224 Ibid.

225 Ibid., Report Number 430.

226 Ibid., Report Number 410.

227 *Intermediate Education Board for Ireland. Reports of Inspectors 1909–10. From No. 1 to No. 81. Vol. I.* Report Number 17.

period.[228] However, in a few schools, such as the Royal School in Raphoe, it was given every day, while those at the Grammar School in Bandon had Swedish drill three times a week.[229] At the Collegiate School in Limavady, drill was taught once a week only.[230] At the Royal Academy in Belfast, girls undertook Swedish drill and boys were given gymnasium while at the Upper Sullivan School in Holywood, County Down, only the girls were given drill, on a Monday, illustrating further the inconsistent nature of its provision in Irish intermediate schools.[231] Many of the decisions affecting the provision of forms of physical education at that level appear to have simply been down to individual preferences, with, for example, the headmaster at St Patrick's Collegiate School in Newbridge, County Kildare, of the view that the provision of exercise on wet days was unnecessary, as pupils received 'a large amount' of this on their daily journeys to and from the school.[232]

The First World War and Physical Training in Intermediate Schools

Approximately 200,000 Irishmen saw active service in the British armed forces during the First World War and around 30,000 of these were killed.[233] Some intermediate school pupils inevitably entered military service during this conflict.[234] At St Jude's School on the Ormeau Road in Belfast (a school which had enjoyed back-to-back victories in the final of the Cliftonville FC-organised Schools Cup for soccer), most of the

228 Ibid., Report Numbers 432 and 436.
229 Ibid., Report Numbers 406 and 430.
230 Ibid., Report Number 421.
231 *Intermediate Education Board for Ireland. Reports of Inspectors 1909–10. From No. 1 to No. 81. Vol. I.* Report Number 19 and *Intermediate Education Board for Ireland. Reports of Inspectors 1909–10. From No. 401 to 436 Volume IV.* Report Number 417.
232 *Reports of Inspectors 1909–10. From No. 401 to 436 Volume IV.* Report Number 427.
233 Bartlett, *Ireland: A History*, 382.
234 Ferriter, *The Transformation of Ireland*, 159.

boys of military age and physique were said to have joined the army by 1915.[235] By November of that year, Dublin club Olympia FC, Leinster Minor Cup winners in 1914, had twenty-two members serving in the war, with their minor team's captain, RF Kinninmont, becoming a Corporal with the South Irish Horse.[236] In a November 1917 report of activities at the High School, Dublin, which was based in Harcourt Street, it was stated that 'systematic Swedish drill and gymnastics had been introduced, and medals were given for the best boy in each form at the end of the season'.[237] The school's record of providing military men was also noted, and apparently 'as the boys reached the age for service nearly all of the members were only too anxious to serve. They had now between four and five hundred old boys who had joined the forces and three of their masters were at the front.'[238]

Support for the war effort also came in other forms. In July 1916 it was noted in the press that '"Prize Day" in the principal schools in Ulster has become a misnomer since the outbreak of war because so many pupils have voluntarily foregone their prizes with a request that the teachers apply the value to one of the war charities'.[239] Physical drill and outdoor games continued to be provided at the Ladies' School in Cookstown, where that same month the girls requested that the value of their special class prizes be used instead 'for the relief of prisoners in Germany'.[240] Some technical schools also showed their support and attempted to raise greater public awareness of events on the continent. In January 1917, the Municipal Technical School in Derry organised a 'War Work and Art and Crafts Exhibition' which included a physical drill display by students of the Day Technical School.[241]

Exhibitions and competitions therefore continued throughout the war years. The pupils of the Dominican Convent, Wicklow, gave a physical culture display which contained elements of the Swedish system such as the

---

235   *Belfast Newsletter*, 11 December 1915.
236   *Evening Herald*, 27 November 1915.
237   *Dublin Daily Express*, 24 November 1917.
238   Ibid.
239   *Mid-Ulster Mail*, 1 July 1916.
240   Ibid.
241   *Londonderry Sentinel*, 20 January 1917.

use of barbells, dumb-bells, swinging clubs, scarf drills and figure marching under the instruction of Mr Wright in March 1915, for which a number received medals.[242] In April 1917, the Loreto Convent, Balbriggan held their annual physical drill display, with medals presented by the Mother Superior and Mr Harte, the drill instructor.[243] The following month, pupils at the Loreto Convent, Gorey also gave their annual physical drill display under the instruction of Miss Farrley 'before many of the parents and friends and a large number of other invited guests'.[244] Physical training was also simply seen as a form of release from schoolwork. It was noted in the annual report of the principal at Knock Intermediate School and Kindergarten in June 1916, 'drill and singing formed a very pleasant relaxation from the ordinary studies'.[245] Public classes for those interested were also provided in some areas. In November 1916 a Belfast-based Mr Degville advertised his dancing and Swedish drill service in the national press, promising to visit towns in the province of Ulster when hired.[246] By the start of the following month he had established a weekly beginners' class at Donegall Square at a price of ten shillings for twelve lessons.[247] Both public and private tuition of pupils allowed instructors the opportunity to gain employment. In April 1917, 'the pupils of the Misses Devlin gave a very attractive display of dancing and physical drill in the Ulster Hall' in Belfast, and it was noted that the instructors held 'a deservedly high reputation as teachers of dancing and deportment'.[248] While the numbers of these instructors at the time is unclear, some clearly managed to become highly sought after. In March 1918, following the Loreto College, St Stephen's Green students' annual display of physical drill, the death of their former instructor, Mr Harte, was noted. It was also stated that 'in Mr Wright, his successor, they had the best instructor in the three kingdoms'.[249] He had been 'for many years

242   *Freeman's Journal*, 22 and 24 March 1915.
243   *Drogheda Argus and Leinster Journal*, 8 April 1916.
244   *Enniscorthy Guardian*, 6 May 1916.
245   *Northern Whig*, 27 June 1916.
246   *Belfast Newsletter*, 30 November 1916.
247   Ibid., 11 December 1916.
248   Ibid., 3 April 1917.
249   *Freeman's Journal*, 21 March 1918.

an advocate of physical culture in all schools, primary and intermediate'.[250] As noted earlier, he had taught in a number of schools in Dublin and Wicklow and was well established on the physical instructor circuit by the end of the decade.

As stated earlier, the influenza pandemic impacted on the organisation of school games, particularly in Clongowes Wood.[251] Both Swedish and physical drill continued to maintain a place within Irish Schools by the third decade of the twentieth century. In March 1920, a display of physical drill was given by the Loreto Convent North Great St George's Street pupils with medals also awarded.[252] In December 1920, the Friends' School in Lisburn sought 'a resident mistress for Swedish drill and games'.[253] Physical training in intermediate schools still lacked a uniform syllabus and many schools continued with what was suited to their school structure, ethos and the resources they had available. Games continued to be held in high esteem in many schools, and in 1921 Campbell College's rugby first team won the first of six Ulster Schools' Cups in that decade.[254] However, no major changes were made regarding the provision of physical training within the curriculum in Irish Intermediate schools. As shown in Chapter 1, the proposed McPherson Education Bill of 1919–20 was defeated and as Coolahan states, 'an undoubted factor ranged against the success of the bill was the imminence of some form of home rule legislation and the idea that a large-scale recasting of the educational system should be left to the new administration'.[255] He adds that this failure to take action 'left intermediate education in its chronic position' and 'thus it was a rickety and run-down intermediate education machine that the new Independent Irish Free State inherited at the transfer of powers in February 1922'.[256]

---

250 Ibid.
251 Milne, *Stacking the Coffins*, 157.
252 *Irish Independent*, 2 March 1920.
253 *Belfast Newsletter*, 21 December 1920.
254 'Roll of Honour: Danske Bank Ulster Schools' Cup' Retrieved from <https://www.ulsterrugby.com/rugby-in-ulster/rugby-development/schools/roll-of-honour/> [Accessed 20 June 2020].
255 Coolahan, *Towards the Era of Lifelong Learning*, 59.
256 Ibid.

Conclusion

By the end of the first decade of the twentieth century, many second level
or intermediate schools had physical drill instructors and games masters and mistresses, but, as shown earlier, there were some which rejected
the provision or physical exercise, particularly where space was limited
or where attendance numbers were small. At times, pupils were encouraged to organise games independently, although many schools did assist
and some encouraged cooperation between students and staff through
the forming of pupils' committees and team captains. In boys' intermediate schools, sports that were deemed to be generally more suitable
to males, such as rugby, soccer and Gaelic football, were offered, while in
girls' schools the choice of sport was more focused on those less physically
rough such as tennis or dancing, and hockey was usually deemed the most
suitable team game for girls. Evidence for the sport of camogie, which was
founded as 'camoguidheacht' in 1904, is scarce to the point where the
inclusion of rounders was more noticeable in the 1909/1910 inspectors'
reports on girls' schools, but this can perhaps be explained by the temporary decline of camoguidheacht from 1907 until 1911.[257]

Competitive team sports were beginning to become a strong part of
the ethos of schools with the organisation of cups fundamental to this.
Schools were eager to show an emphasis on physical exercise, albeit a peripheral one, in their advertising of their subjects and facilities, while students'
prowess was rewarded through medals at annual speech days and glowing
praise in the provincial and national press.[258] Despite this, it was the more
academic subjects which were deemed to be of most value for positions of
employment. Some schools such as Campbell College also included military training for their pupils, While the Christian Brothers were naturally
eager to promote what they saw as nationalist sports such as Gaelic football

257   Ríona Nic Congáil, '"Looking on for Centuries from the Sideline": Gaelic
        Feminism and the Rise of Camogie' in *Éire-Ireland*, vol. 48, no. 1 & 2 (2013),
        168–90.
258   See, for example, *Belfast Newsletter*, 28 July 1911 and *The Daily Express*, 30
        December 1911.

and hurling, there is less evidence that codes which were portrayed as being overtly British in some sections of the press were deliberately excluded by Catholic-leaning schools at this point. Chapter 3 considers the treatment of physical drill in the Irish Free State, and illustrates how the weak foundations in the subject's status in the pre-partition era quickly gave way to pressure from teachers as it officially became optional in the primary school curriculum by the second half of the 1920s. In addition, it discusses how the Irish Government looked to Czechoslovakia in an indirect attempt to improve PE in its primary and second level schools in the 1930s.

CHAPTER 3

Reduction and Disorganisation: PE in Irish Free State Schools, 1922–1937

Introduction

This chapter discusses the status of physical drill in Irish Free State schools from the First National Programme Conference in 1922 until 1937. While physical drill was initially a mandatory subject in Irish primary schools in the Free State, in the middle of the 1920s a governmental decision was taken which was to have an impact on the physical and mental health of Irish schoolchildren for much of the twentieth century.[1] The move by the Department of Education to reduce physical drill from an obligatory to an optional subject following a vote between members of the Second National Programme Conference in 1925 is therefore examined. It will show that despite much support from educational representatives around the country, pressure from the INTO in relation to overloading of the curriculum led to the subject's reduction in status.[2] Facilities, resources and the physical fitness of some teachers was a problem, while some teachers were not overly interested in teaching the subject in the early years of the Irish Free State. In addition, an overwhelming focus on the development of the Irish language also meant that the teaching of physical drill was in decline in primary schools by the latter part of that decade despite the attempts of General Richard Mulcahy to draw attention to

---

1 Curran, 'The Irish Government and Physical Education in Irish Primary Schools, 1922–37' 43–60 and 'Physical Drill in Irish Free State Schools and the National Programme Conference, 1925–6', BSSH Conference, 2019, Hope University Liverpool.
2 Ibid.

the subject's plight.[3] With a change in government in 1932, when the Cumann na nGaedheal party was replaced by that of Fianna Fáil, and the decision to amend the system of physical training in the Irish Army, it appeared that more attention would be given to physical exercise in Irish schools. Systems of physical training across Europe were examined and the Czechoslovakian Sokol system was chosen as being the most suitable for Irish needs. Despite efforts by military men to introduce the Sokol system of physical training into some Irish schools in the 1930s, this was hampered by a lack of guidance from the Department of Education with the result that there was a failure to coordinate a nationwide system for its implementation in primary and second level schools.[4] This chapter also assesses the views of the GAA on attempts to develop the Sokol system within Irish society and illustrates that while some county board members were opposed to it, it was embraced by others, particularly in County Cavan.[5]

Physical Education in Primary Schools

Physical Drill's status as a compulsory subject in Irish primary schools remained secure within the curriculum in the initial years of the Irish Free State, which saw the Department of Education becoming functional in 1924 with Eoin MacNeill having become the first Minister of Education for the new government two years previously.[6] At the National

---

3   Ibid.
4   Curran, 'The Sokol System of Physical Training in Irish Schools in the 1930s.' ESAI Conference 2019, Radisson Hotel Sligo.
5   Ibid.
6   Brendan Walsh, 'History of Education in Ireland' in Brendan Walsh (ed.), *Education Studies in Ireland: The Key Disciplines* (Dublin, 2011), 34–71, 53 and Antonia McManus, *Irish Education: The Ministerial Legacy, 1919–99* (Dublin: The History Press Ireland, 2014), 19–33. Prior to MacNeill's appointment, John J. O'Kelly was initial Minister for Education but withdrew from the Dáil in January 1922 after the signing of the Treaty. Michael Hayes replaced O'Kelly and became minister in the

Programme Conference, which concluded in January 1922, it had been confirmed by TJ O'Connell, the INTO's general secretary, that it would be one of eight obligatory subjects, with Professor Corcoran of the National University of Ireland influential in compiling this structure.[7] Like history and geography, which were to be combined, and singing, it was to be taught through Irish and simplified. The Swedish system of physical training was recommended with a half an hour per week to be given. However, by 1925, rising dissatisfaction amongst teachers about the structure and quantity of the curriculum had led to the hosting of a second National Programme Conference, with a number of meetings held late in the year. It was at one of these in November that, along with a number of other subjects, physical drill's status was voted upon.[8] Opponents of its compulsory inclusion voiced issues with facilities, space and teachers' knowledge of how it should be taught with the INTO charge led by the teaching union's president, Cornelius P. Murphy. Despite positive sentiments about its value from a number of conference members, including Brother Kelleher, a delegate representing the Christian Brothers, it lost its obligatory status on a vote of nine to two. The vote to decide its status had been called for by the Irish language writer Pádraig Ó Siochfhradha, who was against its maintenance as a compulsory subject. Efforts by General Richard Mulcahy for the decision to be re-examined were fruitless after it became an optional subject and by the end of the decade, it was being neglected in some counties.[9]

Suggestions also came from other politicians in the Dáil but lacked any real traction and messages regarding its teaching and status became mixed and confused as some schools encouraged it more than others. In

---

Dáil and had responsibility for intermediate and higher education. Finian Lynch, who was minister for education in the Provisional Government, was responsible for primary education.

7   For a full examination of the treatment of physical drill in primary schools in this period, see Curran, 'The Irish Government and Physical Education in Irish Primary Schools, 1922–37' 43–60.

8   Ibid.

9   Ibid.

April 1929, Sir J. C. Craig stated in the Dáil that 'simple physical exercises' would be beneficial in warming children up in schools in cold weather. He encouraged the Minister for Education, John Marcus O'Sullivan (1926–32), who had taken over from MacNeill in 1926, to do more in areas where physical training was not taking place.[10] However, investment in the development of a national policy for PE was certainly not a priority. The aims of the Cumann na nGaedheal government in this decade, with the nation still recovering from physical damage inflicted during the Revolutionary period, were chiefly, according to Bartlett, 'financial rigour of the most stringent kind, a firm adherence to the rule of law, glacial tolerance of minorities and a desire to consolidate the "revolution"'.[11] In addition, 'except in respect of the Irish language – and this was a vital exception – there was absolutely no plan to transform Ireland socially or economically; if anything, the reverse'.[12]

Correspondence sent from Seosamh O'Neill of the Department of Education to the Swedish Consulate in Dublin in September 1929 implies that the provision of physical training in Free State schools was being well catered for.[13] O'Neill was responding to a request for information regarding the state of physical training in Irish primary and secondary schools, and was eager to portray a positive image. He stated that

> although Physical Training is not compulsory in the National (Primary) or in the Secondary Schools, about 95 % of the children in attendance in the National Schools receive instruction in Physical Training, and in a large and increasing number of the Secondary Schools, Physical Training is included and is on charge, as in the Training Colleges, of specially competent instructors.[14]

10   *Irish Independent*, 18 April 1929 and 'In Committee on Finance-Vote no. 45-Office of the Minister for Education (Resumed).' Dáil Éireann Debate. Vol. 29, No. 4.17 April 1929. Retrieved from <http://oireachtasdebates.oireachtas.ie/debates%20 authoring/DebatesWebPack.nsf/takes/dail1929041700036?opendocument&high light=physical%20training> [Accessed 7 December 2017].

11   Bartlett, *A History of Ireland*, 420.

12   Ibid.

13   ED/12/ 22858. Gymnastics and Physical Training in Primary Schools and Training Colleges. Letter from Seosamh O'Neill to H. Errickson, Swedish Consul, September 1929.

14   Ibid.

Figure 13. Handball at Good Counsel College, New Ross, County Wexford, 1931.
Courtesy of the National Library of Ireland.

O'Neill added that Irish step-dancing was 'frequently a part of instruction in Physical Training in National Schools' while 'in the larger centres of population the organisation of games, such as hurling, [Gaelic] football and handball (pictured above in Figure 13), for the boys of these schools is growing'.[15]

Other reports told a different story about how much physical training pupils were receiving. In 1930, an inspector's report on the division covering part of Dublin, Louth, Meath, Westmeath, Kildare, Leix, Offaly, Tipperary and Limerick noted that 'drill is now taught in only a few schools'. It was felt by the inspector that 'generally the work done is very good' although 'sufficient variety' was not given in Swedish exercises, while at times games

15   Ibid.

were neglected.[16] A scarcity of this in schools was also linked to physical deficiencies and its lack of attention in schools was highlighted in medical reports. Welshman has stated that in England, 'in the late 1920s and early 1930s' PE was seen as a form 'of preventative medicine.'[17] The same narrative can be seen in Irish medical reports on schools at this time. A School Medical Service was in place in the Irish Free State by the late 1920s.[18]

In March 1932 Fianna Fáil replaced Cumann na nGaedheal in power in the Irish Government following the election, with Eamon de Valera becoming Taoiseach, but there was no immediate impact in terms of attitudes to physical education.[19] In August 1932, at a meeting of the County Dublin Board of Health, J. J. Shiel noted 'the absolute neglect of physical training in national schools' after Dublin Medical Officer of Health [MOH], Dr Harbison, had reported upon physical ailments such as defected teeth and diseased tonsils caused by poor hygiene amongst pupils in four national schools in Dublin.[20] General Mulcahy, speaking in the Dáil three months later, also drew attention to the lack of overall progress made in developing physical training as a subject since its official downscaling in importance in 1926. He noted that much progress had been made in improving medical inspections and treatment of school children, but also stated that 'there is no systematic arrangement for the building up of the child physically.'[21]

He added that there was no department expenditure on physical training and questioned whether or not making money available to adult athletic training was of any value given that he felt it 'should be devoted to

---

16   *Report of the Department of Education 1929–30* (Dublin: The Stationery Office, 1930), 43.

17   Welshman, 'Physical Education and the School Medical Service in England and Wales', 38.

18   Susan Kelly, 'Education of Tubercular Children in Northern Ireland, 1921 to 1955' in *Social History of Medicine*, vol. 24, no. 2 (2010), 407–25, 411.

19   Ferriter, *The Transformation of Ireland*, 358.

20   *Irish Independent*, 3 August 1932.

21   'In Committee on Finance-Estimates for Public Services.-Vote 45-Office for the Minister for Education (Resumed)' Dáil Éireann Debate, 2 November 1932.' Retrieved from <http://oireachtasdebates.oireachtas.ie/Debates%20Authoring/DebatesWebPack.nsf/takes/dail1932110200020?opendocument&highlight=physical%20training> [Accessed 7 December 2017].

nurturing the roots which would give the most satisfactory return – even now – and which would be much more organic in its results than taking adult men and giving them athletic training'.[22] General Mulcahy also voiced concerns that too much attention was being given to the Irish language and this was having a detrimental effect on a number of school subjects.[23]

Despite the promotion of a policy of Gaelicisation in Irish schools, developing a uniquely Irish system of physical training remained elusive and teachers were generally left to their own devices. In the 1933 publication, *Notes for Teachers: Physical Training*, they were advised to consult a number of English Board of Education publications on the actual subject, something which drew condemnation from one newspaper correspondent under the guise of 'Grand National'.[24] He stated that 'I thought we should buy nothing from England, but now about 12,000 national teachers are advised to pay 5/6 into the British Exchequer!'[25] This was a reference to the ongoing 'Economic War' with Britain, which lasted from 1932 until 1938 and which Bartlett describes as 'a most unequal contest, and Irish farming interests, especially those involved in cattle rearing suffered grievously'.[26] Other Department of Education instructions also alluded to the view that teachers should simply do whatever they could to teach the subject as best they could. *The Report of the Department of Education for 1932–33*, published in June 1934, recommended that although it was not obligatory at primary school level, teachers who had received 'any training in the subject' were 'encouraged to take it up'. It was stated that

> a large proportion of the teachers are fully alive to the importance of the subject …. notwithstanding the difficulties due to want of training of the older teachers, lack of facilities and accommodation in many of the large schools in the towns and cities, etc., some forty percent of the school-going children are receiving instruction in the subject.[27]

22   Ibid.
23   *Irish Examiner*, 3 November 1932.
24   *An Roinn Oideachais, Oideachais Náisiúnta. Notes for Teachers: Physical Training* (Dublin: The Stationery Office, 1933), 1–4 and *Irish Independent*, 27 April 1933.
25   *Irish Independent*, 27 April 1933.
26   Bartlett, *Ireland: A History*, 441.
27   Ibid., *Report of the Department of Education for 1932–33*, 18.

Some areas benefitted from the organisation of local schools' associations at the time, with a primary schools' athletic association established at Thomastown, County Kilkenny in May 1934, through the initiation of three national school teachers, M. Walsh, J. Reidy and P. Laffan, but this was generally based on voluntary involvement and failed to develop on a national level.[28] In June 1934 a special meeting of the Cavan committee of the INTO took place there with J. H. Fitzsimmons, the official handicapper of the National Athletic and Cycle Association (of Ireland) [NACA], submitting 'a comprehensive scheme for the promotion of athletics in primary schools'.[29] The scheme received letters of support from new Minister for Education Thomas Derrig; Dr T. P. O'Reilly, who was the County MOH for Cavan; Dr R. J. Rowlette, TD; P. C. Moore, solicitor and President of the NACA; J. J. McGilton, honorary secretary of the NACA and Dr Seán Lavan. In particular, it was stated that Minister Derrig was 'very keen on the furtherance of athletics and physical culture in schools and colleges, and would be very glad that every parish should have its annual school sports'.[30] It was also noted that 'any suitable scheme for the promotion of athletics in primary schools' would have his 'hearty approval' and he wished it well.[31] As will be seen later with the Sokol system, Minister Derrig was keen to encourage some attempts by organisations to take on the development of a system for physical training in schools, but was less inclined to push to have its teaching made compulsory.

The Provision of Physical Training Courses for Trainee Teachers and Qualified Teachers

In a 1933 circular, Minister Derrig noted 'the importance of physical exercises in the schools' and advised 'a member of the staff who has been

28   *Irish Press*, 22 May 1934 and *Sunday Independent*, 24 June 1934.
29   *Sunday Independent*, 24 June 1934.
30   Ibid.
31   Ibid.

trained within the last decade of years' to take responsibility for the subject in larger schools, while acknowledging that not every school could cater for its teaching.[32] Physical training continued to maintain a place in teacher-training colleges for those studying to become primary school teachers. The syllabus for Physical Training for students in National School Teacher Training Colleges by 1929 was based on three main themes.[33] In first year, it was focused on 'Practical physical exercises, including exercises of the Swedish system' and 'Practice in commanding and teaching' and also the theory behind physical training.[34] The course in the second year was the same as that for first year students except with 'exercises and lectures more advanced'.[35] By 1932, all the national school teacher training colleges in the Irish Free State were said to have professional 'professors of drill'.[36] Certainly they had some training in the subject, although their levels of expertise seem to have varied. At St Patrick's Training College, Drumcondra, drill was taught for three hours a week by Patrick Pigott, who held an M.A. and H.Dip. in Education. G. Webb of the Irish School of Physical Drill was employed at De La Salle Training College in Waterford, where he taught four half-hour lessons every week. At Our Lady of Mercy Training College in Blackrock, Mary J. Dunne, who held Bachelor of Commerce and Higher Diploma in Education qualifications, taught the subject for two hours per week. She was a trained teacher and in 1927 had been awarded the Ard Teastas. Therefore she was 'fully qualified to teach drill through the medium of Irish' and had won gold medals for drill having been a student of Sergeant Major Wright. As well as being a Professor of Education at Mary Immaculate Training College in Limerick, Miss E. Murphy was in charge of drill and

32 Department of Education Archives. Department of Education Circular, Revised Notes on Physical Training 1933. Cir. 4/33.

33 ED/12/22858. Gymnastics and Physical Training in Primary Schools and Training Colleges. Syllabus in Physical Training for Students in the Colleges for the Training of National School Teachers (1929).

34 Ibid.

35 Ibid.

36 ED/12/31032. Revised Notes for Teachers' Drill. Physical Training in National Schools, Preparatory Colleges and in Training Colleges. Professors of Drill. (1932).

gave three forty minute lessons in the subject per week. At the Church of Ireland Training College, J. T. Gillespie was responsible for teaching it, although it is not clear for how long each week.[37] Therefore the subject remained very much a part of the training required for primary school student teachers despite the optional status of physical drill by the early 1930s, and as shown earlier in the training colleges in the early 1900s, military instructors were not always the preferred choice.

Physical Education and Second Level Schools

A commission on secondary education, founded by the Dáil, met for the first time in September 1921.[38] Amongst its aims were to construct a programme which would cater for 'the national requirements' with the Irish language receiving 'its due place'.[39] Early in 1922 a draft report was published in the press and circulated amongst headmasters and teachers in secondary schools for review.[40] Six committees were appointed to deal with a number of subjects although none were dedicated to PE.[41] Key recommendations were sent to the Dáil by the end of 1922 and while some proposals were rejected, it was to form the bedrock of the secondary schools' programme which became functional on the first day of August, 1924.[42] A special committee set up to coordinate primary, secondary and technical programmes reported in February 1922 that 'it was considered desirable to have a national graded system for all schools, primary and secondary' but 'no decisions were arrived at'.[43] Attitudes towards the provision of physical exercise remained slow to change. Thomas O'Donoghue,

37   Ibid.
38   Coolahan, *Irish Education*, 75.
39   Ibid.
40   *Irish Independent*, 14 January 1922 and *Irish Examiner*, 19 January 1922.
41   *Irish Examiner*, 19 January 1922.
42   Coolahan, *Irish Education*, 76.
43   *Irish Examiner*, 10 February 1922.

in noting the failure of the Dáil Commission to address physical training in secondary schools, has stated that 'there was no perceived need for the development of the subject' as notions surrounding the physicality of country life remained in relation to agricultural work and travel to school by foot or bicycle.[44] In addition, many schools already had systems of physical training in place, as shown in the previous chapter. The Intermediate Education (Amendment) Act had been passed in June 1924 and the Intermediate and Leaving Certificate examinations replaced the previous grading system, but physical training was not deemed an examination subject.[45] O'Donoghue has also written that the Irish State did not make subjects like PE compulsory as 'it might have resulted in pressure to put money into facilities over which there would be no control'.[46] In addition, as the majority of schools were small, they were unable to raise the fees needed for practical subjects, while private management was also a factor in not changing the programme as the State had only 'limited authority' in relation to secondary schools.[47] Therefore, under the new system implemented in 1924, physical training was not compulsory at secondary school level and 'this was a continuation of the situation as it existed under the Intermediate Education system'.[48]

The lack of government guidance in regard to the development of physical training within the second level education system was a source of concern to the NACA. At a meeting of their County Dublin board, held early in November 1924, it was resolved that members of the medical profession, university, colleges and schools' authorities and athletic bodies throughout Ireland should be contacted in regard to the 'holding of a conference with a view to the establishment of a system of physical training and education for the youths of Ireland on lines similar to those adopted in other countries'.[49] A conference was duly arranged at the Royal College of Surgeons.

44   Thomas O'Donoghue, 'The Dáil Commission on Secondary Education 1921–1922' in *Oideas*, 34 (Autumn, 1989), 61–74, 66.
45   Coolahan, *Irish Education*, 76.
46   O'Donoghue, 'The Policy of the State on the promotion of Physical Education in Irish Secondary Schools, 1924–1973', 28.
47   Ibid., 27–8.
48   Ibid., 8.
49   *Irish Independent*, 5 November 1924.

P. Lynch, KC, who was chairman of the Dublin board of the NACA, was at the forefront of this initiative.[50] In discussing the reasoning behind the conference, he referred to national prestige, the science of Olympic training and the United States of America where 'a special degree' was available for university students who graduated in physical culture and training, and noted Ireland's 'backward position' in regard to opportunities for those interested in this aspect of education.[51] The conference concluded with a committee of five being elected to take steps 'to have physical training recognised as part of the course in all schools and colleges'.[52] The honorary secretary of the Leinster branch of the Irish Hockey Union, J. S. McMahon, noted how physical training was part of the course in most secondary schools and felt that primary schools should be targeted with a view to bringing them up to 'the standard of the Swedish schools'.[53] Dr R. J. Rowlette was of the opinion that a small committee should be set up to investigate the system in other countries, particularly those in Scandinavia.[54] The NACA's president, J. J. Keane, supported the idea of implementing physical training into the schools' curriculum and felt that their proposition would receive favour from then Minister for Education, Eoin MacNeill.[55]

However, the attendees do not appear to have made much progress with their plan. In November 1925, 'the Scout' writing in the newspaper *Football Sports Weekly*, complained that despite the committee's formation, 'so far no report of its labours has seen the light of day' and urged them to 'wake up'.[56] This came despite the NACA's involvement in the promotion of the All-Ireland Schools and Colleges' championships at Croke Park in May 1925, with the performances of students at Roscrea, Blackrock College and Clonmel High School praised in the press.[57] The

50   *Irish Independent*, 7 November 1924.
51   Ibid.
52   *Donegal News*, 15 November 1924.
53   Ibid.
54   Ibid.
55   Ibid., and 'Ministers for Education from 1921 to Date' <https://www.education. ie/en/The-Department/Ministers/Ministers-for-Education-From-1921-to-Date. html> [Accessed 14 September 2017].
56   *Football Sports Weekly*, 7 November 1925.
57   Ibid., 29 May 1925.

following year's programme indicates that athletic events were held for juveniles (under 14s), juniors (under 16s) and seniors (under 18s) on Whit Monday.[58] Schools also encouraged competitions in other codes. In May 1926, the Schools' junior and senior cricket cups draw had ten entries at each level, with teams mainly based in Dublin.[59] Competitive soccer struggled to recover from its poor start in schools in the late nineteenth century. A schoolboys' league for soccer was initiated in Dublin in the 1920s, but this had only limited success and in 1933 a new league was established by the Leinster FA after complaints from senior clubs about the lack of structures for underage players.[60] In the summer of 1934 a cup for Dublin schoolboys was established.[61] However, there is no indication that schools were overly interested in this. In 1938 the FAI noted that the game's development was being obstructed in schools and colleges and in 1943, they sought assurance from the Ministry of Education that it was not being discouraged in schools.[62] A lack of encouragement of soccer remained and it was not until 1968 that the first secondary schools' cup was held, following the success of the Easter Vacation League, initiated in the 1950s.[63] In the mid-1970s the Department of Education agreed to fund the coaching of young soccer players.[64]

Some secondary schools did have state of the art facilities for physical training of pupils. St Columba's College of Rathfarnham, described as a 'Public School (Incorporated by Royal Charter)' had a swimming bath and 'large playing fields' amongst other facilities on its seventy acre site near the Dublin mountains.[65] A number of other secondary schools also highlighted that they encouraged physical training and publicised their events in the

58   Ibid., 1 May 1926.
59   Ibid., 8 May 1926.
60   *Evening Herald*, 3 September 1920 and *Sunday Independent*, 1 October 1933.
61   *Evening Herald*, 24 May 1934.
62   FAI Archives, P137/24. Junior Committee Minutes 24 Feb. 1938 and P137/29 Junior Emergency Committee Minutes, 2 September 1943.
63   Curran, *Irish Soccer Migrants*, 86–7 and *Evening Herald*, 17 May 1968.
64   FAI Archives, P137/17. Coaching and Development Committee Meeting, 30 July 1976.
65   *Belfast Newsletter*, 3 January 1925.

press. One writer claimed that Cork's secondary schools were 'pioneers in the most important matter of physical training' in Ireland, with junior and senior boarders at Loreto Convent, Fermoy, well-trained in Swedish drill as well as being able to perform exercises involving barbells, flags, musical bells and hoops at an event in March 1929 under the supervision of their physical training teacher, T. J. O'Sullivan of Cork.[66] In 1931, the boys of the Presentation Brothers' school in Cobh gave a similar display having been trained by G. Bygrove.[67]

However, many of these efforts were self-driven by schools themselves. The lack of state support in providing fields for youths' physical training was referred to by General Eoin O'Duffy at an address he gave at an athletics meeting of colleges at Cistercian College, Roscrea, in May 1932.[68] He also stated that 'athletics should be officially recognised as part of the school curriculum, and should be under the supervision of the inspection staff'.[69] This rhetoric came as part of O'Duffy's efforts to promote and revive athletics, and in February 1933 at the NACA's Congress in the Dolphin Hotel, Dublin, as president of the organisation, he suggested that the Minister Derrig be approached about the development of a national stadium in Phoenix Park and a National Council 'to further physical training'.[70] General O'Duffy also felt that 'proper facilities' should also be made available for the physical training of school pupils and a committee was set up to approach and interview the Minister on the matter.[71] However, the outcome of this idea that the government should intervene was not immediately successful.

66   *Irish Examiner*, 27 March 1929.
67   Ibid., 3 June 1931.
68   *Irish Independent*, 10 May 1932.
69   Ibid.
70   Ibid., 20 February 1933.
71   Ibid.

The Military and Physical Training in Second Level Schools

O'Donoghue et al have stated that the Swedish Ling movement was 'the earliest of the international physical education traditions to be established on a formal basis in Ireland' and 'this movement existed in the nation side-by-side with military practices in physical training, which were periodically linked to the work in schools'.[72] The Army School of Physical Training, which was established in 1922 at Keane Barracks before coming under the control of the Army School of Physical Culture eight years later and relocated at the Curragh, was responsible for the training of army physical training instructors.[73] As well as undertaking this work in the army, these men also visited primary, vocational and secondary schools, 'thus establishing an association between national security and fitness in the mind of the public'.[74]

Competitions remained an important part of showcasing the results of the work done in schools. At a meeting of the Irish Nurses Union in Dublin in May 1930, Dr Mary O'Leary, School Medical Officer, stated that ex-army officers from the Physical Culture School were being employed by the Christian Brothers to drill pupils in the open air. She noted that 'drill was observed in some of the schools, but it was to be hoped that the managers of the other schools would follow the Christian Brothers' example'.[75] In 1926, a physical culture competition was inaugurated amongst Dublin's Christian Brothers Schools with training taking place under 'capable and highly qualified instructors'.[76] The 1928 finals were held at the gymnasium at Portobello Barracks with seven schools involved.[77] Three years later, the Synge Street Christian Brothers organised a sports and physical culture display at Croke Park with the proceeds going to the school. There were approximately 18,000 spectators present.[78] 1,400 Synge Street pupils

72 O'Donoghue, Harford and O'Doherty, *Teacher Preparation in Ireland*, 110.
73 Ibid., 110–11.
74 Ibid., 111.
75 *Evening Herald*, 2 May 1930.
76 *Irish Independent*, 23 May 1928.
77 Ibid.
78 *Irish Press*, 1 October 1931.

took part and 'showed evidence of careful training by their instructor, Mr T. Gallagher' while guests included General Mulcahy, General O'Duffy, Dr Seán Lavan and Dr T. P. McLaughlin.[79] The Garda Síochana and Artane bands played throughout the day, illustrating the significance attached to this event.[80]

Moran has stated that 'it was cost effective for the government to maintain the physical education link with the army' while 'school managers were comfortable with the contribution of military PTIs on their staff'.[81] He has also noted that PE was introduced into Vocational Educational Schools in Dublin in 1928, following an agreement between the Department of Education and the Department of Defence which saw soldiers being given part-time instruction roles in schools.[82] He states that 'the most prominent Army Instructor at the time was M. J. Doogan, a Royal Dublin Fusilier, who transferred to the Irish Army and introduced physical training to the technical schools before the 1930 Vocational Education Act was passed'.[83]

Following investigations by the Commission on Technical Education of 1926–7, the Vocational Education Act of 1930 was implemented as it was felt that technical and continuation education was not receiving sufficient attention.[84] Through this Act, technical education committees were replaced by Vocational Education Committees and school building was also increased with forty-six finished by 1936.[85] Moran states that the Commission on Technical Education recommended physical culture as one of a number of subjects to be taught in technical schools in urban areas.[86] It was General Mulcahy who pushed for the Minister of Defence to develop the subject within technical schools in Dublin as he pointed to the availability of a school gym in the city and Commissioner P. J. Hernon's encouragement of the initiative.[87] As a result of this, M. J. Doogan took on

79   Ibid.
80   Ibid.
81   Moran, 'The Role of the Military in the Development of Physical Education', 86.
82   Ibid., 51.
83   Ibid., 51–2.
84   Coolahan, *Irish Education*, 95–6.
85   Ibid., 97.
86   Moran, 'The Role of the Military in the Development of Physical Education', 52.
87   Ibid.

the role of fostering the subject's growth in these schools following military recommendation that he should take up the role.[88] Some regional educational boards also explored the idea of implementing physical drill more thoroughly in their respective areas. The County Westmeath Vocational Educational Committee [VEC], for example, discussed the possibility of 'making provision for physical drill instruction' at Mullingar and Athlone technical schools in September 1931 with £50 being provided towards instruction in both schools.[89]

The Preparatory Colleges and Physical Training

Despite the government's tendency to look to the military to undertake physical training in schools, it would be incorrect to assume that the military had a monopoly on the teaching of physical training in Irish schools and it is clear that it was instead a mix of existing teachers, those deemed as specialists in the subject, and military personnel who were engaged in its teaching. Under a system implemented in the new Free State, the progress of Gaeltacht students towards teacher training was prioritised rather than that of non-Gaeltacht residents, with college places kept for them although the latter may have received higher marks in the final secondary school examinations.[90] The preparatory colleges had been established in 1926 as second level institutions to prepare Gaeltacht students for teacher-training college, and by 1932 there were seven of these in place. The employment of part-time instructors in drill and physical culture for these colleges had been discussed in 1928.[91] Along with three colleges for Catholic boys, Coláiste Éinne (Marlborough House, Glasnevin, County Dublin, which was later transferred to Galway),

---

88   Ibid., 53–4.
89   *Irish Examiner*, 4 September 1931.
90   Interview with primary school teacher number seven, 3 July 2019.
91   ED/12/31032. Revised Notes for Teachers' Drill. Physical Training in National Schools. Instruction in Drill in the Preparatory Colleges. 15 June 1932.

Coláiste Caoimhin (Glasnevin) and Coláiste na Mumhan in Mallow (County Cork), there were three Catholic girls' preparatory colleges, Coláiste Brighde (Falcarragh, County Donegal), Coláiste Íde (Dingle, County Kerry) and Coláiste Muire (Toormakeady, County Mayo) and one co-educational preparatory college, Coláiste Mobhi, which was for Protestant boys and girls and was located in Phoenix Park.[92] By 1932, with the exception of Coláiste Éinne, all preparatory colleges were 'partially equipped.'[93] Physical training was given by non-military staff at Coláiste Caoimhín in Glasnevin, where each of the three divisions received half an hour per week from Brother McDonagh, while at Coláiste Moibhi, Mary J. Dunne gave one hour in training per week. She was a qualified teacher who specialised in physical training and, as stated earlier, was also part-time instructor at Our Lady of Mercy Training College, Blackrock.[94]

At Colaiste Íde in Dingle, each division received half an hour's training every Saturday from a trained national school teacher, Siobhan Ní Ruairc, while the students also participated in Irish dancing. Half an hour's training was given weekly to each division at Coláiste Brighde in Falcarragh, with instruction given by Treasa Nic Aodhain, although she was not qualified in the subject. At Coláiste Muire, Tourmakeady, half an hour per week was given to four divisions on separate days. Training was given by Máire Ní Chathasaigh, who had experience in the subject, and Máire Ní Lordain, who was a national school teacher. A former member of the Order of the Irish Christian Brothers, Domhnall Ó Ciabhain, gave two periods of half an hours' training per week at Coláiste na Mumhan in Mallow.[95]

Given that they were not all fully qualified in physical training, the recruitment of military men was naturally a preferred option in some colleges. Military involvement in preparatory colleges developed following correspondence between the Departments of Education and Defence in

---

92   *Report of the Department of Education for 1932–33*, 8.
93   Ibid., 11.
94   *Revised Notes for Teachers' Drill. Physical Training in National Schools. Instruction in Drill in the Preparatory Colleges.* 15 June 1932.
95   Ibid.

1933.[96] Following this, the Department of Finance sanctioned 'the detailing of Army Instructors for imparting physical training to students in three preparatory colleges'. These were identified as Coláiste Caoimhín, Coláiste Einne and Coláiste na Mumhan, and an army instructor was also to be provided in one training college, St Patrick's Training College, Drumcondra in October 1933.[97] It was also stated that this was subject to instructors' participation 'not interfering with their military duties'.[98] The preparatory colleges were to be given the services free but training colleges would have to pay, as the former were 'under the direct administration of the Department [of Education]' while the training colleges were 'controlled, subject to the general jurisdiction of the Department, by the Authorities of the College'.[99] By the early 1930s, drill was therefore taught in the preparatory colleges through the assistance of the military and other staff.[100] Irish dancing was also taught 'in all the colleges' under staff supervision, while Gaelic games including hurling, football and handball were played in the boys' colleges. Camogie, basketball and tennis were played in the girls' colleges.[101]

Additional Courses in Physical Training for Teachers

In the early 1930s plans were also made to advance physical training courses for primary and second level teachers who were already active in schools. In 1932, the Department of Education reported that 'special summer courses' would be available for teachers employed by VECs, with six courses

96   Military Archives, Cathal Brugha Barracks. Department of Defence Files, 2/ 92315. Instruction. P.T. Schools and Colleges, Dublin Area. 1948-Memorandum. February 1955.
97   Ibid.
98   Ibid.
99   Ibid.
100 *Report of the Department of Education for 1932–33*, 10.
101 Ibid., 11.

intended.[102] One of these was to be 'in physical training for teachers who
are prepared to take this as an additional subject'.[103] In July 1933, around
fifty vocational school teachers from around the country took part in 'a
course of intensive study under the auspices of the Ministry of Education
at the Technical Schools' in Rathmines.[104] Along with physical training,
the course consisted of Irish literature, mathematics, practical geography,
school organisation, field work and was run by five instructors.[105] Some
other technical schools such as that in Ballsbridge provided courses 'to
enable the teachers to include physical training as part of the curriculum
of the new vocational schools throughout the country'.[106] The *Report of
the Department of Education for 1932–33*, stated that because the subject
had apparently not been receiving 'the attention it deserves' in either the
Training Colleges or Preparatory Colleges, 'many of the young teachers
had not acquired a proper sense of the value of a good course in physical training, and the teaching of the subject in the schools has suffered
correspondingly'.[107] By 1934, with permission of the Minister of Defence,
Frank Aiken, 'an extensive course of Physical Training' had been given to
students of Preparatory Colleges and Training Colleges located 'near the
large Army centres', which included Athlone, Dublin, Cork, Limerick,
Galway and the Curragh. Attempts were being made 'to improve the position in these colleges in which it is not feasible to make the services of
the Army Instructors available', while additional time was to be given to
the subject in all colleges.[108] Winter evening courses were also being held
twice a week at the same barracks for young males teaching in schools.[109]

---

102   *Report of the Department of Education for 1931–32* (Dublin: The Stationery Office,
      1933), 54.
103   Ibid.
104   *Irish Press*, 14 July 1933. See also *Report of the Department of Education for 1932–
      33*, 82.
105   Ibid.
106   *Irish Press*, 20 July 1934.
107   *Report of the Department of Education for 1932–33*, 18.
108   Ibid.
109   Ibid., 19.

Minister Derrig noted in the Dáil in April 1934 that as well as the aforementioned course for training vocational school teachers held in 1933, 'a number of very brief courses' had taken place at national school level through the instruction of the army in both English and Irish.[110] While he felt that there would be 'no difficulty in the larger centres in getting further assistance from the Army in the way of providing instructors' he also stated that they did not have 'very many instructors in the country, outside the Army'. He also noted that they did have 'a number of ex-Army men', although they had no institution 'in which this instruction could be carried on in a specialised way', but it was being given in training colleges.[111] He concluded by stating that

> For the present, until some better arrangement is made for the provision of whole-time teachers of physical training, we shall have to depend on those part-time courses which are carried out by the Army authorities. I would be very glad indeed if we could have the co-operation of the teachers' organisation generally in organising these courses.[112]

The first full-time summer courses in physical training were held in the summer of 1934 with forty-five full-time VEC teachers in attendance at two separate centres for males and females in Dublin, with sixteen men and sixteen women reaching the required standard of qualification to enable them to teach the subject.[113] In the summer of 1935 the Department of Education again ran two courses in physical training for VEC teachers, one for men and the other for women, with the Irish equivalent terms of instruction also provided.[114] It was noted in the Department of Education's Annual Report that forty-five teachers again attended and 'both of their

110   'In Committee on Finance-Vote No. 45-Office of the Minister for Education.' Dáil Éireann Debate. Vol. 51, No. 12. 11 April 1934. Retrieved from <http://oireachtasdebates.oireachtas.ie/debates%20authoring/DebatesWebPack.nsf/takes/dail1934041100023?opendocument&highlight=physical%20training> [Accessed 7 December 2017].

111   Ibid.

112   Ibid.

113   *Report of the Department of Education 1933–34*, 78.

114   *Irish Press*, 13 June 1935.

courses had as their aim the provision of a restricted course of training which would enable teachers in small centres to give instruction in Physical Culture in addition to their ordinary duties'.[115]

These developments were well received by a number of those involved in the development of second level education. At the Annual Congress of the Irish Technical Education Association, held in the Mansion House, Dublin, in June 1934, the Very Reverend Canon PJ O'Beirne noted in his presidential address that since the Vocational Educational Act of 1930, 'much had been accomplished', particularly in terms of the numbers of students attending courses. As a result of the previous summer's courses, the number of centres where PE was provided had increased, and he felt that 'it should be the aim of every Local Committee to secure for each vocational school in its area a suitable sports field'.[116] In his presidential address at the Annual Congress of the Vocational Education Officers' Organisation, held in Parnell Square in July 1934, A. Weldon noted how physical training arrangements were enthusiastically being taken up.[117] At the following year's Congress of the Technical Education Association, a resolution was adopted in favour of training full-time teachers and physical training organisers in the subject.[118]

Moran has noted that after this initial spurt, 'these in-service courses were not repeated in subsequent years' as 'the Department had other priorities for their teachers' with the result that 'sufficient numbers were not available to study physical training'.[119] However, the government remained keen to utilise military instructors within schools, and their usage was cheaper than building a new specialised institution for the instruction of teachers in physical training.[120] Moran has also found evidence through his interviews with former military Physical Training schools' instructors that 'school managers were happy to employ a military person in their schools as

---

115   *Report of the Department of Education 1934–35* (Dublin: The Stationery Office, 1936), 87.
116   *Evening Herald*, 6 June 1934.
117   *Sunday Independent*, 22 July 1934.
118   Ibid., 21 July 1935.
119   Moran, 'The Role of the Military in the Development of Physical Education', 56.
120   Ibid., 87.

they were impressed by the type of discipline displayed by military teachers through sport'.[121] Although there are no clear figures available for the employment of military men, as opposed to graduates with PE qualifications in schools, it is evident that the government saw their army's role in the teaching of physical training as a significant one at this time.

The Failure of Sokol within the Irish School System

Although the 1935 summer course programme consisted of 'Swedish exercises and gymnastics, organisation of school games and athletics, swimming and lectures on physiology', it was also noted that 'in the men's course advantage was taken of a display of the Sokol system of Physical Culture at the Curragh to enable the teachers to get an insight into other methods'.[122] In the early 1930s, Sokol became the preferred method of physical training in the Irish Army.[123] O'Donoghue has also stated that the Sokol system was chosen by the army as they felt their physical training system was out of date while they were also conscious of the threat of the Blueshirts and the Irish Republican Army [IRA] in the early 1930s.[174] General Aodh MacNeill felt that previously, the training had 'been too stereotyped and unimaginative'.[125] The decision to choose Sokol followed investigations of physical training systems in Czechoslovakia, Germany

---

121 Ibid., 89.
122 *Report of the Department of Education 1934–5*, 87.
123 Military Archives, Cathal Brugha Barracks. 2/32357. Physical Training. Promotion of Physical Training in the Army. Proposal to employ a continental (P.T.) expert. Information regarding P.T. in foreign countries. Secretary of the Minister of Defence to the Secretary of the Minister of Finance, 8 November 1933.
124 O'Donoghue, 'The Attempt by the Department of Defence to Introduce the Sokol System', 337–8.
125 Military Archives, Cathal Brugha Barracks. 2/32357. Physical Training. Promotion of Physical Training in the Army. Proposal to employ a continental (P.T.) expert. Information regarding P.T. in foreign countries. General Aodh MacNeill, Leathan Miontuairisce to Director, No. 1 Bureau, 3 January 1933.

and Sweden.[126] Colonel McCorley was appointed Director of Training of General Head Quarters in 1932, and was, according to one *Irish Press* writer, 'instrumental' in Sokol being introduced as 'the standard of physical training in the army' having been asked to carry out an inspection of these continental systems.[127] Lieutenant Joseph Tichy of the Czechoslovakian Artillery Corps was selected by the authorities of the Czechoslovakian Army to introduce the system into the Irish Army and eventually into the Free State schools.[128] However, adopting the system in schools was not straightforward, despite positive sentiments from Ministers Aiken and Derrig and Dr Burke of the Department of Education in 1935.[129] While local authorities were said to be enlarging playgrounds in rural schools in January 1937, Sokol and Swedish drill exercises were being provided 'only in a few schools' and had 'not yet been introduced in any of the primary schools in country districts' according to one *Connacht Tribune* reporter.[130] Most notably, Sokol was taught in some second level schools in Dublin, Cork, Kildare and Galway, but success was limited.[131] Some headway was made in primary schools in parts of Donegal. These attempts by Corporal McIntyre were welcomed by the County Donegal Medical Officer of Health, Michael Bastable, who stated that

> To those who have seen large impressive displays of Sokol training by school children on the continent, it is a matter for rejoicing that even at this hour we are about to see its inception in this country and particularly in our national schools. In the past it has been pathetic at times to see how eagerly the little scholars seized on the necessarily meagre hints thrown out by the School Medical Officer during the physical examination, and strutted around at the lunch-interval with expanded chest and head erect … so may we take the Sokol to ourselves, and evolve a Gaelic tradition in its usage.[132]

126   Ibid.
127   *Irish Press*, 21 November 1946.
128   *Irish Independent*, 13 June 1934.
129   Ibid.,16 July 1935.
130   *Connacht Tribune*, 16 January 1937.
131   Ibid.
132   *Derry Journal*, 25 January 1937.

Figure 14. A Sokol display at Good Counsel College, New Ross, County Wexford,
c.1930s. Courtesy of the National Library of Ireland.

Despite these positive comments, it proved impossible to fully implement the Sokol system (pictured in Figure 14) throughout the country's
schools.[133] One contemporary account by Ellen Cooney notes that along
with 'financial reasons', a lack of cooperation from the Department of
Education led to training in Sokol being 'discontinued' in Donegal.[134] She
has also stated that Sokol training and boxing for boys in Athlone had ceased
within a few years due to 'the transfer of the soldiers who gave the instruction'.[135] The migration of soldiers was a common cause of the failure of teams
to develop in some sports at the beginning of the twentieth century.[136] There

133   *Irish Press*, 31 January 1939.
134   Cooney, 'The Tendency towards Physical Training in the Sokol Way', 36.
135   Ibid., 38.
136   Curran, *The Development of Sport in Donegal*, 62.

is also evidence that the army were reluctant to allow non-military personnel to attempt to take on the Sokol method without their assistance.[137]

There is some indication that the Sokol System may not have been fully embraced by some sections of Irish society, particularly given the strong emphasis on developing an Irish-Ireland in the national and regional press and the criticism given to the promotion of 'foreign' games, which the GAA actively discouraged through their 'Ban'.[138] In particular, in 1934 it was criticised in *The Catholic Bulletin* by J. J. Murphy, who felt that the GAA should have been involved in developing 'an Irish National Plan of Physical Culture' rather than allowing attempts to have the Sokol system implemented.[139] Derry GAA County Board member P. Fox also expressed discontent in January 1937 that the Donegal MOH had welcomed Sokol within schools there, as he felt that hurling was a more suitable form of physical training in schools.[140] In fact, as MOH Bastable had also indicated, the Sokol system was intended to be modified 'by the characteristics of the Irish people' with commands given through Irish.[141]

Despite this, there is scarce evidence that the GAA's Central Council took any major notice of the Sokol system. As noted earlier, primary school leagues were organised in Dublin in the early part of the twentieth century, and the GAA, in what it saw as its role as an All-Ireland sporting body, had contacted both the Ministry of Education in Northern Ireland and the Department of Education about procuring playing fields for schools in 1928.[142] However, progress was slow. In May 1928 J. O. Glen, the private secretary to the Northern Ireland Minister of Education, James Caulfeild, wrote to the GAA to state that a meeting about the matter was unnecessary

137   Military Archives, Cathal Brugha Barracks. 2/41656. Physical Training. Sokol Drill. Particulars of Exercises etc. Application by Newry Christian Brothers Schools. Captain Seán O'Neill to Brother P. W. Newell, 6 June 1935.

138   Curran, *The Development of Sport in Donegal*, 199–222.

139   J. J. Murphy, 'Physical Culture Plans: A Plea for a National Principle' in *The Catholic Bulletin*, vol. XXIV, no. 7 (1934), 577–84, 584.

140   *Derry Journal*, 3 February 1937.

141   *Leinster Leader*, 24 August 1935.

142   Gaelic Athletic Association Archives. Dublin Schools League Minute Book 1917–1920 and Gaelic Athletic Association/CC/01/03 (1925–1929). Central Council Meeting Minutes, 26 May 1928.

as the Ministry was 'already fully alive to the necessity of playing fields for all types of schools in Northern Ireland and has this question constantly in view'.[143] While a GAA deputation did have a number of meetings with Department officials in Dublin, in January 1929, the Minister for Education, John Marcus O'Sullivan, wrote to say that given that the 'very rough estimate of the cost involved in providing such playing grounds would be £110,000', they could do nothing to assist.[144]

Although the GAA was involved in fundraising and in the provision of scholarships at St Enda's College by the early 1930s, by the latter half of the decade 'the most serious impediment to the further expansion of the schools organisation' was still 'the lack of proper playing fields'.[145] It was also noted in the secretary's annual report at the end of 1936 that 'thanks mainly to the teachers of all ranks, the area in which primary schools games are now played regularly has been considerably extended and the general standard of competition raised'.[146] An account of progress in primary schools in Leinster, given at the GAA's annual congress in April 1938, illustrated that 'satisfactory reports were received from most counties' although neither the subject of physical education nor the Sokol system was directly commented upon.[147] Certainly by the GAA's fiftieth anniversary in 1934, national school teachers were in a firm position to promote Gaelic games in schools, with one writer in the national press noting that year that 'you'll find a national school teacher in every club-because the colleges where these men are trained are truly Gaelic'.[148] Some GAA county boards, such as that in Donegal, had a number of national school teachers in key administrative

143 Gaelic Athletic Association/CC/01/03 (1925–1929). Central Council Meeting Minutes, 30 June 1928.

144 Ibid., 19 January 1929.

145 Gaelic Athletic Association/CC/01/04 (1929–1932). Secretary's Report for the Year Ended 31 December 1931 and Central Council Meeting Minutes, 24 September 1932 and Gaelic Athletic Association/CC/01/06 (1934–1938). Secretary's Report for Year Ended 31 December 1936.

146 Gaelic Athletic Association/CC/01/06 (1934–1938). Secretary's Report for Year Ended 31 December 1936.

147 Gaelic Athletic Association/CC/01/06 (1934–1938). Annual Congress report for Leinster, 17 April 1938.

148 Curran, *The Development of Sport in Donegal*, 146.

positions, and were able to utilise their educational networks to advance these codes in schools.[149]

Protest about Sokol's initiation into schools did come from others. One *Drogheda Independent* writer, alarmed at some press reports of its popularity in July 1935, claimed that it was 'the name given to an anti-religious athletic organisation that was conceived in the minds of the pagan propagandists of Central Europe'.[150] He felt that it was 'about time that an emphatic protest was made by our Catholic organisations' and called for the Navan branch of the Catholic Young Men's Society [CYMS] to 'give a lead'.[151] However, it is more likely that it was the lack of a definitive lead given by the Department of Education for its full implementation which deterred its progress rather than any public protest. Some GAA teams were in fact happy to embrace it. The Cavan Gaelic football team which won the All-Ireland championship in 1935 benefited from a physical training programme based on 'the new Sokol exercises under the direct supervision of Capt. John P. Murphy'.[152] Displays at times took place at events which included GAA matches, with army Sokol teams from the Curragh giving a Sokol exhibition at the Knockanna Sports in aid of new schools in Wicklow in June 1936.[153]

A resolution passed by the Carrickmacross Urban District Council to be put forward at the Annual Conference of Municipal Authorities of Ireland in 1937 that the Sokol system be introduced on a compulsory basis in Ireland's schools illustrates the haphazard nature of attempts to develop its potential more thoroughly at that point.[154] In particular, it was noted that more needed to be done in providing land for this through the passing of legislation.[155] However, the majority of schools do not seem to have attempted, or have had the manpower, finances and resources, to introduce it. Despite the failure of Sokol to take root comprehensively in the Irish

149   Ibid.
150   *Drogheda Independent*, 20 July 1935.
151   Ibid.
152   *Sunday Independent*, 29 September 1935.
153   *Wicklow People*, 20 June 1936.
154   *The Liberator*, 4 September 1937.
155   Ibid.

education system, an announcement by Minister Derrig in December 1936 that a committee was to be established to investigate the state of Physical Education in Irish schools offered fresh hope that something more satisfactory would be offered with the full support of the Irish government.[156]

Conclusion

The removal of physical drill as a compulsory subject from the primary school curriculum did not result in any major uproar or discontent from teachers or parents. With the lack of any sporting representatives on the National Programme Conference in 1925, there was a distinct scarcity of advocates for its maintenance, despite some efforts to keep things as they were. Opinions clearly certainly varied over the value of physical drill and many chose not to remember it with any great fondness. In 1940, when a discussion arose in the Dáil regarding physical training, Taoiseach Eamon de Valera stated that

> As far as I remember, there used to be a sort of thing that was called physical drill. I remember that I had some sort of physical drill in the primary school – some kind of marching, and so on – and I think I remember having something in the nature of a physical drill in the secondary schools. However, from my memory of any physical drill that I saw in these schools, it did not appear to me that it was very much worthwhile bothering about. [157]

While the value of the subject, and its British military connotations and the lack of space to develop it in many schools have been addressed earlier, the drive to Gaelicise Irish society meant that the Irish language and culture were to be prioritised within primary schools and this meant

156   Physical Education. The Report of the Committee, 1.
157   'In Committee on Finance.-Vote 45-Oifig an Aire Oireachais.' Dáil Éireann Debate. Vol. 80, No. 13. 6 June 1940. Retrieved from <http://oireachtasdebates.oireachtas. ie/debates%20authoring/DebatesWebPack.nsf/takes/dail194006060018?open document&highlight=physical%20training> [Accessed 7 December 2017].

reducing the time given to subjects that were deemed less significant. This was in some ways understandable given the treatment of Irish in the pre-partition years, but Irish educationalists in the new Free State failed to come up with their own version of physical training within the curriculum. Certainly, Gaelic games and Irish dancing were encouraged, but by the early 1930s Irish teachers were still being advised by the Minister of Education to consult English literature on the subject, while the Swedish system of physical training was also encouraged.

One Irish newspaper report at that time highlighted how far the Irish system for developing sport in general was behind a number of European countries where athletic success was linked to national prestige. Russia's government was said to have put aside £8 million for physical training.[158] The reporter called for a ministry of sport to be established in line with other parts of Europe and it was noted that in New York, 600,000 boys and 150,000 girls were 'committed to participate regularly in some form of sport' with the USA 'regarded as the greatest athletic power of all' given their success at the 1932 Los Angeles Olympics.[159] Despite the achievements of Irish representatives Bob Tisdall and Pat O'Callaghan, the Irish government were not overly concerned with international athletic developments.[160] They did, however, have the foresight to look for help. The decision of the Irish Army in the early 1930s to adopt the Sokol system offered hope that this particular method may be taken on in Irish schools. While it was adopted in some schools, a lack of a clear organisational plan to implement it throughout the country, and a scarcity of government funding, meant that it was destined to fail. Training existing teachers in physical drill was difficult enough given the problems in transferring this to the school setting from the training colleges, and enthusiasm was not always there to teach it, particularly amongst those less physically fit. Primary school teachers' views on inspectors and what they wanted to see in classrooms also meant that many felt other subjects should be prioritised rather than one that appeared to lack any real academic relevance. Adopting an entirely alien

158   *Irish Independent*, 21 December 1933.
159   Ibid.
160   Goldblatt, *The Games*, 170.

method of physical training in the mid-1930s illustrates a lack of clarity of the Irish government's part regarding what should be done in terms of providing a system of physical training in schools that could be easily taken on and that would mean something to a largely Catholic population that was still trying to establish its national identity in the aftermath of partition from the United Kingdom. As shown in this chapter, while military instruction in training courses and in schools was important, and was clearly encouraged by the government, this was not the only way in which physical training was taught in colleges and schools. Despite the failure of Sokol on a national level, some promise had been shown, and the government's decision to investigate the state of physical training in Irish schools in 1936 offered the opportunity to establish a new structure for the teaching of PE in the Irish Free State. Chapter 4 addresses the results of this and other examinations into physical training in Ireland during the immediate years after this as the nation was plunged into the Emergency and as its relatively newly gained independent was being tested.

False Dawns: PE in Independent Ireland, 1938–1953

Introduction

Writing in August 1938, one Irish-based journalist stated that in schools on the continent, 'physical culture almost takes preference over the purely educational subjects, and while we may have no desire to follow in the footsteps of the dictator countries, we might take a headline from them in this important matter'.[1] Given that Independent Ireland officially remained neutral during the Second World War, which began in September 1939, there was deemed to be less need to place an emphasis on developing physical training in Irish schools as had taken place in nations such as Italy and Germany.[2] However, the period from 1938 until 1943 saw the completion of three Irish government-backed investigations on the state of PE and athletics in the country and, in the late 1930s and early 1940s, it looked as if the provision of compulsory physical training in Irish schools was going to be taken seriously.[3] Despite generally encouraging recommendations from the committees appointed, they were not implemented as other matters were prioritised. Plans drawn up by the INTO in 1947 for PE, and those in a Department of Education committee report, which both called for the subject to be given a more central place in the

---

1   *Drogheda Independent*, 20 August 1938.
2   Bartlett, *Ireland: A History*, 452.
3   TAOIS/S11053. Physical Education. The Report of the Committee. 1938; Report of the Committee appointed by the Government to Examine the Question of the Promotion of the Revival of Athletics. 1939 and Proposals for Promoting the Revival of Athletics and General Physical Training. Report of the inter-departmental committee. 18 June 1943.

curriculum of primary schools, were ultimately ignored.[4] In examining the state of PE during the Emergency and its immediate aftermath from the perspective of pupils themselves and from County Medical Officers of Health, this chapter also highlights how it was being neglected. It also looks at calls from sporting and other public bodies for the Department of Education to take action to improve the status of the subject at both primary and secondary level.

The Report on Physical Education, 1938

The Department of Education's report on PE, completed in April 1938, illuminates the state of the subject in schools in Dublin and a number of regional counties to some degree.[5] The committee, named by Minister Derrig in December 1936, consisted of four officials of the Department of Education, L. Ó Muirthe, P. Ó Cochláin, Dr P. E. Ó Suilleabháin and T. K. Whitaker.[6] Two military men, Captain Hogan and Commander Coote, were appointed, while Dr Seán Lavan, who had previously supported the NACA's scheme for athletics in primary schools, was also invited to join. In January 1937 another member of the Defence Forces, Colonel O'Higgins, was brought on board.[7] Sixteen meetings were held by the committee while they visited a number of Irish colleges and schools to inspect the physical training that the students were receiving. Practices in two colleges, St Patrick's Training College, Drumcondra, and the Church of Ireland Training College were observed, while they also went to Alexandra College for girls, and the Curragh Camp National School for boys and girls. The reason given for their selection was that they held organised courses of instruction in PE, although, given that physical drill, as noted earlier, was being taught in Ireland's teaching colleges, it is not

---

4   Coolahan, *Irish Education*, 44.
5   Physical Education. The Report of the Committee, 1938, 1.
6   Ibid.
7   Ibid.

clear why all of those operational in the late 1930s were not included.[8] It appears the committee simply chose to focus on a number of those close to Dublin only, for reasons of transport and convenience, although they also ignored Our Lady of Mercy Training College in Blackrock.

An unnamed Army Instructor who was a sergeant in the national defence forces was responsible for conducting the PE training in St Patrick's College as Patrick Pigott had been replaced, while an ex-British Army Non-Commissioned Officer undertook its teaching in the Church of Ireland Training College. The courses in Alexandra College were taught by a teacher who had completed a three years' training course in an unnamed institution which was authorised to award a Diploma in the Swedish gymnastics system.[9] Students attending the Curragh Camp National Schools at that time were trained after school had finished for the day by instructors who were registered with the Army School of Physical Culture.[10] Therefore the committee's assessment of training courses was also influenced by their own military connections. O'Donoghue et al have stated that the committee's views were also swayed by Commander Coote, who was more in favour of the Swedish Ling tradition than that of Sokol, as the former system had a 'scientific approach to the teaching of gymnastics for the promotion of health and a rejection of the mass methods of delivery which were central' to the latter.[11] Indeed, there is scarce acknowledgement of the Sokol system in Irish schools throughout the report, illustrating further its failure to have any major impact.

Following this examination of the state of the courses taught in their selected institutions, the committee recommended that teachers needed to generally have minimum education qualifications along with sufficient PE training.[12] In utilising statistics from national schools, they highlighted that 'some form of physical training was given in about 2,000 National Schools out of a total of 5,243 and in a good many Secondary Schools' while vocational schools had seen a gradual introduction of the subject.[13]

8   Ibid.
9   Ibid., 1.
10   Ibid., 2.
11   O'Donoghue, Harford and O'Doherty, *Teacher Preparation in Ireland*, 111.
12   Physical Education. The Report of the Committee, 1938, 2.
13   Ibid.

They concluded that there was 'no uniformity of method and no proper understanding of the aim to be achieved' in schools where physical training was a part of the curriculum. This, the committee felt, meant that 'such physical training as it is given cannot but be haphazard, unscientific and of little or no value'.[14]

The government's committee also examined, in some detail, the progress of physical training in schools in a number of counties throughout Ireland. They noted that in County Westmeath a half hour was given weekly to the subject in the junior division of one unnamed national school, while it took place in forty-four national schools in the Tipperary South riding area, but again was 'given mainly to the junior standards', which strengthened their view on the sporadic nature of its teaching noted above. Along with viewing PE films, they also looked to the opinions of medical authorities, through utilising annual reports of County Medical Officers of Health from 1936, to show how 'a system based on scientific principles' had much support in other European countries and in the United States of America.[15]

Reports were gathered from County MOHs in Dublin, Cavan, Carlow, Waterford, Donegal and Kilkenny and these illustrate that conditions in Irish schools had not changed since the reports at the beginning of the decade, noted in the previous chapter.[16] Some annual reports published in the press also continued to highlight the concern of county medical officials with the lack of physical training available to children and the effects this had on posture.[17] A lack of physical training and instruction in hygiene was also linked to the spread of disease. In July 1938, Dr Harbison recommended that an organised system of PE should be implemented in schools and noted there had been 306 cases of diphtheria, 50 cases of malnutrition, 141 of dental defects and 28 of anaemia in Dublin that month and 100 children were found not to have received any vaccinations.[18]

14   Ibid.
15   Ibid.
16   Ibid., 3.
17   See, for example, *Irish Examiner*, 3 June 1938 and *Ballina Herald*, 16 August 1941.
18   *Irish Independent*, 17 August 1938 and *Irish Press*, 17 August 1938.

PE in Other European Countries on the Eve of the Second World War

The 1938 Report on PE is also valuable in its assessment of practices for the teaching of the subject in a number of what the committee described as 'the more progressive European countries'.[19] They had procured international literature and through correspondence, were able to report on how systems for PE operated in Sweden, Denmark, Finland, Germany, Czechoslovakia, Great Britain, and, to a lesser extent, Russia, Italy and France.[20] The League of Nations held meetings and conferences on physical education and fitness in 1937 and 1938, during which the value of 'community and not competition' was highlighted, and had compiled documents on related policies.[21] Irish Taoiseach Eamon de Valera was actively involved in the League, but there is nothing in the PE committee's report on his views on these related international PE meetings at that time.[22] The PE committee's conclusion from evidence available from the above countries was that 'great importance' was given to it and a proper system of PE was needed in Ireland, as the health benefits were to be seen elsewhere.[23]

As Cronin has written, in some European nations in the 1930s, 'sport as a physical activity that was linked to conceptions of the nation and strength was a powerful force'.[24] In the years between the First and Second World Wars, the fascist governments in Germany, Italy, Spain, Portugal and that of the communist Soviet Union were eager to encourage sport 'as an activity that encapsulated strength and beauty' while 'sport in this context was a stage for the preparation of the body for military service, and also a vehicle through which the regime could prove its ideological superiority by

19 Physical Education. The Report of the Committee, 1938, 8.
20 Ibid.
21 Vanessa Heggie, *A History of British Sports Medicine* (Manchester: Manchester University Press, 2011), 72–3 and 90.
22 Ferriter, *The Transformation of Ireland*, 370.
23 Physical Education. The Report of the Committee, 4 and 8.
24 Cronin, *Sport: A Very Short Introduction*, 42.

defeating other nations in a host of different sports'.[25] Guttmann has noted how in Germany, 'the National Socialist approach to "Physical Culture" was equally confused and contradictory' like that in Fascist Italy with, despite an early condemnation of modern sports, the hosting of the 1936 Olympics and Hitler's praise for boxer Max Schmeling.[26] Although systems for physical training in schools differed 'in matters of detail' in Russia, Italy and France, the 1938 PE Report committee noted that they were based on similar principles to Czechoslovakia, Denmark, Finland, Germany and Sweden.[27] They offered a rather potted history of developments in these countries and also noted an increase in funding for physical fitness in Britain through the Physical Training and Recreation Act of 1937.[28]

Despite their observations on structures in other countries, the 1938 PE Report committee recommended that the PE system which they hoped to introduce and develop would be one that would need to be modified to 'meet the needs of Irish children and the conditions of life peculiar' to Ireland.[29] Given these nationalist sentiments, it is surprising that there was no clear outline of what this would entail in terms of communications with sporting bodies, but this does hint at a desire to adhere to the GAA's games and ethos, and was in line with the overall policy of the Gaelicisation of Irish education which was being promoted within Irish schools.[30]

The Proposed Central Institute of Physical Education

The new system would require a specialist training college for PE to be built. The committee felt that 'the first essential requirement' in inaugurating a national system for PE in Ireland would be to set up a Central

25   Ibid.
26   Guttmann, *Sports*, 293–5.
27   Physical Education. The Report of the Committee, 1938, 8.
28   Ibid.
29   Ibid.
30   Coolahan, *Towards the Era of Lifelong Learning*, 34.

Institute of Physical Education which had a full range of equipment and was fully staffed.[31] It was there that Department of Education organisers of PE would be trained, along with secondary and vocational school teachers of the subject, while national school teachers could undertake refresher and other special courses. The committee also drew up a list of nine subjects for the curriculum at the proposed Central Institute.[32]

PE would, the committee recommended, become 'in due course … a compulsory subject in all schools' with a minimum of three periods a week devoted to it. At secondary school level, it was suggested it should become a subject for Certification exams and 'a compulsory subject for students in preparatory colleges'.[33] In training colleges, the subject would become 'an integral part of the course of studies' and a mandatory subject in the exams.[34] With the training to be made available, it was hoped that all national school teachers would be able to teach the subject competently at that level. However, the committee also felt that they would require the assistance of Department of Education organisers.[35] As most national schools in Ireland were said to be small and located rurally, it was felt that the only way the subject could be taught economically and to a satisfactory level was with their assistance, as this was said to be common in many countries in Europe. There were also plans that national school teachers could take on PE teaching in post-primary schools. Trainee primary teachers 'of special aptitude' would also be given the opportunity to do a third year of training in the Institute to acquire the Institute's Diploma in Physical Education, while a bonus would be given, as an incentive, to those holding this in line with the awarding of a bonus to national school teachers who had special qualifications such as a university degree. Those who had obtained a Diploma from the Institute would be required on

31   Physical Education. The Report of the Committee, 1938, 9.
32   Ibid. These included anatomy; physiology, including dietetics; theory and practice of gymnastics; pedagogics; hygiene and first aid; remedial gymnastics; games and sports, and play leadership leading to scientific recreation; athletics, aquatics and equitation and dancing and singing.
33   Ibid.
34   Ibid.
35   Ibid.

the staffs of secondary and vocational schools. Equipment for exercises in national schools, the committee felt, would be 'neither elaborate nor expensive and could be largely home manufactured'.[36] In urban areas, preparatory and training colleges, secondary and vocational schools would require gymnasia, sufficient outdoor space for recreation and, if possible, swimming pools.[37]

There were two major considerations noted in establishing a Central Institute of Physical Education. The first was the provision of necessary capital to obtain a site of sufficient size and to erect a new or to reconstruct an existing building. The second was the appointing of staff with qualifications in Irish.[38] The committee also felt that the site should be located in Dublin as 'it may be necessary for students of the Institute to attend lectures in one or other of the universities' and they identified two existing buildings which might be suitable for the Institute, while noting that each college would need to 'lend itself readily and economically to adaption'.[39] These sites were named as Coláiste Mobhí, Phoenix Park and St Patrick's Training College, Drumcondra, although they felt satisfied that Coláiste Mobhí was more suitable 'in every respect' and noted how new living quarters could be found for those accommodated there.[40] The Minister for Education, Thomas Derrig, along with officers of his Department, visited the recommended sites and Coláiste Mobhí had been decided upon.[41]

Information relating to staffing, accommodation and equipment was obtained from Carnegie Physical Training College, Leeds.[42] The new Institute's staff would be made up of a Director and two full-time assistants, one male and one female, along with 'the necessary part-time non-resident lecturers for special subjects such as anatomy, physiology, dancing and hygiene'. Part-time lecturers would be required to have completed a

36   Ibid.
37   Ibid.
38   Ibid., 11.
39   Ibid.
40   Ibid.
41   Secretary for the Minister of Education to the Secretary of the Taoiseach, 9 January 1943, TAOIS/S11053.
42   Ibid.

PE course or at least be interested in the subject. The committee calculated that the capital expenditure involved in building and equipping the new Institute would not be more than £120,000, although this would be 'very much reduced' if Coláiste Mobhí was acquired. They also estimated that 'annual charges in respect of Physical Education' would be around £19,000.[43] In order to speed up the development of PE as a taught subject in all Irish schools and to make it a compulsory subject, 'short courses for teachers of suitable age and aptitude' would be introduced. Department of Education statistics for 1935–6 illustrated that there were 13,487 primary school teachers and 2,879 secondary school teachers employed.[44]

The Committee recommended that 'no time should be lost in establishing the Central Institute'.[45] They also felt that the system for providing school meals needed to be improved and extended, although they acknowledged that nutrition and housing conditions were matters for parents and the Public Health Authorities.[46] In recognising the concerns of the medical health officers, noted above, it was also recommended that those in charge of PE in the schools work closely with school medical officers so that children would not perform exercises beyond their capacities and that any postural defects be prevented or cured.[47] The Central Institute would also contribute to improving 'the standard of health and physical fitness and the general moral tone of the nation'.[48] Following this investigation, 'concrete proposals were about to be prepared and submitted to the government when war broke out' in September 1939.[49] Although

43   Physical Education. The Report of the Committee, 1938, 11 and 15. These costs were calculated in comparison with the building of the Preparatory College in Ballyvourney, County Cork, which was said to have cost £82,500. The college could accommodate 120 resident students, teaching and domestic staff. The additional costs of the Central Institute would come from 'the increased cost of building and equipping the new Central Institute'.
44   Ibid., 11.
45   Ibid., 12.
46   Ibid.
47   Ibid.
48   Ibid.
49   Secretary for the Minister of Education to the Secretary of the Taoiseach, 9 January 1943.

the Phoenix Park site was accepted provisionally, it was taken over by the Defence forces for the war and 'it was decided to postpone further action until the financial situation clarified itself'.[50]

The Report on the Revival of Athletics, 1939

While the PE committee's findings were under consideration in the Department of Education, another report related to the development of physical training and athletics was submitted. This had been completed by a government-appointed cabinet committee, established on 13 December 1938 to examine the revival of athletics, although naturally there was some overlap with the development of PE.[51] It consisted of the Minister Aiken, Minister Derrig, the Minister for Posts and Telegraphs, Oscar Traynor, the Attorney General, Patrick Lynch and Seán Moylan, Parliamentary Secretary to the Minister for Industry and Commerce.[52] The Minister for Industry and Commerce (Seán Lemass) and the Minister for Lands (Gerald Boland) were later appointed to the committee on 16 May 1939.[53] In the first four months after the initial appointments, three meetings were held. At the first meeting on 15 December 1938, athletics in the country was naturally discussed and specific references were made to physical training in schools, the Sokol system and coaching for athletes. The committee decided that it would be best if the Government did not attempt to mediate in the dispute between the NACA and the Amateur

50   Ibid.
51   Report of the Committee appointed by the Government to Examine the Question of the Promotion of the Revival of Athletics. 1939, 1 and Secretary for the Minister of Education to the Secretary of the Taoiseach, 9 January 1943.
52   Report of the Committee appointed by the Government to Examine the Question of the Promotion of the Revival of Athletics. 1939, 1–2.
53   TAOIS/S11053. Minute from P. Ó Murchadha, Private Secretary, Department of Industry and Commerce, to the Parliamentary Secretary for the Minister of Industry and Commerce, Seán Moylan, 15 March 1940.

Athletic Union of Éire.[54] At the second meeting, on 18 January 1939 the committee decided to follow suggestions made by Minister Aiken, and when they met again on 14 March they made five main recommendations based on these.[55] They felt that in promoting athletic activities, a start should be made with school pupils. They also recommended that a scheme for the promotion of athletic activities should be promoted by the Department of Education in all schools, and, in echoing the key recommendation of the Committee on Physical Education, called for the establishment of a School of Physical Instruction to train games' and physical instructors. These instructors were to be made available for employment by local committees and half of their salaries were to be paid by a State grant. Finally, they suggested that 'the Land Commission should be requested actively to utilise the powers regarding the provision of sites for sports fields and playing grounds contained in the Land Act, 1933' and, if required, 'these powers should be extended to include the provision of sites for handball alleys, swimming pools and village halls'.[56]

However, not everyone was in favour of these proposals. On 26 January 1939, committee member Seán Moylan prepared a memorandum which was circulated at a meeting of the committee on 22 June 1939. In the memorandum, Moylan highlighted that all of the recommendations were not agreeable and was of the opinion that they were 'merely proposals to introduce Physical Education into the schools which is a matter for the Department of Education'.[57] It was also stated that athletics should be linked to cultural development, and 'the making of an athletic programme into a matter of study, duty or compulsion' was not supported. Physical instruction would only be part of the scheme 'when a general interest has been developed in the question of physical fitness'.[58] This attitude was at

54   For an examination of this conflict see Tom Hunt, 'The National Athletic Association of Ireland and Irish Athletics, 1922–1937: Steps on the Road to Athletic Isolation' in *Sport and Society*, vol. 19, no. 1 (2016), 130–46.

55   Report of the Committee appointed by the Government to Examine the Question of the Promotion of the Revival of Athletics. 1939, 2.

56   Ibid.

57   TAOIS/S11053. Parliamentary Secretary Seán Moylan to the Minister for Industry and Commerce, Seán Lemass, Memorandum 26 January 1939.

58   Ibid.

odds with the earlier recommendations of the 1938 Report on Physical Education despite the research procured from other countries, while the previous INTO issue of the perceived overloading of the primary school curriculum was highlighted. It was stated in the memorandum that

> I am not convinced that the provision of trained physical culture instructors is a wholly desirable thing. It will be found difficult to allocate time from an already heavily burdened school programme to such instruction. The physical activities of the children should be recreational rather than studiedly instructive and their leisure time is better occupied with sport or fun created by themselves from opportunities afforded them than it would be with any form of directed activity. Again, if the work is to be undertaken it must be done so in all schools, and without detailed knowledge of its success in an experimental stage or in another country the cost would not be justifiable.[59]

This document, which was undoubtedly influenced by Minister for Industry and Commerce, Seán Lemass, appears to have had considerable impact. At the June committee meeting, Minister Lemass, who had joined the committee in May, recommended a scheme to organise athletics 'on a county or some such basis' having stated that 'the Committee's previous recommendations had been disposed of'.[60] He discussed the appointment of County Athletic Officers who would guide local committees in obtaining playing fields and he also hoped to see the development of inter-district athletic competitions, with a national stadium being built in Dublin. It was there, he envisaged, that 'periodic national games' would be hosted. Patrick Lynch agreed with Lemass's views and suggested that a Central Advisory Committee should be established to oversee the scheme.[61] Gerald Boland gave advice on the Land Commission's policy regarding the distribution of land for sporting activities, and those present agreed to consider Lemass's proposed scheme.[62] Boland informed

---

59   Ibid.
60   TAOIS/S11053. Minute from P. Ó Murchadha, Private Secretary, Department of Industry and Commerce, to the Parliamentary Secretary for the Minister of Industry and Commerce, Seán Moylan, 15 March 1940.
61   Ibid.
62   Ibid.

the committee that facilities could only be provided as part of the Land Commission's usual work in dividing land.[63] A draft scheme was prepared, but with the outbreak of war, the committee's meetings ground to a halt. They later agreed when contacted individually by Lemass's private secretary, P. Ó Murchadha, that 'as the expenditure of a not inconsiderable amount of public money would be involved in the promotion of a scheme such as was visualised' the scheme could not be considered further at that time.[64]

In April 1940, the new Minister for Lands, Thomas Derrig (1939–43), stated that in regard to the allocation of land for sport, he agreed with the objections of his predecessor, Gerald Boland, that 'the provision of sports fields etc., should be undertaken by the Land Commission independently of its normal operations as it would involve diverting the attention of the staff from more urgent work'.[65] On 16 December 1942 at a meeting of the Cabinet Committee on Economic Planning, it was agreed to ask the Department of Education to consult with the Department of Defence to prepare proposals for reviving athletics and general physical training. The cabinet also agreed to ask the Department of Defence to consider creating a full-time post in relation to the promotion of athletics and the appointment of an officer who would be suitable for this on retiring from the Defence Forces.[66]

The Department of Education submitted copies of the 1938 PE Report to the Cabinet Committee on Economic Planning on 9 January 1943.[67] Minister Derrig's secretary communicated that if it was deemed 'desirable to proceed with the scheme in the present circumstances' the Minister would

---

63 TAOIS/S11053. Letter from Secretary to the Minister for Lands to the Secretary to the Department of the Taoiseach, 5 April 1940.

64 Minute from P. Ó Murchadha, Private Secretary, Department of Industry and Commerce, to the Parliamentary Secretary for the Minister of Industry and Commerce, Seán Moylan, 15 March 1940.

65 TAOIS/S11053. Letter from Secretary to the Minister for Lands to the Secretary to the Department of the Taoiseach, 5 April 1940.

66 TAOIS/S11053. Revival of Athletics and Physical Training. Department of the Taoiseach, 17 January 1944.

67 TAOIS/S11053. Secretary for the Minister of Education to the Secretary of the Taoiseach, 9 January 1943.

submit a detailed proposal to the Government.[68] Later that month, it was
noted that the Cabinet Committee were of the view that the Taoiseach,
Eamon de Valera, and the Minister for Defence, Oscar Traynor, should
discuss the promotion of athletics but the question of proceeding with the
proposals of the reports on Physical Education and the Revival of Athletics
were deferred.[69] The Taoiseach let the Cabinet know at the end of the
month that little progress had been made in his talks with the Minister for
Defence.[70] In addition, the Department of Defence told the committee
that they had recommended to the Department of Education 'the con-
vening of an Inter-departmental committee with a view to the submis-
sion of proposals'.[71] This new committee's report was completed in June
1943 but was not submitted to the Department of the Taoiseach until 6
December of that year.[72]

The Report on the Revival of Athletics and Physical Training, 1943

The Inter-departmental Committee consisted of two members of the
1938 Physical Education Report group, Dr P. E. Ó Súilleabháin and
P. Ó Cochláin; two high ranking army men, Colonel S. Ó Suilleabháin,
Colonel Seán Collins Powell; P. Breathnach, R. Kent and the secretary,
D. Ó Laoghaire.[73] They felt that much of the background work had been
completed through the 1938 Committee which reported to the Minister
for Education, and as a result they only held three meetings. These took

68   Ibid.
69   TAOIS/S11053. Revival of Athletics and Physical Training. Department of the
     Taoiseach, 17 January 1944.
70   Ibid.
71   Ibid.
72   Ibid.
73   TAOIS/S11053. Proposals for Promoting the Revival of Athletics and General
     Physical Training. Report of the inter-departmental committee. 18 June 1943, 1.

place in the Department of Education on 31 May, 8 and 18 June 1943. Their proposals were divided into three sections, (1) permanent measures; (2) interim measures towards a realisation of the first category and (3) measures that could be taken immediately.[74]

The outlining of the permanent measures was strongly influenced by the 1938 Report and the ten points were almost entirely the same as the previous committee's recommendations, as the 1943 Committee felt that 'the recommendations made in that report should form the basis of any permanent scheme for the revival of athletics and general physical training'.[75] Therefore they reiterated the need for a Central Institute of Physical Education to be founded immediately. They also recommended that 'certain essential qualifications for admission to the Institute be prescribed' and that scholarships to be utilised in the Institute should be awarded.[76] PE, they felt, should be compulsory in all schools while it was to be taught by 'ordinary teachers' at primary school level and by those who would obtain the Diploma of the Institute in secondary and vocational schools and in training and preparatory colleges.[77]

As the founding of the Central Institute could not take place while the Emergency was ongoing, the committee, as noted, proposed a number of interim measures. They proposed that a Recreational Council consisting of approximately twenty members be established representing 'religious, educational, cultural and recreational interests, of the Departments of Education, Local Government and Public Health, Defence, and Finance'.[78] They also recommended that the Council would act through local committees in order to encourage and promote physical, cultural and recreational activities 'on a national basis'.[79]

Although the Committee felt that they could not give an estimate of the funds needed for the running of the Recreational Council, they noted that financial assistance would be required for Head Office and staff; for

74 Ibid.
75 Ibid.
76 Ibid., 2.
77 Ibid.
78 Ibid.
79 Ibid.

teachers' and play leaders' training; for the payment of organisers and teachers; the provision of facilities and equipment and to promote competitions and displays.[80] They acknowledged that some financial provisions may already exist through various Acts but felt that for full implementation of their proposals 'special grants' would have to be given by the State.[81] The Committee also recommended that State grants for the scheme would be supplemented by local rates with the local committees to receive part of the Central State grant in proportion to the amount given through local rates with 'special consideration' given to poorer areas.[82]

The third category of measures, those that the Committee felt could be taken at once, were placed under three headings. These were defined as the army, the schools and the general public. In relation to the army, it was noted that physical training courses were taking place in the Army School of Physical Culture. The next course to be held there would consist of fifty to sixty students who were selected 'on a territorial basis from the Reserve, Volunteer and Temporary Officers and NDOs'.[83] The Committee hoped that those who qualified at these courses would, after demobilisation, take an active part in 'the general scheme of physical education as play leaders, youth leaders and physical education instructors'. Schemes were also said to be under consideration 'to extend physical training through the Local Defence Force, the Construction Corps and Second Line Units.'[84] By June 1943 figures for the Local Defence Force had reached 106,000, and despite having only 20,000 enlisted in September 1939, following a recruitment campaign the Emergency Army numbered almost 41,000 in the summer of 1941.[85]

---

80   Ibid., 3.
81   Ibid., These included the Museums and Gymnasiums Act, 1891; the Local Government (Ireland) Act, 1898; the Vocational Education Act, 1930; and Section VIII of the Local Government Act, 1941.
82   Ibid.
83   Ibid.
84   Ibid., 4.
85   'The Emergency 1939–1945' Retrieved from <http://www.military.ie/info-centre/defence-forces-history/the-emergency-1939-1946/> [Accessed 2 November 2017].

The Committee felt that 'a scheme based on athletics and recreation rather than on physical training as a formal subject should be initiated' in schools in order to make a start and considering the resources available. They proposed that a space be found in the school timetable and 'the drawing up of a programme to be fitted into the general work'. In citing the section 'Irish, General conversation' on page 32 of the Department of Education's *Notes for Teachers*, they recommended that PE might be fitted into the more general playground games which, it was stated in this publication, could be utilised to help children learn Irish. The Committee also recommended that a minimum of one hour per week 'from the time devoted to Irish and English' should be given 'to systematic training through Irish in recreational activities'.[86] During that period, instruction might include subjects such as Physical Training; health and hygiene; community singing of Irish and Anglo-Irish marching songs; step and figure dances; athletics; team games, and where it was possible, swimming and lifesaving. Different age groups would benefit from a varied syllabus.[87]

A number of proposals were also made, which, they felt, would benefit the general public. It was recommended that playgrounds be acquired, and this would be more advantageous if these were as near as possible to local schools and under the control of local committees.[88] Given that 'some instruction' was already being given in physical training at primary, secondary and vocational level, and in the Preparatory and Training Colleges, it was recommended that six organisers of Physical Education, including two women, be appointed immediately by the Department of Education. They also proposed that one out of every four school inspectors appointed be qualified in PE and that 'one such inspector' should be appointed as soon as would be possible. Students undertaking practical physical training in the Preparatory and Training Colleges should receive a minimum of three hours per week each, while they also recommended that 'an experimental course of ten months for fifty men and women be instituted in Dublin by the Department of Education'. This would take place along the lines of the

86 TAOIS/S11053. Proposals for Promoting the Revival of Athletics and General Physical Training. Report of the Inter-Departmental Committee. 18 June 1943, 4.
87 Ibid., 5.
88 Ibid., 7.

Special Course for Irish Teachers while those admitted would be picked on the basis of examination and interview results 'designed to test the candidates in Irish and general knowledge, personality, interest in Physical Education, leadership, etc.'.[89] They recommended that a state scholarship of 40/- be given to each student while Army instructors would also participate.

In order to introduce PE more thoroughly in the schools, summer courses would also be implemented 'for all types of teachers' with the State providing travel and accommodation expenses.[90] The texts would also have to be outlined in advance while a Special Certificate would be given to those successful in the related theoretical and practical exams. A Higher Certificate in Physical Education, for those who completed the experimental course noted above, would be operational until the Institute of Physical Education was established, while the syllabus and certification tests would be drawn up by the Department of Education in collaboration with the Army.[91]

The Committee also suggested that the universities be encouraged to implement year-long courses in PE to allow graduates to teach it in secondary and vocational schools.[92] They also felt that the Civic Institute, which already provided practical training for those undertaking the Diploma in Social Science, should be contacted in regard to organising practical courses for potential play leaders over the summer months.[93] They also recommended that Radio Éireann be contacted to broadcast material on Physical Education, health and hygiene in their forthcoming school and general programmes, while texts on various aspects of Physical Education were to be compiled by 'competent persons' with publication undertaken by the Stationery Office.[94] Badges to illustrate levels of expertise in the subject's courses would also be introduced, while it was felt that the scheme provided 'an excellent means of promoting the use of the Irish language'. Therefore, the Committee believed that the scheme's activities should 'as

89   Ibid., 7–8.
90   Ibid., 8.
91   Ibid.
92   Ibid., 8–9.
93   Ibid., 9.
94   Ibid.

far as possible, be conducted through the medium of Irish and through Irish only in the schools'.[95]

The Failure to Act on the Recommendations of the Three Reports

In early December 1943 Education Minister Derrig's private secretary contacted Taoiseach Eamon de Valera's private secretary to state that he had considered the reports made available and reiterated the point that the establishment of a Central Institute had been considered previously but stated that any further action would be postponed 'for the present' with the proposed site being taken over by the military.[96] While he felt that the establishment of a Recreational Council, one of the 1943 Committee's interim measures, would be beneficial and would be a useful propaganda exercise in terms of raising general interest levels, he was of the opinion that 'even these measures ... will require some consideration before a decision can be reached on them'.[97] In relation to the Inter-departmental Committee's proposed measures to be undertaken at once, he felt that 'it is to be feared that a grave difficulty exists in the lack of trained personnel'. Regarding the one hour per week the Committee proposed, he felt that 'there should be at least one young teacher in the school interested and enthusiastic and reasonably competent' and in addition, 'it would presume that instructors are available who are fully qualified in physical education'.[98] He added that 'it is a matter of some doubt, however, whether in fact there are any such fully trained men instructors or many fully trained women instructors available in this country'.[99] He also felt that while the

95 Ibid.
96 TAOIS/S11053. Letter from Private Secretary of the Minister for Education to the Private Secretary of the Taoiseach, 6 December 1943.
97 Ibid.
98 Ibid.
99 Ibid.

army instructors would be of value, it was 'questionable whether these in-structors would be sufficiently well acquainted with elementary anatomy and physiology to appreciate the function of the different exercises'.[100]

In the case of the proposed appointment of six organisers of PE, the Minister recommended that none should be appointed without a recog-nised qualification. He stated that 'a beginning might be made with one organiser fully qualified' but that person would have to be qualified in Irish and would have to spend time abroad undertaking the necessary training in Physical Education. He ended the letter by stating that

> this Department recommends that, until the time is opportune for the organisation of physical education on a sound basis, that is after the war, all that can be done for the present is (1) by propaganda to create an interest in physical education (2) to con-vince teachers, managers of schools and all others interested in the physical welfare of the youth and the general well-being of the nation of the importance of physical education, games and athletics and (3) to secure their willing co-operation and to encourage such games, athletics and other out-door recreational activities as will tend to improve the general standard of physical fitness among the school children and the youth generally of the country.[101]

On 20 December 1943, the Cabinet Committee on Economic Planning stated that they wished to prioritise viewing a memorandum that the Irish Tourist Board had prepared and that they would defer considering the Inter-departmental Committee report.[102]

Proposals for the development of PE in Irish schools were dealt an-other blow in January 1944 when the Minister for Defence, Oscar Traynor, gave his views on the Inter-departmental Committee's report having read the Minister of Education's comments.[103] It was noted that he had 'grave doubts' if the recommendations of the report would help promote the re-vival of athletics. While he felt they 'would no doubt be of value and enable

100   Ibid.
101   Ibid.
102   TAOIS/S11053. Cabinet Committee on Economic Planning. Extract from Minutes of Meeting held on 20 December, 1943. Revival of Athletics.
103   TAOIS/S11053. Private Secretary for the Minister for Defence to the Private Secretary of the Taoiseach, 15 January 1944.

a useful basis for athletic development to be established', without specialised athletic training and regular practice, it would be unlikely that the athletics revival could be successful. Minister Traynor contradicted Minister Derrig in stating that army staff were trained in anatomy and physiology, but saw the fact that instruction had to be given in Irish as 'one of the main difficulties' in employing army personnel in the capacity of instructors of physical training.[104] He also felt that the Minister of Education's suggestion that only one organiser be appointed initially would 'result in considerable delay' and was likely to jeopardise progress, particularly if the organiser had to go abroad for training for a period of two years as he recommended. Finally, Traynor noted that in regard to the Cabinet Committee's request in December 1942 that the Department of Defence create a post promoting athletics that a retired army man would take up, there was 'no suitable officer for appointment to such a post'.[105] In February 1944, the Taoiseach agreed to discuss the revival of athletics with Seán Moylan, the Minister for Lands, but this did not lead to any changes in the system for physical education in Irish schools.[106]

De Valera, who, as RV Comerford has noted, was a rugby enthusiast, had stated in the Dáil in June 1940 that games should be encouraged in schools, but felt that procuring playing fields was expensive. However, he noted that, if playing fields connected to schools could be obtained, then 'a system of regular exercises which we generally refer to as physical drill' could be incorporated. He concluded by stating that he 'would not like to make any promise in regard to that matter, or in regard to playing fields' but would 'look into it'.[107] Given Moylan and Lemass's misgivings about government involvement in developing physical education in Irish schools,

---

104   Ibid.
105   Ibid.
106   TAOIS/S11053. Cabinet Committee on Economic Planning. Revival of Athletics. Minutes from Meeting Held on 21 February 1944. 29 February 1944.
107   'In Committee on Finance.-Vote 45-Oifig an Aire Oireachais.' Dáil Éireann Debate. Vol. 80, No. 13. 6 June 1940. Retrieved from <http://oireachtasdebates.oireachtas. ie/debates%20authoring/DebatesWebPack.nsf/takes/dail194006060018?open document&highlight=physical%20training> [Accessed 7 December 2017] and RV Comerford, *Ireland: Inventing the Nation* (London: Hodder Arnold, 2003), 226.

and Traynor's lack of enthusiasm, it is perhaps unsurprising that nothing came of the matter at this time.

Physical Training Initiatives in Schools

While members of the government deliberated over what to do with PE in Irish schools, some sporting organisations and educational institutions took the initiative themselves and continued to help in the promotion of forms of physical training for school pupils. Members of the NACA continued to push for a better system of PE in Irish primary schools. At the Cork City NS Sports at Douglas in June 1938, run in conjunction with the Cork NACA, the performance of St Patrick's NS was notable, with chairman and national school teacher, P. Dynan, hopeful that other schools would follow their example.[108] A Schools' Boxing Board, backed by the Dean of Cork, had been established in Cork earlier that year.[109] A motion that the Connaught Convention of the NACA request the Department of Education give a certain period every day for physical training exercises in every school, was adopted at their Convention in February 1946.[110] However, it was noted by Rev. Brother Cashin, who seconded this, that 'it would be hard to have it enforced', as he reflected that physical training's status was reduced in the 1920s 'to give more time for studies and for learning the Irish language'.[111]

The Emergency clearly impacted on schools' sport in the early part of the decade. While the government enquiries about the state of physical training and athletics rumbled on in the early 1940s, the Department of Education's report for 1940–1 noted that in all Continuation Education schemes 'there was a successful organisation of social activities for students of the day schools' and 'as in previous sessions, football, hurling and

---

108   *Irish Examiner*, 18 June 1938.
109   Ibid., 9 March 1938.
110   *Connaught Telegraph*, 23 February 1946.
111   Ibid.

camogie teams were formed'.[112] However, 'the inter-school and inter-scheme matches, so prominent a feature previously, had to be largely curtailed owing to transport difficulties'.[113] As Terence Browne has stated, 'private motoring became almost impossible by 1942 and was replaced by many resurrected horse-drawn vehicles' as the rationing of fuel impeded the former.[114] The Department of Education's Report for 1943–4 highlighted that in the majority of secondary schools, games were well covered although those travelling long distances to attend day schools had neither the time nor the opportunity to participate fully.[115] In the following year's report, similar sentiments were expressed while it also was noted that girls did not receive as much athletic training as boys and that more opportunities should be provided.[116]

The Development of Physical Training Courses

The state of the training of teachers in PE remained a concern. One account written by two army men, Captain TG Teahan and Lieutenant PM Cashin, published late in 1943 highlighted that 'there was still a great scarcity' of fully qualified physical training instructors in Ireland, although some had attended Ling College in Dublin and the Army School of Physical Culture.[117] The authors felt it was 'strange that there was not a general demand by parents for Physical Education in all schools, for

112 *Report of the Department of Education 1940–41* (Dublin: The Stationery Office, 1942), 30.

113 Ibid.

114 Terence Browne, *Ireland: A Social and Cultural History 1922–2002* (London: Harper Perennial, 2004), 164.

115 *Report of the Department of Education 1943–44* (Dublin: The Stationery Office, 1945), 26.

116 *Report of the Department of Education 1944–45* (Dublin: The Stationery Office, 1946), 27–8.

117 *Kerry Champion*, 25 December 1943.

it is parents who see the physical deficiencies in their children.[118] They
called for a National College of Physical Training to be developed where
qualifications could be obtained, as there was 'a grave danger of more
harm than good resulting to students, should an unqualified instructor
be employed.[119]

Some attempts were made to further develop physical training
courses for teachers. In July 1947 the City of Dublin Vocational Education
Committee hosted a three-week refresher course for physical training
teachers at the School of Domestic Science in Cathal Brugha Street.[120]
The course was directed by Director of the League of Health and Beauty,
Kathleen O'Rourke, and consisted of practical and theoretical elements.[121]
A branch of the League of Health and Beauty was founded in Belfast in
1934 and O'Rourke had established one in Dublin that same year.[122] Ten
men and nine women, most of whom were employed in schools in the city,
took part in the City of Dublin refresher course.[123] O'Rourke had previously
articulated her views of the state of PE in Independent Ireland. Speaking
at a display by the Women's League of Health and Beauty at the Mansion
House in November 1940, she stated that 'physical training was in a difficult state of transition' in Ireland 'because of a certain apathy to physical
education, which was a constant reproach to both parents and educationists.[124] She added that 'physical education should occupy a definite place
in the curriculum of the schools and be the basis of general education.[125]

O'Rourke had taught physical training in leadership training camps
in Scotland in the summers of 1938 and 1939.[126] She also conducted physical training classes and lectures in Ireland for teachers of the Department

118   Ibid.
119   Ibid.
120   *Irish Independent*, 16 July 1947.
121   Ibid.
122   Conor Heffernan, 'Fitness and Fun that's Not Just for Mum: The Women's League
      of Health and Beauty in 1930s Ireland' in *Women's History Review*, vol. 28, no. 7
      (2019), 1017–38, 1021.
123   *Irish Independent*, 16 July 1947.
124   *Evening Herald*, 8 November 1940.
125   Ibid.
126   *Irish Press*, 25 October 1946.

of Technical Education in 1935, 1941 and 1943.[127] By May 1950, she was running the Dublin College of Physical Education, which was based at Pembroke Street and which offered a course of three years' duration for females who wanted to become PE teachers.[128] This was recognised by the Department of Education, with a curriculum which included 'education, recreation and remedial gymnastics, dancing, swimming, games, anatomy, physiology, pathology, theory of gymnastics and teaching'.[129] The course was said to be suitable for employment in schools, factories, welfare centres and League of Health classes.[130]

Despite these efforts, a lack of qualifications was a problem for those seeking posts in physical training within schools, with the Cork City Vocational Education Committee noting in July 1948 that for the post of female physical training teacher, there was only one applicant, but she did not have the Ceard Teastas, a required qualification to teach in secondary schools in the Republic of Ireland. Therefore she could only be appointed temporarily for twelve months until she obtained this.[131] The following year, at a meeting of the same organisation, school principal, J. F. King, noted that there were nine applicants for the position of part-time physical training teacher at the Technical Institute in Cork, 'but none of them possessed evidence of having been trained as a teacher of physical training'.[132] Although the committee agreed that all nine applicants be called for an interview, King stated that 'it was necessary for prospective teachers to go to England to get proper training and a diploma in physical culture'. He added that the teacher they had was giving adequate service despite not being fully qualified.[133]

In 1952, the Minister of Education Seán Moylan (1951–4) issued a circular to VEC Chief Executive Officers, stating 'that Irish should, as far as

---

127   Ibid.
128   Ibid., 6 May 1950.
129   Ibid.
130   Ibid.
131   *Irish Examiner*, 13 July 1948.
132   Ibid., 1 March 1949.
133   Ibid.

possible, be the medium of instruction in Physical Training'.[134] Therefore committees advertising for part-time teachers in these subjects were required to specify that 'a satisfactory knowledge of oral Irish' was needed on the part of candidates.[135] An oral test, 'the standard of examination of the Technical Instruction Branch in advanced Irish' was to be undertaken by the candidates under the inspection of the Department of Education's CEO and if no one passed the test, the committee could still approve of a candidate for the post, but this position would be re-advertised at the end of 'the current session'.[136] The need for aspiring physical training teachers to possess this certificate further complicated the process of obtaining a full-time position in a school in the Republic of Ireland.

Along with facilitating teachers who were officially deemed to be not fully qualified to teach the subject, some second level schools continued to rely on military instructors for the teaching of physical training. Some schools benefited from the availability of instructors with an interest in the Sokol system and its presence lingered on in some areas.[137] O'Donoghue et al have stated that despite the promise shown by the Army involvement in the teaching of physical training in Irish schools in the 1930s, their influence declined in the 1940s and 1950s, 'although in the City of Dublin VEC schools and in some primary and secondary schools around the country, physical education continued to be taught not only by ex-Irish Army physical training instructors, but also by some who had been in the British Army'.[138] By April 1945, Coláiste Ciaran (Bray), St Fintan's High School (Sutton) and St Helen's (Booterstown) were availing of the services

134   Department of Education Archives. Department of Education Circular, Irish qualifications required in the case of part-time teachers of choral singing and of physical training. Cir. 6/52. (1952).
135   Ibid.
136   Ibid.
137   Cooney, 'The Tendency towards Physical Training in the Sokol Way', 37; *Connacht Tribune*, 11 June 1938, *Sligo Champion*, 27 May, 5 August and 16 September 1939; *The New Ross Standard*, 15 July 1938 and *The Standard*, 3 July 1936, *Irish Press*, 16 June 1941 and *Westmeath Independent*, 8 September 1945.
138   O'Donoghue, Harford and Doherty, *Teacher Preparation in Ireland*, 112.

of an army physical training instructor.[139] In 1946 Company Sergeant John Kavanagh and Sergeant A. Dowling, army physical training instructors, participated in training at Artane School to prepare 600 boys for a display at Croke Park which took place on 2 September 1945.[140] The evidence in the Department of Defence files does not suggest any huge involvement of the army in schools in the Dublin or Wicklow area at this time. Granting permission for physical instructor participation in physical training of students was subject to clearance due to interference with normal military duties, and a request from Glasthule Presentation College for one to be provided in 1948 was rejected as a suitable timetable arrangement could not be found.[141]

The Views of Pupils and Educational Bodies' Efforts to Implement Change

There is some evidence in the press which highlights how school pupils felt about the state of PE at this time. At the annual Public Debate of the Presentation Brothers College Literary and Debating Society, held in University College Cork in May 1946, one student noted how 'physical training was almost completely neglected, and games were played chiefly to garnish the schools with laurels'.[142] A fellow student agreed that sport was played in some schools solely for the honour of winning, and that

139   Military Archives, Cathal Brugha Barracks. Department of Defence Files, 2/92315. Instruction. P.T. Schools and Colleges, Dublin Area. Commandant M. Gray, Operations Officer, Eastern Command, to Chief Staff Officer, 17 April 1945.

140   Military Archives, Cathal Brugha Barracks. Department of Defence Files, 2/92315. Instruction. P.T. Schools and Colleges, Dublin Area. Letter from Command Operations Officer D. A. Kelly to Chief Staff Officer, Department of Defence, 26 August 1946.

141   Military Archives, Cathal Brugha Barracks. Department of Defence Files, 2/92315. Instruction. P.T. Schools and Colleges, Dublin Area. Letter from Secretary A. J. Hyland to Reverend Brother Lewis, 1 December 1948.

142   *Irish Examiner*, 25 May 1946.

there was a lack of choice in the games played.[143] The following year, a *Sunday Independent* essay writing competition for schoolboys highlighted that pupils would have liked more physical training and to have a gymnasium in every school.[144]

A number of those interviewed for this book highlighted the lack of emphasis placed by primary schools on PE during their childhoods in the 1940s. One man who later became a primary school teacher recalled of his primary school years in rural Ireland that 'at that time, at the end of the war years and in the post-war years, the main problem of all parents wasn't PE, it was a matter of having enough to eat-there was rationing'.[145] In addition, he stated that

> it's very hard to explain now, where were they going to get a ball? I mean, the ball's made of rubber, leather ... a football, at that time, was a novelty. We played at school-it used to be if you had a stocking, the stocking was filled with hay. Or the next one was-the pig's bladder .... See rubber was scarce, I remember the rubber coming in ... it came in bales-there'd be tubes about 18 inches-that's the raw rubber, very, very heavy, you know, they floated ashore during the Battle of the Atlantic.[146]

Similarly, a female primary school teacher who grew up during the war noted the lack of formal PE in her locality, which was also in a peripheral Irish county, when she stated that 'there was no PE in the primary schools that I attended. We did our own PE outside playing out in the fields, hanging off trees, different things like that. We spent most of our childhood outdoors.'[147] In addition, a male primary school teacher who began school near the end of the 1940s remembered playing football in the school yard at lunch time, but 'other than that there was no PE whatsoever in primary school'.[148]

Some efforts were made to remedy this situation at that time. As Coolahan has written, the INTO's proposals in their 1947 publication, *A*

---

143   Ibid.
144   *Sunday Independent*, 14 December 1947.
145   Interview with primary school teacher number ten, 25 July 2019.
146   Ibid.
147   Interview with primary school teacher number seven, 3 July 2019.
148   Interview with primary school teacher number nine, 24 July 2019.

Plan for Education, including 'a more child-centred focus for the school programme and a much wider subject range embracing literary, aesthetic, practical and physical education subjects' were not implemented while 'the relationships between government and teachers were very strained at the time'.[149] INTO efforts to secure better pay and working conditions were rejected despite strike action with Ferriter of the view that Minister Derrig's attitude 'seemed to reflect the arrogance of 15 years of uninterrupted power in rejecting calls for Ireland to follow the educational reforms being put in place in post-war Europe'.[150] The INTO noted in their document that in terms of Physical Training, 'one of the most obvious defects' of the school system in Ireland was 'that it demands of pupils what might be described as perpetual immobility'.[151] It was also noted that 'the present attitude to physical training may be judged from the lowly place which "Drill" occupies on the programme. It might be said, indeed, that "Drill" is regarded, not as a subject proper, but as a recreational interlude. Certainly it is seldom taken seriously.'[152] They added that

> Physical training, we submit, should be restored to a place of honour on the school curriculum. It is the birthright of every child, and it caters for an instinct that finds no expression in purely bookish subjects. There are several excellent systems from which we can choose, notably the Swedish and Sokol systems, and there is no reason why we should not evolve a composite system suited to our own needs. The planning of such a system is a task for experts, and we shall content ourselves with calling attention to the need for it.[153]

Despite this, they did offer some indication of what they would like to see, stating that their 'concept of physical training however, is far wider than any system of planned exercises. It would include, first, our own native dances, and second, the provision of playing fields and systematic training in games.'[154] They also noted later in their publication the poor

149   Coolahan, *Irish Education*, 44.
150   Ferriter, *The Transformation of Ireland*, 532.
151   *A Plan for Education. Issued by the Irish National Teachers' Organisation* (Dublin: INTO, 1947), 48.
152   Ibid., 49.
153   Ibid.
154   Ibid.

state of many schools and that the 'system of primary education is not a State-system but a State-aided system. The schools, with few exceptions, are owned by local trustees, and the Manager – who in most cases is the parish priest – is the local authority.'[155] Delays in securing finance from the State, with around 50 per cent of 5,000 national schools said to be 'defective' in 1944, illustrate that in many national schools, basic facilities were still inadequate.[156]

These INTO views on physical training appear to express a turnaround from the organisation's views on the subject noted in the pre–First World War years and in the mid-1920s. Similarly, a Department of Education committee report, completed in 1947 with a focus on amending the primary school-leaving age to 12 and redeveloping the second level system in accordance with this, proposed that drawing, nature study and physical education become mandatory subjects, but there were no major policy changes implemented at this time.[157] It is worth noting that at that point, in the aftermath of the Second World War, no international pressure was brought to bear on the Irish government to improve matters in this regard. The poor standards did not go unnoticed, however. One group of teachers from Wales who undertook a trip to visit a number of unnamed schools in Ireland in 1949 were 'surprised' at 'the lack of attention' physical training was given in primary schools.[158] In particular, they commented that 'physical training was not included in any time-table, except during the summer term' and suggested that it may have been down to the lack of a main hall in many primary schools.[159] The reporter noted that this was not really an excuse, although 'so very few of the primary schools' had 'spacious playgrounds'.[160]

In 1948 General Richard Mulcahy became Minister of Education as Fianna Fáil were defeated in the General Election and a coalition government was formed.[161] His appointment offered hope that physical education

---

155   Ibid., 85.
156   Ibid., 84–5.
157   Coolahan, *Irish Education*, 44.
158   *Irish Independent*, 29 March 1949.
159   Ibid.
160   Ibid.
161   McManus, *Irish Education: The Ministerial Legacy, 1919–99*, 80.

would be given more attention and initially it was as the Minister arranged for information to be procured about facilities for the subject in training colleges and its position in vocational schools.[162] Following this, it was noted that there were only thirty physical education teachers for almost 18,000 students and that Irish trainee teachers who undertook physical education courses in Britain generally did not return as they took up positions there. Despite this, and discussions over the role of Ling College, no concrete action was taken regarding the development of a specialised training college for physical education at this time.[163]

The establishment of a Council of Education by General Mulcahy further offered the opportunity to reflect on curricular issues such as physical education. The Council, which initially contained twenty-nine members, had been appointed in April 1950 with the Very Reverend Martin Brennan as chairman.[164] There were eleven members of the clergy named on the committee while the majority of the others had education qualifications of various levels.[165] Padraig Ó Siochfhradha, who had been against the inclusion of compulsory physical drill in 1925, was also on the committee, which later gained new members due to some deaths in the early 1950s. There were also two resignations.[166] As Antonia McManus has stated, it was 'an unrepresentative council as trade unions were not represented, and neither was there a representative appointed from the inspectorate'.[167] Representatives of parents were also absent while similarly there were no sporting delegates chosen.[168]

As Minister for Education, General Mulcahy was of the view that he lacked any real power to make substantial changes to the education system.

162 O'Donoghue, 'The Policy of the State', 111.
163 Ibid., 111–13.
164 *Department of Education. Report of the Council of Education as presented to the Minister of Education. (1) The Function of the Primary School (2) The Curriculum to Be Pursued in the Primary School from the Infant Age up to 12 Years of Age* (Dublin: The Stationery Office, 1954), ii.
165 Ibid.
166 Ibid.
167 McManus, *Irish Education: The Ministerial Legacy, 1919–99*, 82–3.
168 Ibid., 83.

His comments on the function of his role as Minister during his first term in the position illustrate that in any case, he felt that the position was not one of any great significance. In 1948 he had declared that it was 'a very, very narrow one' while the following year he stated that the Minister's role was 'to watch out for causes of irritation, and having found them, to go around with the oil-can', highlighting that he saw the role as a fixer of problems rather than a visionary one.[169]

The formation of a separate national organisation for sport offered some promise. In July 1950 delegates representing thirteen sporting organisations met to adopt a constitution for the Sports Federation of Ireland at the National Boxing Stadium in Dublin.[170] As well as acting as a 'Central Organisation' to coordinate all sports, one of their objectives was 'to encourage systematic physical education and to stimulate a more general practice of athletic exercises in Ireland, with particular reference to the youth of the country'.[171] The GAA was notably absent but representatives from boxing, fencing, soccer, athletics, rowing, table tennis, motor yacht racing, lacrosse and roller hockey were all initially present.[172] In April 1951 the National Council of the Sports Federation of Ireland appointed a subcommittee to prepare a memorandum on physical education with a view to submitting this to the government.[173] However, it appears that no immediate action regarding physical education was taken. In any case, by the following year, the Sports Federation of Ireland was more concerned with securing government funding and the organisation of a pools' scheme.[174] Gaining financial assistance from the government for sporting initiatives was difficult. In November 1952 Minister for Justice, Gerald Boland, who had been involved in the 1939 cabinet committee which discussed the revival of athletics, stated that he was not in favour of raising money for sport through pools or lotteries controlled by the State.[175]

169   McManus, *Irish Education: The Ministerial Legacy, 1919–99*, 81.
170   *Irish Independent*, 3 July 1950.
171   Ibid.
172   Ibid.
173   Ibid., 20 April 1951.
174   Ibid., 25 October 1952.
175   *Irish Press*, 27 November 1952.

A report by the Commission on Youth Unemployment, completed in 1951, echoed the recommendations of the 1938 Report on PE but again, no affirmative action was taken by the government at this time regarding the subject. This had been established in 1943 under the chairmanship of Most Reverend Dr John Charles McQuaid. The Commission and its sub-committees had met on 241 occasions and reviewed 'a considerable number of documents and heard 296 witnesses'.[176] In addition, 'about 461 organisations and individuals furnished replies to questionnaires'.[177] Amongst the recommendations was the setting up of an Institute for Physical Training, which the Department of Education was said to have been considering.[178] The Commission also recommended that the subject be made 'an integral part of the curriculum of all schools' and 'that assistance be given towards the establishment of classes in physical education in boys' and girls' clubs'.[179] It was also stated that the matter was receiving 'special attention' from the Department of Education although one reporter claimed that 'the annual reports have ignored the subject', with teachers who had the facilities to teach it being encouraged rather than required to do so.[180] However, as will be seen, the Irish Government again failed to take decisive action.

O'Donoghue has highlighted the influence of the Catholic Church on medical matters at that time and believes that in rejecting Dr Noel Browne's Mother – and – Child scheme along with the Irish Medical Association, and in looking to the Irish Constitution and the rights of parents to educate their children, outlined in Article 42, the Church were reluctant to allow the role of the physical education teacher to be developed in a way that would interfere with their moral belief system.[181] Despite this, and as shown elsewhere in this book, he also notes that they were encouraging of athletics and games within the education system.[182] An exception was in the Christian Brothers' treatment of soccer, which was banned in many

176   *Irish Independent*, 12 October 1951.
177   Ibid.
178   Ibid.
179   Ibid., 13 October 1951.
180   Ibid.
181   O'Donoghue, 'The Policy of the State', 116–20.
182   Ibid., 119.

schools by the 1950s with physical violence and other punitive measures undertaken against those playing it.[183] Female religious orders, many of which had founded convents, primary and secondary schools, also continued to promote physical education, including those at the Sisters of Charity Convent, Lady Lane and Spring Garden Alley, Waterford (pictured in Figure 15). However by then, government enthusiasm for a nationwide programme to improve the structure and centralisation of the subject's teaching had withered.

Figure 15. Ball games at the Sisters of Charity Convent, Lady Lane and Spring Garden Alley, Waterford, 1949. Courtesy of the National Library of Ireland.

183   Curran, *Irish Soccer Migrants*, 82–3.

Conclusion

The results of the Irish Free State government-backed investigation into the development of PE in schools, along with those of two further related reports within the war years, centred on the revival of athletics and physical training, failed to later gain sufficient overall support at governmental level.[184] While the coming of the Emergency was undoubtedly a hindrance to plans to increase PE's development in Irish schools, concerns over financial considerations, training and organisation also hampered the progress of the subject's status.[185] Despite the sizeable evidence in favour of developing a system of PE for Irish schools, opposition to initiating a scheme mainly came from Seán Moylan, a member of the 1938 PE Committee, and Seán Lemass, and this lack of unity over the matter meant that it was not adequately pursued. Oscar Traynor, a former soccer player who later became president of the FAI, was surprisingly reluctant to push for athletics to take on a more adequate structure.

In their overall neglect of PE, the Irish Free State's government was not unique in this regard. The work of Sait Tarakçıoğlu has shown that in Turkey, plans to implement PE on a compulsory basis on the eve of the Second World War went unfulfilled because of the state of the country's economy during the war, while the culture of sports and PE there was not as developed as those in areas such as Italy and Germany.[186] As will be shown, the state of the Irish economy in the 1950s, with emigration rampant, was not conducive to investing in the development of the type of infrastructure

---

184   Physical Education. The Report of the Committee, 1.

185   Report of the Committee appointed by the Government to Examine the Question of the Promotion of the Revival of Athletics. 1939, 1 and Secretary for the Minister of Education to the Secretary of the Taoiseach, 9 January 1943.

186   Sait Tarakçıoğlu, 'A Failed Project in Turkey's Sports History: The Law on Physical Education of 1938' in *International Journal of the History of Sport*, vol. 31, no. 14 (2014), 1807–19, 1815.

advocated in the 1938 PE report. In addition, conservative attitudes shown by Eamon de Valera did little to encourage any major government-backed developments in sport during his time as Taoiseach.[187] Chapter 5 examines how PE was viewed in Northern Ireland from the early 1920s until the opening of the Ulster College of Physical Education in 1953.

187   Browne, *Ireland: A Social and Cultural History*, 202. De Valera stepped down and was replaced by Lemass as Taoiseach in 1957 and became Irish president two years later.

Towards a Specialised Training College: PE in Northern Ireland, 1922–1953

Introduction

In Northern Ireland, the development of PE was in some ways reflective of events in the field in England in the years immediately prior to the Second World War, but, as will be shown, there were distinct differences. Holt and Mason have written that 'in sport, as in so many other respects, Northern Ireland was unique' and 'in no other part of the United Kingdom was sport so bitterly divided and politicized'.[1] While a number of colleges and related courses for PE had been developed in England and Scotland, it was not until 1953 that a specialised college for the subject was opened in Northern Ireland, located at Dalriada, outside Belfast. The Ulster College of Physical Education [UCPE] was a non-residential teacher-training college for females, with fifteen students initially enrolling in the three-year course.[2] PE had been taught in many of Northern Ireland's schools, but the facilities and levels of staff expertise in the subject meant that standards remained low in comparison with other nations in Western Europe, despite the area being part of the United Kingdom.[3] Although the need for a PE college in Northern Ireland had been dismissed by government authorities in Belfast in the immediate aftermath

---

1   Holt and Mason, *Sport in Britain 1945–2000*, 138.

2   PRONI, ED/25/32. Government of Northern Ireland Reports of the Ministry of Education. *Report of the Ministry of Education for the Year 1953–4* (Belfast: H.M. Stationary Office, 1954), 11.

3   PRONI, ED/13/1/2293. Proposed Establishment of Physical Education College 1947–1954. Memo on Proposed Physical Education College, 12 December 1949.

of the British Government's Physical Training and Recreation Act of 1937, by the early 1940s the realisation that a facility of this nature was necessary was becoming apparent to key figures in the Northern Ireland government. It was the 1947 Education Act and the expansion of schools which cemented this belief. However, the general failure of Northern Ireland candidates in their applications for a scholarship system, based in England's physical training colleges, had also highlighted to key policy makers that something needed to be done to increase the number of Northern Ireland-based PE teachers, and to improve their levels of qualifications and expertise to teach the subject. This chapter traces the provision of courses for training in PE in Northern Ireland, beginning with an assessment of the status of PE as a subject in the early years of the new Northern Ireland State before examining the decision taken by the Ministry of Education to provide specialised training for the subject for second level teachers. Finally, events preceding the opening of the UCPE in Belfast in 1953 are assessed.

The Early Development of PE in Northern Ireland's Schools

In Northern Ireland, political power, the police and the top public service jobs were very much in the grip of unionism and as Bartlett has stated, 'the sectarian structure and nature of its society' did not change much during the early years.[4] In fact, 'if anything there was a consolidation of the forces keeping Catholics and Protestants apart'.[5] D. H. Akenson has noted that, following partition in 1921, 'the government of Northern Ireland inherited an educational machine which had serious mechanical difficulties' and that the new State 'did not succeed to a mechanism of education but to three separate, self-enclosed systems: national education, intermediate education, and technical education'.[6] In addition, he

4   Bartlett, *A History of Ireland*, 438.
5   Ibid.
6   Akenson, *Education and Enmity*, 12.

states that 'like a great, untracked locomotive, each of these educational engines went its own way with little effort at overall guidance and coordination being made by the central government'.[7] Ciaran O'Neill has stated that 'the decision of the Catholic Church not to engage with the government (Lynn) commission in 1922 facilitated structural segregation north of the border, creating an underfunded voluntary sector in 1923 which persisted until 1968 when denominational and largely independent providers became either controlled or "maintained" schools'.[8] As Jonathan Bardon has noted, Minister of Education Lord Londonderry's 1923 Education Act had 'incorporated most of the Lynn committee's recommendations that the state pay all teachers' salaries in elementary schools, which were to be in three categories'.[9] These included the first of these, 'those fully maintained by local authorities and the state'. In the second group, known as ' "four-and-two" schools', the committee's management consisted of four people who had been chosen by trustees or managers, while the local education authority also selected two members. Schools within this second category 'were eligible for capital grants and got half the cost of repairs, equipment, heating, lighting and cleaning'. However, the third classification, the voluntary schools, only received 'a contribution towards heating, lighting and cleaning'.[10]

While Londonderry, who held the ministerial position from 1921–6, planned to establish 'a system of publicly controlled elementary schools open and acceptable to all interests and to all sections of the population', with religious education being provided in a non-denominational structure, this was rejected by the Catholic Church, who wanted to maintain their own schools and were eager to promote a nationalist ethos.[11] Protestant

---

7   Ibid.
8   Ciaran O'Neill, 'Literacy and Education' in Eugenio Biagini and Mary E. Daly (eds), *The Cambridge Social History of Modern Ireland* (Cambridge: Cambridge University Press, 2017), 244–60.
9   Bardon, *A History of Ulster*, 502.
10   Ibid.
11   Seán Farren, 'Denominationally Integrated Education in Northern Ireland-Panacea or Civil Right' in *Paedagogica Historica: International Journal of the History of Education*, vol. 35, sup 1, (1999), 353–68, 358–9.

churches were also reluctant to submit their schools to the proposed system as their management of these was limited.[12] In 1930, the government agreed to change its regulations with concessions being given to the Protestant churches, including mandatory 'bible instruction' while church representatives were guaranteed positions on local authority and school educational committees. As Seán Farren has also stated, 'the result was that public elementary schools became, in effect, Protestant' and 'as voluntary institutions, Catholic schools received an increase in capital and maintenance grants but at a level considerably below the one hundred per cent funding available to public elementary schools'.[13] As Bardon has also noted, James Caulfeild had succeeded Lord Londonderry in 1926 and following his preparation of a new bill, and subsequent amendments, 'the 1930 Education Act allowed two school systems to operate, the Catholic one partly funded from local and central government sources, and the fully funded one attended almost exclusively by Protestants because "simple Bible instruction" was in effect mandatory'.[14]

N. C. Fleming has written that following the formation of the Northern Ireland government in Belfast in 1921, 'the work of the new Ministry of Education was initially hampered by delays in transferring staff and powers from Dublin and London, and by the political violence and uncertainty which accompanied the creation of Northern Ireland'.[15] Improving physical training in schools was not, therefore, prioritised by the Ministry of Education in the initial years of Northern Ireland State and it appears that no major changes were made to the previous system in regard to the subject. As noted, prior to partition in 1921, physical drill had been compulsory in all Irish primary schools since 1900 and while a less structured system was prevalent in second level schools, physical training and games were generally commonplace.

---

12   Ibid., 359.
13   Ibid.
14   Bardon, *A History of Ulster*, 504.
15   N. C. Fleming, 'Education since the Late Eighteenth Century' in Liam Kennedy and Philip Ollerenshaw (eds), *Ulster since 1600: Politics, Economy and Society* (Oxford: Oxford University Press, 2013), 211–27, 218.

The Northern Ireland Ministry of Education's School Programme, which was implemented for the 1924–5 school year following the Final Report of the Departmental Committee of the Education Services in 1921, favoured the incorporation of Swedish drill and dancing.[16] Physical exercises and games were also commonplace.[17] In addition, 'the appointment of specially trained games teachers in larger schools or combination of smaller schools' was encouraged while swimming was also recommended as a part of the physical training programme where facilities were available.[18] However, schools deemed examination subjects more worthy of instruction than physical training, and the specialised nature of teaching and providing accommodation for the subject were being noted as factors in its neglect by the mid-1920s.[19]

As indicated in newspaper reports at the time, even the most basic efforts to remedy this situation could prove unsuccessful. In October 1926, the Belfast Education Committee, which was chaired by S. Donald Cheyne, JP, appointed Herbert L. Atkinson of Jesmond, Newcastle-Upon-Tyne, as public elementary schools' physical training and games organiser.[20] The fact that a candidate from Ulster was not selected was criticised by some members of Belfast Corporation, with the result that the appointment was reversed although a suitable replacement does not seem to have been found.[21] This failure to appoint an organiser at this time meant that the development of the subject was hindered and government reports, at times, hint at this lack of overall development.

Perceptions of the value of physical training at primary level remained focused on its disciplinary merits rather than the expression of any great joy or release for the pupils, but games did appear to be receiving more formal attention. The Ministry of Education's annual report for 1926–7 stated that in regard to elementary schools, 'according to the time-table at least

16 McGourty, 'The Boys' Physical Education Curriculum in Secondary Schools in Northern Ireland', 27.
17 Ibid.
18 Ibid.
19 Ibid., 28.
20 *Belfast Newsletter*, 23 October 1926.
21 *Belfast Telegraph*, 2 November 1926 and *Belfast Newsletter*, 2 and 3 November 1926.

one period per week is given to Physical Training, but its practical application to the manner, deportment and carriage of the pupils is too often lost
sight of in the interval between lessons'.[22] However, it was noted that 'on
the whole, the subject is fairly well taught'.[23] It was also stated that 'a comparatively new development is the attention paid to organised games', with
Belfast said to have 'given a valuable lead' as football teams were involved in
inter-school matches.[24] Provincially based schools were also getting more
involved in games and it was hoped that their teachers would 'realise the
important lessons which can only be learned by organised team work'.[25]

   The development of competitive schools' sport remained focused in
Belfast, however. In 1925, the Belfast Education Authority's Director of
Education, Rupert Stanley, stated that a committee had been formed 'in
order to organise competitive sports in the public schools in the city'.[26] By
the late 1920s the Belfast Education Committee's Elementary School Sports
Association was operational following the organisation of fundraising
dances, with the aim of promoting 'friendly rivalry and sport amongst children of all classes and creeds in the public elementary schools'.[27] Although
the IFA had their own soccer competition for schools in operation at that
stage, they formed a committee to meet with the Education authorities
about this.[28] By 1928, the Northern Ireland Technical Day Schools had
an association for physical training, with cups for boys' football and girls'
hockey.[29] Cricket continued to maintain a place in some institutions such
as the Royal School Armagh, pictured in Figure 16.[30] Despite this, the value

22   PRONI, BCT/7/5/3. Government of Northern Ireland Reports of the Ministry of
     Education. *Report of the Ministry of Education for the Year 1926–7* (Belfast: H.M.
     Stationary Office, 1927), 24.
23   Ibid.
24   Ibid.
25   Ibid.
26   Irish Football Association Papers, IFA Council Minutes, D4196/2/4,
     24 November 1925.
27   *Belfast Newsletter*, 27 November 1926 and 5 March 1927.
28   Irish Football Association Papers, IFA Council Minutes, D4196/2/4,
     24 November 1925.
29   *Fermanagh Herald*, 17 November 1928.
30   *Football Sports Weekly*, 29 May 1926.

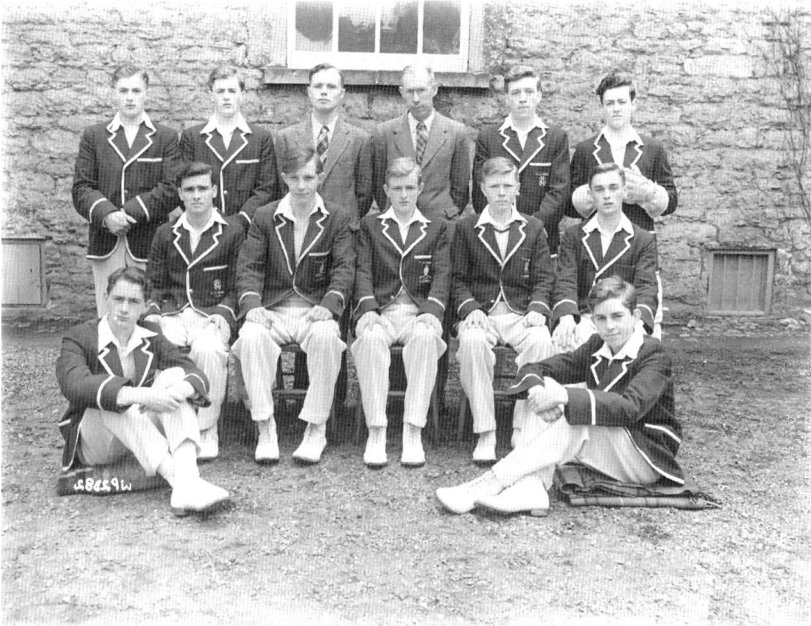

Figure 16. The Royal School Armagh cricket team c.1930. Courtesy of PRONI.

of physical training over games in a disciplinary sense was highlighted by authorities in some more regional areas. One inspector's report on developments in the west of Northern Ireland in 1926 noted that drill instruction was 'generally well attended to' although its positive effects were 'not always to be seen in the bearing and manner of the pupils'.[31]

As Sugden and Bairner have noted, in Northern Ireland, 'an anglophile and largely Protestant muscular Christianity has existed alongside a Celtic and recognisably Jesuit approach to the teaching and playing of sports and games'.[32] Annual reports illuminate the emphasis on winning, tradition and

31 PRONI, BCT/7/5/3. Government of Northern Ireland Reports of the Ministry of Education. *Report of the Ministry of Education for the Year 1925–6* (Belfast: H.M. Stationary Office, 1926), 23.

32 John Sugden and Alan Bairner, *Sport, Sectarianism and Society in a divided Ireland* (London: Leicester University Press, 1993), 97.

team prestige, with a reviewer of activities in July 1922 at Campbell College, said to be 'one of the largest, best equipped and most successful schools in the United Kingdom', referring to the ongoing success of their rugby team while the cricket team was said to be 'the equal of its predecessors'.[33] As Holt and Mason have stated, the tradition of games 'was alive and well in private education and continued to prosper throughout the twentieth century' and 'high status schools had high-achieving parents, who believed in sport as physical and moral training, insisting their hefty fees were invested in good facilities and plenty of competitive games for boys and girls'.[34] By the end of the decade, pupils at the Royal School at Portora (see Figure 17) had a 'first class instructor' for physical training while they also had use of a 104 feet swimming bath. The school also owned six racing boats for activity on the Erne and an 'up-to-date sanatorium and gymnasium'.[35] Similarly, pupils at Foyle College utilised the local waterway as well as their own indoor facilities for competitions and practice, with a boat club in existence there by the late 1930s (pictured in Figure 18).[36]

Dónal McAnallen has illustrated that it was not until after partition in 1921 that the choice of sports became more pronounced in Northern Ireland's Catholic schools, although he also notes that at St Patrick's College Armagh, the decision had been taken to 'abandon soccer' by the spring of 1917 in the aftermath of the 1916 Rising, in line with their nationalist ethos (see Figure 19).[37] Physical drill continued to be taught there (see Figure 20) and in many other Catholic schools such as the CBS in Newry, soccer was also rejected.[38] While the MacRory Cup was operational for Gaelic football teams in 1923, the Ulster Colleges' GAA Council was not founded

33   *Belfast Newsletter*, 20 July 1922.
34   Holt and Mason, *Sport in Britain 1945–2000*, 16.
35   *Belfast Newsletter*, 10 April 1929.
36   See *Londonderry Sentinel*, 29 September 1900, 8 October 1908 and *Irish Independent*, 10 July 1939.
37   Dónal McAnallen, 'Partition, Sport and Education in Ireland, 1921–72.' Paper given at Paper given at Sport and Education in Ireland and Britain Conference, Public Record Office of Northern Ireland, Belfast, 27 September 2019. See also Curran, *Irish Soccer Migrants*, 84.
38   *Irish Independent*, 20 August 1917 and Curran, *Irish Soccer Migrants*, 84.

Figure 17. Portora Royal School boxers, 1928. Courtesy of Robert Northridge.

until 1928.[39] Michael McGrath has noted that in early 1930s, 'a significant minority of Catholic schools did not play Gaelic games'.[40] However, competitions later broadened as the failure of a number of Christian Brothers Schools to compete successfully at MacRory Cup level saw the initiation of the Rannafast Cup for under 16s in 1938 and the Corn na nÓg cup for under 14s was inaugurated ten years later. In 1963 the Mageean Cup was established for hurling purposes.[41] In 1946 the first All-Ireland colleges' senior

---

39 'MacRory Cup: The stats' Retrieved from <https://www.irishnews.com/sport/gaafootball/2019/11/01/news/macrory-cup-the-stats-1748138/ [Accessed 27 October 2020] and 'Ulster Schools GAA' Retrieved from http://www.danskebankulsterschoolsgaa.com/history/> [Accessed 27 October 2020].

40 Michael McGrath, *The Catholic Church and Catholic Schools in Northern Ireland* (Dublin: Irish Academic Press, 2000), 251.

41 'Ulster Schools GAA'.

FOYLE COLLEGE BOAT CLUB.
1ST IV. 1939.

Figure 18. Foyle College Boat Club first team, 1939. Courtesy of William Lynn.

Gaelic football championship competition, the Hogan Cup, was won by St Patrick's College Armagh, illustrating the GAA's policy of organising its games on an all-Ireland basis.[42]

The teaching of physical training in Northern Ireland primary and intermediate schools was influenced by curriculum guidance from England while exercises undertaken followed Swedish methods, although the time allocated varied from school to school. After a request from the Polish Embassy in May 1930 seeking information on physical culture in Great Britain, the Secretary to the Cabinet in Northern Ireland, CH Blackmore, noted in his reply that

> A course in Physical Exercises is given in practically every public Elementary School in Northern Ireland. The time given to this subject varies from half-an-hour per week

42   *Sunday Independent*, 29 November 1964.

Figure 19. St Patrick's College Armagh Gaelic football team 1927–8. Courtesy of PRONI.

to fifteen minutes daily on 4 days per week. The latter practice is being adopted in an increasing number of schools. In all cases the exercises performed follow the lines of the syllabus for Physical Training for Schools issued by the Board of Education in London, and based broadly on the Swedish system of Gymnastic exercises.[43]

It was also stated that 'the curriculum prescribed by regulation for all recognised Secondary and Day Schools' included physical training while 'gymnastic exercises based on the Swedish system for the most part are given to the pupils of practically all these classes of schools'.[44] Given that Northern Ireland's public elementary schools were, as noted, effectively

43   PRONI, CAB/9/D/57/1 Physical Education 1930–1935. Letter from CH Blackmore to the Under Secretary of State, 27 May 1930.

44   Ibid.

Protestant by the 1930s, there was less official recognition of what was taught in Catholic schools, which remained 'voluntary institutions' whose authorities looked to their own religious beliefs and nationalist culture in common with the official government policy in Dublin.[45] In addition, as Farren has also noted, by the 1940s, 'since secondary schools were almost completely outside the control of the Ministry of Education, all but 3 of the 70 secondary schools were conducted under voluntary auspices' and 'the ministry could not dictate their curriculum'.[46] He also states that 'like its counterpart in the south, the ministry's influence was directly exercised through the syllabuses it set and the examinations it conducted. As independent institutions, most secondary schools were free to offer whatever curricula they considered appropriate.'[47]

Sports days were also part of pupils' development in the inter-war years (see Figure 21) and some organisers allowed for parental involvement such as those of the Christian Brothers (Brow-o-the-Hill), who held their annual sports at the Brandywell in Derry in July 1933.[48] Along with all the teaching staff, the St Columb's College annual sports, which took place at the same venue in June 1937, attracted the support of 'many past pupils, both clergy and laymen, who displayed great interest in the various events'.[49] The performance of 15-year-old Mary Keenan at the Donaghmore Convent School Sports in June 1937 earned her the school's Perpetual Challenge Cup, which was presented by the local priest, the Very Reverend Canon Finnegan.[50] In winning six events, she had 'as opponents many who were her seniors'.[51] Team games such as hockey remained popular in many educational establishments such as the Armagh Girls' High School (Pictured in Figure 22), while lacrosse was played at some such as Richmond Lodge School, Belfast.[52] By 1930, Inter-School cups were growing in popularity in

45   Farren, 'Denominationally Integrated Education in Northern Ireland-panacea or Civil Right', 353–68, 359.
46   Farren, *The Politics of Irish Education 1920–65*, 157.
47   Ibid.
48   *Derry Journal*, 3 July 1933.
49   Ibid., 14 June 1937.
50   *The Mid-Ulster Mail*, 3 July 1937.
51   Ibid.
52   *Belfast Newsletter*, 1 December 1931.

Figure 20. St Patrick's College Armagh PE class 1928. Courtesy of PRONI.

Belfast, with many teachers involved in training teams and managing the competitions, while the Belfast Education Authority's provision of fields was 'a valuable aid' to children's physical development.[53] League competitions were operational in a variety of codes with the Ulster Secondary Schools camogie league attracting teams from Ballycastle (Antrim), Newry and Kilkeel (Down) by the winter of 1934.[54] For convent schools, the playing of camogie was also an expression of their community identity and beliefs, with St Ita's Camogie club ceili, held at the local Convent High School

53   PRONI, BCT/7/5/3. Government of Northern Ireland Reports of the Ministry of Education. *Report of the Ministry of Education for the Year 1929–30* (Belfast: H.M. Stationary Office, 1930), 14.
54   *Ballymena Observer*, 30 November 1934.

Figure 21. A school sports day in Northern Ireland in the 1920s. Courtesy of PRONI.

Hall in Magherafelt, County Derry, concluding with the singing of the Irish national anthem in May 1935.[55]

Difficulties in the Provision of Facilities

By the late 1920s, official attitudes appear to indicate an adequate level of satisfaction with the standard of physical training in Northern Ireland's schools, but problems with facilities were also acknowledged. In 1928, the Ministry of Education's annual report noted that in some schools the work carried out in regard to physical training continued to be 'of a stereotyped character partly because of the lack of suitable playgrounds' despite the increase in games.[56] It was also noted that outdoor games

---

55   *The Mid-Ulster Mail*, 11 May 1935.
56   PRONI, BCT/7/5/3. Government of Northern Ireland Reports of the Ministry of Education. *Report of the Ministry of Education for the Year 1927–8* (Belfast: H.M. Stationary Office, 1928), 16.

Figure 22. Armagh Girls High School hockey team 1933–4. Courtesy of PRONI.

and swimming in Belfast had recently undergone 'a very marked development'.[57] The problem of playgrounds as a venue for physical training in elementary schools was also discussed in the Ministry of Education's report for 1928–9. It was outlined that 'playgrounds in a large number of cases' were 'unsuitable', while many schools had none. In more rural areas, these were said to be 'so wet and muddy in bad weather that the children have to play on the public roads, a practice which is becoming increasingly dangerous'.[58] By the end of the decade, along with physical training, the elementary school curriculum in Northern Ireland included English, arithmetic, geography, history, drawing, music, needlework, domestic

57   Ibid.
58   PRONI, BCT/7/5/3. Government of Northern Ireland Reports of the Ministry of Education. *Report of the Ministry of Education for the Year 1928–9* (Belfast: H.M. Stationary Office, 1929), 11.

economy, horticulture, nature study, elementary science and Irish but these subjects were not taught in all schools.[59]

As Bartlett has stated, the Great Depression brought on by the Wall Street Crash of 1929 'hit Northern Ireland hard' and by 1932 nearly 80,000 people were unemployed in Belfast while poverty and disease were rife and housing, healthcare and state benefit systems were inadequate.[60] By 1935, 'physical culture' was obligatory in public elementary schools in Northern Ireland and was also taught 'in all Preparatory, Intermediate and Secondary Schools' while it was supplemented in the majority of schools by games 'such as football for boys and hockey for girls'.[61] Despite this, problems remained in many schools. One headmistress at a Belfast school felt in June 1935 that physical training had been neglected by the Ministry of Education and had 'not yet reached the dignity of an "inspected subject", as it has been in England for many years', although she also stated that England lagged 'far behind' other European countries.[62] One of the main difficulties in teaching the subject in Coleraine Academical Institution and employing a physical training instructor on a full-time basis by the late 1930s was 'the provision of a suitable gymnasium'.[63] J. H. Robb, the Parliamentary Secretary to the Ministry of Education, stated in November 1935 that 'a better system of physical training' was needed in the schools and that any suggestions would be welcome, which suggests a lack of direction.[64]

In 1936, the Ministry of Education James Caulfeild (1926–37) noted that 'only a small proportion' of intermediate and secondary schools were able to provide 'a separate room' for physical training, 'or equipment of any kind'.[65] Only thirty to forty minutes per week were allocated to physical

59   PRONI, BCT/7/5/3. Government of Northern Ireland Reports of the Ministry of
      Education. Report of the Ministry of Education for the Year 1927–8, 15–20.
60   Bartlett, *Ireland: A History*, 436–7.
61   PRONI, CAB/9/D/57/1 Physical Education 1930–1935. Letter from W. A.
      Houston to the Secretary to the Cabinet, 7 June 1935.
62   *Belfast Newsletter*, 24 June 1935.
63   Ibid., 7 August 1939.
64   Ibid., 2 November 1935.
65   PRONI, BCT/7/5/3. Government of Northern Ireland Reports of the Ministry
      of Education. *Report of the Ministry of Education for the Year 1935–6* (Belfast: H.M.
      Stationary Office, 1936), 20.

training 'in most schools' despite the British Medical Association recommending in a report on physical training that 'three normal periods of gymnastic training' should be given to all pupils in public and secondary schools along with the time given to swimming and field games.[66] It was also noted that in Northern Ireland's intermediate and secondary schools, the provision of 'alternative physical activities for children not interested in or fit for the ordinary school games, football and hockey' was being neglected.[67] There was said to be 'some difficulty in providing specialist teachers for this work' and it was felt by the Ministry of Education that 'a little more co-operation between governing bodies might lead to more frequent appointment of specially qualified instructors'.[68] In 1937, the Ministry of Education's annual report noted 'the poor facilities for physical training in most schools' and 'the extremely limited time generally allotted to this important element of the curriculum'.[69] It was recommended that each class should be given physical exercises daily along with 'the fixed lesson once or twice a week by an expert'.[70]

Developing physical training in technical schools was also difficult in some areas, with mixed attitudes shown towards the value of its inclusion. Some relied on local contacts to provide teachers, with the principal of Enniskillen Technical School expressing his gratitude to a Mr Seale who had helped them acquire the services of Mr Buchanan, who taught the Day commercial students the subject in 1928.[71] By October 1929 Larne Technical School was still without a playing field, despite their annual report noting that physical training was 'being considered of great importance by the Ministry'.[72] By the winter of 1933 they had managed to appoint an

66   Ibid.
67   Ibid.
68   Ibid.
69   PRONI, BCT/7/5/3. Government of Northern Ireland Reports of the Ministry of Education. *Report of the Ministry of Education for the Year 1936–7* (Belfast: H.M. Stationary Office, 1937), 22.
70   Ibid.
71   *Fermanagh Herald*, 1 December 1928.
72   *Belfast Newsletter*, 16 October 1929.

instructor for physical training despite the subject being omitted from the curriculum there until then.[73]

Some technical schools needed to be forced to take action to provide physical training. In 1931, the Strabane and Castlederg Regional Committee passed a resolution 'deleting physical training and all games' due to the expenditure involved at Strabane Technical School, particularly in regard to running a school soccer team.[74] In July 1932, after discussion with an inspector from the Ministry about its provision in the Strabane Day Commercial School, they reluctantly agreed to include physical training and to appoint both male and female instructors for the subject.[75] The inspector, W. G. Pirie, addressed them on its necessity and stated that it 'was taught in nearly all the schools in Northern Ireland' and agreed to speak to the Ministry about the lack of attention they had received in the past. One committee member stated that in terms of accommodation, Strabane had 'only a ram-shackle' while there were also complaints over the cost in paying instructors.[76] In August 1932, Strabane Urban District Council agreed to let the local Town Hall for the purpose of physical training classes for Strabane Technical School (see Figure 23) for two hours on two evenings per week.[77] Somewhat later, in September 1937, the new Technical School in Strabane, which included a physical training and science room, was opened.[78]

Pre–Second World War Teacher Training and PE Qualifications

Holt has noted that in Britain, unlike in other European countries where physical training in schools was developed more in line with state policy,

---

73   Ibid., 29 November 1933.
74   *Belfast Newsletter*, 5 December 1931.
75   *Strabane Chronicle*, 9 July 1932.
76   Ibid.
77   Ibid., 6 August 1932.
78   Ibid., 11 September 1937.

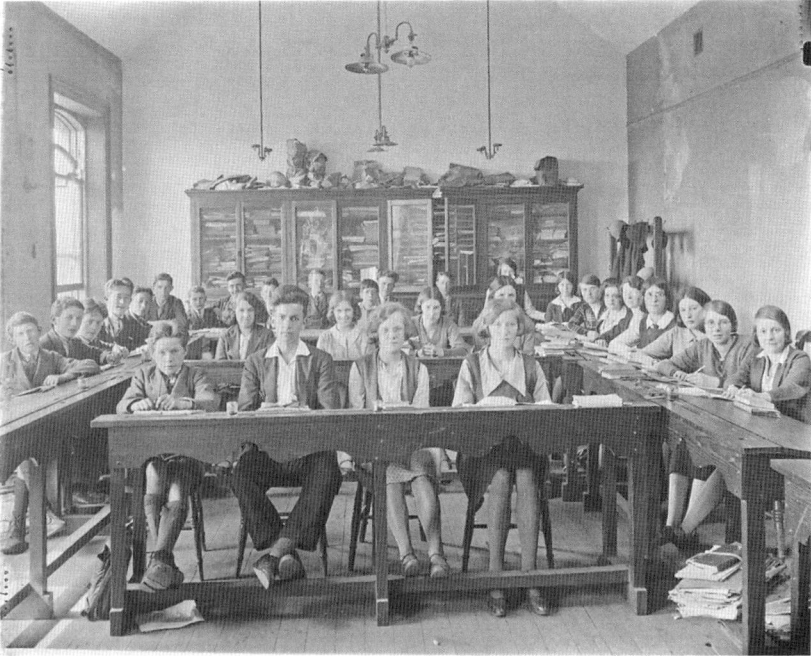

Figure 23. Strabane Technical School c.1930s. Courtesy of PRONI.

'there was a very restricted physical education "establishment" in the form of specialist colleges for teacher-training'.[79] In addition, 'these institutions were concerned mainly with gymnastics and confined largely to women until after the Second World War'.[80] He has also stated that 'games were not even made compulsory in state schools until 1944 despite the importance of athleticism in private schools' as 'the small-state tradition of the Victorians was strong and resilient'.[81] As Patricia Vertinsky has noted, by the late 1930s there were seven specialist female colleges for physical training in Britain, with institutions based in Hampstead,

79   Holt, *Sport and the British*, 344.
80   Ibid.
81   Ibid.

Dartford, Chelsea, Liverpool, Bedford, Dunfermline and Nonington.[82]
P. C. McIntosh has written that with the opening of Carnegie College
of PE in Leeds in 1933, a year's training course was available for male
teachers who had finished 'two years' general training' or who had completed a university degree.[83] Both the Loughborough course, initiated
in 1935, and that begun at Goldsmith's College in 1937, were similar to
that at Carnegie College.[84] However, McIntosh also states that there
were two main differences between these courses and the physical education courses in the women colleges. Firstly, the men's courses 'were only
open to teachers who had already qualified to teach other subjects' as
the Board of Education 'had decided that specialist training in physical
education for men must not exclude a general training as it had done in
the women's colleges'.[85] In addition, there were many of those training at
Carnegie College who received grants from the government while female
colleges, with the exception of Chelsea College, were 'private enterprises
which had to pay their way on the fees of the students'.[86] Following negotiations about the nature of the exclusion of female colleges from 'the
general pattern of teacher training', London University decided to award
a diploma for female students, with examinations in this award initially
held there in 1932.[87]

In Northern Ireland, a co-educational teacher-training college was
established at Stranmillis in Belfast through the Ministry of Education in
October 1922, although there was no specialised college for those wishing
to teach PE.[88] Prior to this, some students from the north of Ireland had attended Marlborough Street Training College in Dublin, but after partition

---

82   Patricia Vertinsky, 'Re-examining *Women First*: Rewriting the History of the 'End
      of an Era" in David Kirk and Patricia Vertinsky (eds), *The Female Tradition in
      Physical Education: Women First Revisited* (London: Routledge, 2016), 1–20, 15.
83   McIntosh, 'Games and Gymnastics for Two Nations in One', 206.
84   Ibid.
85   Ibid.
86   Ibid.
87   Ibid.
88   PRONI, ED 25/1/1 9125. Ministry of Education Northern Ireland. Report of the
      Ministry of Education 1922–23 (Belfast: H.M. Stationary Office, 1923), 56.

it closed and the Northern Ireland government moved to secure the property at Stranmillis Housing Estate.[89] The Northern Ireland government also made a temporary arrangement whereby 'a limited number of students' attended the Church of Ireland Training College at Kildare Place in Dublin while instruction also took place in connection with Trinity College Dublin.[90] The Northern Ireland Ministry also approved training courses undertaken by female students at St Mary's College, Belfast and in England for male students at Strawberry Hill, Middlesex.[91] Physical Training was also included on the curriculum at Stranmillis Training College for Elementary Teachers, with an instructor specialising in Swedish methods of physical training employed.[92] This was largely a Protestant college as Catholics generally attended St Mary's College on the Falls Road or St Mary's College in Strawberry Hill.[93] The Ministry of Education were reluctant to fund the hiring of specialised physical training instructors in primary schools and teachers at that level were expected to teach the subject themselves as part of their duties.[94]

In 1925, having considered the status of diplomas available at a number of colleges specialising in physical training in England and Scotland, W. A. Houston, the assistant secretary to the Northern Ireland Minister of Education, Lord Londonderry, noted that they would keep their regulations as they were. They would not mention any 'particular diplomas' in their advertisements as it was felt that 'for some time to come' they would 'probably have to accept as physical teachers persons who have somewhat

---

89   Ibid.
90   Ibid.
91   *Belfast Newsletter*, 15 November 1932.
92   PRONI, CAB/9/D/57/1 Physical Education 1930–1935. Letter from CH Blackmore to the Under Secretary of State, 27 May 1930.
93   McGrath, *The Catholic Church and Catholic Schools in Northern Ireland*, 52.
94   ED/14C/385. 1922–27 St Mary's Girls National School. Newcastle. Inspection of PT. Extracts from general report dated 15th September 1926, by Mr John D. MacManus, Inspector to St Mary's Girls' Public Elementary School, County Down. Roll Number 15,306. Postal Address Newcastle. Efficiency of the instruction, and ratings assigned to teachers; Letter from William J. Nolan to the Secretary of the Minister of Education, 22 Jan. 1927 and Letter from the Assistant Secretary to the Minister of Education to W. J. Nolan, 3 February 1927.

inferior paper qualifications' as this would leave them with 'as free a hand as possible'.[95] The Ministry did approve of diplomas from colleges which qualified for membership of the Ling Association, along with the British Association for Physical Training and the Liverpool Physical Training College.[96] In particular, correspondence from Irene M. Marsh, the principal of Liverpool Physical Training College, illustrates that 'many Irish students' had attended the college by the mid-1920s as it was 'the nearest [Physical Training] college to Ireland' where adequate qualifications could be obtained.[97]

Recruitment of those with specialist teaching qualifications from English colleges was not uncommon in Northern Ireland's Intermediate schools. At Ashleigh House School, which had 'a well-equipped gym' attached by June 1922, the girls there gave 'a most interesting demonstration of physical education' in the school garden, under the direction of Miss E. A. Stollery, who held a diploma from Chelsea College of Physical Education.[98] In June 1924, the staff of the Royal Academy in Belfast was strengthened by the appointment of Miss Doris Morton, who held a first class diploma from Liverpool Physical Training College, 'as games mistress and physical instructress for the girls' school'.[99]

While the Ministry did not 'prescribe a syllabus for Physical Culture' for second level school trainee teachers, it was noted by the middle of the 1930s that persons who had a diploma from the Ling Association of Teachers of Swedish Gymnastics, the Bergman Osterberg Physical Training College (Dartford) or the Diploma in Theory and Practice of Physical Education of the London University were certified to teach the subject. By the following year, this list also included the Diploma of the Incorporated British

---

95   PRONI, ED/13/1/1490. Physical Training. Recognition of Diplomas, Vocational Courses 1928–1932. Letter from W. A. Houston to Mr Smyth, 12 November 1925.

96   Ibid.

97   PRONI, ED/13/1/1490. Physical Training. Recognition of Diplomas, Vocational Courses 1928–1932. Letter from Irene M. Marsh to the Secretary of the Ministry of Education, 12 October 1925. See also *Northern Whig*, 26 March 1904.

98   *Belfast Newsletter*, 22 June 1922.

99   Ibid., 20 June 1924.

Association for Physical Training.[100] By the summer of 1936 the Northern Ireland Ministry of Education was organising summer vacation courses in Belfast in physical training, and these were restricted to public elementary, secondary and technical school teachers.[101]

The 1938 Northern Ireland Physical Training and Recreation Act and the War Years

In February 1937, the British government circulated its proposals 'for extending facilities for physical training and recreation' and established two national advisory councils, with one for Scotland and one for England and Wales and funding of £2 million to be given along with annual charges costing £150,000 over three years.[102] Grants were to be given to organisations such as the National Playing Fields Association and the Central Council of Physical Recreation to develop the supply of leaders and teachers. Local authorities were to be given extended powers, particularly in regard to providing community centres through the new Bill while it was also proposed to establish a national college for the development of physical training teachers and leaders.[103]

Despite this, Welshman has written that the Act was 'an amateurish British response to the physical training schemes developed by other

100   PRONI, ED/13/1/1490. Physical Training. Recognition of Diplomas, Vocational Courses. Letter from the Secretary of the Ministry of Education to Miss P. McAlinney, 14 March 1936.
101   Ibid.
102   *Belfast Newsletter*, 5 February 1937.
103   Ibid. and 19 February 1937. See also Holt and Mason, *Sport in Britain 1945–2000*, 19–22. The Central Council for Recreative Physical Training was established in England in 1935 and by 1944 had become known as the Central Council of Physical Recreation. It was extended to Northern Ireland in 1949. See Curran, *Irish Soccer Migrants*, 72–4.

European countries'.[104] Physical Education in England, according to Carter, 'relied on schools and voluntary organisations' in the early 1930s 'whereas in Germany, Italy, Czechoslovakia and Russia, the state had invested heavily' in educating teenagers in the subject.[105] Holt has noted that British funding 'was exceedingly modest in scope' when compared to 'the vast sums spent on "Kraft durch Freude" by the Third Reich and Mussolini's "Dopolavoro" programme'.[106] The provision of this Act was motivated by the Conservative government's fear of German rearmament. It was not until the latter half of the twentieth century 'that the state accepted a prime responsibility for the provision of sports facilities culminating in the setting up of the Sports Council with its slogan "Sport for All"' in 1972 after an Advisory Council was established in 1965.[107] In addition, Holt has written that despite assistance in providing facilities for physical training undertaken by bodies such as the Central Council of Physical Recreation, the National Playing Fields Association and the National Council for Social Service, 'all of these organizational initiatives stopped well short of full-blooded state intervention'.[108]

Having considered the United Kingdom 1937 Physical Training and Recreation Act in April 1937, a number of members of the cabinet in Belfast including Lord Charlemont and J. H. Robb decided that 'the circumstances in Northern Ireland did not require anything so pretentious as the organisation which was being set up in Great Britain'.[109] They felt that 'nothing in the nature of a central college of Physical Education would be necessary, and it was agreed that there would be no question of setting up local committees outside the machinery of the Local Authorities themselves'.[110] However, they did agree to investigate the facilities for PE in Northern

104   Welshman, 'Physical Culture and Sport in Schools in England and Wales, 1900–40', 54–75, 71.
105   Carter, *Medicine, Sport and the Body*, 70.
106   Holt, *Sport and the British*, 344.
107   Ibid., 271.
108   Ibid., 344.
109   CAB/9/D/72. Physical Recreation and Training 1937–43. Physical Training and Recreation Meeting, 9 April 1937.
110   Ibid.

Ireland and a Physical Training and Recreation Committee was established. By July 1937, the survey of the Physical Training and Recreation facilities in Northern Ireland was completed.[111] The results were gathered from a questionnaire circulated throughout an unspecified number of unnamed primary, secondary, technical schools and training colleges and then completed by principals, with mixed results in terms of facilities, teachers' qualifications and schools' abilities to provide regular PE to a satisfactory level.[112]

Following these findings, plans for improvements were brought into place. By November 1937 a draft scheme of Physical Training and Recreation had been drawn up by the Committee representative of the Ministries of Education, Finance, Home Affairs and Labour, with a view to incorporation within a Bill and presentation to Parliament in March 1938.[113] In particular, they noted that the contrast between physical training in Northern Ireland and in mainland Britain:

> The Physical Training and Recreation Act, which became law in England and Wales on 13 July, 1937, is designed mainly to develop and encourage physical training for adolescents and adults of both sexes and does not relate to the provision of facilities for the purposes mentioned in connection with schools. The representatives of the Ministry of Education on the Departmental Committee, have, however, stressed the fact that in Northern Ireland, physical training is by no means so well developed in the schools as in Great Britain, nor are the facilities usually provided here at all commensurate with those available across the water. They have urged, therefore, that in dealing with the subject here attention should be given to this aspect of the matter, pointing out that little progress can be expected from adolescents and adults if physical training is not a regular feature of life at school.[114]

In April 1938, the British Government announced details of the Northern Ireland Physical Training and Recreation Bill. £65,000 was to be made available over three years to develop physical fitness and related facilities

---

111   FIN/18/7/254. Physical Training and Recreation. Physical Training and Recreation Facilities in Northern Ireland. July 1937.

112   Ibid., 1–2.

113   PRONI, ED/ Scheme of Physical Recreation and Training, 26 November 1937. By July 1937 R. R. Bowman of the Ministry of Labour was also involved.

114   Ibid.

in Northern Ireland.[115] An Advisory Council, paid by the Ministry of Education, was to be appointed by the Prime Minister, James Craig, with grants to be given to 'local authorities or voluntary organisations' to promote physical training and recreation facilities.[116] Grants could also be given 'towards the expenses of managers and governing bodies of schools recognised, other than public elementary schools, in providing facilities for physical training and recreation.'[117] They could also be made towards funding 'of any central voluntary organisation.'[118] It was also stated that where grants were to be made available to schools, 'non-pupils' would also be able to avail of their facilities for physical training and recreation, while a 'new or existing voluntary school' could also be given a grant towards facilities such as gymnasia, swimming baths and playing fields.[119]

The Northern Ireland Physical Training and Recreation Act was given Royal Assent on 15 June 1938.[120] The act was implemented 'to provide for the development of facilities for, and the encouragement of, physical training and recreation, and to facilitate the establishment of centres for social activities.'[121] The purpose of the Act was said to be quite similar to the British one passed the previous year, and was 'intended mainly to assist in the development of physical training for adolescents and adults of both sexes', although in the Northern Ireland Act provision was also included for 'assisting managers of secondary and technical schools to promote this form of education amongst the pupils.'[122] An Advisory Council for Physical Training and Recreation was to be established, along with a Grants Committee, while it was also intended 'to empower the Ministry of Education to make grants to local authorities, voluntary organisations and school managers,

115   *Irish Independent*, 18 April 1938.
116   Ibid.
117   Ibid.
118   Ibid.
119   Ibid.
120   PRONI, BCT/7/5/3. Government of Northern Ireland Reports of the Ministry of Education. *Report of the Ministry of Education for the Year 1937–8* (Belfast: H.M. Stationary Office, 1938), 9.
121   Ibid.
122   Ibid.

for the purpose of helping the latter to provide playing-fields, gymnasiums and other facilities for physical training'.[123]

In addition, the Ministry of Education had the power to pay part of the salaries of physical instructors and leaders.[124] Finance was to be provided from Parliamentary funds for the Act's purposes and local authorities were to be given 'enlarged powers' to carry out measures while a section was also included which would enable the Ministry to assist 'in paying the expenses of training instructors of physical education at an approved college'.[125] The aim of the Act was to extend the popularity of physical training and recreation throughout Northern Ireland.[126]

In line with the passing of the Act, the Northern Ireland government also appointed a joint Organiser and Inspector of Physical Training in November 1938, with L. Bain Dickinson of Allanton, Scotland, recruited to take up the position in the New Year.[127] Dickinson was games' master at Dollar Academy and his new position came 'under the Ministry of Education' while his main duty was to 'advise the Ministry on matters coming with the scope' of the new Act.[128] He later noted that in relation to PE on the eve of the war there had only been 'one qualified training college lecturer, and ten qualified women teachers and five qualified men teachers in the whole of Northern Ireland'.[129] Despite his appointment, and the formation of an Advisory Council and a Grants Committee, progress was slow and the beginning of the Second World War in the autumn of 1939 saw attention diverted elsewhere. Dickinson spent the years from 1940 until the end of 1944 as Staff Physical Fitness Officer at the RAF's Northern Ireland headquarters as well as in the headquarters of the RAF's No. 27 group in Cirencester, Gloucestershire and did not take up the role again until 1945.[130] The Grants Committee was temporarily suspended. However,

123   Ibid.
124   Ibid., 9–10.
125   Ibid., 10.
126   Ibid.
127   *Belfast Newsletter*, 23 November 1938.
128   Ibid.
129   Ibid., 29 March 1954.
130   Government of Northern Ireland Reports of the Ministry of Education. *Report of the Ministry of Education for the Year 1937–8*, 10.

'in view of the effect of the black-out and other war time considerations', by November 1940 it had been reconstituted 'with more limited powers'.[131]

Belfast had been bombed by the Luftwaffe in April and May 1941 and as Bardon has written, 'the Northern Ireland government failed to make adequate preparations to protect its citizens'.[132] Evacuation of schoolchildren did not take place until April 1941 in Belfast with around 30,000 eventually arriving in rural areas. Later that year, German military interest became more focused on Russia, allowing schools in Belfast to reopen 'shortly after the main raids, and despite public warnings of the danger, gradually the students trickled back'.[133] The number of displaced pupils dropped to 278 by the final year of the war in 1945.[134] However, as Akenson has also stated, 'the effect of unfamiliar home situations, interrupted schooling, overcrowding and inadequately equipped schools upon the children can only have been educationally dysfunctional'.[135]

Despite these difficult conditions, the issue of PE was not overlooked for long. At the end of December 1941, in a report on the public health service in Belfast, Dr Thomas Carnwath criticised the system of physical training in public elementary schools and stated that 'the work requires organisation under a competent director, and should be regarded as an essential part of the curriculum'.[136] In February 1942, the Belfast Education Committee approved the appointment of a female organiser of physical training from April 1943 and a male organiser for after the war would end in accordance with financial provisions available.[137] This had been recommended in the Carnwath report, along with a number of other proposals including the establishment of special schools for children with disabilities and the provision of school meals.[138] It was not until February 1944, when Joan Burnett-Knight (pictured in Figure 24) from London, who had held a similar position with the

131   *Belfast Newsletter*, 11 November 1940.
132   Bardon, *A History of Ulster*, 563.
133   Akenson, *Education and Enmity*, 151.
134   Ibid.
135   Ibid., 151–2.
136   *Belfast Newsletter*, 29 December 1941.
137   Ibid., 12 and 24 February 1942.
138   Ibid.

Brighton and East Sussex education authorities, was appointed as physical training organiser (on a salary of £400 along with a war bonus), that the female position was filled.[139] She had seven years' organising experience and was the best qualified of eleven candidates.[140] However, it appears she was unable to take up her duties until November 1944 due to travel restrictions between England and Northern Ireland during the war.[141] Like Atkinson and Dickinson who had been selected to organise PE there before her, Burnett-Knight was not a native of Northern Ireland but had been trained within the British system. In this way, the Belfast Education Authority was not unlike the IFA in recruiting those from England who had experience of coaching and physical training there, such as Walter Winterbottom, who assisted in their coaching in the late 1940s.[142]

As female PE organiser, Burnett-Knight was required to be healthy and have acquired a 'diploma of a recognised Physical Training College and have had teaching experience'.[143] The list of duties included giving advice to the Education Committee, via the Director of Education, J. Stuart Hawnt, 'on policy in physical education, buildings, equipment and playing fields' while she was also expected to supervise and inspect physical training in Belfast's public elementary schools which had around 40,000 children in attendance.[144] As organiser, she was expected to 'advise and assist teachers responsible for Physical Training in the schools, with a view to increasing the value of physical education'.[145] 'Similar duties' were

139   Ibid., 3 March 1944 and PRONI, ED/13/1/2081. Physical Training Organisers Appointment 1943–1946. Letters from J. Stuart Hawnt to the Secretary of the Ministry of Education, 12 February 1944 and 27 February 1945.
140   ED/13/1/2081. Physical Training Organisers Appointment 1943–1946. Letter from J. Stuart Hawnt to the Secretary of the Ministry of Education, 21 July 1943 and 29 February 1944.
141   ED/13/1/2081. Physical Training Organisers Appointment 1943–1946. Letter from J. Stuart Hawnt to the Secretary of the Ministry of Education, 27 February 1945.
142   Curran, *Irish Soccer Migrants*, 72.
143   ED/13/1/2081. Physical Training Organisers Appointment 1943–1946. Belfast Education Authority. Appointment of Organiser of Physical Training (Woman). Conditions of Appointment. Undated.
144   Ibid.
145   Ibid.

to be undertaken in relation to Technical High Schools and Technical Colleges.[146] Burnett-Knight, who had attended Bedford Physical Training College from 1929–32, also had to organise swimming instruction for public elementary school children and to arrange and conduct refresher courses for physical training teachers and assist voluntary youth organisations and clubs. She also had to develop recreative physical training in evening institutes.[147] Having led the Northern Ireland section of the British team at the Lingiad gymnastics games in Stockholm in 1949, Burnett-Knight kept her position until 1950 and later moved to West Germany to work as Organiser of Physical Training in the British Families Education Service (BFES) in February 1951.[148] In April 1952, the Belfast Education Committee appointed Dublin woman Doreen M. Byrne as female organiser for PE.[149]

The Provision of Physical Training Courses for Northern Ireland Teachers

By the middle of the war the idea that a PE college was needed was being circulated. In March 1943, the report of a committee established by the Minister of Education, J. H. Robb (1937–43), to examine Youth Welfare in Northern Ireland, was released to the press. Amongst their recommendations, they stressed 'the need for the employment of properly trained Physical Instructors in schools' and felt that, after the war,

---

146   Ibid.
147   Ibid., and Private Papers of Joan Burnett-Knight. Application for Physical Education Advisor (Woman) 1947, 1. I am grateful to Sheelagh Watford for granting me access to these papers.
148   *Belfast Newsletter*, 23 July 1949 and Private Papers of Joan Burnett-Knight. Recommendation for Miss J. L. Burnett-Knight by Sergeant H. Priestley, Director of the British Families Education Service, Dusseldorf, 11 February 1956.
149   *Irish Independent*, 19 April 1952.

Figure 24. Joan Burnett-Knight coaching netball to youth leaders at Balmoral in 1950.
Courtesy of Sheelagh Watford.

consideration would be given to the foundation of a Physical Education College there.[150] They also recommended that 'modern training should be made available by means of summer schools and winter classes'.[151] In October 1943 a permanent Youth Welfare Committee superseded the Advisory Council set up under the Physical Training and Recreation Act of 1938, and had 'both advisory and executive functions'.[152] It was established through the Northern Ireland Youth Welfare Bill.[153]

In July 1943, in a memorandum dealing with the Youth Welfare Committee Report, Director of Education Dr J. Stuart Hawnt also stated that Northern Ireland should have its own physical training college for teachers who wanted to study the subject specifically.[154] The Gibbon

---

150 PRONI, ED/13/1/2292. Physical Education and Physical Training 1945–1948. Secretary for Ministry of Education of Northern Ireland to Secretary for Minister for Finance, 28 March 1947 and *Belfast Newsletter*, 8 March 1943.
151 *Belfast Newsletter*, 8 March 1943.
152 Ibid., 15 September 1943.
153 Ibid., 30 October 1943.
154 Ibid., 29 July 1943.

Committee, which was formed to report on the training of teachers, also recommended this move.[155] It was stated in this report, published in 1947, that there were only fourteen fully qualified PE teachers in Northern Ireland, with twelve females and two males noted, while Scotland had 670 PE teachers, illustrating that the number of qualified female PE teachers had risen slightly while the figure for male teachers had actually dropped since before the war.[156] In addition, in Britain, the McNair Report of 1944 had recommended that PE teachers should be given the same respect as those of other subjects, and that their training should be more closely linked to other teachers' training.[157]

Similar views were articulated at a meeting of a new PE association founded early in 1944, at which Dr Hawnt was heavily involved. In February 1944, an Association of Physical Education for Northern Ireland was formed in The Boys' Brigade House, May Street, Belfast with Dehra Parker, the parliamentary secretary to the Ministry of Education, presiding.[158] It was at this meeting that Dr Hawnt again articulated his desire to see a PE college established. He felt that in Northern Ireland 'they still had a long way to go in regard to PE as an aspect of their general educational programme. One of the difficulties was the shortage of trained leaders.' Dr Hawnt also commented 'that the province (sic) was capable of supporting a physical education college of its own, and the sooner they got it, the better'.[159]

During the war, Northern Ireland-based female students who normally would have attended PE colleges in England instead generally trained at Ling Physical Training College in Dublin.[160] However, following issues over salary scales and the credibility of the Fellowship Diploma of the

155   PRONI, ED/13/1/2292. Physical Education and Physical Training 1945–1948. Secretary for Ministry of Education of Northern Ireland to Secretary for Minister for Finance, 28 March 1947.
156   McGourty, 'The Boys' Physical Education Curriculum in Secondary Schools in Northern Ireland', 30.
157   Ibid.
158   Belfast Newsletter, 21 and 26 February 1944.
159   Ibid.
160   PRONI, ED/ Rhona E. Jackson. Confidential Report on Ling Physical Training College, 24 Upper Mount Street, Dublin. 1942.

British Association of Physical Training available there, in March 1949 the
Ministry of Education ceased to recognise this award as a qualification to
teach PE in Northern Ireland's schools.[161] Naturally, this led to issues as a
number of teachers who had gained this from Ling College were teaching
in Northern Ireland, so the Ministry of Education held a special PE examination, mainly consisting of candidates who had attended Ling College,
in October 1951, with a view to strengthening their qualifications.[162]

A scholarship system for Northern Ireland students was operational by
the late 1940s, but this was not a success. The Northern Ireland Ministry of
Education decided to award 'a limited number' of PE scholarships, beginning in September 1947, at PE colleges in Britain such as Carnegie (Leeds),
Bedford, Loughborough and IM Marsh College of Physical Training in
Liverpool.[163] By the end of 1949, however, it was noted by the Ministry of
Education that the scholarship arrangement had been unsatisfactory, as the
students from Northern Ireland, 'on account of their inadequate training in
the schools' had not been able 'to compete on equal terms with the other
students'. In addition, 'because of their limited experience' the courses were
said to be unsuitable for the Northern Irish students.[164] This strengthened
the notion that Northern Ireland should have its own PE college, and it
was noted that there was a 'deplorably low standard-perhaps the lowest
in Western Europe' in terms of the quality of PE in Northern Ireland's

---

161   PRONI, ED/13/1/ 2337. Grammar Schools: Qualifications required for recogni-
      tion of teachers-special examination for teachers' qualifications in physical educa-
      tion, 1951. Letter from Harry McClure to Rhona E. Jackson, 23 March 1946 and
      Letter from R. S. Brownell, Secretary for the Minister of Education, to Mr Glen.
      Qualifications of Teachers. Physical Education, 24 May 1950.
162   PRONI, ED/13/1/ 2337. Grammar Schools: Qualifications required for recogni-
      tion of teachers-special examination for teachers' qualifications in physical educa-
      tion, 1951. Special Examination for Teacher's Qualification in Physical Education,
      1951, List of candidates.
163   PRONI, ED/13/1/2292. Physical Education and Physical Training 1945–1948.
      Ministry of Education for Northern Ireland. Physical Education Scholarships,
      1947. Secretary to Ministry of Education of Northern Ireland, circular to
      Secondary School Teachers, 15 April 1947.
164   PRONI, ED/13/1/2293. Proposed Establishment of Physical Education College
      1947–1954. Memo on Proposed Physical Education College, 12 December 1949.

schools.[165] This was mainly due to the scarcity of teachers with adequate training in the subject. As well as the Gibbon Committee and the Youth Welfare Committee, noted above, the Ulster Headmasters' Association and the Ulster Headmistresses' Association had made representations for the need for a PE college.[166]

By the summer of 1946 the Association of Physical Education for Northern Ireland had become known as the Northern Ireland Physical Education Association [NIPEA] and held its first summer school of Physical Education over a two week period in Bangor.[167] Joan Burnett-Knight was responsible for organising the course.[168] She recalled that 'owing to the difficulty in finding adequate facilities and the lack of experience of those whose co-operation had to be obtained' organising the event was 'no mean task'.[169] The summer school took place over the course of two weeks and around 140 male and female teachers and youth leaders attended it, with accommodation given in three hostels while five local halls were used for the classes.[170]

In August 1947 the NIPEA held its second summer school of PE, again over a two week period at Bangor.[171] The Association was supported by the Bangor Borough Council, while halls for activities were provided by the Church Committees and 'other bodies'.[172] The 1947 Teachers' course was opened on 4 August by the Minister, Samuel Hall-Thompson, who had replaced Robert Corkery (who was only in the ministerial position for less than a year), in March 1944, with the association's president, Dehra Parker, taking the chair.[173] Tutors included Inspectors of Physical Education,

165   Ibid.
166   Ibid.
167   PRONI, ED/13/1/2162. 1946–1947. Larkfield Training College. Bangor Summer School of PE. Second Summer School of Physical Education Booklet, 1.
168   Ibid., 5 and Private Papers of Joan Burnett-Knight, Application for Physical Education Advisor (Woman) 1947, 2–3.
169   Private Papers of Joan Burnett-Knight, Application for Physical Education Advisor (Woman), 2–3.
170   Ibid.
171   PRONI, ED/13/1/2162. 1946–1947. Larkfield Training College. Bangor Summer School of PE. Second Summer School of Physical Education Booklet, 1.
172   Ibid., 5.
173   Ibid.

L. B. Dickinson, and Misses L. R. Hogg and Rhona E. Jackson and Joan Burnett-Knight, along with a number of representatives of schools and colleges in Northern Ireland and from England and Scotland. There were also two visiting lecturers involved, Miss C. O'Dowd, the Inspector of Nursery-Infant Education, and Mr W. J. McClure, senior lecturer in education at Stranmillis College of Education. The event was hosted by Mr G. McDermott of St Malachy's College.[174] A number of the courses given were based on the 1933 Syllabus of Physical Training for Schools.[175]

Some courses also took place in other regional areas. In the autumn of 1947 'a sessional course in Physical Education for men teachers was held in Newry' and 'an average nightly attendance of nearly fifty teachers was maintained from schools in South Down and South Armagh', but it appears that there was still a shortage in the number of those competent to teach the subject.[176] In view of the general shortage of expertise in the subject, in February 1945, Inspector Dickinson had written to the Staff Inspector of Physical Training at the London Ministry of Education, Major SJ Parker, to ascertain his views on the use of ex-service men as PE teachers in secondary and technical schools in Northern Ireland.[177] It appears he was agreeable to the move as after the war the Northern Ireland Ministry of Education had a scheme in place entitled 'Emergency Training of Teachers' with training given to former members of the Merchant Navy and HM Forces.[178]

The overall training of teachers had stalled temporarily during the war. The training of male teachers in Northern Ireland had been suspended from 1939 to 1942 and there was also a reduction in the numbers of female

---

174   Ibid., 6.

175   Ibid.

176   PRONI. So/1B/883. Government of Northern Ireland Reports of the Ministry of Education. *Report of the Ministry of Education for the Year 1947–48* (Belfast: H.M. Stationary Office, 1949), 8.

177   PRONI, ED/13/1/2680. Recognition of Certain Courses for Teaching Purposes. Men with Service in HM Forces as Specialists in Physical Training. Letter from L. B. Dickinson to Major S. J. Parker, 12 February 1945.

178   PRONI, ED/13/1/2166. Larkfield Training College. Short Courses in Physical Education for Men and Women Students. Secretary to the Minister of Education to A. J. Kissock, 30 January 1948.

teachers during the war years.[179] The Ministry of Education stated that this was 'a primary reason for the shortage of trained teachers in the intermediate war years'.[180] However, following the release of service men and women, and the conclusion of the war in Europe in May 1945 and in the Pacific three months later, the Larkfield Emergency Training College was established at Dunmurry, County Antrim in 1946 with a view to catering for new students who were available after their work in the war effort.[181] The first course for ex-service men and women under the Emergency Training Scheme began at Larkfield in May 1946 and in July 1947 forty-eight students received certificates from the prime minister having completed their studies.[182] By the end of March 1948, a total of 149 students had passed out from Larkfield Training College.[183] The college functioned 'in improvised premises and with a temporary staff' and until its closure in 1949 was home to a course directed towards mature students who had not been studying regularly and had experience of previous employment.[184] The Ministry deemed it a 'great success' with 365 men and forty women completing the sixteen months' course while 'on the score of numbers alone the substantial contribution made by Larkfield to the acute shortage of teachers was invaluable'.[185]

In order to further strengthen numbers, 'short intensive courses in Physical Education' were scheduled at Campbell College for male and female students of Larkfield College in April 1948.[186] The male and female

179   PRONI, ED/25/31. Government of Northern Ireland Reports of the Ministry of Education. *Report of the Ministry of Education for the Year 1952–3* (Belfast: H.M. Stationary Office, 1953), 13.
180   Ibid.
181   Ibid., 13–14.
182   PRONI, BCT/7/5/5. Government of Northern Ireland Reports of the Ministry of Education. *Report of the Ministry of Education for the Year 1948–9* (Belfast: H.M. Stationary Office, 1949), 38.
183   Ibid.
184   Ibid., 14.
185   Ibid.
186   PRONI, ED/13/1/2166. Larkfield Training College. Short Courses in Physical Education for Men and Women Students. Letter from Assistant Secretary to the Minister of Education to R. Groves, 22 March 1948 and Letter from Assistant Secretary to the Minister for Education to A. E. Lewis, 22 March 1948.

courses were conducted by the Inspectors of Physical Education, L. B. Dickinson and Rhona E. Jackson respectively, although it appears the latter course took place at Princess Garden School at Colinmore.[187] Dickinson was assisted by another inspector, F. W. Smith, while 'demonstration lessons' were given by PE teachers and pupils from city schools.[188] Later that year, both Dickinson and Jackson again supervised similar courses for Larkfield students.[189] In November 1949, around 250 male and female teachers attended a one day course in physical training in Omagh, which was under the supervision of Dickinson, Jackson and Hogg.[190] The course was organised in Omagh by A. Gibson, Chief Education Officer.[191] In the 1950–1 school year the Ministry of Education also ran ten-week courses in art and physical education in Belfast for trained primary school teachers with a view to appointment in intermediate schools.[192]

The Impact of the 1947 Education Act

Developments in Northern Ireland in the immediate post-war years shadowed those on the British mainland. As Holt and Mason have stated,

187 Ibid., and Letter from Assistant Secretary to the Minister of Education to A. E. Lewis, 22 April 1948.

188 PRONI, ED/13/1/2166. Larkfield Training College. Short Courses in Physical Education for Men and Women Students. L. B. Dickinson to Major Pomeroy, 23 March 1948.

189 PRONI, ED/13/1/2166. Larkfield Training College. Short Courses in Physical Education for Men and Women Students. Assistant Secretary to the Minister of Education to R. Groves, 6 Aug. 1948 and Assistant Secretary to the Minister of Education to the Secretary of the Church of Ireland Young Men's Society, 21 October 1949.

190 *Ulster Herald*, 3 December 1949.

191 Ibid.

192 PRONI, ED/13/1/2456. Teachers' Courses: One Term (Ten Week) Course for Physical Education (25 September to 2 December 1950). Ministry of Education for Northern Ireland. Qualification of teachers for appointment to Intermediate Schools. One term courses. Circular G. 1950/16.

'the 1944 [Butler] Education Act was an important landmark' there as it 'opened up secondary education for all at least up to the age of fifteen' and abolished fees 'for all state secondary schools' while it also 'compelled all local education authorities to provide adequate facilities for recreation and physical training'.[193] Under the 1947 Education Act, Northern Ireland's education system had been amended 'to bring it into line with the British system' and this meant 'changes in the grading of schools as well as of teachers, and in the methods of recruiting teachers'.[194] Bardon has noted that 'the principal task was to convert elementary schools into the new primary and secondary schools'.[195] From around 5 years of age until they reached 11 years old, when they then undertook a qualifying examination for placement in the next level, children attended primary schools.[196] Around one-fifth were to gain places in grammar schools, with the remainder to attend intermediate or technical schools. Despite this plan, 'the traditional grammar schools successfully resisted direct control and preserved their identity largely intact'.[197] In addition, 'all continued to charge fees and to take in a proportion of pupils who had not passed the examination; yet all obtained direct grants from the state and were not therefore "public schools" in the British sense'.[198]

As Ferriter has stated, 'education, of course, was another pillar of the welfare state' and the 1947 Education Act 'instigated a new structure for primary, secondary and further education, and single, reconstituted education committees for each county and city'.[199] Through this Act, education authorities were obliged to offer free services to all schools in terms of meals and milk, transport, books, stationary and medical treatment. In addition, mandatory free education was to be given to all pupils up to fifteen years old.[200] This move followed the Butler Act of 1944 with the subsequent

193   Holt and Mason, *Sport in Britain 1945–2000*, 21.
194   *Irish Independent*, 31 January 1956.
195   Bardon, *A History of Ulster*, 595.
196   Ibid.
197   Ibid.
198   Ibid.
199   Ferriter, *The Transformation of Ireland*, 453.
200   Ibid.

paper, *Education Reconstruction in Northern Ireland*, published late in that year, advocating a change in structures in education there.[201] However, as Bardon notes, 'the 1947 act did less to break down social barriers in the region than might have been expected'.[202] He has stated that delays meant that 'the full social and political impact of educational advance was not felt until the mid-1960s' and 'education reform had a modernising effect in Northern Ireland only within the limits of a strictly segregated system'.[203]

By the late 1940s, Minister Hall-Thompson was more seriously considering the development of a college for PE Training in Northern Ireland, 'with a view to ensuring that facilities are available to provide for an adequate supply of properly qualified teachers of Physical Education' for schools. It was noted in 1947 that 'the present situation in regard to physical education in Northern Ireland is unsatisfactory; there is probably no aspect of education in which Northern Ireland is so far behind Great Britain and most other countries'.[204] It was also felt that only a small number of places would be available to potential teachers from Northern Ireland within colleges of PE in Britain, and that they would soon decline to accept any Northern Ireland students 'in view of the educational developments' then taking place in Britain.[205] In light of these factors, the Ministry found that it was 'essential that a College of Physical Education should be established in Northern Ireland as soon as possible, if the educational developments foreshadowed in the new Education Act are not to be seriously impeded'.[206] Minister of Education, Harry Midgley (1950–7), who succeeded Lieutenant Colonel Samuel Hall-Thompson (1944–50) in that role, later stated that 'after the war there had been an abnormal demand for places in physical training colleges across the water'.[207]

---

201   Akenson, *Education and Enmity*, 157–9.
202   Bardon, *A History of Ulster*, 595.
203   Ibid., 596.
204   PRONI, ED/13/1/2292. Physical Education and Physical Training 1945–1948. Secretary for Ministry of Education of Northern Ireland to Secretary for Minister for Finance, 28 March 1947.
205   Ibid.
206   Ibid.
207   *Belfast Newsletter*, 27 June 1956.

The Ulster College of Physical Education

The expansion of schools meant that more fully qualified teachers would be required, the Ministry of Education felt, 'to staff adequately the posts which should be provided in Grammar Schools, Technical Schools, the new Intermediate Schools and in connection with the Youth Service'.[208] The new PE College, would, it was initially proposed, run courses based on similar lines to those in Britain, with a one-year course for men and a three-year course for women who had passed the Senior Certificate Examination at secondary school level. Ardnalee House, Craigavad, County Down had been inspected with a view to purchase as a site for the new college, although the Ministry of Education later decided that a site at Dalriada, Jordanstown, County Antrim would be more suitable as it was only six miles from Belfast and had good public transport services.[209]

The Ministry had initially looked at a proposal to set up a 'mixed' college for physical training but this idea was dropped, with three main reasons identified, these being 'the difficulty of organising such a "mixed" college', the authorities of the Roman Catholic Church's opposition to a 'mixed' college and thirdly, the offer of Loughborough College to establish a special class for male students from Northern Ireland.[210] Consideration was later given to establishing a PE College for women only in Northern Ireland, with the view that it would offer a three-year training course for those specialising in physical education. A one-year course would also be provided for students from universities and training colleges. It was also intended to provide a research centre for PE in order to foster interest in the subject throughout Northern Ireland.[211]

208   Ibid.
209   PRONI, ED/13/1/2292. Physical Education and Physical Training 1945–1948. Secretary for Ministry of Education of Northern Ireland to Secretary for Minister for Finance, 28 March 1947. and PRONI, ED/13/1/2293. Proposed Establishment of Physical Education College 1947–1954. Memo on Proposed Physical Education College, 12 December 1949.
210   Ibid.
211   Ibid.

While the Roman Catholic authorities were opposed to a residential college for women as well as a 'mixed' college, they had agreed to allow female students to attend the Physical Education college for women 'only as non-residential students'.[212] Estimates for the number of PE teachers needed were given as 'at least 600' by the Ministry, with 'about 300' of these women. It was also noted that there were only twenty qualified female teachers of physical education in Northern Ireland, with thirteen of these fully qualified and teaching in grammar schools while the remainder, said to hold 'semi-specialist qualifications', taught in intermediate schools.[213] It was stated that 'a fair estimate for the ultimate demand', with marriage and retirement taken into account, would be '150 semi-specialists and 150 specialists'.[214]

It was also felt that the establishment of a PE College 'would cost no more, and possibly less, to train women students at a college in Northern Ireland' than it was costing the Ministry to award Physical Education scholarships taken up at colleges in England.[215] The Ministry therefore decided that costs would not be problematic, while it was noted that inspectors were of the opinion that courses organised would not need excessive staffing. There would be a sufficient number of students given the number of candidates for the English scholarships (fifty-two), and the appointment of lecturers could be accommodated by selecting Northern Ireland students who were training in England when they had completed their courses there.[216]

A female-only college also appears to have been favoured because of differences in the recognised courses in physical training for male and female which were available in Britain and the short supply of female PE teachers in Northern Ireland. It appears that the Ministry of Education were of the view that the problem of maintaining a 'reasonably adequate number' of male physical education teachers could be satisfactorily overcome by arranging for them to attend one-year specialist courses in PE

212   Ibid.
213   Ibid.
214   Ibid.
215   Ibid.
216   Ibid.

colleges in England, and at Stranmillis College in Belfast (which was implemented from 1956–7).[217] However, it was noted that 'a similar arrangement did not prove practicable for women' as the 'recognised course' for
women as students of physical training was 'a three-year one not preceded
by general training'. In addition, the Ministry of Education stated that 'it
soon became evident that it would only be possible to meet the demand
for women physical education specialists by the establishment of a college
for the purpose in Northern Ireland'.[218]

Early in 1950, new Minister of Education, Harry Midgley, gave his backing
for the 'immediate purchase of Dalriada' in a letter to the Minister for Finance,
John Maynard Sinclair.[219] In May 1951, it was noted at Stormont that 'negotiations were in progress for the purchase of suitable premises, and £7,620 was
included in the estimates for that purpose'.[220] Northern Ireland, it was felt,
'should keep abreast of the rest of the United Kingdom' in regard to physical
training and 'especially as the number of places which could be allocated to
Northern Ireland students in colleges in Great Britain were limited'.[221] By the
end of 1952, a large vacant house had been bought at Dalriada by the Northern
Ireland Ministry of Education.[222] It was also reported that the new PE centre
would eventually accommodate forty-five trainees at a time.[223]

After the informal opening of the UCPE in September 1953, the arrangement whereby female students would be awarded scholarships at PE
colleges in England came to an end, although those already undertaking
these continued at that time, with six women completing their scholarships

---

217 PRONI, ED/25/36. Government of Northern Ireland Reports of the Ministry of
     Education. *Report of the Ministry of Education for the Year 1957–8* (Belfast: H.M.
     Stationary Office, 1958), 13.

218 Ibid.

219 PRONI, ED/13/1/2293. Proposed Establishment of Physical Education College
     1947–1954. Letter from Minister of Education to Minister of Finance, 27
     February 1950.

220 *Belfast Newsletter*, 23 May 1951.

221 Ibid.

222 *Irish Independent*, 30 December 1952.

223 Ibid.

in three-year physical education courses that year.[224] Arrangements for the awarding of PE scholarships to male students from Northern Ireland continued, with eight men given scholarships for a one-year course in 1952, and six of these men completed these at Loughborough College in 1953.[225]

Conclusion

With the foundation of the UCPE, an important step had been taken, although men with aspirations of becoming physical training teachers in Northern Ireland, such as Derry Gaelic footballer Jim McKeever and future Northern Ireland international footballer Hubert Barr, who attended Loughborough College in the 1950s, continued to migrate to take up courses in the subject to gain sufficient qualifications to teach it.[226] The introduction of a PE course at Stranmillis in 1956 was a help, but places were limited. PE in Northern Ireland's primary schools enjoyed a higher status than that south of the border for much of the twentieth century. Therefore, claims that the standard of physical education in Northern Ireland was the worst in Western Europe by the late 1940s seem harsh when placed in comparison with the subject's development further south noted in the previous chapter.[227] The development of the subject had also been badly affected in England and Wales during the war with Welshman

---

224 Ibid., and Ida M. Webb, *The Challenge of Change in Physical Education: Chelsea College of Physical Education-Chelsea School, University of Brighton 1898–1998* (London: Falmer Press, 1999), 7.

225 Ibid.

226 *Irish Independent*, 14 February 1953 and 'Northern Ireland's Footballing Greats: Hugh Barr' Retrieved from <http://nifootball.blogspot.com/2006/07/hugh-barr.html> [Accessed 19 August 2020].

227 PRONI, ED/13/1/2293. Proposed Establishment of Physical Education College 1947–1954. Memo on Proposed Physical Education College, 12 December 1949.

noting that it 'suffered from the persistent shortage of decent facilities and qualified teachers'.[228]

What is less clear from government reports is how Catholic pupils in Northern Ireland fared in terms of the provision of PE in comparison with Protestant students. Bardon has stated that in insisting 'on total clerical control' over Northern Ireland's Catholic schools in the 1920s, 'the Catholic hierarchy felt it had done well in the circumstances' but one outcome of this was that 'a generation of Catholic children suffered from inadequate and outmoded facilities by comparison with their Protestant peers'.[229] However, he feels that 'even if some Catholic schools had accepted "four-and-two" management, as did some Christian Brothers schools, they still would have been disadvantaged' as 'there is no doubt that Westminster had allowed the Unionist government with its unassailable majority to discriminate against Catholics in education provision'.[230] It appears likely that facilities for PE in some Catholic schools in Northern Ireland would therefore have been worse than schools there which received greater levels of government funding.

While teachers did receive training in physical education at primary level, it was secondary level where students' appreciation of PE appears to have really suffered in some schools. Like in sports coaching, developments in physical education training in Northern Ireland were more reflective of those in England, and, despite earlier recommendations, it was the 1947 Education Act and the expansion of schools which was the key to the decision to finally develop a college for Physical Education in Belfast. Chapter 6 assesses the failure of the Republic of Ireland's Government to take significant action to develop the subject in Irish schools in the period from 1954 until the appointment of an inspector for PE, Michael McDonough, in the early 1960s.

228   Welshman, 'Physical Education and the School Medical Service in England and Wales', 47.
229   Bardon, *A History of Ulster*, 505.
230   Ibid.

A Slow Struggle for Recognition: PE in the Republic of Ireland, 1954–1965

Introduction

This chapter assesses the failure of the Republic of Ireland's governments to take significant action to develop PE in Irish schools in the period from 1954 until 1965. An initial report of the Council of Education, published in 1954, drew on evidence provided by the Sports Federation and called for a fuller inclusion of physical training within the primary school curriculum.[1] However, despite positive sentiments from the Minister for Education, General Richard Mulcahy (1954–7), and his successor, Jack Lynch (1957–9), recommendations that it be developed were ignored for much of this decade. It will be shown that opposition from primary school teachers themselves to widening the curriculum remained in place by the middle of the 1950s. This chapter also assesses the continued role of pivotal figures such as Kathleen O'Rourke in the provision of teacher training for female secondary school physical training teachers. Despite the poor state of the Irish economy in the 1950s, with emigration widespread, in 1957, the privately funded St Raphael's Physical Education College for females was officially opened and key developments in the increase in student numbers and the provision of facilities there are explored in this chapter.[2] It also looks at attempts by VECs to develop training in the subject for males, particularly in Dublin. By the late 1950s, the Dublin VEC was offering scholarships for men interested in

---

1   *Department of Education. Report of the Council of Education as Presented to the Minister of Education*, 118 and 314.

2   *Irish Examiner*, 13 June 1957.

undertaking teacher training at Loughborough College.[3] However, it was not until 1963 that the Irish government decided to appoint an inspector for PE and this reflected wider changes in the expansion of Irish education in this decade and is indicative of the modernising attitude shown by Minister for Education from 1959 to 1965, Dr Patrick Hillery.[4] The appointment of Captain Michael McDonough as PE Inspector of the Department of Education in 1965 illustrated a greater urgency to develop the subject within Irish schools and is reflective of a wider European influence in education in Ireland in this decade.[5] In addition, it looks at the efforts of representative bodies, and those in the media, such as writer Ulick O'Connor, a champion at both pole vaulting and boxing, to raise awareness of the need for Irish pupils to have regular physical education and for the provision of a specialist training college for PE teachers.[6] This chapter concludes by assessing the recommendations of a report on physical education drawn up by Captain McDonough. These included the establishment of a Council for Physical Education and Sport, the setting up of a specialist training college for the subject's teaching and his view that it should become a compulsory subject at primary school level.[7]

The Council of Education's Report on Primary Schools and Its Impact on PE

The Council of Education's report on the primary school's function and curriculum, published in 1954, while not recommending any major changes, urged that physical education, drawing and nature study be included as obligatory subjects, and that scholarships for secondary school

---

3   *Irish Independent*, 6 April 1956.
4   *Evening Herald*, 30 January 1963.
5   *Irish Press*, 8 July 1968.
6   *Irish Times*, 7 October 2019.
7   McDonough, 'Physical Education and the Sports Complex in the Community School', 32–3.

pupils be increased.[8] However, as Coolahan states, 'even these modest proposals got little backing and curricular policy remained much as it had been'.[9] In particular, it had been agreed by the Council that the curriculum was too narrow and that 'physical training, besides helping to develop a healthier and happy child and generally producing a keener mind, can be used in conjunction with the teaching of music and assist in the maintenance of good order and decorum in the school-room'.[10] In addition, they felt that 'to provide a standard curriculum for all schools is preferable to prescribing a certain number of obligatory subjects for schools of each type'.[11]

The differences between what was available in urban and rural schools were also noted. Their recommendations in regard to these additional compulsory subjects were driven by a desire to see small rural schools maintaining 'as high a standard in the matter of curriculum as the largest town school, thus discouraging the inclination of rural children to travel to town-schools in search of extra subjects'.[12] The Council also stated that the system was imperfect without the full inclusion of PE and the evidence they had received (which included submissions from the Sports Federation of Ireland) was in support of this opinion.[13]

The Council suggested that the teaching of the subject should consist of two elements, physical and hygienic.[14] While they were against the use of drill as it was too regimented and artificial, it was felt that 'some ordered exercises should be provided to improve deportment and to correct defects of carriage and physique', particularly as facilities for teaching the subject were not adequate.[15] The aim of the new programme of physical training was to be 'the development of carriage and physical alertness, good posture

---

8   Coolahan, *Irish Education*, 45.
9   Ibid.
10   *Department of Education. Report of the Council of Education as Presented to the Minister of Education.* 122 and 272.
11   Ibid., 122.
12   Ibid.
13   Ibid., 188 and 314.
14   Ibid., 188.
15   Ibid., 190.

in sitting, and the general cultivation of health'.[16] To this end, half an hour per week was to be devoted to the subject outside of school breaktimes and other recreational activities.[17] Where possible, physical training was to be held outside the classroom in the open air.[18] They were also of the view that

> drawing, nature study and physical training, if efficiently taught, within the limits of the programme suggested for them, should aid considerably the more efficient teaching of the other subjects and hence that time taken from other subjects to provide for their teaching will not reduce the standard of proficiency in those other subjects.[19]

Despite this, the report contained a notable objection in the form of a Minority Report from Council member Liam Forde, who noted previous problems with having too broad a curriculum and felt that

> the suggestion that time can be found for the teaching of Drawing, Nature Study and Physical Training, by cutting down on the written work in both Irish and English, is ridiculous. The standard in both those subjects is, if any, already too low to permit of further reduction. The suggestion furthermore shows a complete lack of knowledge of the working of a Primary School.[20]

Therefore, this move to strengthen the role of PE within the curriculum was objected to internally on the grounds that it was already too full. While the INTO's 1947 plan seemed to indicate a change of heart in regard to PE's fuller inclusion, conservative attitudes expressed much earlier in the twentieth century still lingered. Accepting responsibility to deal with the matter of PE was also an issue. It was not that government ministers were not aware of the need to provide PE on a more regular basis. They were reluctant, however, to be seen to be providing funding for the development of Irish sport in general, and this excuse was often dragged up when challenged about Ireland's poor international standing in the athletics world and in relation to international competitions. In November 1955, General Mulcahy, the Minister for Education, told Mr

16   Ibid.
17   Ibid., 192.
18   Ibid.
19   Ibid., 122.
20   Ibid., 308.

John McQuillan of the Independent Party in the Dáil that 'he fully recognised the importance of physical education and it was the constant
endeavour of the Department of Education to make the maximum provision, consonant with other requirements, for the subject in the various
schools that received grants'.[21] However, he felt that the provision of athletic facilities was not the responsibility of the Ministry and, when questioned on Ireland's poor international standing in track and field, said
that he would like to see someone not connected to the Department to
deal with the issue.[22]

The *Irish Independent*'s editorial, which had consistently called for action
to be taken in relation to the state of PE in Irish schools, noted in November
1955 that the public had scarce evidence that the Department of Education
was concerned with the subject, and that their recent reports barely mentioned it.[23] It was also stated that there had been a lack of urgency in regard
to the facilities:

> indeed in the building of new schools there has been a lamentable failure to grasp op-
> portunities. Even many rural schools built during the last twenty or thirty years were not
> provided with sufficient space to allow the children to play organised field games such
> as football, hurling and camogie, although most of these schools are adjacent to suitable
> fields which doubtless could have been purchased at a reasonable price.[24]

One primary school teacher stated, when interviewed for this book, that
school facilities at that time frequently left a lot to be desired and school
sites were often cheaply acquired, or donated, and in his own locality all
the primary schools appeared to have been built on high ground, which
was inadequate for games and sport.[25] While acknowledging that the
Minister was 'strictly accurate' in stating that he was not responsible for
providing athletic facilities in schools, the *Irish Independent*'s editor felt
that it was the Department of Education's responsibility 'to encourage

---

21 *Irish Independent*, 10 November 1955.
22 Ibid.
23 Ibid., 17 November 1955.
24 Ibid.
25 Interview with primary school teacher number ten, 25 July 2019.

and promote the provision of such facilities'.[26] The sooner this was recognised, it was hoped that Ireland 'may be enabled to regain the honoured place in the world of athletics which it lost so many years ago'.[27] The editor ended his article by stating that 'intellectual development divorced from physical fitness is a very incomplete form of education'.[28]

By the late 1950s, teachers' opposition to the compulsory inclusion of physical training was clearly still notable. In March 1956, the former president of the INTO, Seán Ó Brosnachain, a member of the organisation's Central Executive Committee, voiced his concerns about the faults of education in an address given to Firinne, 'the Irish-speaking branch of Maria Duce', a Catholic group, in Dublin.[29] He rejected the Council of Education's recommendation to include physical training, nature study and drawing and claimed that a 'spurious piece of educational theory' had been 'concocted' by the Council to support their inclusion, despite problems such as the overcrowding of schools with pupils and the overloading of the curriculum.[30] The view that the addition of these three subjects as obligatory would be unhelpful was also expressed in a letter to the *Evening Herald* with the writer of the view that it would be better to promote physical development during the summer months, as it was felt that 'teachers complain the programme is too overcrowded to include these'.[31]

Efforts continued to amend the time allocated to physical education, however. In December 1956, following another review of the Council of Education's report on the primary schools' curriculum and function, Minister for Education, General Mulcahy, recommended widening the curriculum by introducing physical training, drawing and nature study.[32] However, he also noted that consultation would have to be carried out 'with the various interested bodies – ecclesiastical authorities, managers, teachers, with a view to making the necessary arrangements and adjustments'.[33]

26   *Irish Independent*, 17 November 1955.
27   Ibid.
28   Ibid.
29   *Irish Independent*, 12 December 1952 and *Irish Press*, 12 March 1956.
30   *Irish Press*, 12 March 1956.
31   *Evening Herald*, 9 June 1956.
32   *Irish Examiner*, 19 December 1956.
33   *Irish Independent*, 19 December 1956.

Despite the Council's recommendations, and Minister Mulcahy's belated encouragement, the Department of Education was slow to take action and there was no mention of developing physical training, drawing or nature study in the curriculum in the Department of Education's report for 1954–5, which had been published by March of 1957.[34] It would appear that opposition from teachers to the subject's more comprehensive inclusion remained a major stumbling block.

The failure to take action continued to be heavily criticised in some sections of the national press as the decade drew to a close. In June 1957, *Sunday Independent* writer Ulick O'Connor, who was also a sports correspondent at the *Observer*, claimed that 'the Department of Education is apparently satisfied with the "half-hour" drill systems that are given weekly in the secondary schools. These are often a joke-thirty minutes' arm swinging with the boys still in their ordinary clothes. The National School curriculum ignores physical training completely.'[35] He added that in Ireland, 'the government actually places obstacles in the way of physical training instead of helping it. A monstrous duty and levy of 60 p.c. is placed on sports goods and gymnastic equipment coming into Ireland.'[36]

Some national school teachers were anxious to clarify that they felt they were, in fact, adequately catering for the physical education needs of the nation's children. A response to O'Connor came in June 1957 from a writer under the penname of 'Galway Teacher', who claimed that the idea that the subject was being neglected in the curriculum was inaccurate. He pointed out that:

> Not alone is physical training catered for in the school curriculum - it is also optional on the 'leath la saor' [free half day] and the wonderful organisation of the Galway Diocesan Schools' Sports and the West Connemara Primary Schools' Sports shows the tremendous work being done for young Ireland in this respect. I would like to inform Mr. O'Connor that each primary teacher has to undergo a complete course in Physical Education and Hygiene for the purpose of passing this knowledge to his pupils. The system used is the Swedish one of Ling.[37]

34 Ibid., 27 March 1957.
35 *Sunday Independent*, 23 June 1957.
36 Ibid.
37 Ibid., 30 June 1957.

Those training to become primary school teachers in the 1950s did indeed have to undergo a course in PE at college. Not everybody felt that it was adequately catered for, however. One primary school teacher interviewed for this study, who trained at St Patrick's College Drumcondra at that time, felt the subject was not taken very seriously, recalling that 'the emphasis was on three things – the three Rs – it was the three Rs and only the three Rs …. I mean, you must look back, that was the late '50s …. I mean times weren't that rosy in this country at the time, you know'.[38] In addition, he felt that it was very much left to the teachers to do what they wanted in regards to PE, as he noted of his time on teaching practice in a school where the teacher was an intercounty Gaelic footballer:

> there was no word whatsoever [of physical education] … he [the teacher] had a massive class of about thirty-five to forty children. And he used to take them up every day - when the rest of the school would be in, he would take his class out, up to the football field, and let them run riot there, you know. He would try to get them to use as much energy as they could, so that when they would come back they would settle down, you know. But there was no emphasis whatsoever on PE.[39]

On graduating and moving to a rural school to teach his own class, the teacher interviewed noted a lack of space and facilities as being detrimental to any notions of teaching the subject:

> It was one thing that was never mentioned. In my time, an inspector never, ever mentioned it. It was the *one* thing that nobody ever mentioned, never, never. Anyhow, I started in 1958, I had something like forty children in third and fourth class. Now, the schoolyard, if all the children in the school were out at the one time, there would be barely room to stand for everyone, you know. How could you have any PE … and in the classrooms, they were sitting on top of each other.[40]

This lack of playground space available in schools did not go unnoticed in the Dáil, with Jack Lynch stating in 1961 that 'in rural areas it is the invariable practice to try to secure a field adjacent to the school', but

---

38   Interview with primary school teacher number ten, 25 July 2019. This was a reference to reading, writing and arithmetic.
39   Ibid.
40   Ibid.

as shown above, this was not always practical.[41] One teacher who was trained at St Patrick's College in the late 1950s noted when interviewed how athletic techniques were well taught to trainee teachers by a military man. However, he also stated that when he graduated, 'there was never any mention of PE' in any of the initial schools in which he taught.[42] He added that it 'was largely left to the teacher – you could do it, or don't do it as the case may be, nobody was going to insist, like they would with the three Rs'.[43]

At this point, it was clear that the subject was receiving more attention in Northern Ireland's schools. Writing in the *Sunday Independent* in April 1959, Ulick O'Connor again voiced his dissatisfaction that PE in the Republic of Ireland's schools was being neglected. He was of the view that the facilities for the subject in Northern Ireland far outweighed those in the Republic of Ireland. He had received this information from a teacher in Stranmillis College, Belfast, and stated that in comparison to how the subject was treated there,

> Down here the subject of physical education is treated in a scandalous way by the Department of Education. I enquired about the matter a while ago. A Department official produced a typewritten sheet. This is handed out to the teachers. From it they are supposed to 'instruct' children in physical exercises. It was nothing more than a huge joke. To make it more ridiculous the subject was optional.[44]

This form of instruction offered illustrates the lack of in-service training provided in the subject at that time.[45] While primary school trainee teachers clearly did receive instruction in the subject at college, transferring this training into a school setting was generally not required in the 1950s, and in any case most schools had neither the space nor facilities for

---

41 'Dáil Éireann Debate – Tuesday, 6 Jun 1961. Vol. 189. No. 10. Ceisteanna – Questions. Oral Answers. – Physical Training in National Schools.' Retrieved from <https://www.oireachtas.ie/en/debates/debate/dail/1961-06-06/52/> [Accessed 2 November 2020].

42 Interview with primary school teacher number nine, 24 July 2019.

43 Ibid.

44 *Sunday Independent*, 26 April 1959.

45 Ibid.

it. Similarly, there was no major emphasis placed by the Department of Education at that time on upskilling primary school teachers who may have qualified as teachers in previous decades.

The Foundation of St Raphael's Physical Education College for Females

By the early 1950s, some headway was being made in improving training facilities for females interested in a career teaching PE at secondary level. In August 1954, it was agreed by the Dominican Sisters that the Dublin College of Physical Education would become part of the Maria Assumpta Training Centre, Dominican Convent, Sion Hill, Blackrock, County Dublin.[46] Kathleen O'Rourke had been 'a Dominican girl' and approached them about incorporating her college into the Sion Hill teachers' training centre.[47] She was also involved in founding the Central Remedial Clinic, while she also worked in maternity hospitals in the city and, as noted earlier, ran League of Health classes.[48] A number of girls trained at O'Rourke's Dublin College of Physical Education had gained positions under education committees in England as well as in Ireland. It was also noted that in general, in Ireland, 'the demand for teachers' had 'far increased beyond the supply'.[49] In that decade, career options available to the majority of people in Ireland were scarce, as one primary school teacher recalled of how he had got involved in teaching:

> In my time, to have a job, of any kind, was your ambition, because there was a lot of unemployment in Ireland … I sort of drifted into it - you were either a teacher or a guard or you went on the boat to England. Broadly speaking, you didn't sit down like they do today and have 150 choices, wondering what you should do.[50]

46   *Irish Press*, 13 August 1954 and *Irish Independent*, 13 June 1955.
47   *Irish Press*, 3 July 1947 and *Irish Independent*, 13 August 1954.
48   Ibid. and *Irish Independent*, 21 January 1956.
49   Ibid.
50   Interview with primary school teacher number nine, 24 July 2019.

Similarly, one female primary school teacher also noted of that time that 'there weren't many options for you, after you finished secondary school you either got a job in the civil service or you got into [teacher] training college or you did nursing'.[51]

The move to amalgamate O'Rourke's Dublin College of Physical Education with Maria Assumpta Training Centre was backed by the Department of Education, who approved the Diploma of Physical Education available there as they had done to that available at the Dublin College of Physical Education.[52] Writing in 1954, one reporter stated that 'few schools, outside the progressive city Vocational groups, have full-time physical training teachers on their staff, and few have the necessary gymnastic space or equipment'.[53] It was also noted that 'most of them have part-time teachers, and physical culture is relegated to the more leisurely periods in the education programme'.[54]

O'Rourke and a number of her female colleagues also attempted to establish a national body for PE, but this appears to have been less successful in gaining momentum and the support of other organisational bodies, let alone the Irish government.[55] In September 1954 the Irish Association of Physical Education was founded in Dublin with a committee formed under her presidency.[56] It was announced that they planned to launch 'a campaign to have physical education recognised as an essential subject of general education'.[57] The number of officers elected, however, was quite small and included only O'Rourke, who was chairperson; the aforementioned Mr M. J. Doogan, of the High School of Commerce, Rathmines; Mrs M. McHugh, Collins Barracks and Mr J. J. Conway of Sandymount. The honorary treasurer was Mrs K. Scally of Upper Leeson Street.[58] By November 1954 the Association was said to have expanded and consisted

---

51   Interview with primary school teacher number seven, 3 July 2019.
52   *Irish Independent*, 26 March 1956.
53   Ibid., 5 November 1954.
54   Ibid.
55   *Irish Press*, 8 September 1954.
56   Ibid., 6 May 1950 and 25 September 1954.
57   Ibid., 25 September 1954.
58   Ibid.

of 'teachers and parents, medical people and all those interested in the promotion of physical culture' and planned to host 'a big gymnastics convention' in Dublin in January 1955.[59] However, like the Sports Federation of Ireland at that time, there is scarce evidence that the organisation had much influence in persuading the government to take the subject of physical education more seriously or in attracting politicians as members.

The integration of the Dublin College of Physical Education physical training course at the Maria Assumpta Training Centre was an important step in bringing what was generally a peripheral training course into a more educational setting and offered a more concrete structure for the training of physical education teachers. The initial three-year course there in 1955 provided 'complete training for Teacher's Diploma in Theory and Practice of Educational and Remedial Gymnastics – and in all branches of Games, Dancing and Swimming'.[60] Students were required to have passed the Leaving Certificate 'or Matriculation or an equivalent examination' to gain entry.[61] Plans were made for the provision of facilities, with the college opening in the autumn of 1955, and O'Rourke maintained her role as principal after the changeover.[62]

In June 1957 a new building for physical training was completed at Sion Hill. Named as St Raphael's Physical Education College, it was officially opened and blessed by the Archbishop of Dublin, Most Reverend Dr McQuaid while Minister for Education Jack Lynch also attended the ceremony.[63] The new St Raphael's college had a 'fully equipped gymnasium' with showers, dressing and equipment rooms and the building's completion was impressive enough for it to be given the Triennial Gold Medal, which was awarded by the Royal Institute of Architects of Ireland.[64] In 1958 five students graduated from St Raphael's.[65] This figure had quintupled by early 1962, with Ling also producing a similar number of graduates at

59   Irish Independent, 5 November 1954.
60   Ibid., 13 June 1955.
61   Ibid.
62   Irish Press, 13 August 1954 and Irish Independent, 13 August 1954.
63   Irish Examiner, 13 June 1957.
64   Irish Independent, 8 August 1962.
65   Irish Press, 27 February 1969.

that point.[66] By the autumn of 1962, St Raphael's also had lecture rooms, a library, facilities for drama and dancing and music rooms.[67] In the winter of 1964 it was announced by the principal, Sister Mary Rose Catherine O'Nolan, who had taken over the role the previous year, that an increase in student enrolment was planned for September 1965.[68] This was because, she believed, PE was 'becoming much more a part of secondary school life'.[69] The implementation of Teilifís Éireann in 1961 saw PE gain more exposure through the medium of television with St Raphael's College students featuring in a programme, *Sport and You*, broadcast in December 1964.[70] In July 1965, a film in which 'educational gymnastics and modern dance' were used by the students to demonstrate 'the most up-to-date techniques and methods of physical education', *Physical Education in Ireland*, was released, having been made on behalf of the college authorities by the Raven Group in cooperation with Silverpine Studios in Bray.[71] The film was later made available to Irish schools offering courses in the subject.[72]

The Provision of Physical Education Training Courses for Males

Attempts to organise structures for the training of male physical education teachers in the Republic of Ireland remained poorly supported

66   'Dáil Éireann Debate – Tuesday, 27 Mar 1962. Vol. 194. No. 4. Ceisteanna – Questions. Oral Answers. – School Physical Training Courses.' Retrieved from <https://www.oireachtas.ie/en/debates/debate/dail/1962-03-27/71/?highlight%5B0%5D=physical&highlight%5B1%5D=training&highlight%5B2%5D=physical&highlight%5B3%5D=training> [Accessed 2 November 2020].
67   *Irish Independent*, 8 August 1962.
68   *Evening Herald*, 10 December 1964.
69   Ibid.
70   *Irish Press*, 18 December 1964.
71   *Irish Independent*, 3 December 1965, *Irish Examiner*, 4 December 1965 and *Kilkenny People*, 17 December 1965.
72   *Irish Press*, 29 November 1965.

by the Irish government. In June 1957, Ulick O'Connor noted that 'the summer school for training athletic instructors which is run voluntary every year in Newman House receives not a sausage from the government'.[73] This was a reference to the Summer School of Athletics which was held at St Stephen's Green and was in its fifth year in 1957.[74] It had the Department of Education's recognition as 'an approved summer course for primary and vocational teachers' and was intended 'to ensure that all schools and clubs will have at least one member qualified to give fundamental instruction'.[75] The course was designed to teach attendees basic techniques in running, jumping and throwing and was open to teachers, students and athletes.[76] From 1955, male primary school teachers were allowed 'five weeks' vacation with pay' to participate in the Dublin-based course, run by chief coach Jack Sweeney for a week at the end of July.[77] In July 1957 Minister for Education Jack Lynch stated that Ireland was 'far behind in the matter of physical education, the facilities for which, in the way of equipment and trained teaching personnel, are with very few exceptions, practically non-existent in this country'.[78] He hoped that the School of Athletics would soon receive 'adequate recognition from his Department, if red tape could in this matter be overcome', but progress was slow.[79]

Financial Support for Training PE Teachers

The provision of scholarships by Vocational Education Committees in a few Irish cities offered some financial support for males with aspirations

---

73   *Sunday Independent*, 23 June 1957.
74   *Irish Independent*, 23 July 1957.
75   Ibid. and *Irish Press*, 5 March 1955 and 22 July 1958.
76   *Irish Independent*, 23 July 1957.
77   *Irish Press*, 5 March 1955.
78   *Irish Examiner*, 23 July 1957 and McManus, *Irish Education: The Ministerial Legacy, 1919–99*, 93.
79   *Irish Examiner*, 23 July 1957.

of gaining qualifications in physical education in migrating to training colleges in England. In April 1957 it was announced that the Dublin VEC was offering six scholarships for young men aged between 21 and 26 with a view to becoming physical training instructors in boys' classes in Dublin.[80] These scholarships included the fees for an initial six-week course at Loughborough College along with £50 for expenses such as travelling and text books.[81] Applicants had to be university graduates in arts, commerce or science, have a 'good knowledge of Irish' and a recognised VEC teaching qualification. They also had to agree to teach for five years and had to pass a two-year probationary period as part of this. When qualified, they would also hold positions as classroom teachers in the VEC schools in Dublin 'so that in later years, when they find physical instruction too strenuous, they may be relieved without terminating their employment with the committee'.[82] This indicates that physical training was seen by the Dublin VEC as an occupation for a young person at this time. An unspecified number of applications ranging between forty and fifty were received, and the selected candidates undertook the course.[83] In the summer of 1958 ten men, six from Dublin and one each from Waterford, Kilkenny, Louth and Limerick attended a six-week physical training course at Loughborough College, with the Department of Education supplying £25 of the £45 fee for each one.[84]

Other VECs also attempted to train their physical training teachers. Cork VEC had sent one student abroad for this purpose in the 1940s but this does not appear to have become an annual arrangement.[85] In April 1959 they agreed to arrange a vocational school teachers' summer course in physical culture on the advice of Minister Lynch, a former All-Ireland hurling and Gaelic football winner, whom, it appears, was eager to promote the subject in his own locality at least.[86] Minister Lynch had stated that

80   *Irish Independent*, 6 April 1957.
81   Ibid.
82   Ibid.
83   *Evening Herald*, 15 April 1957.
84   *Irish Examiner*, 29 May 1958.
85   O'Donoghue, 'The policy of the State', 113.
86   *Irish Press*, 15 April 1959.

sending men to Loughborough, which only the Dublin VEC could afford to do, was inadvisable and that facilities in Ireland could be utilised with summer courses being initiated.[87] He also felt that 'the vocational service had very many good young teachers who had excelled in different games and these could teach physical training'.[88] In addition, he noted that the Cork VEC had 'excellent equipment available in the schools under their control' and their physical training instructor was fully qualified.[89] In the summer of 1959, the City of Dublin VEC held 'a special short course' for Dublin Vocational School male physical training instructors, in cooperation with the Leinster branch of the Irish Amateur Swimming Association, for the first time.[90] It was also noted that this was the first year that swimming that been on the curriculum and an emphasis was placed on swimming and life-saving in the course.[91] The scholarship scheme with Loughborough does not appear to have been very successful in the long run. Although Dublin VEC-backed students initially 'attended two six-week courses at Loughborough during the summer vacation and had a further one or two short courses from Loughborough staff in subsequent years', the scheme had gone into decline by the mid-1960s.[92]

In the late summer of 1962 PE was taught in 358 out of the 542 secondary schools in the Republic of Ireland.[93] Thirty-two of the 280 vocational schools had full-time qualified teachers to teach the subject, while in the remainder 'physical instruction and/or organised games' were part of extra-curricular activities. Twenty-five qualified instructors completed training every year in 'the private training colleges for physical education'.[94] In 1964, there were a total of thirteen 'whole-time vocational teachers' registered for the subject in the Republic of Ireland, with four having 'special qualifications' such as a Diploma in Physical Education while nine possessed

87   *Irish Examiner*, 24 February 1959.
88   Ibid.
89   Ibid.
90   *Evening Herald*, 2 July 1959.
91   Ibid.
92   *Investment in Education. Annexes and Appendices*, 23.
93   *Irish Independent*, 8 August 1962.
94   Ibid.

'mainly certificates from Loughborough College' and 'a few had army qualifications'.[95] As noted, male teachers had no centres for PE teaching, and boys' second level schools often had to 'rely mainly on former army personnel'.[96] Therefore it can be assumed that the majority of the Republic of Ireland's secondary school teachers with accredited teaching qualifications for PE were female by the mid-1960s.

The Military and Physical Training in Irish Schools

The prospects for males hoping to pursue physical training teaching as a career remained uncertain and by the mid-twentieth century, the military was still utilised to provide instruction in some schools and the training colleges. It was noted in the *Irish Independent* in March 1956 that 'the demand for teachers of physical education is far in excess of the number who are trained, and the prospects of employment are very bright indeed'.[97] Despite this, it was also stated that 'it is true at the same time that there are few full-time appointments in schools at present in the Republic, and most of the teachers do part-time work'.[98] The following year, one *Irish Examiner* reporter stated that 'in the past, ex-army physical training experts have contrived to make a living for themselves by taking secondary school pupils for training for a few hours each week. Soon, perhaps, there will be little scope for such freelances.'[99]

The military were, at times, still reluctant to release their staff for instructors in some schools, as the following case shows. While the Department of Defence had sent a physical instructor to St Fintan's High School in Sutton since October 1944, early in February 1955 they informed

---

95   *Investment in Education. Report of the Survey Team Appointed by the Minister for Education in October, 1962* (Dublin: The Stationery Office, 1965), 289.

96   *Investment in Education. Annexes and Appendices*, 23.

97   *Irish Independent*, 26 March 1956.

98   Ibid.

99   *Irish Examiner*, 13 June 1957.

the Reverend Superior there that this arrangement could not continue.[100] This was because Company Sergeant Kavanagh's service with the Defence Forces was due to expire on 19 February, and due to 'the training requirements of the service', the Department of Defence did not think another instructor would be available to continue his work in the school.[101] St Patrick's College were also contacted about the termination of his role there.[102] The principal of St Patrick's College, the Reverend Killian Kehoe, replied to say that they 'were being unfairly treated' by the Department of Defence and that they would struggle to find another instructor at that stage in the college year. He asked that Company Sergeant Kavanagh be allowed to continue until the end of the academic year 'at least' and noted that a contract had been entered into in relation to the matter in 1938.[103] Following a review of the position, the Deputy Adjutant General, Colonel T. Gray, stated that no such contract existed from that time. However, in 1941, when Company Sergeant Kavanagh had been appointed to the position, 'provision was made in the establishment of the C[ommand] T[raining] depot, Eastern Command, for a Coy/Sergeant as P.T. Instructor-Schools and Colleges'.[104] In addition, it was noted that 'this appointment disappeared in the 1946 Establishments'.[105]

After the 1946 Establishments, Company Sergeant Kavanagh was allowed to continue as PT Instructor in the schools and colleges, but it appears that his position in the O/C 1st Battalion was problematic and there were calls that he be transferred 'as he was blocking an appointment which it was necessary to fill' and which he could not take up due to his

100   Military Archives, Cathal Brugha Barracks. Department of Defence Files, 2/92315. Instruction. P.T. Schools and Colleges, Dublin Area. Letter from Secretary M. P. Healy to the Reverend Superior, St Fintan's High School, 8 February 1955.
101   Ibid.
102   Ibid.
103   Military Archives, Cathal Brugha Barracks. Department of Defence Files, 2/92315. Instruction. P.T. Schools and Colleges, Dublin Area. Letter from Reverend Killian Kehoe to Minister for Defence, General Seán Mac Eoin, 9 February 1955.
104   Military Archives, Cathal Brugha Barracks. Department of Defence Files, 2/92315. Instruction. P.T. Schools and Colleges, Dublin Area. Leathan Miontuairisce, Deputy Adjutant Gray, 15 February 1955.
105   Ibid.

lack of Irish.[106] In December 1954 a vacancy arose in the 2nd Battalion and he was posted there. However, this was again awkward as the appointment of Company Sergeant required that full-time service was required, but he was engaged with PT Instruction three days a week in total and it was necessary that a Sergeant was employed to take up his military duties.[107]

Colonel Gray noted that 'the matter came to a head' when he applied to have his service extended before it was due to end on 19 February 1955.[108] With the present arrangements, 'the O/C 2nd Battalion and O/C Eastern Command were not prepared to recommend continuance in service' and Kavanagh himself stated that he did not wish to continue unless these arrangements would be continued. However, he was willing to continue until he had made arrangements with the College Superiors in question that he be retained as a civilian instructor.[109] The Adjutant General recommended that, with Kavanagh having completed thirty-two and a half years' service in the military, and recovering from an illness at that time, he 'be discharged with all convenient speed' after his sick-leave ended on 27 March 1955.[110]

Despite this, Kavanagh was allowed to retain his position as Physical Instructor until September 1955, as he was 'granted an extension of Service with the Permanent Defence Force'. This followed complaints from the Reverend Superior at St Fintan's High School about the planned cessation of his position and work in the school.[111] Both St Helen's of Booterstown and Coláiste Ciaran of Bray had declined to continue with the accommodation of Company Sergeant Kavanagh's physical instruction after his fee had been raised to £1 an hour in 1952.[112] This increase had been brought

106 Ibid.
107 Ibid.
108 Ibid.
109 Ibid.
110 Ibid.
111 Military Archives, Cathal Brugha Barracks. Department of Defence Files, 2/92315. Instruction. P.T. Schools and Colleges, Dublin Area. Letter from Secretary M. P. Healy to the Reverend Superior, St Fintan's High School, April 1955.
112 Military Archives, Cathal Brugha Barracks. Department of Defence Files, 2/92315. Instruction. P.T. Schools and Colleges, Dublin Area. Letter from M. Ó Corráin to the Secretary of the Minister of Defence, 23 January 1952 and Letter from R. Q. O'Driscoll to the Secretary of the Department of Defence, 28 January 1952.

in due to an increase in the cost of maintaining an Army Sergeant.[113] The army did not immediately appoint anyone to replace Company Sergeant Kavanagh in his role as physical instructor.[114] They did, however, contact the Department of Finance in November 1956 about gaining the Minister's sanction in regard to the provision of Permanent Defence Forces physical training instructors, subject to a number of conditions.[115] Of primary importance was that it did not interfere with instructors' military duties, while they also wanted to ensure that the Department of Defence received travelling allowances and subsistence allowance for the attendance of instructors at schools. They also stipulated that school and college authorities, with the exception of the preparatory college authorities, paid prescribed fees based on instructors' remuneration, maintenance and accommodation.[116]

Therefore the military were not always enthusiastic about supplying their staff as physical training and drill instructors in Irish schools, and the fact that they took this up with the Minister of Finance illustrates that tensions existed between the Department of Defence and some schools and colleges. In any case, the value of military instruction in colleges was not always appreciated. One primary school teacher interviewed for this study felt that some trainee students took a lackadaisical approach to drill instruction in the training college he attended in the 1950s as it did not have any academic standing, while there was also a tendency to question the instructor's academic credibility.[117] One teacher who had attended a preparatory college in the west of Ireland noted that there was a much

113 Military Archives, Cathal Brugha Barracks. Department of Defence Files, 2/92315. Instruction. P.T. Schools and Colleges, Dublin Area. Letter from Private Secretary J. Boland to Brother T. N. MacDonnchadha, Headmaster, St Fintan's High School, 23 February 1952.

114 Military Archives, Cathal Brugha Barracks. Department of Defence Files, 2/92315. Instruction. P.T. Schools and Colleges, Dublin Area. Letter from Lieutenant Colonel Harpur to the Director of Training, Army Headquarters, 1 August 1956.

115 Military Archives, Cathal Brugha Barracks. Department of Defence Files, 2/92315. Instruction. P.T. Schools and Colleges, Dublin Area. Letter from the Secretary of the Department of Defence to the Secretary of the Department of Finance, 19 November 1956.

116 Ibid.

117 Interview with primary school teacher number ten, 25 July 2019.

wider variety of sport available there than in St Patrick's College in the 1950s, with the result that he did not enjoy the PE course there at all.[118]

There is evidence that 'some schools and colleges' were still 'standing aloof' when it came to embracing the GAA's codes.[119] In his 1954 report to the Annual Congress of the GAA, general secretary, P. J. O'Keeffe, stated that only a small number of college students played Gaelic games and while priests and Brothers were fundamental to the development of the GAA's sports in vocational schools, attempts to develop hurling were difficult.[120] O'Keeffe felt that 'the efforts to spread the game in the counties fringing the hurling areas or to secure any firm footholds in other districts are disappointing'.[121] This was despite the introduction of 'special competitions, cheaper hurleys' and 'grants to schools' although the game was progressing well in Dublin. He added that there was only so much the GAA could do in schools when he stated that 'our hopes for the great revival … must be centred in the primary schools; not that the GAA should aim at controlling juvenile competitions which should be left to the parents of the boys and to the managers and teachers'.[122] Some embraced this view more than others, with the GAA organising parish leagues in a number of counties such as Donegal (see Figure 25).[123]

By the early 1960s the situation regarding physical training in St Patrick's Training College had improved. J. P. O'Keeffe, a former Army Commandant, became responsible for the training of PE at St Patrick's College in 1960, with his appointment as full-time director marking 'the first time that physical education was given official status' in the college, although as shown above, other army men had previously been employed there.[124] This was done with a view 'to give future teachers a basis for imparting knowledge to their pupils' although in most schools, facilities

---

118   Interview with primary school teacher number twelve, 26 July 2019.
119   *Evening Herald*, 6 April 1954.
120   Ibid.
121   Ibid.
122   Ibid.
123   Seán MacConaill (ed.), *Idir Pheil agus Pobal: A History of the GAA in the Parish of Ardara* (Ardara: Black Lion Books, 2004), 212 and 220.
124   *Evening Herald*, 30 January 1963.

Figure 25.   Brackey National School team 1960, who featured in the Ardara Parish
Schoolboys' Gaelic Football League, established in 1959. Courtesy of John McConnell.

were 'far from being the best'.[125] In the opening years of that decade the
Department of Defence was still supplying men to instruct in physical
training in educational institutions, as in the case of the preparatory second
level school, Coláiste Iognáid in Galway, while they also rejected proposals from schools such as that in Castle Park, Dalkey, when it did not
suit their schedules.[126] Commandant O'Keeffe was given the award of Best
All-round Army Athlete in 1956 and had also studied physical education
in England, Sweden and Denmark.[127] He later hosted a television series
on physical fitness in the summer of 1964.[128] In December 1965 he was the

125   Ibid.
126   Military Archives, Cathal Brugha Barracks. Department of Defence Files, 2/92315.
      Instruction. P.T. Schools and Colleges, Dublin Area. Department of Defence
      Secretary to Fr Piaras Ó h-Uiginn, 29 September 1960 and Department of Defence
      Secretary to D. S. Pringle, 3 October 1960.
127   *Irish Press*, 3 July 1964.
128   Ibid.

first Irishman to become a Fellow of the American Association of Health, Physical Recreation and Education.[129]

Dr Patrick Hillery Becomes Minister for Education

In its 1959 Report, the Department of Education noted that in secondary schools, the state of PE was still not satisfactory, but schools generally had playing fields for games, especially those for boys.[130] However, they admitted that this was not enough for all pupils' needs, particularly those who were not interested in field games and those for whom the games were not suitable. They also felt that there were many ways of putting PE into practice in a classroom, although they did not state what these were.[131] It is clear that they had not formulated any structured plan for PE at this point. At the opening of an extension to the City of Waterford Technical School early in June 1959, Minister Lynch 'emphasised the importance of physical training and courses for apprentices'.[132] He also again reiterated that more needed to be done, but was less forthcoming on what this should be, with one report noting his view that 'the time had come when they would have to approach physical education as a fundamental part of the whole education set-up …. they had, unfortunately, a most haphazard system in this field and in other aspects of education, also, they needed clearer thinking and more realistic planning'.[133]

That same month, Lynch was succeeded by Dr Patrick Hillery as Minister for Education. In July of that year, Dr Hillery stated in the Dáil that he was considering introducing PE more fully into all national schools as it was named as only an optional subject at that point.[134] The following

---

129   *Irish Press*, 6 December 1965.
130   *Department of Education Report for 1958–59* (Dublin: The Stationery Office, 1960), 10.
131   Ibid.
132   *Irish Independent*, 2 June 1959.
133   Ibid.
134   Ibid., 16 July 1959.

year, he noted that its status was still being reviewed.[135] Some politicians were eager to see this improved, with Deputy Patrick Giles of Fine Gael stating in May 1960 that physical training was 'badly needed in the schools' and linked this to poor physical development. He added that developments in regional Ireland were behind those in the nation's capital when he claimed that 'you can always know the country boy or girl in Dublin ... by the long step and the hump on the back'.[136] The *Irish Independent*'s editorial again criticised the lack of Department of Education input into physical training in June 1960 and felt that it was 'no wonder so many Irish boys and girls are ungainly and awkward in their bearing and deportment'.[137] It was also noted that a contrast existed in primary and secondary schools as the latter had more independence in the time and space that they could allocate to sport:

> Indeed, the Department seems, judging by the blanks in the annual report, to disclaim all responsibility. Only in the secondary schools – which, significantly enough, are not under direct control of the State – is provision made for organised games. The number of primary schools with a playing field could probably be counted on the fingers of one hand; most of them have playgrounds only in name.[138]

Some sporting organisations hoped to put pressure on the Minister so that stronger action would be taken. In July 1960, having drawn courage following a lecture by Victor Obeck, the Director of Athletics at New York State University, which took place at the National Stadium in Dublin, a delegation of sporting organisations present decided to try to meet with the Minister for Education to urge him to have physical education taught in all schools.[139] While the meeting's outcome is unclear, the NACA continued to air their displeasure at the condition of the subject in Irish schools. In January 1961 some of their officials were reported to be 'disturbed because of the absence of physical education' in primary schools.[140]

135   Ibid., 20 May 1960.
136   *Irish Examiner*, 26 May 1960.
137   *Irish Independent*, 20 June 1960.
138   Ibid.
139   *Evening Herald*, 15 July 1960. These included the Irish Athletic Boxing Association, the Amateur Athletic Union, the NACA, Foras Eireann, the Basketball Association and the Catholic Secondary Schools' Athletic Federation.
140   *Connacht Sentinel*, 10 January 1961.

Support for a full inclusion of the subject also came from some members of the clergy involved in second level schools. At the annual congress of the Irish Vocational Education Association at Kilkee, County Clare, in June 1961, Very Rev. J. M. Butler, a parish priest in Wexford, 'moved a motion asking the Department of Education to provide physical education for the students in all schools'.[141] This was an oversimplification of the situation by both organisations as trainee teachers did indeed receive training in the subject, and had done so since the early 1900s, and it did have a position in the curriculum, albeit a peripheral one. However, conditions in schools and the place of physical education in the curriculum meant that it was not being adequately catered for in many areas. Despite this, in some more affluent schools, such as Clongowes Wood College, pupils continued to have access to a range of indoor as well as outdoor games, including table tennis, pool and billiards, pictured in Figure 26.[142]

Figure 26. Indoor pursuits at Clongowes Wood College, c.1960s.
Courtesy of Declan O'Keeffe.

141   *Irish Examiner*, 9 June 1961.
142   I am grateful to Declan O'Keeffe for this information.

In April 1962, the Council of Education, in their second report prepared for the Minister for Education, which focused on secondary schools, stated that athletic games were 'an important if not essential part of physical education but they have their disadvantages. They need to be supplemented by specifically planned and systematic physical exercises.'[143] It was also posited that 'physical education is a most important part of the school education programme' and the Council recommended that the Department of Education 'secure the services of an expert or experts in an advisory capacity and prepare suitable specimen syllabuses for the schools.'[144] In the period from 1954 then until the report was finalised in 1962, the Council, chaired by Right Rev. Monsignor Martin Brennan, the holder of a Ph.D. and Diploma in Education, had held thirty meetings and committees of the Council had met 136 times, and had 'considered memoranda from nearly 70 organisations and individuals.'[145] Without directly referring to this report, in May 1962 Minister Hillery again acknowledged that PE was being neglected although he noted that 'organised games and athletics received due attention in most of the secondary schools.'[146] He also asked school headmasters 'to give the matter serious consideration with a view to taking whatever steps that might be necessary to improve the situation.'[147]

The fact that the subject was continuously being deliberated upon without concrete action impacted on the development of young athletes to some extent. At the opening of the NACA's annual summer school in July 1962, president of the organisation, Seán Ó Tuama, stated that 'despite the athletic improvement marked in the Irish championships in Killarney and the additional impetus given to athletics in recent years through the Santry Stadium', the schools' response was 'disappointing'.[148] He noted that 'both the number of entries and the attendance at the annual Primary Schools' Sports in Croke Park' had remained poor.[149] In addition, he called for the

143   *Irish Press*, 26 April 1962.
144   Ibid.
145   Ibid.
146   *Irish Examiner*, 22 May 1962.
147   Ibid.
148   *Irish Press*, 25 July 1962.
149   Ibid.

Department of Education to take a more active part in 'the training and recruitment of proper instructors and coaches in the schools'.[150] Ó Tuama also noted how unfair it was that training of young athletes only took place 'as a spare-time activity' and called for 'a new deal for school athletics and physical education'.[151]

Wider changes were important in drawing attention to the need for a more inclusive education system. Of key significance to higher education's transformation in the Republic of Ireland was the government-commissioned *Investment in Education* report, published in 1965. This was overseen by the Organisation for Economic Co-operation and Development (OECD) and was undertaken between 1962 and 1965.[152] As Brendan Walsh has written, this was 'a turning point in how the state understood provision, particularly at second and third level'.[153] John Walsh has stated that it highlighted the 'elitist nature of university institutions' and how 'university education remained the preserve of a small privileged elite until the mid-1960s'.[154] In particular, an emphasis on university preparation for profession careers was notable and while the ideals of John Henry Newman and liberal education were worth respecting, in reality these did not fit the needs of the majority of people in Irish society.[155] The climate surrounding the OECD examiners' analysis had a strong influence on the policy changes announced by Minister Hillery. In 1963, he proposed the development of Regional Technical Colleges which was 'the first significant government initiative' in the attempted diversification of the Higher Education system which had been focused on the elite status of universities.[156] *Investment in Education* highlighted that 'all Department-trained teachers and all teachers of art, domestic science and physical education

---

150   Ibid.
151   Ibid.
152   John Walsh, 'The Transformation of Higher Education, 1945–80' in Andrew Loxley, Aidan Seery and John Walsh (eds), *Higher Education in Ireland: Practices, Policies, Possibilities* (Basingstoke: Palgrave Macmillan, 2014), 5–32, 7.
153   Walsh, 'History of Education in Ireland', 56.
154   Walsh, 'The Transformation of Higher Education, 1945–80', 8.
155   Ibid.
156   Ibid., .20–1.

receive formal instruction in teaching theory and practice during their course of training'.[157] However, while providing a brief account of the state of PE in Irish schools and in the teaching colleges, it failed to offer any recommendations for improving its status.[158] The government remained reluctant to help with developing physical education courses for secondary school teachers. *Investment in Education* reported that neither Ling nor St Raphael's were funded initially by the State.[159] In addition, the Secondary Teachers' Registration Council recognised only the qualifications of St Raphael's, although the PE qualifications there and at Ling College were recognised for vocational school teaching.[160]

The Appointment of an Inspector for Physical Education

In January 1963 Minister Hillery announced that he planned to appoint an inspector 'to control physical education in the schools' and to 'co-ordinate all present systems and plan future programmes'.[161] While the Department of Education kept in touch with educational developments abroad, in appointing a PE inspector they were 'striking out on their own' and did not 'propose following foreign methods', echoing the views of the 1938 Physical Education Report's committee.[162] Dr Hillery was 'a keen golfer himself and sportsman' who was, through this move, showing 'signs of fitting the Irish education system to the requirements of the 1960s'.[163] It was also noted in the press that the Department of

157   *Investment in Education. Report of the Survey Team Appointed by the Minister for Education in October, 1962* (Dublin: The Stationery Office, 1965), 291.
158   See, for example, Ibid., and *Investment in Education. Annexes and Appendices to the Report of the Survey Team Appointed by the Minister for Education in October, 1962* (Dublin: The Stationery Office, 1965), 23.
159   Ibid.
160   Ibid.
161   *Evening Herald*, 30 January 1963.
162   Ibid.
163   *Limerick Leader*, 2 September 1963 and *Sunday Independent*, 8 September 1963.

Education was intending 'to introduce in schools a section devoted to physical education similar to that in the US and Germany' while as well as the appointment of an inspector, ten teachers were to be selected to receive 'special training' in England.[164] At the Fianna Fáil Ard Fheis in November 1963, Dr Hillery stated that he 'had been trying recently to get an extra half-hour per day allocated to subjects like physical education such as swimming'.[165] He also noted that 'in the reconstructed training colleges there would be provision for swimming pools so that teachers would be able to give instruction in life saving and swimming' and that 'he would sanction such courses by the vocational schools'.[166] In November 1963 the position of 'Organising Inspector of Physical Education' was advertised in the national press.[167] It is clear the Department of Education was seeking someone who was relatively young and physically active, as applicants were required to be no older than thirty-five years old 'with extensions' while essential requirements included experience of 'satisfactory' levels of training and teaching of PE and an adequate knowledge of the Irish language.[168]

The move by the Department of Education to appoint a PE inspector reflected wider international trends. One reporter noted in August 1964 that PE was 'now considered to be of such importance towards the development of a sound and healthy youth that the Council of Europe's cultural committee has established a special division for this aspect of its work'.[169] This was to see 'official coaches visit member countries, lecturing' and also 'giving demonstration in latest developments to physical leaders'.[170] Moran has stated that in November 1962 the Department of Education sent the Reverend Thomas Lonergan as Ireland's representative to a Council of Europe-backed Convention on Sport and Physical Education in Schools.[171] This took place in Bonn and during the event, Ireland's lowly

164   *Irish Examiner*, 9 September 1963.
165   Ibid., 21 November 1963.
166   Ibid.
167   *Irish Press*, 30 November 1963.
168   Ibid.
169   *Irish Independent*, 28 August 1964.
170   Ibid.
171   Moran, 'The Role of the Military in the Development of Physical Education', 106.

position in terms of the teaching of PE was noted.[172] Following communications with David Lewis, who was Council of Europe Administrator of the
Committee for Cultural Cooperation, a 'Mutual Assistance Programme'
was established.[173]

In the United Kingdom, PE was said to have developed 'from a mere
PT exercise into a training backed by scientific research and years of study'.[174]
In August 1964, a two week- long Council of Europe Physical Education
course was held at University College Dublin's Iveagh Gardens under the
instruction of 'Liverpool Irishman' John Kane, a lecturer in physical edu-
cation at London University who had given talks throughout Europe as
a research committee member of UNESCO's International Council of
Sport and Physical Education, and three other international coaches.[175]
The course had been organised by the Irish Secondary Schools' Athletic
Association and was assisted by the Council of Europe and the Willwood
Athletic Foundation.[176] Kane hoped that it 'would result in a greater importance being attached to the teaching and study of physical education'.[177]
Forty-eight participants received certificates from the Minister for Defence,
Gerald Bartley, at the end of the course, which was linked to the NACA-
backed Summer School of Athletics.[178] Some other organisations also hosted
training courses in PE, with the Boys' Brigade involved in that held in conjunction with the Army Physical Training Corps at Portobello Barracks
in December 1964.[179]

Despite this progress, the government remained steadfast in their
attitude towards not assisting the overall development of athletics. In
November 1964 the Taoiseach, Seán Lemass, told Seán Dunne of the Labour

---

172 Ibid., 106–7.
173 Ibid., 107.
174 *Irish Independent*, 28 August 1964.
175 *Irish Examiner*, 5 August 1964 and *Irish Independent*, 24 August 1964. UNESCO's
      International Council of Sport and Physical Education was founded in 1960. This
      was renamed as the International Council of Sport Science and Physical Education
      in 1982. See Carter, *Medicine, Sport and the Body*, 69.
176 *Irish Examiner*, 5 August 1964 and *Irish Independent*, 24 August 1964.
177 Ibid.
178 *Irish Examiner*, 5 August 1964 and *Irish Press*, 19 August 1964.
179 *Evening Herald*, 3 December 1964.

party in the Dáil that 'the government had not formulated any plans in relation to the promotion of athletics, as they considered that, in keeping with their amateur tradition, that was a matter best left to the athletic organisations'.[180] However, they intended to consider proposals that may help the development of athletics. He also noted that they had aided the cost of the Eamon Ceannt Athletics Stadium at Sundrive Park, Dublin, and that the Department of Education had 'made provision for physical education and sport within the school system and that assistance had also been given towards the building of swimming pools by the Department of Local Government'.[181] It was also stated that 'a very high standard of performance was reached at the annual schools and college athletics championships', although the level of attendance received less attention.[182] In addition, the Department of the Gaeltacht had also provided funding towards a swimming pool, tennis courts, playing pitches and a handball alley.[183]

In March 1965, Lemass reiterated this policy on sport when he responded to a questionnaire forwarded to him by Des Murphy, a writer with the *Irish Independent*.[184] Murphy was keen 'to ascertain the official Government view towards sport in Ireland' following the setting up of the Advisory Sports Council in Britain in the aftermath of the Wolfenden Report, and in light of the role of sport in 'the controlling policy of Communist Governments, the morale-boosting success of international teams and individuals, and the all-round benefits to production of a healthy population'.[185]

While Lemass had declined Murphy's request for an interview on the subject, 'owing to pressure of business', he indicated in the questionnaire that he had no intention of following any wider models of government policy and sport, and stated that he would welcome proposals from Ireland's 'major athletic organisations' before taking any action towards establishing a council or providing financial assistance for athletics.[186]

180   *Irish Independent*, 4 November 1964.
181   Ibid.
182   Ibid.
183   Ibid.
184   Ibid., 9 March 1965.
185   Ibid.
186   Ibid.

Lemass was dismissive of the American system of providing university scholarships, and felt that 'winning international prestige should be the least' of Ireland's concerns.[187] He added that it was 'facilities for recreation, and the stimulus of competition for Irish athletics' that were more important. While he suggested that participation in international competition should be welcomed and was that it was helpful in setting standards and in improving international relations, Ireland 'should not attach undue importance to national prestige in this connection because international athletics and sport should be primarily contests between individuals and teams rather than between nations'.[188] He also stated that he felt participation was more important than winning, and rather dismissively noted that most Irish people 'can never expect to acquire proficiency of international standard'.[189] Lemass was very clear about government provision of aid for sporting organisations when he stated that

> I do not think the Government should support professional sporting events, although last year we exempted the income of professional as well as amateur sporting organisations from liability for income tax, provided their profits are used for the benefit of sport. If the main aim is, as it should be, to encourage and facilitate amateur sports, then on the basis I have indicated, Government help would be useful, but not in such degree as to relieve sporting organisations of the major obligation of maintaining and financing themselves.[190]

He also wanted to see disagreements between sporting organisations settled before any Sports Council could be established, but indicated that the Government would not intervene in bringing about resolutions.[191]

The appointment of Dundalk-born Captain Michael McDonough as Inspector of PE in April 1965 offered fresh hope as he then engaged in assessing the condition of the subject in Irish schools.[192] Captain McDonough had been senior instructor in the Army School of Physical Culture at the

187   Ibid.
188   Ibid.
189   Ibid.
190   Ibid.
191   Ibid.
192   O'Donoghue, 'The Policy of the State', 133.

Curragh Camp and was the son of former Chief Superintendent, T. S. McDonough, who was NACA president by the following year.[193] In October 1965, Captain McDonough submitted his report to the Department of Education.[194] He identified 'the lack of qualified lecturers in the training colleges' and 'the absence of an official syllabus' as the biggest cause of the poor position of physical education in Irish primary schools.[195] He noted that there were some primary schools which had no programme for PE, and where it existed, it was based on drill. New Minister for Education George Colley (1965–6) had stated in May 1965 that 'all recognised secondary schools' were officially 'required to provide for the teaching of physical training or organised athletic games'.[196] However, Captain McDonough noted that in post-primary schools, 'in general the physical educational programme is based on recreational activities. Some schools base all their programmes on one or two games.'[197] McDonough stated that in this type of school, 'the training of an elite few to represent the school' was prioritised and 'in certain schools' there was 'a fanatical loyalty to one game to the near exclusion of all other physical activity'.[198]

He felt that vocational schools were 'the weakest' in regard to implementing physical education, although this differed in Dublin city as 'there were a reasonable number of teachers employed in the post-primary sector'.[199] McDonough's report was based on what he described as 'a very brief inspection of the situation' but he had also been voluntarily involved in school athletics 'for a number of years'.[200] McDonough recommended

---

193   *Nationalist and Leinster Times*, 29 July 1966.
194   *Irish Press*, 8 July 1968 and McDonough, 'Physical Education and the Sports Complex in the Community School', 32.
195   McDonough, 'Physical Education and the Sports Complex in the Community School', 32.
196   'Dáil Éireann Debate – Tuesday, 18 May 1965. Vol. 215. No. 11. Ceisteanna – Questions. Oral Answers. – Physical Education.' <https://www.oireachtas.ie/en/debates/debate/dail/1965-05-18/58/> [Accessed 4 November 2020].
197   McDonough, 'Physical Education and the Sports Complex in the Community School', 32.
198   Ibid.
199   Ibid.
200   Ibid.

that a Council for Physical Education and Sport be founded, while he also suggested that a National College of Physical Education be established.[201] In addition, he wanted to see the organisation of in-service courses as a short-term remedy, while he also recommended that a compulsory syllabus be provided in primary schools. He believed that the appointment of additional qualified inspectors should be made while he also wanted a developmental plan to be drawn up for vocational schools.[202] Many of these proposals reflected the needs outlined in the 1938 Physical Education Report, but by the middle of the 1960s, with the Irish economy in a more prosperous state than it had been for some time, and more attention being paid by the Irish government to wider European health and fitness standards, it appeared that they were finally in a position to act on them.[203]

Conclusion

Despite the progress noted above, the Republic of Ireland still lacked a PE college for males and females. It was not that there was no public awareness of this, and numerous sporting bodies and journalists had attempted to draw attention to the state of PE in Irish schools. Relationships between military officials and colleges and schools were at times frosty and some educationalists were also beginning to question the role of the military in teaching the subject. James McCabe, a man qualified as a vocational teacher in Irish, rural science and commerce and a holder of a teaching certificate in PE from Loughborough College, had suggested in the press in April 1964 that an Irish college be established on the model of Loughborough College in England. He wanted to see

201   Ibid.
202   Ibid., 32–3.
203   For a discussion of the turnaround in Ireland's economic fortunes in the late 1950s and early 1960s see Browne, *Ireland: A Social and Cultural History*, chapter 8.

training supplied there for those intent on studying PE with metal-work and woodwork also incorporated into the course, as the Republic of Ireland had no permanent college for this type of training at that time.[204] He also felt that training in PE by army men was 'a very faulty policy … casually attracting such men who happen to be available to fill the meagre hours allotted to physical education on school curricula'.[205] McCabe noted how, at Loughborough, PE could be studied as a major or minor subject as part of the degrees available there, although 'the tone of the college' was 'set by a PE bias' and degrees were also awarded in handicraft and engineering.[206] Facilities at Loughborough included 'an ultra-modern, well-equipped gymnasium and an indoor heated swimming pool' which was 'generously surrounded by lush playing fields, which have included in them ball and volley-ball courts'.[207] By the mid-1960s, structures for the training of male physical education teachers in the Republic of Ireland often amounted only to temporary courses and lagged far behind this. In addition, no funding was given to the two ladies' physical training institutions at that point.

This came despite the fact that in October 1965 the Irish Federation of Physical Culture estimated that there were over 300 physical education teachers needed in Irish schools.[208] At the premiere of the film, *Physical Education in Ireland*, noted above, at St Raphael's College of PE in December 1965, Minister for Education George Colley commented that public interest in the subject had 'increased greatly in recent years, particularly among school managers and teachers'.[209] The Minister also noted Ireland's tradition of 'enthusiasm and respect for physical prowess' and the country's reputation in athletics, which was creditable 'for a small country'.[210] At this point, with Captain McDonough's appointment, it appeared that

204 *Irish Press*, 30 April 1964.
205 Ibid.
206 Ibid.
207 Ibid.
208 Ibid., 22 October 1965.
209 *Irish Independent*, 3 December 1965.
210 Ibid.

governmental ministers were finally showing sufficient interest in the provision of physical training, but, as will be seen in Chapter 8, it would still be
some time before a permanent, government-funded structure for training
teachers in the subject would be fully implemented. Chapter 7 addresses
PE in Northern Ireland in the period from 1954 until 1972.

Towards the Troubles and Beyond: PE in Northern Ireland, 1954–1972

Introduction

This chapter begins with an examination of the development of the Ulster College of Physical Education from 1954 until the early 1970s when it became amalgamated into the new Ulster College, following the recommendations of the Lockwood Report in 1965.[1] Despite the provision of a co-educational faculty for second level PE trainee teachers by 1972, the facilitation of physical training places for males who wanted to obtain degrees in the subject in Northern Ireland had been unsatisfactory for a long time.[2] While PE was, according to the Ministry of Education, officially compulsory in elementary schools since the 1920s, its position in post-primary schools was less concrete and attitudes to its teaching in some schools remained conservative. Although the Ministry of Education was content that progress was being made by the late 1950s, the Wolfenden Committee was more open about the situation, particularly in regard to the use of space. Its report in 1960 highlighted issues in the sharing of sports facilities between Catholics and Protestants, but the provision of amenities such as playing fields was to remain a problem in Belfast.[3] This chapter also addresses the mixed reactions of the Ministry of Education and school authorities to these findings. It will also show that a number of headmasters were opposed to these, although the Minister for Education from 1957 to 1962, Morris May, generally agreed with the Wolfenden

1   *Belfast Telegraph*, 7 December 1965.
2   Ibid., 6 June 1972.
3   *Irish Press*, 29 September 1960.

Committee's views of the state of PE in Northern Ireland's schools.[4] Some schools remained reluctant to take on sports which they felt did not suit their ethos, with a number of grammar school principals stubbornly resisting calls to include association football at the expense of time allocated to rugby within their provision of games.[5] By the late 1960s, the development of sport centres within colleges such as Stranmillis was improving, thereby strengthening facilities for the training of teachers.[6] However, the rise in sectarian conflict undoubtedly impacted on the running of PE in some areas. This chapter concludes with the onset of the Troubles in 1968, and assesses how this violent sectarian conflict initially impacted on the day-to-day running of schools and the organisation of PE. In doing so, it illustrates attitudes to teacher training, teaching itself and competitive schools' sport through the views of Catholic and Protestant post-primary school teachers.

The Development of the Ulster College of Physical Education

On 26 June 1956, the UCPE was officially opened at Dalriada, Jordanstown, by Lady Wakehurst, who gave certificates to the fourteen female students who had completed three years there as the college had been operational since September 1953.[7] It was the ninth female physical training college to be established in Britain and its principal was Oonagh Pim.[8] In 1953, she had come back from England, where she had worked in

4   *Belfast Telegraph*, 29 September 1960.
5   Curran, *Irish Soccer Migrants*, 74–7.
6   Interview with Northern Ireland second level PE teacher number four, 26 September 2019.
7   PRONI, ED/ 13/1/2716A. Formal Opening of the Ulster College of Physical Education. Opening of the College and Presentation of Diplomas by her excellency the Lady Wakehurst. Thursday, 26 June 1956, at 2.30 p.m.; *Irish Press*, 26 June 1956 and *Belfast Telegraph*, 1 June 1981.
8   Webb, *The Challenge of Change in Physical Education*, 7.

a teaching and organisational capacity, to take up the position.[9] Born in Dublin, she was a graduate of the Bergman Osterberg Physical Training College in Dartford.[10] Early in 1956, plans had been unveiled to take on more students at UCPE. While the initial graduates' course there was for the duration of three years, in February 1956, R. S. Brownell, the secretary of the Ministry of Education, issued a circular to 'principals of all recognised schools', and chief education officers, regarding an upcoming one-year PE course for graduates and non-graduates.[11]

The requirements for entry to the course were of a high level. Applicants needed to have a university degree or to 'have completed a general course of training as a teacher in an approved training college'.[12] It was also open to those completing less specialised degrees and applicants needed to undertake a medical examination and to complete an aptitude test. They were also required to 'be of good physique with special aptitude for physical training and games'.[13] Those successful in their applications had to agree to certain provisions. They had to sign an undertaking that, on obtaining the qualifications offered in the course, they would teach physical education in Northern Ireland for at least two years. Serving teachers were required to give up their salaries while undertaking the course (although they could still be given incremental credit on completion), and have approval from local education authorities or managers that they could leave their position to complete it.[14]

Students of the three-year course at the UCPE were also, as noted, competitively chosen and had to have a pass grade in the schools' Senior Certificate or 'equivalent examination'.[15] Scholarships were available for

---

9   *Belfast Telegraph*, 11 February 1963.
10 Seán Farren, Linda Clarke and Theresa O'Doherty, *Teacher Preparation in Northern Ireland: History, Policy and Future Directions* (Bingley: Emerald, 2019), 61.
11 Ed/13/1/1247. Training of semi-specialists: fourth year course in physical education (women) at Ulster College of Physical Education 1956–7 and proposed 1957–8. R. S. Brownell to Chief Education Officers and Principals of all Recognised Schools. Training Scholarships for a one-year course in Physical Education for women teachers, 1956–7. Ulster College of Physical Education. 19 January 1956.
12 Ibid.
13 Ibid.
14 Ibid.
15 *Irish Independent*, 26 March 1956.

candidates living in Northern Ireland for the non-residential college, and
they had to be at least 17 years old to obtain a place on the course.[16] Some
schools offered scholarships for the PE course. For example, by the middle
of the decade Coleraine High School was awarding two entrance scholarships to students.[17] Some experience of the study of biology, anatomy
and physiology, chemistry, physics or music was an advantage in selection
for the physical education course. The curriculum at the UCPE included
principles of education, anatomy and physiology, health education, theory
and practice of educational gymnastics, school remedial exercises, games,
dancing, swimming and athletics. Students also undertook English language and literature and appreciation of music classes.[18]

The extension of courses was related to the demand for qualified PE
teachers. In 1956 Oonagh Pim welcomed what she saw as a change in views
of the subject's importance in schools when she stated that 'a new attitude
had replaced the old fallacy that the physical side was one of the byways
of the educational process'.[19] There was also some wider recognition that
being fit and healthy could contribute to the demands of society in the late
1950s. In his presentation of diplomas to UCPE graduates in July 1957, Sir
Eric Ashby, the vice-chancellor of Queen's University, Belfast, emphasised
the need for physical fitness in order to hold down a job, particularly as
'modern life was becoming so strenuous'.[20] In her report, principal Pim felt
that individuals needed to become more independent of their families as
they focused on their careers, which appears to have been an issue for some
students at UCPE.[21]

As college principal, Pim liked to keep up to date with wider developments in PE. She represented UCPE at the third International Congress
in Physical Education and Sports for Girls and Women, which was held

16   Ibid.
17   *Belfast Newsletter*, 18 November 1955 and 18 December 1956.
18   *Irish Independent*, 26 March 1956.
19   Ibid.
20   *Belfast Newsletter*, 5 July 1957.
21   Ibid.

in London in the summer of 1957.[22] This was held over the course of a week and 'practical lecture-demonstrations' took place with an emphasis on modern educational dance, movement and gymnastics.[23] On the final day, 400 members of the Congress attended an exhibition of games given by 800 boys and girls on the London County Council's playing fields.[24]

Attitudes towards PE in Northern Ireland's schools were slow to change in some areas, despite the progress made in female teacher training, and some education authorities remained focused on their financial situation. At a meeting of the Tyrone Education Committee in late February 1955, C. A. Beattie stated that 'in former days children walked miles to school, some in their bare feet, but nowadays, they were carried in taxis, and, to give them exercise, large sums of money were spent on physical training equipment'.[25] He felt that 'if some of the children walked to school they would not require the physical training'.[26]

There also seems to have been a lack of clarity over whether or not it was a mandatory subject in schools. In November 1955, in response to a query from Dr Nixon of the Unionist Party in North Down as to whether 'participation in games and physical training was compulsory for schools under his control or in receipt of grants from his ministry', Harry Midgley stated that 'in all primary schools physical education was a compulsory subject of the curriculum'.[27] He also noted that 'in all other types of schools in receipt of grants from the Ministry there were, strictly speaking, no compulsory subjects, but the Ministry approved and encouraged the giving of physical education and games practice to all pupils other than those who were excused participation on medical grounds'.[28]

---

22 O. M. Pim, 'Third International Congress in Physical Education and Sports for Girls and Women' in S. O'Hagan (ed.), *Ulster College of Physical Education Jordanstown* (Belfast: UCPE, 1957), 6–7.

23 Ibid., 6.

24 Ibid.

25 *Belfast Newsletter*, 1 March 1955.

26 Ibid.

27 Ibid., 30 November 1955.

28 Ibid.

Throughout her time as principal, Pim was also eager to strengthen the
notion that PE was a subject worthy of being fully integrated into schools
and to emphasise that the theory behind its teaching was an important
part of being a teacher in the subject. In July 1959, at the annual graduation ceremony of UCPE, which had an enrolment of fifty-two female
students at that time, she stressed the importance of reading for physical
education teachers and stated that they 'must be easy to understand and
grammatical' while speaking. They also had 'to write up reports, and put
up notices' and 'take an intelligent part in staffroom discussions and school
activities'.[29] Pim also encouraged the fifteen graduates present 'to develop
the habit of reading as a means of gaining pleasure and extending experience'.[30] She also wanted to dispel the notion PE was the only subject they
were taught at UCPE.[31]

One late twentieth-century reporter later noted that Pim had watched
over the UCPE students 'like a mother hen'.[32] Apparently, 'she was a stickler
for dress, and no track-suits were allowed in the dining room or even during
teaching practice; gym skirts and blouses were the order of the day'.[33] It
was also noted that 'indoor facilities in those days were limited to gymnasium and dance hall and a nice, comfortable ladies college image was
fostered'.[34] Clearly she was intent on promoting a professional image for
the subject of PE and saw public appearance as being fundamental to that.
Despite progress in the number of college positions for PE students, issues
remained regarding the appointment of full-time PE teachers in secondary
schools, with some school principals still reluctant to encourage this. At
the UCPE graduation ceremony in June 1958, Pim stated that 'there were
many opportunities for the specialist of physical education' and that 'if a
programme of physical education was fully implemented in a school ....
the specialist will not have time to offer another subject'.[35] She noted that

29   *Belfast Telegraph*, 1 July 1959.
30   Ibid.
31   Ibid.
32   Ibid., 1 June 1981.
33   Ibid.
34   Ibid.
35   Ibid., 1 July 1958.

some principals felt that it was better if the PE teacher could offer a second subject, but this was an incorrect assumption. She added that 'I appreciate that there are some secondary schools whose numbers do not justify a full-time specialist, yet surely a joint appointment would be the means of bringing a wide-range of subjects to an age range that needs specialist knowledge to give it satisfaction'.[36]

By the early 1960s, the UCPE was also developing connections with other colleges in Belfast.[37] At the 1960 UCPE graduation ceremony, Pim offered thanks to 'the Ministry of Education for the scope and width given to the college course, to Queen's University for facilities made available in the departments of anatomy, physiology, physical education and in the Institute of Clinical Science and to Stranmillis College' where students had cooperated 'in extra-mural activities'.[38] Ivan C. Gray, the headmaster of Friends' School, Lisburn, in presenting diplomas to nineteen UCPE students at that same graduation ceremony, stated that a revolution had taken place in the subject over the past thirty years as 'in that time it had developed from "drill" to "physical training" to "physical education." '[39] Some public performances were arranged to demonstrate components of the new curriculum. In November 1961, a number of Belfast pupils took part in a modern dance performance at the King George VI Youth Centre.[40] This event had been organised by the NIPEA with a view to publicly demonstrating what former UCPE students were teaching in schools.[41] It was presided over by Rhonda E. Jackson of the Ministry of Education and a talk was given at the event by Oonagh Pim.[42]

Public perceptions about the UCPE remained, however. In February 1963, in an interview with the *Belfast Telegraph*, Pim admitted having a 'bee in her bonnet' about 'misapprehensions about the college's function'.[43] She

36   Ibid.
37   *Belfast Telegraph*, 28 June 1961.
38   Ibid.
39   Ibid., 28 June 1961.
40   Ibid., 10 November 1961.
41   Ibid.
42   Ibid.
43   Ibid., 11 February 1963.

noted that 'physical education is not just playing games and doing exercises. It is very much part of living, of our way of thought.'[44] She added
that she did not see the subject as 'something that is done in a hall or gym.
It is the enjoyment and health you get from moving about, from dancing,
climbing, swimming.'[45] She remained vociferous in her attempts to change
attitudes towards the physical education teaching profession. In June 1965,
in her UCPE diploma graduation presentation address, she was critical of
local education committees' attitudes in their appointing of teachers.[46] In
particular, she wished that 'a way could be found to build a rather more
reliable public image of the teacher of physical education.'[47]

Naturally, not every school principal failed to see PE's value, but parental attitudes were difficult to change. Speaking at a prize-giving ceremony
at Dunlambert secondary school in Belfast in October 1964, headmaster,
Sam Lynn, in discussing the formation of a young citizens' club to combat
vandalism, stated that 'so far as most parents were concerned, subjects like
physical education, religious instruction, music and the arts, were all very
well in their way, but not that important'.[48] He felt that 'in future, however,
both parents and the schools would have to pay more attention to these
subjects, and give them greater scope in the curriculum'.[49] Lynn added that
'a boy who left school interested in gymnastics and sport, music, painting,
sculpting and modelling, had a much fuller, more creative, and less destruc-
tive life ahead of him.'[50]

Pim felt that the UCPE was well situated 'on the shores of Belfast
Lough in about 30 acres of ground' and added that it was not a residential
college, as 'most of the students and staff' lived nearby in lodgings.[51] Despite
her comments on the relatively isolated location of the college, which was
situated away from Belfast city centre and meant less opportunities for

44   Ibid.
45   Ibid.
46   Ibid., 21 June 1965.
47   Ibid.
48   Ibid., 18 October 1964.
49   Ibid.
50   Ibid.
51   Ibid., 11 February 1963.

the students to socialise there, there were some opportunities for extra-curricular activities. Student life at UCPE at the start of the 1956–7 academic year was improved when an entertainments' committee was formed within the college, with students organising two events known as 'hops' for incoming and returning students. In the New Year, two dances were organised for each term, with the College Dress Dance taking place in March and the Graduation Ball in summer.[52] A sports' day was also organised and took place in June 1957.[53] Sporting fixtures were arranged against other colleges. Six tennis matches, against external opposition, were held that year while a hockey team made up of third year students travelled to Scotland to play matches against Dunfermline Physical Training College and Glasgow University.[54] In September 1956 a number of UCPE students took part in a Question Time programme on education which was broadcast by the BBC.[55] It was announced in November 1957 that two all-weather blaes pitches, similar to those in use at Stranmillis Training College, were to be developed for hockey at the UCPE at Jordanstown.[56] In 1961 Pegasus Hockey Club was formed and consisted of past students from UCPE and Stranmillis Training College, while by the late 1960s the UCPE Athletic club had been established.[57] The UCPE also fielded a team in the Ulster Senior Hockey League and Shield, and hockey remained a popular sport in many Protestant schools in Northern Ireland (see Figure 27).[58]

While Pim, a Quaker, said little directly about the religious ethos of the college, it was open to Catholic as well as Protestant students.[59] Speaking in 1995, then Labour MP Kate Hoey and future British Minister for Sport, stated that on entering the UCPE in 1964, that out of twenty students in her year, eight were Catholics and this was the 'highest proportion' they 'had ever had.'[60] She also noted that 'it was, for many, the first time that

52   'College Reports' in O'Hagan (ed.), *Ulster College of Physical Education*, 34–8, 34.
53   Ibid.
54   Ibid., 36.
55   Ibid., 37.
56   *Belfast Newsletter*, 19 November 1957.
57   *Irish Press*, 29 October 1966 and 13 and 27 March 1969.
58   Ibid., 4 March 1970.
59   Farren, Clarke and O'Doherty, *Teacher Preparation in Northern Ireland*, 61.
60   *Belfast Telegraph*, 11 September 1995.

Figure 27. Londonderry High School's hockey first team, 1958.
Courtesy of William Lynn.

they had contact with anyone from another religion. It was terrific because
of the discussions that went on.'[61] The students, she stated, did not regularly go out socialising but put on their own games and an annual play.[62]
Farren et al have written that 'given earlier controversies over separate
arrangements for Roman Catholic student-teachers, there is no evidence
of any objection to Catholic students enrolling in the completely secular
UCPE, nor of the Protestant churches seeking any representation in its
management.'[63] In addition, they note that the UCPE courses did not provide religious education.[64]

61   Ibid.
62   Ibid.
63   Farren, Clarke and O'Doherty, *Teacher Preparation in Northern Ireland*, 61.
64   Ibid.

The Training of Male PE Teachers

In the early 1950s, opportunities for men to gain secondary school qualifications in PE in Northern Ireland remained less straightforward and migration to a specialised college in mainland Britain was the only option. This may have been down to a greater demand for female PE teachers, given that the occupation was at that stage traditionally seen as one more suited to women. Some efforts were made to improve this, however. Early in 1954, a new recreation centre, said to have 'a membership of approximately 140' and estimated to be 'one of the most modern in the United Kingdom', was opened on Annadale Grammar School grounds.[65] This was developed by the Belfast Education Authority with the aim of supplying a centre for youths' physical recreation, while it was 'to provide training facilities for men youth leaders proposing to take the Northern Ireland award in physical recreation sponsored by the NIPEA, and recognised by the Ministry of Education'.[66] It was also intended that it would 'provide further training and refresher courses for teachers and for instructor leaders on the committee's panel'.[67] Coaching 'in major games' was also to be offered using the nearby Carolan Road playing fields while social training was also to be given to youths, 'particularly in matters concerning respect of private and public property'.[68]

Despite this initiative, a shortage of PE teachers remained evident in this decade. In August 1955, the County Derry Education Committee noted at a meeting that there was a short supply of physical training instructors in Northern Ireland, with no applicants for two physical training instructor vacancies they had advertised.[69] This resulted in them passing a resolution 'calling upon the Northern Ireland Association of Education Committees to urge the Ministry of Education to set up a training centre in Northern Ireland for Ulster boys, or make provision for such training

65   *Belfast Newsletter*, 12 January 1954.
66   Ibid.
67   Ibid.
68   Ibid.
69   Ibid., 22 and 23 August 1955.

in the general teachers' course'.[70] It was noted by Director of Education, R. B. Hunter, 'that as the school building programme progressed, more physical training instructors would be needed'.[71] He stated that Loughborough College was 'attended by a very small number of Northern Ireland students' and 'was believed to be the only source of supply [for Northern Ireland boys' schools] in the United Kingdom'.[72] Reverend James Johnston of Magherafelt claimed at the same meeting that 'recently he had to beg the Ministry of Education in England for a physical training instructor for the Rainey Grammar School, Magherafelt'.[73] Deputy Director, H. Geough, stated that he had been notified 'that representation was being made to the Ministry to give students, who completed the present three year course [in education], the option of taking a course in physical training the following year. The committee's action would support this representation.' The Reverend W. J. W. Bruce stated that 'this course would be most desirable, as the teacher would not only be qualified to teach physical training, but also general subjects'.[74]

Pressure was also asserted upon the Ministry of Education from other educational organisations. At the annual meeting of the Association of the Northern Ireland Education Committees, held in Enniskillen in October 1955, 'a resolution was passed which called upon the Ministry of Education to give urgent consideration to the training of specialist teachers in physical education in Northern Ireland'.[75] R. B. Hunter, who was also involved in this body, stated that 'in spite of advertisements it was impossible to get such trained men for schools which quite often had the most elaborate equipment'.[76] These events appear to have led to the decision to establish a one-year course in PE for those already completing three-year education degrees at Stranmillis College from 1956 onwards.[77]

---

70   Ibid., 22 August 1955.
71   Ibid.
72   Ibid.
73   Ibid.
74   Ibid.
75   Ibid., 10 October 1955.
76   Ibid.
77   *Report of the Ministry of Education for the Year 1957–8*, 13.

Scholarships for men continued to be limited, however. In 1958, the Ministry gave nineteen women the three-year scholarship award at the UCPE while eighteen women who had been in receipt of this award completed it that year.[78] In addition, two men were awarded one-year scholarships in physical education while six men also successfully completed scholarships in the subject that year, although the male scholarships were for colleges in mainland Britain.[79]

The idea that some primary school teachers could move to teach in secondary schools was formally circulated. In April 1958, Minister for Education, Morris May, made an appeal for 'more suitably qualified applicants for posts in secondary intermediate schools' at the Ulster Teachers' Union annual conference.[80] He stated that 'with increasing development in these schools the lack of teachers in certain subjects such as physical education, science, woodwork and metalwork was causing considerable concern'.[81] Minister May called on qualified primary school teachers to undertake these positions to become more involved in teaching in intermediate secondary schools.[82] However, it was the Lockwood Report of 1965 which led to more decisive action being taken in regard to a co-educational PE college for second level teachers being developed. The Lockwood committee had been established in November 1963 to give advice on facilities for higher technical education and universities.[83] While this report is more commonly linked to the decision to establish a second third level institution in Coleraine rather than in Derry city, it can also be seen as being influential in the decision to facilitate the training of male physical education teachers along with that of females in a new institution in Belfast.[84]

---

78   PRONI. ED/25/37. Government of Northern Ireland Reports of the Ministry of Education. *Report of the Ministry of Education for the Year 1958–59* (Belfast: H.M. Stationary Office, 1959), 86.
79   Ibid.
80   *Belfast Telegraph*, 9 April 1958.
81   Ibid.
82   Ibid.
83   Ibid., 6 February 1965.
84   Bardon, *A History of Ulster*, 625–6.

Plans had already been underway to develop the UCPE prior to the Lockwood recommendations. By 1964, the Ministry of Education had decided to extend the college, which, it was felt, would 'enable places to be provided for a considerably larger number of students' in the courses there at that time.[85] This development 'would provide almost double the number of existing students' as 'there was still a great need for qualified women teachers of physical education in the schools'.[86] However, it appears this was surpassed by the views of the Lockwood committee, made public the following year, as a new co-educational facility which would cater for teacher training in physical education was recommended. In December 1965, Jordanstown was chosen as the site for the new Ulster College of Further Education, which had been suggested in the Lockwood Report.[87] The Lockwood Report had advised that the new college campus consist of the Regional College of Technology, the College of Art and Design, the College of Domestic Science and the College of Physical Education.[88] It was also recommended that colleges of commerce, management, music and drama were to be developed.[89] Legislation for the college was later ratified through the Ulster College Act (Northern Ireland) 1968, and an independent Board of Governors was established through this, with the board financed by the Ministry of Education and responsible for administrating its own matters.[90]

Despite the absence of a co-educational college for second level PE teachers, some progress continued to be made in training teachers in the subject within primary schools. In August 1965, one *Belfast Telegraph* reporter noted that 'every young man or woman at a [primary] teacher-training college takes physical education (the term P.T. – physical training – is no

85   PRONI. ED/25/42. Government of Northern Ireland Reports of the Ministry of Education. *Education in Northern Ireland in 1964* (Belfast: H.M. Stationary Office, 1965), 24.
86   *Belfast Telegraph*, 19 March 1964.
87   Ibid., 7 December 1965.
88   *Irish Press*, 8 January 1970.
89   Ibid.
90   PRONI. D4327/4/2. *Ulster College. The Northern Ireland Polytechnic. Annual Report to 31 August 1972* (Belfast, 1972), 3.

longer used) as part of their courses, while many specialise in this sphere of education'.[91] It was also reported that 'there is an average of three teachers on every school staff who can take charge of sporting activities, while many schools bring in outsiders-people who have made a name for themselves in a particular sport-to coach their pupils in that sport'.[92] Unlike in the Republic of Ireland, there was less emphasis on military instruction at this point, although army men maintained a presence in some schools such as the Royal School at Portora, where from 1948 to 1979 the Director of Physical Education was Major J. T. Wheeler, who also taught swimming and life-saving on a cross-community basis in Enniskilllen along with his wife from 1960 onwards.[93] In 1965, the Residential Coaching course was held at Orangefield for the seventh year, with fifteen courses being held and around 1500 pupils and teachers involved.[94]

As noted above, by the late 1950s a qualification in PE was available as part of an education degree for second level trainee teachers at the Protestant Stranmillis College, but it was not a degree in physical education as taken in Loughborough or St Luke's College, Exeter. Students could undertake 'a common teaching course' at Stranmillis for three years, which qualified them to teach in a primary school, and then the fourth and final year was spent undertaking their specialist subject such as physical education, with the result that they would get a teaching certificate with a specialisation in the additional subject.[95] One former PE teacher interviewed also noted that candidates' chances of obtaining a place on the Stranmillis course were helped by their own sporting careers along with the appropriate qualifications.[96] One other former PE teacher stated of the course that

91 *Belfast Telegraph*, 11 August 1965.
92 Ibid.
93 *Fermanagh Herald*, 20 August 1960 and Miles Henry and Ian Burn, *Portora. The School on the Hill: A Quatercentenary History* (Enniskillen: The Royal School Portora, 2008), 90–1. I am grateful to Robert Northridge for drawing my attention to this reference.
94 Ibid.
95 Interview with Northern Ireland second level PE teacher number four, 26 September 2019.
96 Ibid.

It was quite good, quite involved, so it was. We did other subjects as well, like we would have done education as one of the main [ones], we would have done English, and you also had to take a second subject and I took geography. But final year was probably quite intense, it was nearly all physical education-[that was] pretty comprehensive in the Department at that time.[97]

Students undertook two teaching practices each year while at Stranmillis with the initial practice in a primary school and later in secondary school.[98] This usually lasted for two of the four years, but in the final year while undertaking the physical education specialisation, placement was for a full term.[99]

By the late 1960s, Stranmillis, with its 'excellent facilities for physical education', under the head of the department there, Jimmy Bogan, was producing twenty-four PE teachers, with twelve males and twelve females graduating each year.[100] One former PE teacher recalled that the curriculum was 'very broad' and students took a range of major and minor sports (see Figure 28).[101] The PE Department there was 'very busy and worked extremely hard' according to a fellow graduate of Stanmillis, who also recalled that Bogan, who was an ex-army man and a 'very good organiser', took the students 'for just about everything'. He added that they 'even did a session with a golf pro … judo, boxing, we did the lot'.[102] He also stated that 'if they didn't have the expertise they brought somebody in and that is exactly how the place was run'.[103] At the Catholic St Joseph's training college, facilities for the subject were apparently not as good and fourth year students there used to come to Stranmillis to do their final year practical

---

97   Interview with Northern Ireland second level PE teacher number ten, 16 November 2019.
98   Interview with Northern Ireland second level PE teacher number four, 26 September 2019.
99   Ibid.
100   Ibid.
101   Interview with Northern Ireland second level PE teacher number five, 4 October 2019.
102   Interview with Northern Ireland second level PE teacher number eight, 31 October 2019.
103   Ibid.

Figure 28. King's Scholars Rugby first XV 1967–8, consisting of Stranmillis College students, who won the McCrea Cup and were captained by Stewart McKinney. Courtesy of Mervyn Elder.

work with the students there.[104] This college had grown out of St Mary's College with a men's department founded in 1949 at Trench House.[105] In 1961 it was renamed as St Joseph's Training College.[106] One former PE teacher stated that relationships between students from both religious backgrounds were good and that there was little disruption in Stranmillis due to its location on the outskirts of Belfast.[107]

With the opening of the Ulster College at Jordanstown in 1971, students no longer needed to attend Stranmillis to gain a qualification in teaching PE at second level.[108] The UCPE remained in operation until it

---

104 Interview with Northern Ireland second level PE teacher number four, 26 September 2019.

105 'History of St Mary's University College' Retrieved from <https://www.stmarys-belfast.ac.uk/general/history/default.asp> [Accessed 16 November 2020].

106 Ibid.

107 Interview with Northern Ireland second level PE teacher number nine, 13 November 2020.

108 Interview with Northern Ireland second level PE teacher number four, 26 September 2019.

was incorporated into Ulster College.[109] In January 1970 it was announced that £2.3 million was to be given for the new college's development at Jordanstown.[110] The UCPE was therefore amalgamated with the former Belfast College of Art and Design and the College of Domestic Science to form the Ulster College, although the latter two initially remained at York Street and Garnerville respectively.[111] Within the Faculty of Education there were three schools, including Domestic Science, Educational Studies and PE.[112] In May 1970, Derek Birley, who had been a deputy director of education in Liverpool, was appointed as the director of Ulster College, which was also known as the Northern Ireland Polytechnic.[113] By June 1972 the Ulster College had been operational for over a year with a School of Physical Education in the Faculty of Education.[114] Oonagh Pim maintained her position as principal of PE until she retired in August 1972.[115]

The Development and Provision of PE in Schools, 1954–1960

By the mid-1950s, PE maintained a reasonably solid presence in many schools in Northern Ireland, although structures for its teaching were by no means uniform across primary and second level schools. As noted above, in 1955 Harry Midgley had stated that it was compulsory in

---

109   Webb, *The Challenge of Change in Physical Education*, 7.
110   *Irish Press*, 8 January 1970.
111   Webb, *The Challenge of Change in Physical Education*, 4 and PRONI.SO/1/A/573. Government of Northern Ireland Reports of the Ministry of Education. *Education in Northern Ireland in 1971* (Belfast: H.M. Stationary Office, 1972), 14.
112   PRONI. D4327/4/2. *Ulster College. The Northern Ireland Polytechnic. Annual Report to 31 August 1972*, 6.
113   *Fermanagh Herald*, 9 May 1970.
114   *Belfast Telegraph*, 6 June 1972. The Ulster College became known as the Ulster Polytechnic in 1978. See *Ulster Yearbook 1983* (Belfast: General Register Office, 1983), 107.
115   *Belfast Telegraph*, 1 January 1973. Oonagh Pim was awarded an OBE in the New Year Honours 1973.

primary schools, but the subject was not on every school's programme.[116] In 1956 it was stated in a Ministry of Education Circular that PE 'was to be given five teaching periods per week of forty minutes each – almost as much as English and mathematics' in post-primary schools.[117] At this point, gymnastics had become more common within the curriculum, although as McGourty has noted, male teachers were more resistant than females to taking this on as part of their lessons and many continued with the Swedish system.[118] One PE teacher interviewed recalled that pupils at his Belfast primary school in the late 1950s had been introduced to 'a sound physical education curriculum' and his interest in the subject was fostered by the quality of teaching he himself received.[119] After moving to a secondary school, this continued with a number of the staff being intra-provincial rugby players. While secondary schools were not allowed to enter the Ulster grammar schools' athletic sports, they did field teams in soccer and rugby competitions.[120] Pupils at his secondary school were given two PE lessons per week, along with a games' afternoon and they played rugby matches on Saturday morning.[121] The level of affluence of a school could clearly influence the facilities available, with one PE teacher recalling that at primary school in a working class Belfast area they played mostly ball games as they had no resources for 'gymnastics or anything complicated like that'.[122] Some schools benefited from past pupil patronage in their development of sports facilities. Portora School's new outdoor swimming bath pictured in Figure 29, initiated by Major Wheeler, was partially financed as a war memorial gift through the Old Portora Union in that decade.[123]

116   *Belfast Newsletter*, 30 November 1955.
117   McGourty, 'The Boys' Physical Education Curriculum in Secondary Schools in Northern Ireland', 31.
118   Ibid.
119   Interview with Northern Ireland second level PE teacher number four, 26 September 2019.
120   Ibid.
121   Ibid.
122   Interview with Northern Ireland second level PE teacher number five, 4 October 2019.
123   *Belfast Newsletter*, 1 June 1957 and *Impartial Reporter*, 5 February 2009.

Figure 29. Swimming at the Royal School, Portora, in the late twentieth century.
Courtesy of Robert Northridge.

While sporting timetables were commonplace by then in most of the more prestigious Belfast schools, other related initiatives were also established for school children in the 1950s. A cycling school was in operation in Belfast having begun as a pilot scheme at Ashfield Boys' Secondary School in 1957 through the organisation of the Royal Society for the Prevention of Accidents and Belfast Education Authority.[124] 1500 children passed the test and were given awards within the first five years. PE Advisor for Belfast, R. H. Williams, hoped that the scheme would be extended to every school in the city, as it appears it was being neglected in grammar schools.[125]

A desire to maintain the traditional school ethos was detrimental to the development and teaching of other sports and was clearly noticeable in some grammar schools. The selection of teachers specialising in certain sports was not uncommon and had led to the IFA complaining to Minister Hall-Thompson, about this practice in Grosvenor High School, where rugby was the preferred code, in 1948.[126] In 1954, the majority of grammar schools in north-east Ulster, generally recognised for their rugby-playing strength, including the Royal Belfast Academical Institution [Inst], Down

124   *Belfast Telegraph*, 7 December 1957.
125   Ibid., 15 January 1962.
126   *Belfast Newsletter*, 8 April 1948.

High School and Grosvenor High, refused to entertain the proposals of the IFA and the Minister for Education, Harry Midgley, that soccer be introduced into their schools.[127] Difficulties in accommodating soccer that were noted included organisational problems with facilities, players and teachers; school prestige; the fixture list, travelling costs, the opposition of parents and soccer's links with professionalism.[128] However, in August 1958, it was announced that fifty soccer-playing schools under the Belfast Education Committee would obtain a professional football coach, following recommendations from the Director of Education, Dr J. Stuart Hawnt, and PE Advisor, R. H. Williams.[129] Belfast's Education Committee was the first in the UK to undertake this move. In England, the FA had a scheme in operation whereby county associations had panels of coaches connected to youth clubs and schools. Councillor Joss Cardwell, IFA Council Member and Glentoran Director, was 'instrumental in getting the proposal to the Education Committee'.[130] He had also been influential in its decision 'to give grammar schools permission to play association football and use their school colours', which had been introduced in November 1955.[131] The development of other sports had benefited from coaching initiatives. Dr Hawnt stated that 'for some time swimming coaches had been employed by the Education Committee with outstanding results'.[132] During the Christmas holidays of 1958, soccer coaching was given to 'the cream of Belfast's school soccer players' by four coaches, including R. H. Williams, at the North Road playing fields.[133] Despite this, soccer continued to be discouraged in some grammar schools throughout the rest of the twentieth century although some, such as Royal Academical Institution, did eventually loosen their reservations towards it and later offered soccer teams for pupils.[134]

127   Curran, *Irish Soccer Migrants*, 74–8.
128   Ibid.
129   *Belfast Telegraph*, 22 August 1958.
130   Ibid.
131   Ibid.
132   Ibid.
133   Ibid., 29 December 1958.
134   Curran, *Irish Soccer Migrants*, 98.

While Gaelic football mainly remained as a sport played in Catholic schools, some efforts were made to initiate cross-community understanding of all codes at this time. One PE teacher who attended a leading Protestant Day School in the north-west of Northern Ireland recalled that his teacher, who had inspired him to take up a career in PE teaching, 'did just about everything' including organising Gaelic matches against a nearby Catholic school. In what appears to be a unique attempt at developing cross-community sports in the pre-Troubles era, students would play a half of rugby and a half of Gaelic football, with matches held on a home and away basis.[135]

The development of playing fields did receive some attention in Belfast. In 1955, the Youth Committee for Northern Ireland reported that there was 'no doubt that lack of foresight and inadequate planning in the past' were 'the primary causes of the present lamentable shortage of open spaces and playing fields' in the city.[136] It was also felt that this was 'a contributing factor in juvenile delinquency and in maintaining at a high annual figure the number of accidents occurring to children playing in city streets'.[137] Following a survey of the playing fields in the Belfast area undertaken between December 1956 and June 1957, it was recommended in the related report that legislation and grants be improved and that 'school playing fields should be made available and education authorities should be encouraged to provide hard porous pitches'.[138] In July 1957, the Belfast Education Committee backed work to begin on a thirteen-acre site near the Holywood Road with school playing fields to be laid down for use by pupils in the locality in the sports of soccer, rugby, cricket and hockey. This first portion of the job was expected to take three years with the rest done in instalments and £13,000 was provided.[139]

135 Interview with Northern Ireland second level PE teacher number eight, 31 October 2019.
136 PRONI. LAI/3AL/6/3. *Government of Northern Ireland. Ministry of Education. Youth Committee. Report for the period June 1952 to June 1955* (Belfast: Her Majesty's Stationery Office, 1955), 4.
137 Ibid.
138 PRONI. LAI/3AL/6/3. *Government of Northern Ireland. Ministry of Education. Youth Committee. Report for the period October 1955 to October 1958* (Belfast: Her Majesty's Stationery Office, 1958), 7.
139 *Belfast Newsletter*, 19 July 1957.

In November 1957, the Youth Committee of Northern Ireland reported that the lack of playing fields 'would have to be tackled with greater urgency, greater vision and "no longer in piecemeal fashion".'[140] Its report, which was forwarded to the Ministry of Education and Belfast Corporation Parks Committee, lamented the lack of progress in Belfast and stated that future planning for the provision of playing fields was 'inadequate' while open spaces and sports grounds were 'fast disappearing', with housing being given greater priority. It was also noted that according to the National Playing Fields Association, 'there should be six acres of open space for every 1000 inhabitants' and this meant 'approximately 1000 pitches for Belfast which had 52 public pitches with another 18 planned'.[141] The Youth Committee's report was debated in the House of Commons in April 1958 and nine party members were in favour of its adoption. The Minister for Education agreed that 'there was a woeful deficiency of playing fields and other recreational facilities in Belfast and district'.[142] In July 1958, the Minister for Education announced that the maximum rates of grants given for 'playing fields and certain other facilities' was 'to be increased to 65 per cent'.[143]

In 1960 the Ministry of Education reported that PE was making 'good progress' in primary schools, with demonstrations and courses being 'well attended by teachers'.[144] In addition, it was noted that 'the increasingly generous provision of apparatus, including indoor and outdoor climbing frames' was aiding progress.[145] A public swimming bath had been opened in Derry city, which had helped 'many children in the city schools to be

140 Ibid., 1 November 1957.
141 Ibid. This organisation had been founded in 1925 'as a charity to protect the UK's sports fields, recreation grounds and public spaces'. See Carter, *Medicine, Sport and the Body*, 28. A branch had been formed in Belfast in Belfast in 1930. See *Belfast Newsletter*, 23 August, 1930.
142 *Belfast Newsletter*, 1 November 1957.
143 *Belfast Telegraph*, 8 July 1958.
144 PRONI. ED/25/38. Government of Northern Ireland Reports of the Ministry of Education. *Report of the Ministry of Education for the Year 1959–60* (Belfast: H.M. Stationary Office, 1960), 9.
145 Ibid.

given swimming instruction' while a swimming class training course also took place.[146]

At secondary school level, indoor and outdoor PE facilities were stated to be getting better.[147] It was noted that 'a number of schools now have hard-surfaced pitches; others are enlarging their grass playing fields'. The situation in regard to staff with qualifications in physical education was 'improving slowly' and 'the majority of schools' had specialists in the subject. However, the supply of PE teachers was still 'inadequate for present requirements'.[148] While general teaching standards in the subject were 'steadily improving', it was noted that 'the meagre allocation of time for physical education, especially in the senior classes' was significantly reducing the impact of gymnastics and dance training.[149] Games were said to hold 'a prominent part of the physical education programme' with 'an increasing number of representative teams in hockey, netball, rugby, basketball and tennis' emerging. There was also said to be an increase in the number of boys and girls participating in athletic county championships (see Figure 30). Despite this, some schools had an 'excessive' number of inter-school matches which led to problems in accommodating those not on teams.[150]

The Wolfenden Report on British Sport, 1960

Official government reports in Northern Ireland generally failed to take the religious make-up of Northern Ireland into account when reflecting upon the state of PE in schools there. This was particularly exposed when, in September 1960, the Wolfenden Committee Report on British Sport was published.[151] This report had been commissioned by the Central

---

146   Ibid.
147   Ibid., 13.
148   Ibid.
149   Ibid.
150   Ibid.
151   *Irish Press*, 29 September 1960.

Figure 30. Belfast Boys' Model School Athletic team who won the 1959–60 Ulster Secondary Schools' Athletic Championship. Courtesy of Mervyn Elder.

Council of Physical Recreation in London in 1957.[152] Holt and Mason have stated that 'Wolfenden was a very significant moment in the history and development of British sport' as it 'was the first time that a body of responsible men and women had sat down to examine the relationship between sport and the welfare of society'.[153] The Wolfenden committee recommended the foundation of a Sports Development Council (in Britain) consisting of six to ten persons 'responsible to the Lord President of the Council or directly appointed by the Chancellor of the Exchequer'.[154] The Council was to receive £5 million a year 'to disburse either by way of non-recurrent grants or in assistance towards the recurrent expenditure of the "composite" bodies (British Olympic Association, Central Council of Physical Recreation and National Playing Fields Association) and the individual national associations concerned with physical recreation'.[155] In

152 Holt, *Sport and the British*, 344.
153 Holt and Mason, *Sport in Britain 1945–2000*, 149.
154 *Belfast Telegraph*, 28 September 1960.
155 Ibid.

1965, the Sports Council was established, as Kevin Jefferys has stated, 'as an advisory body rather than the independent, executive authority proposed in the Wolfenden Report'.[156]

The Wolfenden Committee was advised on the situation in Northern Ireland by Col. E. D. R. Shearer and E. A. J. Edwards. The document took three years to prepare with the committee of eight chaired by Sir John Wolfenden. Wolfenden himself stated that the committee were of the view that 'with the different political and religious affiliations in the Six Counties the maximum use was not got out of all the facilities available for sport'.[157] It was posited that 'religious and political differences have stunted the proper development of sport' in Northern Ireland.[158] They also reported that 'the religious and political problems of the Six Counties are undoubtedly a factor detrimental to any integrated pattern of sports development and to the best use of resources and man-power available'. However, they felt that they were 'unable to offer any helpful comment on these problems'.[159] Wolfenden also stated that 'one profession may have a football ground while another profession may have an athletic pitch'.[160] He felt that 'this differentiation of communities is both wasteful and uneconomic'.[161]

The report noted that developments in sport in Northern Ireland were 'marked by a number of distinctive and difficult factors'.[162] The committee reported that they were under the impression 'that the standard of physical education and games in secondary schools' was not generally 'as high as in most other parts of the United Kingdom' although they recognised 'that strenuous and successful efforts' were underway to amend this.[163] In addition, they were of the view that 'school standards inevitably tend to be

---

156   Kevin Jefferys, 'The Thatcher Governments and the British Sports Council, 1979–1990' in *Sport in History*, vol. 36, no. 1 (2016), 73–97, 77.
157   *Irish Press*, 29 September 1960.
158   Ibid.
159   Ibid.
160   Ibid.
161   Ibid.
162   Ibid.
163   Ibid.

reflected both in the degree of interest and in the standard of performance in post-school recreation'.[164]

Their evidence suggested that it was clear that 'with few exceptions the powers and resources of local education authorities, particularly in regard to the use of school premises and playing fields, were not always harnessed to the service of the voluntary sports bodies'. The committee hoped that this situation would soon be remedied by 'a growing realisation of the value of sport to the community'.[165] They urged

> local authorities and local education authorities to consider very carefully whether they all doing all that they can to promote post-school physical recreation, especially by offering co-operation to the many voluntary agencies concerned, and, in particular, to examine how the facilities under that control can be best used for that purpose - perhaps by being made available free or at sympathetic rates.[166]

Reactions to the Wolfenden Report

Responses to the Wolfenden Report committee's findings on sport in Northern Ireland were mixed. Minister for Education, Morris May, stated that 'the report covered a wide field, and the conclusions were reasonable'.[167] He also mentioned that although 'schools had expert tuition in rugby' and the IFA had started to show films about soccer, 'there was relatively little tuition in athletics'.[168] The Minister of Education's comments on soccer coaching drew criticism from the IFA, with secretary, W. J. Drennan, pointing out in the press that coaching structures for schoolboys and others had actually been in operation, through their coaching committee, since the late 1940s.[169]

164   Ibid.
165   Ibid.
166   Ibid.
167   *Belfast Telegraph*, 29 September 1960.
168   Ibid.
169   Ibid., 30 September 1960. See also Curran, *Irish Soccer Migrants*, 71–4.

A number of grammar school headmasters were opposed to the Wolfenden Report's findings. W. Moles of Grosvenor High School stated that 'standards of physical education and games' were 'appreciably higher' in Northern Ireland, while J. W. Derbyshire of Belfast Royal Academy felt that the standard of games there was 'high'.[170] Foyle College Headmaster, J. S. Connolly, pictured below in Figure 31) stated that the standard of rugby, cricket and athletics was as good as that in mainland British schools. Belfast Deputy Director of Education, William C. H. Eakin, who welcomed the Report's general recommendations, felt that 'Government sources' had not been giving much encouragement and that playing fields were not getting enough attention. He added that the supply of sports facilities should have been given the same status as the provision of hospitals and schools and that the development of swimming facilities needed more money.[171]

Eakin was in agreement with the Wolfenden Committee's view that there should be no Ministry of Sport, but disagreed that standards in PE and games at secondary school level were lower than in Britain.[172] He pointed to the fact that Northern Ireland had 'produced many famous sportsmen' but stated that 'if there is any truth in the viewpoint at all it is a reflection on the poor playing facilities we have had in Belfast for years'.[173] In addition, 'he refuted the idea that religious and political problems were detrimental, among other things, to the best use being made of man-power and facilities available' in Northern Ireland. He also stated that he did 'not think the point arises as all the playing fields are being used to saturation point'.[174]

The editor of the *Belfast Telegraph* noted that the Wolfenden Committee's main criticisms, the scarcity of playing fields and other facilities for sport, 'should be taken in the helpful spirit in which they are offered'.[175] He added that 'our shortcomings have been apparent for a

170   *Belfast Telegraph*, 29 September 1960.
171   Ibid.
172   Ibid.
173   Ibid.
174   Ibid.
175   Ibid.

FOYLE COLLEGE CROSS COUNTRY TEAM · 1966 - 67 SEASON·

BACK LEFT TO RIGHT - J.S. Connolly Esq. J.E. Moore, D.E. Lynn, R.J. Ramsay,
R.J.B. Young, R. Fennell, I.W.N. McMorris, F.G.R. Ward. Esq.
SEATED LEFT-RIGHT - R.S.T. Marshall, D.J. Row, D.D. Bratton (V. Capt.)
T.S. Bratton (Capt.) J.A. Campbell (Sec), R.J. Knowles, S.A. McSparron
FRONT - K.T.A. Taylor · M. Ferguson.

Figure 31. Foyle College Cross-Country team, with their headmaster, J. S. Connolly, in the 1966–7 season. Courtesy of William Lynn.

long time' and that the aforementioned report undertaken by the Youth Committee in 1957 had also highlighted 'how Belfast lags behind cross-channel cities'. Some action had been taken:

> The Government responded by stepping up playing field grants to councils from 50 to 63 per cent. But the question remains whether some further emergency action is called for, when the more accessible open spaces are being swallowed up rapidly

by development. It is here that capital grants from a new sports council could be especially valuable.[176]

He also felt that Northern Ireland should have a representative on a national council for sport and added that 'what in effect, the committee pleads for is increased cooperation in making the best use of facilities, and it is a pity that religious and political differences here have led to the wasting of resources'.[177] However, it was stated that 'the committee is on much less sure ground in suggesting that standards of physical education and games in secondary schools' were lower in Northern Ireland than in Britain.[178]

He was also of the view that the Wolfenden Report was 'a challenge' to Northern Ireland's 'councils, education authorities, sporting bodies, and indeed to the public, to see that all reasonable facilities for recreation and games are readily available'.[179] It was also noted that 'Belfast is surely an ideal place for the sort of experimental multi-sports centre which the committee believes should be established by local authorities'. The editor also felt that in view of British performances at the 1960 Rome Olympic Games, the Wolfenden Committee was right to call for improved coaching 'and an end to tolerance of low standards'.[180]

There is strong evidence that sports facilities in Belfast were still inadequate. By April 1961, with the opening of new playing fields by the Shore Road, the Belfast Education Authority had fifty-three pitches and twenty tennis courts which could be used by schools.[181] The former had grown from a figure of just twenty pitches in the years immediately after the Second World War.[182] However, in March 1961, International Coach to the Amateur Athletic Association, Geoff Dyson, told the Northern Ireland branch of the Central Council of Physical Recreation in Belfast that

176   Ibid.
177   Ibid.
178   Ibid.
179   Ibid.
180   Ibid.
181   Ibid., 11 April 1961.
182   Ibid.

'Northern Ireland is one of the worst spots in Britain in the provision of athletic facilities'.[183] He added that 'much good material turned out by the schools was lost because youngsters leaving schools with some proficiency in field events joined athletic clubs which were not really athletic clubs at all, and which tried to turn them into sprinters and distance runners'.[184] In addition, 'many schools in Britain, and especially in Northern Ireland, were only now setting up athletic training facilities'.[185]

In October 1961, a survey undertaken by J. D. Wheatley on behalf of the Central Council of Physical Recreation found that 'sports facilities in Belfast are so bad that they could hardly be much worse'.[186] The main objective of the survey was to 'provide information for Professor R. Matthew's Belfast Regional Plan'.[187] The CCPR drew up 'a six point recommendation' which included 'a central sports stadium in the province, the immediate provision of 60 new soccer and 20 hockey pitches in the Belfast area and the improvement of existing playing areas in parks'. It was noted that 'the most obvious and most stark fact is the appalling state of the provision of soccer pitches both in quantity and quality'.[188] Wheatley added that immediate action had to be taken as 'patterns of education' were 'changing so rapidly' and since the 1900s little action had taken place 'in relation to the rise in population and the development of urban areas'.[189] Naturally, the findings were welcomed with 'widespread approval by officials of governing bodies of sport in Northern Ireland'.[190]

These developments were much slower than in some international countries where physical exercise was given more emphasis by governments such as the USA, where President Dwight D. Eisenhower had founded the President's Council on Youth Fitness and the Citizens Advisory Committee on the Fitness of American Youth in 1956 following concerns over the

183   Ibid., 30 March 1961.
184   Ibid.
185   Ibid.
186   Ibid., 18 October 1961.
187   Ibid.
188   Ibid.
189   Ibid.
190   Ibid.

fitness levels of Americans.[191] By 1962 the PE programme had been improved through President John F. Kennedy's fitness curriculum which was piloted in a number of states with fitness tests implemented and measurements utilised as opposed to those centred on play.[192] In Communist Russia, 'every organisation of 500 people or more' was said to have two PE specialists, while in France, the Government was set to build 500 gymnasiums throughout the country.[193] Progress in developing PE in Northern Ireland continued to reflect what was happening in the rest of the United Kingdom and while improvements were made in the subject's provision, concerns remained.

In May 1965, Wheatley, who was by then the secretary of the Northern Ireland branch of the CCPR, criticised the Government for 'its lack of interest in stimulating growth in sport and recreation'.[194] He also called for the Northern Ireland Youth and Sports Council 'to be reconstituted, so that its membership could be widened to admit people from all walks of life'.[195] This followed criticisms of the organisation from other quarters. In June 1962 the Northern Ireland Empire Games Council had expressed its dissatisfaction that that the formation of the new Youth and Sports Council was 'too similar to the old Youth Committee which disbanded in January'.[196] The vice-chairman of the Empire Games Council, Captain T. D. Morrison, stated that he could not 'understand why the Minister did not consult the two most important bodies in Ulster (sic) sport – the Central Council of Physical Recreation and the Empire Games Council'.[197]

Wheatley also noted in May 1965 how the Northern Ireland Youth and Sports Council had eighteen members 'drawn from the youth services

191   Gerald Gems, Linda J. Borish and Gertrud Pfister, *Sport in American History: From Colonization to Globalization* (Champaign: Human Kinetics, 2008), 274.
192   *Belfast Telegraph*, 23 January 1962 and Matthew T. Bowers and Thomas M. Hunt, 'The President's Council on Physical Fitness and the Systematisation of Children's Play in America' in *International Journal of the History of Sport*, vol. 28, no. 11 (2011), 1496–511, 1498–501.
193   *Belfast Telegraph*, 23 January 1962.
194   Ibid., 22 May 1965.
195   Ibid.
196   Ibid., 6 June 1962.
197   Ibid.

and sport' and advised the Minister of Education on sport but had 'only produced about two reports'.[198] It was also criticised by Captain T. D. Morrison, then chairman of the Empire Games Council, who felt that a body should be 'set up on the lines of the British Sports Council'.[199] Similarly, Brigadier R. J. Broadhurst, National Playing Fields representative, felt that it needed a professional staff as was in existence in Britain.[200] In August 1965, the Northern Ireland Youth and Sports Council was enlarged to twenty-four members.[201]

Wheatley continued his criticisms at a symposium entitled 'The changing face of physical education', which was arranged by the NIPEA and hosted in Queen's University in March 1966, when he stated that 'a more objective approach to recreational needs' was required.[202] He also stated that they needed 'to measure the balance of the costs of providing a scheme against the benefits of the community to be derived from it'.[203] In June 1966, it was reported that despite Belfast Education Authority having 'provided more outdoor recreational facilities during the past ten years than any other authority, the city' was still 50 per cent 'behind [the number of] facilities recommended by the Ministry of Education'.[204]

A working report on the curriculum in secondary schools, published in 1967, stated that while guidance should be given to pupils regarding how they used their leisure time, it was 'not implied that leisure training should now become a subject on the time-table, but rather that the whole curriculum should help young people to find worthwhile leisure activities'.[205] While the working party which compiled the report admitted that 'the best course of development is not yet clear enough to ask for any fixed pattern of provision' and a more detailed analysis would be needed, they felt

198   Ibid., 22 May 1965.
199   Ibid.
200   Ibid.
201   Ibid., 27 August 1965.
202   Ibid., 25 March 1966.
203   Ibid.
204   Ibid., 7 June 1966.
205   *The Curriculum of Secondary Schools: Report of Working Party* (Belfast: Her Majesty's Stationery Office, 1967), 17.

that 'in the meantime the Ministry and the education committees should look kindly upon any schemes presented to them and should seek ways of making financial assistance available in matters both great and small'.[206]

Some Education Committees did appoint PE organisers in an attempt to improve the subject's status within schools. In January 1967 Albert Lucas was appointed by County Antrim Education Committee as advisor for games and gym in schools in what was said to be a new post in the county.[207] Lucas was given the role of co-ordinating physical education teaching throughout the county and the promotion of inter-schools' competitions. One education spokesman stated that 'there already is cooperation ... but we want more'.[208] Like many other males involved in the subject in Northern Ireland, Lucas had gained his qualifications abroad, gaining a diploma in PE from Loughborough Training College and he was also a Fellow of the British Association for Physical Training.[209]

Major developments generally remained centred in Belfast and its surrounding areas. In August 1967, the Belfast Education Committee recommended installing swimming pools in a small number of secondary and primary schools in the city.[210] The committee intended that pools would be 'provided in extensions being planned in secondary schools to help cater for the raising of the school-leaving age to 16 in 1970' while they also felt their development would deter vandalism as they could be used by youth clubs after school.[211] In June 1968 the Belfast Education Authority hosted a water safety campaign week involving over 35,000 children, with schools also organising essay competitions, poster displays and quizzes based on this theme.[212] At the end of that month a 'Learn to Swim' week was held in Bangor, with five PE teachers giving free tuition to schoolchildren.[213]

206 Ibid., 57.
207 *Belfast Telegraph*, 2 January 1967.
208 Ibid.
209 Ibid.
210 Ibid., 18 August 1967.
211 Ibid.
212 Ibid., 4 June 1968.
213 Ibid., 29 June 1968.

Some efforts were made to improve PE teaching in the west of Northern Ireland. In July 1968, the Minister for Education from 1966 to 1968, Captain William Long, attended a course entitled 'Physical Education in the Primary School' which was held at Omagh Technical College.[214] Fifty teachers, mainly from County Tyrone, participated, with Anna Richmond, senior lecturer at the UCPE, Ruth Blackadder and Elizabeth Pottie tutoring the course.[215] The success of a few Ulster counties in All-Ireland Gaelic football competitions was portrayed by some sections of the press as being related to superior PE structures in schools in Northern Ireland. Following Tyrone's victory over Kerry in the 1967 All-Ireland Vocational Schools' final, a competition established early in that decade, one sports reporter was of the opinion that the system of 'physical education and physical training was taken far more seriously' in Northern Ireland than in the Republic of Ireland.[216] He also noted that Jim McKeever had become head of physical training at St Joseph's Training College in Belfast.[217] A college GAA club had played in the Antrim league but it was not until the 1964–5 season that a committee was elected there to run Gaelic games there while the building of a gym was also beneficial to its growth.[218] McAnallen et al have stated that the return of these graduates and their new expertise 'catalysed radical changes' for Gaelic football coaching in Ireland.[219] With the advent of PE teaching courses for males in Northern Ireland by the 1960s, PE-related migration to English colleges was not as necessary as it had been. As McKeever himself stated in 1969, altogether, St Joseph's and Stranmillis produced twenty qualified PE teachers every year although he was not entirely happy with the situation at primary school level as

214 *Ulster Herald*, 13 July 1968.
215 Ibid.
216 *The Kerryman*, 11 March 1961 and 3 June 1967.
217 Ibid., 3 June 1967.
218 Harry Chivers, 'St Joseph's Training College' in Seán McGettigan (ed.), *Ulster Games Annual 1966* (Belfast: Howard Publications, 1966), 33–4.
219 Dónal, McAnallen, Peter Mossey and Stephen Moore, 'The "Temporary Diaspora" at Play: The Development of Gaelic Games in British Universities' in *Sport and Society*, vol. 10. no. 3 (2007), 402–24, 409.

the teachers there were not specialists in PE, but plans were underway for courses to amend this.[220]

One journalist was of the view that these counties' successes were also related to 'the rapid growth of the intermediate schools' in Northern Ireland.[221] This meant that these schools had more PE instructors with regular classes taking place, while many of them were committed to Gaelic football.[222] He also noted that Down's success in winning three senior All-Ireland Gaelic football championships in the 1960s could be pinpointed to the rivalry between Newry schools St Colman's and Abbey CBS, with eleven of their panel products of these institutions in 1960.[223] He added that 'the mushroom growth of the Intermediate School System is well il-lustrated in the case of Tyrone' where 'all the main centres of population' had 'flourishing, fully-equipped Intermediate schools'.[224] Other sports also benefited. In 1970, one reporter linked the dominance of Ulster hockey over the rest of Ireland to the PE and coaching that was available in some schools in Northern Ireland, with fifteen of twenty-two players selected for an international senior trial in the spring of that year based in the prov-ince of Ulster.[225]

Naturally, these players were also involved in coaching, with many of them attending courses 'at the famed Orangefield Centre in Belfast' which had grown in reputation since courses were initiated there in the 1950s.[226] By the late 1960s, Residential Coaching courses organised and facilitated by the Belfast Education Authority and directed by R. H. Williams, were taking place annually each summer at secondary schools in Belfast such as Grosvenor High School and Orangefield Girls' Secondary School.[227] The organising committee included men from the GAA such as Jim McKeever and Alf Murray, although other sports such as table tennis, soccer, tennis,

220   *Irish Press*, 26 February 1969.
221   *Evening Herald*, 3 October 1968.
222   Ibid.
223   Ibid.
224   Ibid.
225   Ibid., 17 February 1970.
226   Ibid., 3 October 1968.
227   *Irish Press*, 6 July 1967.

basketball, netball, rugby and hockey were taught along with the GAA's codes.[228] A total of 1,200 pupils were said to be involved in 1967 with more regional schools also involved.[229]

However, while advances in PE made in Northern Ireland's schools were probably ahead of those in the Republic of Ireland at this point, the provision of resources and facilities for many school pupils remained insufficient as the decade drew to a close. In 1968, the Northern Ireland Youth and Sports Council reported that while progress had been made by education committee since the early 1960s, in relation to children's playgrounds, 'local education authorities could do more' and it was felt that they should ensure that school playgrounds were accessible outside of school hours, and that more play schemes should be available during school holidays.[230] It also recommended that playgrounds could be staffed for use after school, and that voluntary bodies could be assisted to run the playgrounds. It also felt that playground equipment should be more age-appropriate and that adventure playgrounds be provided.[231] The findings of *Primary Education in Northern Ireland: Report of Advisory Council for Education*, published in 1968, included recommendations that school authorities should assist in the improvement of school buildings, but the committee carried no concerns that PE itself was in need of more development.[232]

This lack of space was noticed by one PE teacher who attended school run by a religious order in Belfast throughout the 1960s.[233] However, he felt this had not affected the teaching he had been given in the subject, and recalled that in secondary school,

228 Ibid.

229 Ibid.

230 PRONI. LAI/3AL/6/3. *Government of Northern Ireland. Ministry of Education. Youth and Sports Council. Report for the period 1965 to 1968* (Belfast: Her Majesty's Stationery Office, 1968), 10.

231 Ibid.

232 *Primary Education in Northern Ireland: Report of Advisory Council for Education* (Belfast: Her Majesty's Stationery Office, 1968), 84–8, 85.

233 Interview with Northern Ireland second level PE teacher number three, 26 September 2019.

We would have had PE in those days twice a week. We would have had approximately two hours a week for physical education every week … we were really, really hampered by the space that we had. But then when you look at it and as I reflected in later years, it's not so much about the space it's about the people who are taking you that make the difference … as I look back now as a teacher myself, the standard of teaching plus the extra -curricular activities were exceptionally good. And I was fortunate to experience a wide range of physical activities which would have been unusual in the sense that most physical activities in those days would have would have centred on games only.[234]

PE in Schools and the Onset of the Troubles

The Catholic-led Civil Rights Movement of the late 1960s was not well received by many unionists and the related violence resulted in the establishment of the Provisional IRA and the deployment of British troops in Northern Ireland.[235] Over 3,500 people were killed between 1969 and 2001 as a result of a violent conflict the British security forces, loyalist paramilitaries and the Provisional IRA.[236] As Holt and Mason have stated, 'sport was profoundly affected by this climate of sectarian hate and violence' and 'instead of representing a national consensus, sport in Northern Ireland both reflected and exacerbated national divisions'.[237] The onset of the Troubles in 1968 and the arrival of British troops in Northern Ireland the following year had an impact on many schools. In August 1969 'several Belfast schools were temporarily occupied by either troops or homeless families but by mid-September all schools were operating normally'.[238] An emergency committee was established by the Ministry in August 'and maintained contact with local education authorities, voluntary school

---

234   Ibid.
235   Bartlett, *Ireland: A History*, 503–5.
236   'Malcolm Sutton. An Index of Deaths from the Conflict in Ireland' Retrieved from <https://cain.ulster.ac.uk/sutton/book/> [Accessed 2 December 2020].
237   Holt and Mason, *Sport in Britain 1945–2000*, 138.
238   *Primary Education in Northern Ireland: Report of Advisory Council for Education*, 85.

managers and teachers' organisations' and two central emergency offices were set up, one in Andersonstown for County Antrim Schools and the other for Belfast schools at the Belfast Education Committee's office.[239] It was reported that 'these offices provided information for parents, teachers and school authorities and were responsible for co-ordinating emergency arrangements'.[240]

These official views did not always reflect the opinions of PE teachers who were based in the city at that time. One former PE teacher who began his employment in a Belfast school in the early years of the Troubles naturally recalled it being 'a dangerous place'. They had to evacuate their swimming facility during bomb alerts and to provide the children with space blankets and take them to the designated safe space. Transport to their playing fields was also difficult, but they did travel to 'some of the worst areas' to play matches and 'were always able to keep sport going'.[241]

The Ministry of Education reported in 1970 that 'the impact of the civil disturbances of the past year on schools was not as serious as had at first been feared' although two schools in Belfast had been seriously physically damaged, these being Donegall Road Primary School and St Gall's Primary School.[242] In 1972 the Ministry stated that 'the operation of some schools was rendered difficult by the unsettled state of the country' as 'the movement of families from place to place produced unexpected fluctuations in enrolment with consequent dislocation of organisation and teaching'.[243] In addition, 'from areas where rioting was frequent there were reports that the children were at times unsettled and lethargic from lack of sleep and rest'.[244] Despite this, they also felt that 'only a small number of the schools

239 Ibid.
240 Ibid.
241 Interview with Northern Ireland second level PE teacher number four, 26 September 2019.
242 PRONI. SO/1A/542. Government of Northern Ireland Reports of the Ministry of Education. *Education in Northern Ireland in 1969* (Belfast: H.M. Stationary Office, 1970), 5.
243 PRONI. SO/1A/573. Government of Northern Ireland Reports of the Ministry of Education. *Education in Northern Ireland in 1971* (Belfast: H.M. Stationary Office, 1972), 9.
244 Ibid.

were affected in this way and in most work proceeded smoothly and peace-fully'.[245] However, as will be seen in Chapter 9, things were to get a lot worse.

Conclusion

By the middle of the 1950s, PE as a subject appeared to be on a relatively solid footing in many of Northern Ireland's schools, although conservative attitudes towards its place within the curriculum remained, particularly if its provision meant what were deemed to be 'additional' expenses had to be put aside for it. This was despite the efforts of Oonagh Pim to establish the female PE teacher as a specialised, professional educator and to move away from traditional notions about the subject's value. Male trainee teachers generally migrated to colleges in mainland Britain in order to earn full PE qualifications in this decade, and a shortage of teachers with a specialisation in the subject remained in some regional areas. By the summer of 1964, teaching jobs were said to be difficult to obtain in Belfast, according to a survey carried out by one Stranmillis College PE student.[246] In particular, students specialising in PE and art were finding it difficult to get work, with one student, Billy Ingram, stating that of ten PE graduates in his group, only three had managed to find jobs.[247] Ingram added that 'if anything, this teacher over-supply is going to increase as the intermediate school building programme nears completion'.[248]

The provision of summer courses and coaches for sports by the Belfast Educational Committee was an important outlet for teachers and pupils in the city, but sports facilities appear to have generally been insufficient for schoolchildren and teenagers there. This remained so despite the fact that throughout the 1960s, a number of new buildings for PE had been

---

245   Ibid., 9–10.
246   *Belfast Telegraph*, 4 June 1964.
247   Ibid.
248   Ibid.

completed in Belfast, but these were generally done to benefit third level students. In July 1966 the new Malone playing fields, part one of the new development of PE facilities at Queen's College, where a new PE Centre was being built, were opened.[249] In October 1966, the Stranmillis College Sports Centre at Shaw's Bridge, Belfast, was opened at a cost of £125,000.[250] By September 1968 work had begun on the £800,000 Queen's University PE Centre and Swimming Pool at Botanic Gardens.[251]

While the Wolfenden committee had noted the issue of facilities for recreation, their claims that the standard of PE in Northern Ireland was lower than in other parts of the UK put the yearly reports by the Ministry of Education into perspective, although naturally this state of affairs was refuted by a number of local educationalists. The decision highlighted by the Lockwood Report to develop a co-educational college for PE teachers was a major step in the provision of a teacher-training college for both male and female second level teachers in the subject, although at that point training was available at UCPE for women while a course for gaining qualifications in the teaching of physical education had also been made available at Stranmillis by the late 1950s.

Despite this progress, concerns remained that not enough was being done more broadly to improve standards of recreation. In October 1971, the Youth and Sports Council for Northern Ireland [SCNI] was reconstituted by the Minister for Education, Captain Long, in his second term in the role (1969–72).[252] In March 1972 it was announced that a new sports body representative of all sports organisations' governing bodies was to be established in Northern Ireland.[253] The beginning of the Troubles in the late 1960s naturally had an effect on Northern Ireland's schools, and increased security measures and heightened tensions within communities impacted upon physical education classes and the movement of school teams. With the introduction of direct rule from Westminster in March

---

249 *Belfast Telegraph*, 7 July 1966.
250 Ibid., 12 October 1966.
251 Ibid., 17 September 1968.
252 Ibid., 6 October 1971.
253 Ibid., 4 March 1972.

1972, 'the leading public responsibility for all things pertinent to physical education, sport and recreation fell within the remit of the Department of Education for Northern Ireland (DENI)'.[254] Chapter 8 examines developments within PE in the Republic of Ireland's schools from the mid-1960s until the opening of the NCPE in Limerick in 1973.

254   Sugden and Bairner, *Sport, Sectarianism and Society*, 97.

A Temporary Transformation: PE in the Republic of Ireland, 1966–1973

Introduction

This chapter assesses the development of physical education in the Republic of Ireland from 1966 until 1973. These were important years in the progress of the subject in Independent Ireland's schools and a number of key events which affected its status at both primary and second level took place in this short period. A significant initiative was the founding of the Physical Education Association of Ireland in 1967 and this became recognised by the Department of Education, the International Council on Health, Physical Education and Recreation [ICHPER] and the INTO.[1] In the summer of 1968, the eleventh annual ICHPER congress was held in St Patrick's Training College, Drumcondra and it served to highlight further, if any more evidence were needed, that Ireland's schools should become more aligned with the state of physical education on an international level.[2] This new era in secondary education, with 'free education' implemented in 1967, also saw funding applications for schools' sports facilities being encouraged by the Minister of Education (1968–9), Brian Lenihan, who had taken up this role in 1968 after the death of Donogh O'Malley (1966–8).[3] Community and comprehensive schools were also established towards the end of the decade.[4] A key development in State recognition towards sport was the appointment in 1969 of Robert Molloy

---

1   *Irish Press*, 3 January 1968.
2   Ibid., 20 July 1968.
3   Curran, *Irish Soccer Migrants*, 90.
4   Coolahan, *Towards the Era of Lifelong Learning*, 136–7.

as parliamentary secretary to the Minister of Education with a special responsibility for physical education, a new position.[5] The foundation of
a National Council for Sport and Physical Recreation or COSAC (An
Comhairle Sport agus Caitheamh Aimsire) in 1971 also illustrated that
more acknowledgement of the role played by sport in society was being
considered by the government.[6] The piloting of PE as a compulsory subject in the Revised Primary Schools Curriculum of 1971 gave the subject
more recognition.[7] These initiatives acknowledged the change in lifestyle
in 1970s Ireland.[8] Integration into the European Economic Community
would also bring challenges and Irish industry and education needed to
be prepared to meet this. These developments culminated in the opening
of the National College of Physical Education in Limerick for second
level trainee teachers in 1973 and this was a pivotal event in the future
training of PE teachers within the Republic of Ireland.[9]

Physical Education Teacher Training in the Late 1960s

Following the findings of the *Investment in Education* report, many of
which highlighted socio-economic inequalities within education, 'a
key policy was to encourage greater participation by pupils with widely
varying abilities and from diverse social backgrounds'.[10] With this in
mind, a free education scheme was introduced by Minister for Education,
Donogh O'Malley, in 1967, with enrolments increasing although the
school-leaving age was not raised to 15 years until 1972.[11] State-run comprehensive schools were first opened in 1966, and by the early 1970s

5   *Irish Press*, 10 July 1969.
6   *Evening Herald*, 23 January 1971.
7   *Irish Examiner*, 24 November 1971.
8   *Evening Herald*, 23 January 1971.
9   *Irish Examiner*, 2 June 1973.
10   Coolahan, *Towards the Era of Lifelong Learning*, 113–4.
11   Ibid., 114.

community schools were operational, while free buses became available for students living further than three miles from their schools.[12]

In March 1967 it was estimated that there were approximately 2,200 full-time lay secondary school teachers in the Republic of Ireland and these were 'divided equally between the sexes'.[13] The number of new teachers joining the profession annually was around 300, 'again divided almost equally'.[14] Minister O'Malley also noted at that time that there were 588 secondary schools with over 103,000 pupils, a huge increase from the figures from 1923–4, which saw only 23,000 pupils in 292 secondary schools.[15] The number of pupils in Vocational Schools had risen from 1,000 in 1930 to 30,000, but it was noted that 'still there were 17,000 children who would not receive any form of post-primary education unless it was provided free'.[16] With the expansion of the second level school system in the late 1960s more PE teachers were required.

Speaking in the Dáil in 2010, Captain McDonough stated that 'in 1965 when I was appointed by the Department of Education to be the first inspector of physical education, there was not much to inspect, except in the girls' schools, and so a development programme was required'.[17] In the years immediately after his appointment as PE inspector, a number of Department-backed courses were organised. In March 1966 it was announced that a Department of Education-run physical education course for male secondary school teachers, held over the duration of three weeks, would take place in July and August in the Dominican College, Newbridge.[18] Course information was sent to schools via a Department of Education circular with the aim 'to give each teacher a basic knowledge of the theoretical

12 Ibid., 136–7.
13 *Irish Farmers' Journal*, 25 March 1967.
14 Ibid.
15 Ibid.
16 Ibid.
17 'Joint Committee on Justice, Equality, Defence and Women's Rights Debate – Wednesday, 13 Jan 2010. Role of Defence Forces in Promoting Physical Fitness: Discussion.' Retrieved from <https://www.oireachtas.ie/en/debates/debate/joint_committee_on_justice_equality_defence_and_womens_rights/2010-01-13/2/> [Accessed 30 October 2020].
18 *Irish Press*, 22 March 1966 and *Munster Express*, 19 August 1966.

and practical aspects of a programme of physical education suitable for post-primary schools'.[19] It was stated in the press that 'the idea is to make a start in expanding the numbers in the country qualified to teach physical education'.[20] The *Irish Press* also noted that previous courses of that type had been run by voluntary organisations, stating that these were mainly focused on track and field. These included the NACA summer school of athletics, with the Willwood Foundation assisting in cooperation with the Council of Europe.[21] Facilities at the new course were provided by the Dominican fathers and army personnel.[22]

Having completed the programme, the forty male teachers who participated took on 'the work of organising physical education classes in the curriculum of their schools'.[23] The forty teachers were, one Department of Education spokesman felt, 'pioneers in the field' with Captain McDonough hoping that a PE training college for males would be established in the future, although he acknowledged that until then, they were reliant on 'these crash courses to enable a headstart to be made'.[24] Captain McDonough stated that the aim of the course was to give 'non-specialist teachers of physical education the philosophy of the subject, within the school curriculum'.[25]

By the following summer, Irish men interested in teaching PE generally still had to look abroad in order to find courses with full qualifications to teach the subject. In May 1967, males interested in becoming PE teachers were advised by one reporter to write to Loughborough Training College or St Mary's College, Strawberry Hill, Twickenham.[26] In addition, qualifications to teach PE could be obtained through study at Chester College; Carnegie College of Physical Education, Leeds; Borough Road College, Isleworth, Middlesex; City of Cardiff Training College; St Paul's College,

19   Department of Education Files. *Department of Education Circular. Summer Course in Physical Education*, Cir. 12/66.
20   *Irish Press*, 22 March 1966.
21   Ibid.
22   *Nationalist and Leinster Times*, 29 July 1966.
23   *Irish Independent*, 5 August 1966.
24   *Irish Press*, 4 August 1966.
25   Ibid.
26   *Irish Farmers' Journal*, 20 May 1967.

Cheltenham and St Luke's College's Exeter.[27] Female students could also apply for the UCPE courses in Belfast.[28] Some VECs again funded a small number of scholarships at English colleges. That same month, Dun Laoghaire Borough Vocational Education Committee decided to sponsor two teachers to attend Loughborough College, with one to participate in a summer course in Education Technology and the other to undertake a course in PE.[29]

At the beginning of June 1967, one *Irish Independent* journalist estimated that around fifty-five qualified teachers were awarded diplomas in PE from the private training colleges for the subject, Ling College and St Raphael's, every year.[30] PE was taught in 334 out of 588 secondary schools in the Republic of Ireland, and there were full-time qualified teachers for the subject in 21 out of 330 vocational schools. It was also stated that 'in the remainder, organised games and recreational activities form part of the extra-curricular activities'.[31] One PE teacher who was a pupil at a prestigious regional second level school at that time recalled that they mainly played Gaelic football as that was the school's tradition and they did not get a fully qualified PE teacher until his final years there, and they then took part in badminton, basketball and swimming.[32] From 1 August 1966, the Department of Education had recognised the Diploma of Ling College 'as an acceptable qualification for the purposes of placing the holder on the register of secondary teachers'.[33] Students were required to have obtained the Leaving Certificate examination by the time they began studying at Ling College.[34]

Some previously established courses continued during the summer months. In the summer of 1967, the Council of Europe Physical Education course for youth leaders, which was organised by the Irish Secondary

---

27 *Irish Independent*, 2 June 1967.
28 Ibid.
29 *Evening Herald*, 20 May 1967.
30 *Irish Independent*, 2 June 1967.
31 Ibid.
32 Interview with secondary school PE teacher, 29 August 2019.
33 *Irish Independent*, 2 June 1967.
34 Ibid.

Schools' Athletic Organisation and assisted by the Willwood Athletic Foundation, took place at Newman House, St Stephen's Green and at Marian College Baths, Ballsbridge.[35] The course consisted of coaching in athletics, swimming, canoeing, life-saving and other sports and was attended by twenty-three pupils who were representative of the Army, schools and clubs as well as Urs Weber of the Swiss Federal School of Gymnastics and a number of other coaches and lecturers from Ireland.[36] By 1968, 'special in-service training courses' in PE were being held for primary and second level teachers each summer.[37]

The Foundation of the PEAI and Dublin's Hosting of the ICHPER Congress

Towards the end of the decade, a number of significant events took place which benefited PE's status in the Republic of Ireland by raising awareness of the need for Irish schools to fall into line with its provision elsewhere. The Physical Education Association of Ireland was founded on 17 September 1967 and became recognised by the Department of Education, ICHPER and the INTO.[38] The PEAI was open to PE teachers registered with the Department of Education.[39] Joe Lennon was elected as president of the PEAI at one of their first meetings in January 1968, while Mona Wren, senior lecturer at St Raphael's Physical Education College, Sion Hill, became vice-president.[40] Along with the appointment of a secretary, treasurer and PRO, there was also a general committee formed along with

35   Ibid., 16 June 1967.
36   Ibid., and *Irish Press*, 5 July 1967.
37   'Dáil Éireann Debate – Thursday, 7 Nov 1968. Vol. 236. No. 14. Ceisteanna – Questions. Oral Answers. – Physical Training in Schools.' Retrieved from <https://www.oireachtas.ie/en/debates/debate/dail/1968-11-07/65/> [Accessed 2 November 2020].
38   *Irish Press*, 3 January 1968.
39   *Irish Independent*, 13 January 1968.
40   *Sunday Independent*, 14 January 1968 and *Irish Independent*, 18 January 1968.

a sub-committee for the forthcoming ICHPER congress at St Patrick's College, with Joe Lennon coordinator of the latter group.[41] In April 1968 the PEAI helped organise a two-day PE seminar in Galway for teachers in conjunction with the Department of Education with eighty teachers participating.[42] Following another course in December 1968, a Connacht Branch of the PEAI was formed.[43] The PEAI had also organised a similar event in Cork in April 1968 and a Munster branch of the organisation was established.[44] By February 1969 the PEAI had 270 full and associate members and one reporter noted how 'much of the energy of the association is devoted to lobbying, in the vital quarters, for more recognition' for the subject in the Republic of Ireland and to try and get a men's PE college established.[45]

The state of PE as a subject in the Republic of Ireland's schools was put into context at the ICHPER congress, which was held in St Patrick's Training College, Drumcondra in July 1968.[46] Representatives from more than 100 nations were in attendance, with the event hosted by the then newly formed PEAI.[47] The congress was officially opened by the Minister for Health, Seán Flanaghan, on 17 July and lasted for five days, and it brought delegates from as far away as Japan, with Dr Roger Bannister amongst the speakers.[48] The theme of the Congress was 'Developing Leadership in Health, Physical Education and Recreation – a universal need'.[49] The congress was the first of five world congresses related to the teaching profession to take place in Dublin that week. It was presided over by Sir Ronald Gould, the president of the World Confederation of Organisations of the Teaching Profession.[50]

41   *Irish Independent*, 18 January 1968.
42   *Tuam Herald*, 30 March 1968.
43   *Connacht Tribune*, 27 December 1968.
44   *Connacht Sentinel*, 9 April 1968 and *Irish Examiner*, 18 and 26 April 1968.
45   *Irish Press*, 27 February 1969.
46   *Sunday Press*, 7 July 1968 and *Sunday Independent*, 7 July 1968.
47   *Sunday Press*, 7 July 1968.
48   Ibid. and *Irish Press*, 8 July 1968.
49   *Sunday Press*, 7 July 1968.
50   Ibid.

At the ICHPER Congress, Sir Ronald Gould urged PE experts 'to press for the development of health, physical education and recreational facilities' and emphasised the need for people to be more physically active in the modern world.[51] Minister Flanaghan stated that every child should have access to 'a competent physical education' which would enable them to live a full life and to educate them on having a proper sense of leisure.[52] He also felt that participation of children in physical exercise was more important than success. The president of the organisation's International Council, Dr Julien L. Falize, stated that 'physical education was now accepted as a universal need in all countries' and a competent physical education teacher needed to be knowledgeable about applied anatomy, physiology, psychology, economics and sociology. This, he added, 'was a far cry from the old concept of merely doing physical exercises'.[53] Demonstrations of PE in Ireland were given by students of Ling College and Scoil Lorcain, Ballyfermot, and a number of delegates were received by the president of the Republic of Ireland, Eamon de Valera, at Áras an Uachtaráin.[54]

At the Congress, the *ICHPER Questionnaire Report 1967–1968* was presented and discussed, with the *Irish Press* noting how Ireland had 'emerged rather badly' from its findings.[55] Published in cooperation with UNESCO, this was 'a survey report of teacher training practices in physical education around the world' and was 'one of three studies first carried out by ICHPER in 1963'.[56] The report had been planned through resolutions passed by the World Confederation of Organisations of the Teaching Profession, which was of the view that all schools should have 'an adequate programme of physical education' in order 'to improve their physical and mental health and their social adjustment'.[57] In addition, they felt that teachers ought to receive sufficient training to carry out their responsibilities. The report

---

51   *Irish Press*, 18 July 1968.
52   Ibid.
53   Ibid.
54   Ibid. 20 July 1968.
55   Ibid.
56   *ICHPER Questionnaire Report. Part II. 1967–1968 Revision. Teacher Training for Physical Education* (Washington, DC: ICHPER, 1968), iv.
57   Ibid.

was compiled through consultation with administrators in fifty-one countries, and was revised in 1967, with information gathered from seventy-two countries.[58]

Part of the report featured an analysis of resources available, with fifty countries reporting that trainee PE students had access to library resources[59] Thirty-one countries stated that research took place in institutions where teachers of physical education were trained.[60] Nineteen countries noted that they had adequate facilities for physical training, with others identifying issues such as a lack of properly equipped gymnasiums and an absence of swimming facilities including showers and changing rooms.[61] The Republic of Ireland's information was submitted by Sister Mary Rose Catherine O'Nolan of St Raphael's College of Physical Education and Edith Hudson of Ling Physical Training College.[62] They reported that library resources for physical education students were 'limited' and that there were no research facilities. In addition, training facilities were said to 'lack space, playing fields and showers'.[63] They also noted how 'the individual college body has the responsibility for the planning of teacher training programs for physical education teachers'.[64] Trainee teachers undertaking the course in PE at all levels were required to gain a Diploma in the subject.[65]

Joe Lennon stated that the PEAI received correspondence each week from males wanting to become PE teachers, but regretted that they had to be directed overseas.[66] He added that it was 'time that we seriously considered that we have a pressing need for specialists and a demand for their services' and he hoped to see a faculty for PE developed in an Irish university.[67] Lennon, the Director of Physical Education at the Franciscan College in

58 Ibid.
59 Ibid., 102.
60 Ibid.
61 Ibid.
62 Ibid., 117.
63 Ibid., 104.
64 Ibid., 50.
65 Ibid., 51.
66 *Irish Press*, 20 July 1968.
67 Ibid. and *Irish Examiner*, 23 July 1968.

Gormanston, and a Down Gaelic football star, was, as noted, chairman of a committee helping to organise the event.[68] He had trained to become a PE teacher at Padgate College, Warrington before being appointed to the staff of Gormanston College and in 1964 had overseen the first national coaching course in Gaelic football, which took place at the Meath venue.[69]

Lennon felt that the ICHPER congress marked the dawn of 'a new and exciting phase in the history of PE' in Ireland and stated that they would do all they could to 'redress the imbalance' in the Republic of Ireland's education system by making sure that the subject became 'an integral part' of the education of Irish society for students and adults.[70] At the close of the ICHPER congress, Captain McDonough was presented with a plaque by the world organisation for his services to PE in Ireland and the PEAI was accepted as a member of the Council's International Executive.[71] The INTO also hosted a six-day seminar in Limerick at the same time as the ICHPER conference, entitled 'Primary Education in a European Context', illustrating a growing awareness of the need to develop a less insular attitude towards PE and other non-core subjects.[72]

Governmental Attitudes towards Physical Education

In April 1968, Minister for Education, Brian Lenihan, promised grants for gymnasium and playground equipment in primary schools while secondary schools were also eligible to apply for funding and building assistance.[73] The Department of Education again backed a number of ad hoc training courses that year. They organised a non-residential course for

68   *Irish Independent*, 18 December 1967.
69   McAnallen et al., 'The "Temporary Diaspora" at Play', 409.
70   *Irish Press*, 23 July 1968.
71   *Irish Examiner*, 23 July 1968 and *Irish Press*, 23 July 1968.
72   *Evening Herald*, 15 July 1968.
73   'Dáil Éireann Debate – Tuesday, 2 Apr 1968. vol. 233. no. 11. Ceisteanna – Questions. Oral Answers. – Physical Education in Schools.' Retrieved from <https://www.oireachtas.ie/en/debates/debate/dail/1968-04-02/35/> [Accessed 2 November 2020].

fifty post-primary male and female physical education teachers from 22 July to 2 August 1968 at St Michael's College, Ailesbury Road, Dublin.[74] A focus was placed on gymnastics and games while courses organised by Bórd Lúthchleas na hÉireann (The Athletics Board of Ireland), the Leinster branch of the Irish Rugby Football Union and the Irish Red Cross Society that year were also associated with the Department's course. This linkage was in the form of 'special lectures in the theory of physical education' which were given at these courses by the staff on the Department's own course.[75] The Department also recognised two GAA courses held at Gormanston College in July and August 1968 with special lectures dealing with PE included.[76]

Government attitudes towards sport hardened, however. In November 1968, when challenged in the Dáil about the need to set up a government commission to investigate Ireland's failure to win any medals at that year's Olympics in Mexico, the Taoiseach, Jack Lynch, stated that it was not necessary to win medals to gain honour and he refuted the claims of deputies P. G. Reynolds and Gerry L'Estrange that there was 'significant public disquiet on the subject'.[77] He felt they had 'initiated a progressive programme for PE in the Department of Education which he hoped would be effective in the long run' and that there would be no point in launching any investigation until the differences between the GAA and other sporting bodies were eradicated.[78] This was a similar argument used by Seán Lemass while Taoiseach.[79]

In January 1969, Lynch, in dealing with a resolution in the Dáil which called for the establishment of a Department of Sport within the government, stated that 'there seemed to be no demand from the public that the State should take over control of sport' and that it should be left to organisations responsible for it.[80] Lynch again noted that there were difficulties in

---

74 *Department of Education Archives. Department of Education Circular, Summer Courses on Physical Education.* Cir. 19/68.
75 Ibid.
76 *Irish Independent*, 12 June 1968.
77 *Irish Examiner*, 7 November 1968.
78 Ibid.
79 *Irish Press*, 8 November 1968.
80 *Irish Independent*, 30 January 1969.

administrating sporting jurisdictions and that some organisations did not recognise each other, with athletics cited as an example, while the GAA's 'Ban' on its members taking part in 'foreign games' was also mentioned. He again refuted the idea that Ireland's athletes had performed poorly at the 1968 Olympics and stated that they had 'acquitted themselves, by and large, very, very well'.[81] While admitting that successive governments had not done enough to encourage physical training in schools, he stated that 'a start has been made' and highlighted that there was now 'a special unit in the Department responsible for physical education in schools at all levels'.[82]

He also noted that he would encourage the Minister for Education 'to do everything possible to expand physical training in the schools'.[83] He also reaffirmed the line that if Ireland's sporting organisations were to 'agree on some form of liaison between them' so that the Government could justify allocating funds and giving assistance to different sports, then they would give financial and administrative assistance.[84] Lynch felt that, for example, the Government could not provide funding for a stadium for one sports organisation, as there would be difficulties with 'exclusive use'.[85] This attitude can be compared to a number of other European countries' funding of sport in that decade as some of these were more aware of the value of sport's role in general well-being and in boosting national pride and identity on an international scale. In 1960 Norway, a country with a population of 3.5 million, which was slightly higher than that of the Republic of Ireland at that time (2.8 million in 1961), gave almost half a million pounds directly to sports organisations through the State, while Finland, which had a population of around 4.5 million, contributed £890,000 to help sport through football pools.[86] In addition, through the CCPR in Britain, half

---

81   Ibid.
82   Ibid.
83   Ibid.
84   Ibid.
85   Ibid.
86   'Census 1961 Volume 1 – Population, Area and Valuation of Each DED and Each Larger Unit of Area' Retrieved from <https://www.cso.ie/en/media/csoie/census/census1961results/volume1/C_1961_VOL_1_T1.pdf> [Accessed 6 October 2020] and *Irish Press*, 28 February 1969.

a million pounds was made available to sporting organisations, while in West Germany, £11 million pounds was given to sport organisations.[87]

A New Training College for PE and Related Developments

Journalists continued in their efforts to push for more governmental recognition of sport. In February 1969, Seán Diffley of the *Irish Press* wrote a number of articles on PE and the state of sport in Ireland. He noted that 'our interests, on the whole, are on winning and losing, but we do not really appreciate the value of sport or its place in our educational and social activities'.[88] In addition, he felt that the public were failing to push for more emphasis on developing sport within society:

> Above all, we have the poorest facilities for sport in Europe and no government aid. And worst of all there is no real demand that the government should help develop sport and when the Taoiseach gave his reasons recently why the government did not intend to do anything, his line of reasoning was accepted almost without a murmur.[89]

On a more positive note, it was announced in February 1969 that the Republic of Ireland was to get a new training college for PE, as part of a new Higher Education institute in Limerick.[90] Minister for Education, Brian Lenihan, stressed that the new PE college would help develop the standard of the subject in the Irish educational system, while he also planned that the new syllabus would be introduced in September 1969, and would also allow more emphasis to be placed on PE.[91] Diffley felt that 'PE has been almost totally absent from most primary schools due to two factors – lack of trained teachers and an over-constricted curriculum'.[92] However, with the removal of the Primary Certificate in 1967,

87   *Irish Press*, 28 February 1969.
88   Ibid.
89   Ibid.
90   *Irish Press*, 22 February 1969 and *Irish Independent*, 2 May 1969.
91   *Irish Press*, 4 March 1969.
92   Ibid.

the Intermediate Certificate became the first examination, with Minister Lenihan of the view that this would lead to more flexibility.[93] The Department of Education also had plans for 'crash courses' in PE for primary schools 'to try and get as high a proportion as possible of the present teachers to gain additional qualifications'.[94] Although there were PE specialists in St Patrick's College Drumcondra with Commandant O'Keeffe still present there and Liam Dugdale based at Mary Immaculate College in Limerick, the Department of Education intended to increase efforts to aid the teaching of PE at primary level through these additional courses.[95]

While noting Captain McDonough's appointment as Inspector of PE in the Schools, the reporter also gave a contrast in stating that the Scottish county of Renfrewshire alone had five inspectors of this type.[96] He also stated that 'many have felt that it was only the spirited lobbying of a comparatively small body of PE teachers, trained in England for the most part, which had managed to prod the Department into making a progressive move'.[97] In addition, the Department of Education was now encouraging applications from schools for building gymnasia and the laying of pitches as physical education was set to become a compulsory subject in the primary and post-primary schools from September 1969 onwards, although this took longer than was anticipated.[98] Minister Lenihan stated that he would welcome any suggestions on PE and noted how the Department of Education had recently become more involved in running coaching courses in cooperation with governing bodies of sport such as the GAA and the Irish Rugby Football Union.[99] Later that year, they also recognised a soccer coaching course for secondary school teachers which was run by the Irish Universities and Colleges Football Union, with a lecturer from the Department sent to discuss 'educational aspects of soccer and sport in general'.[100]

93   Ibid. and Coolahan, *Towards the Era of Lifelong Learning*, 121.
94   *Irish Press*, 4 March 1969.
95   Ibid.
96   Ibid., 25 February 1969.
97   Ibid.
98   Ibid.
99   Ibid.
100   *Irish Independent*, 21 June 1969.

Diffley noted that while progress had been made in the gaining of recognition of qualifications for female physical education teachers, 'when PE teacher training really gets off the ground both Sion Hill and Ling may be faced with the task of enlarging their training facilities'.[101] This was backed up by Edith Hudson, the principal of Ling College, who stated that in the past five years more jobs had become available and there were fewer girls emigrating to teach PE abroad, while in 1968 there were 100 applications for the twenty-five course places at St Raphael's, with a maximum of seventy-four students catered for each year.[102] By 1969 St Raphael's College of Physical Education at Sion Hill had the capacity for eighty-one students and had 121 graduates at this point.[103] Although Sister Mary Rose Catherine O'Nolan was still the principal there, 'the PE expert' was said to be the aforementioned Mona Wren, who had spent three years teaching in Switzerland after becoming a physical education teacher and became vice-principal of St Raphael's in 1957.[104]

Diffley felt that providing male PE teachers was going to 'remain an acute problem for a few years more'.[105] While some men such as GAA player Joe Lennon, rugby international Johnny Moroney and triple jumper Seán O'Dwyer had gone to England to train to become PE teachers, the decision of the British government that 'a prospective PE student must, in future be three years resident in Britain before being eligible for positions in English training colleges' was going to cause difficulties for those from Ireland.[106] Diffley noted that the Department of Education would have 'to grant some kind of scholarship to suitable candidates to enable them to qualify for England' as it would be 'at least three years before the first graduates of the college in Limerick emerge'.[107] As will be shown below, the Department of Education did take concrete action in regard to scholarships later that year.

101   *Irish Press*, 25 February 1969.
102   Ibid., 27 February 1969.
103   Ibid.
104   Ibid.
105   Ibid., 25 February 1969.
106   Ibid.
107   Ibid.

Vocational Education Committees and Physical Education Teaching

The appointment of teachers in the Republic of Ireland's vocational schools continued to be hampered by difficulties surrounding qualifications. In July 1968, Sligo VEC advertised the position of a permanent, full-time PE organiser.[108] However, some traditional attitudes towards the subject's role in schools were slow to die away, with two members of the same committee 'strongly' opposing a request from the headmaster of Ballymote Vocational School 'to sanction expenditure of approximately £500 on the provision of a games court and paths at the school'.[109] These were the chairman, Rt. Rev. Mgr. P. J. Roughneen, PP, VF, and Mr J. Flanagan.[110] It was noted that

> The chairman said that he was not in favour of providing playgrounds at the ratepayers' expense when they would be used for only an hour or so each day. The pupils had football fields and parks in which to play if they wanted and he thought schooltime was for schooling and not for playing. If they wanted to play, they could play as they had done in the old days.[111]

Although the proposal was later passed, it illustrates the difficulties in gaining support for physical exercise in some areas.[112] Some other county VECs, such as that in Laois, struggled to obtain qualified physical education instructors, while the Tralee VEC suggested sending Kerry GAA star Mick O'Connell to England to gain the qualifications needed, having failed to obtain a candidate for the position of physical education instructor in September 1967.[113] By March 1969, the Mayo VEC had advertised the position of PE instructor for a year and had been unable to get a suitable applicant.[114] In May 1969, at the Irish Vocational Education

---

108   *Sunday Independent*, 11 August 1968.
109   *Sligo Champion*, 1 November 1968.
110   Ibid.
111   Ibid.
112   *Western People*, 9 November 1968.
113   *Evening Herald*, 29 September 1967 and *Leinster Express*, 16 November 1968.
114   *Connaught Telegraph*, 6 March 1969.

Association's annual congress, following proposals from County Waterford VEC, some delegates 'called on the Department of Education to recognise that qualifications in physical education available to army PT instructors be recognised as qualifications of diploma level for male teachers of physical education'.[115] The following month, Westmeath VEC were told by the Department of Education that they could not appoint Dublin Gaelic footballer Mickey Whelan as PE instructor without him having the required qualifications.[116] Whelan later emigrated to the United States of America where he became a Hall of Fame awardee for his soccer performances at Westchester Community College. He also undertook a postgraduate degree in PE and biology at Davis and Elkins College in West Virginia following his undergraduate studies.[117] The Donegal VEC also found that five applicants for the position of full-time teacher of PE were not eligible on a full-time basis, with the result that one man was re-appointed on a temporary basis in the summer of 1969.[118]

The development of PE in vocational schools was also hampered by other issues. The Department of Education failed to sanction the building of a gymnasium block at Athenry Technical School in May 1969, a move that drew protest from the Galway VEC.[119] A similar situation occurred later that year in Carlow, with plans for a gymnasium which had been drawn up by the Carlow VEC deemed unacceptable by the Inspector of Physical Education, Captain McDonough.[120] The Department had also rejected plans for school gymnasiums in County Monaghan, with the Monaghan Education Committee's CEO of the opinion that 'the Department seemed to be awaiting the outcome of an experiment in the matter of providing gymnasia'.[121] In addition, in November 1969 Longford VEC noted that there were no playing facilities in three of their technical schools despite a

115 *Irish Press*, 30 May 1969.
116 *Westmeath Examiner*, 21 June 1969.
117 *Westmeath Examiner*, 1 November 1969; *Irish Press*, 23 May 1972 and *Irish Times*, 22 April 2009.
118 *Donegal News*, 19 July 1969.
119 *Tuam Herald*, 31 May 1969.
120 *Nationalist and Leinster Times*, 19 September 1969.
121 *Anglo-Celt*, 28 November 1969.

new timetable for physical education and games being drafted.[122] In January 1971 the Carlow VEC claimed in the local press that they had not received a reply from the Department of Education in relation to their proposal to develop physical education facilities in Tullow and Bagenalstown Technical Schools.[123] Similar concerns were expressed in the provincial press that sufficient PE facilities should be provided in schools so that a wider range of sports could be taught.[124]

The need for PE instructors to obtain a Ceard Teastas remained problematic in some second level schools and many teachers' careers were hindered by the Department of Education's regulation that PE teachers needed to have this certification to teach the subject in a full-time capacity.[125] Waterford VEC made representations to the Department of Education in January 1971 to have their physical education instructor, Jack Frazer of Tallow, recognised as 'a permanent whole-time member of the staff'.[126] Frazer had been a member of the Waterford VEC's teaching staff since 1954 but could not gain this recognition as he did not have a satisfactory level of Irish.[127] Charles Curran of the Waterford VEC described him as 'an outstanding teacher' and stated that his treatment by the Department of Education was 'morally wrong' and 'inhuman' just because Frazer did not possess a Ceard Teastas.[128] However, in April 1971 the Department of Education informed them that Frazer would not gain the recognition they desired as he had not passed the Ceard Teastas examination and 'on the grounds that he lacked the requisite qualifications in physical education'.[129] The Waterford VEC in turn condemned the decision and decided to write to the Department and ask them to define what qualifications were needed

122 *Longford Leader*, 1 November 1969.
123 *Nationalist and Leinster Times*, 1 and 8 January 1971.
124 See, for example, *Donegal News*, 6 February 1971 and *Westmeath Examiner*, 6 February 1971.
125 *Southern Star*, 3 October 1970.
126 *Waterford News and Star*, 22 January 1971.
127 *Irish Examiner*, 16 February 1971.
128 Ibid.
129 *Waterford News and Star*, 23 April 1971.

to teach PE at that level other than having the Ceard Teastas, which appears to have been unclear at that time.[130]

A New Governmental Position for PE: The Appointment of Robert Molloy

Despite these grievances, another positive development was the formation of a new governmental position related to PE. In June 1969, prior to the General Election, Minister for Finance, Charles Haughey, announced that £100,000 was to be given to 'organisations catering for outdoor activities and sport'.[131] After this election, 32-year-old Robert Molloy became parliamentary secretary to the Minister of Education with a special responsibility for physical education, a new position.[132] Galway native Molloy was described as 'an all-round sportsman' who had represented Connacht in rowing and swimming and was a director in his family's wholesale business.[133] In September 1969 he confirmed that the majority of the £100,000 would be spent on youths and on those working with them.[134] In August 1969, he met with the British Minister for Sport, Denis Howell, to discuss the accommodation of Irish PE trainee students in physical education institutions in Britain.[135] As a result of these talks, it was arranged that a number of these men would be accepted in St Mary's College, Strawberry Hill, with scholarships covering travel, accommodation, tuition and other expenses to be provided by the Department of Education for a selection of applicants.[136] The following month, advertisements regarding the scholarships appeared in the Irish national press.

130   Ibid.
131   *Irish Press*, 14 June 1969.
132   Ibid., 10 July 1969 and *Connacht Tribune*, 11 July 1969.
133   *Irish Press*, 10 July 1969.
134   Ibid., 27 September 1969.
135   *Irish Examiner*, 12 August 1969 and *Connacht Sentinel*, 12 August 1969.
136   *Irish Examiner*, 16 August 1969.

Applicants could apply for a 'one-year specialist course' whereby they could obtain 'a college certificate in physical education' but they needed to already have 'a university degree or be qualified under Memorandum V7 of the Department of Education (Technical Instruction Branch)'.[137] There was also a course entitled 'Advanced course in Physical Education' which was for the duration of four years with applicants required to be at least eighteen years old by October 1969, and to have obtained at least a 'C' grade in Leaving Certificate honours Irish and a minimum of one other subject.[138] Those undertaking the latter course were expected to spend the first two years in England and the remainder completing it in Ireland when the new institution for physical education was established.[139] As a result of the first competitions, fifteen students were chosen for the four-year course and five for that of one year.[140]

Among those selected were Galway Gaelic footballer Liam Sammon, an All-Ireland winner, and a number of minor level intercounty players.[141] Sammon had completed a degree at University College Galway and had attended secondary school at St Mary's College, Galway.[142] Others to travel to London to undertake the course included Cork players Billy Morgan and Kevin Kehilly.[143] This arrangement drew complaints from women, with one student writing to the *Sunday Independent* to state that no scholarships were available to females who wanted to pursue a career in PE teaching.[144] By the autumn of 1971 there were thirty-nine male students from Ireland undertaking the PE course at Strawberry Hill.[145] When questioned about this in the Dáil, Deputy Molloy stated that his Department 'had no control

137 *Sunday Independent*, 17 August 1969.
138 Ibid.
139 Ibid. and *Irish Examiner*, 13 September 1969.
140 *Irish Examiner*, 13 September 1969.
141 *Connacht Sentinel*, 16 September 1969 and *Irish Press*, 20 September 1969. See also McAnallen et al., 'The "Temporary Diaspora" at Play', 410.
142 *Connacht Sentinel*, 19 January 1971.
143 *Irish Examiner*, 21 January 1971.
144 *Sunday Independent*, 12 October 1969.
145 Ibid., 10 October 1971.

over the girls' colleges' in the Republic of Ireland but that they were in the process of developing a new college.[146]

In January 1970 Robert Molloy noted that it was an ambition of the Department of Education that 'to have physical education in all schools and to have trained qualified teachers in all post-primary schools'.[147] The same month, it was announced that PE courses would be held in Dublin, Dundalk, Cork, Galway, Sligo and Limerick with a view to familiarising teachers with PE under the new curriculum.[148] An eight-week course for teachers of infants to second class was to begin in January while an eleven week course for teachers of senior classes was to start in April. The Dublin courses were based in Mourne Road, Foxrock and Navan Road.[149] There were two course venues in Cork and activities there were to be supervised by Liam Dugdale, senior lecturer in physical education, Mary Immaculate Training College, Limerick, and Sylvia Lee-Doyle, who had gained a first class honours diploma in the subject at St Raphael's College.[150] In addition, weekend seminars were scheduled as part of each course.[151] Training was to be held on one night a week for the nineteen weeks and it was estimated that around 800 teachers participated with courses oversubscribed.[152] The key themes covered included educational gymnastics, national and creative dance, minor and major games and outdoor activities.[153] Following concerns raised by Waterford Corporation that no course was to be held in their county, Robert Molloy stated that he hoped to organise one the following year but it depended on the availability of a suitable PE lecturer.[154] By the

146   'Dáil Éireann Debate – Thursday, 20 Nov 1969. Vol. 242. No. 9. Ceisteanna – Questions. Oral Answers. – Physical Training in Schools.' Retrieved from <https://www. oireachtas.ie/en/debates/debate/dail/1969-11-20/57/> [Accessed 2 November 2020].

147   *Irish Independent*, 8 January 1970.

148   *Irish Examiner*, 1 January 1970 and *Connacht Sentinel*, 6 January 1970.

149   *Irish Press*, 13 January 1970.

150   *Irish Examiner* 1 and 23 January 1970 and *Irish Independent*, 5 January 1970.

151   *Connacht Sentinel*, 6 January 1970.

152   *Irish Examiner*, 23 January 1970.

153   *Connacht Sentinel*, 27 January 1970.

154   *Irish Examiner*, 29 April 1970.

end of January 1970, the Department of Education was said to have established a physical recreation centre, with Tony Daly in charge.[155]

Not everyone was happy to see PE become more prominent in the schools' curriculum, with one GAA delegate at the Donegal County Board's annual congress in the spring of 1970 concerned that it would replace the Gaelic games (see Figures 32 and 33) in some schools. He stated that 'we must see to it that PE is used to supplement and not supplant the Gaelic games in our schools'.[156] He also felt that Donegal's schools needed more playing pitches.[157] This reflected wider concerns, with the outgoing president of the GAA, Seamus Ó Riain, stating in March 1970 that 'the five-day school week and the extension of physical education had posed problems in relation to GAA games' and that they had discussed this with Robert Molloy.[158] Ó Riain felt that 'nothing could be allowed to interfere with the progress of Gaelic games in the schools and colleges, and the Association had a responsibility to ensure that every assistance was given to the teachers who were so deeply dedicated to the Association'.[159] In turn, the GAA itself received criticism for restricting the access of non-members to its playing fields, with the matter debated at a meeting of the Vocational Education Association in Galway in May 1970.[160]

In February 1970 Robert Molloy announced that he was discussing the prospect of establishing a National Council for Youth and Sport with a number of sporting organisations.[161] He added that the scholarship system was a success and that it would be continued until the new college for PE was opened.[162] Part of the budget of £100,000 allocated towards sport had also been spent on scholarships at St Mary's Physical Education College in London.[163] However, it appears that the Republic of Ireland's two female

155   *Irish Press*, 24 January 1970.
156   *Donegal Democrat*, 6 February 1970.
157   Ibid.
158   *Irish Examiner*, 30 March 1970.
159   Ibid.
160   Ibid., 25 May 1970.
161   Ibid., 17 February 1970.
162   Ibid.
163   *Irish Press*, 24 July 1970.

Figure 32. A vocational schools' Gaelic football match in Breffni Park, Cavan, 1969. Courtesy of John McConnell.

physical education colleges, Ling and St Raphael's, still received little State assistance. Ling had eighty-three students while St Raphael's had eighty by the beginning of 1970, but 'a lack of proper facilities' was given as the reason the numbers were kept down at that level, with Ling receiving applications from 150 ladies in 1969 but only thirty-four could be accepted for first year.[164] The head of the Department of Education's new centre for Physical Recreation, Tony Daly, confirmed at that time that 'the £100,000 is earmarked for the development of youth and sport and any financial help which these colleges would receive will have to come from another source'.[165] This came despite Robert Molloy meeting with the principal of Ling, Edith Hudson, and the principal of Sion Hill, Sister Bede, with the parliamentary secretary promising to look into the matter.[166] In particular,

164   *Irish Independent*, 28 January 1970.
165   Ibid.
166   Ibid.

Figure 33. St Eunan's College Letterkenny, winners of the Ulster Herald Cup in 1969.
Courtesy of John McConnell.

Mrs Hudson stated that Ling needed modernising and that girls were being turned away from their physical education course at a time when there was a shortage of physical education teachers.[167] Both colleges relied fully on student fees.[168]

O'Donoghue et al have noted that Ling differed to St Raphael's in that the teaching of Catholic religious doctrine was mandatory in the latter, where there was more focus on 'child-centred educational gymnastics and educational dance'.[169] By November 1970 both colleges had agreed to cease operations when the NCPE at Limerick was 'in full swing', with both males and females to be trained in PE there.[170] The new college was to be staffed by some of those trained at St Mary's College at Strawberry Hill

167   Ibid.
168   Ibid.
169   O'Donoghue, Harford and O'Doherty, *Teacher Preparation in Ireland*, 113–14.
170   *Irish Examiner*, 7 November 1970.

and accommodation was to be provided for approximately 400 students. The course would be of four years' duration.[171] In September 1971, it was announced by the Department of Education that students of Ling College and St Raphael's would be eligible for grants of up to £175 along with those from a number of other teacher-training colleges.[172] Previously, this had only been available to university students although the trainee teacher grant applicants were required to have at least four 'C' honours grades in their Leaving Certificate and also needed to undertake a means test.[173]

In May 1970 Robert Molloy was appointed Minister for Local Government.[174] He was replaced in his former role by Tipperary-born Michael O'Kennedy, who noted in July 1970 that negotiations were underway to obtain a site for the NCPE in Limerick, with a view to having the college operational in 1972.[175] Plans for the National College were said to be driven by Captain McDonough, Dr John Kane of St Mary's College, Strawberry Hill, Tony Daly and O'Kennedy, with an architect sought in August 1970.[176] O'Kennedy also stated that a PE syllabus had been circulated in all post-primary schools.[177] This also included 'organised athletic games as a suggested area of work' and was to be used in all schools where it was 'feasible to do so'.[178]

171 Ibid.
172 *Irish Independent*, 17 September 1971.
173 Ibid.
174 *Evening Herald*, 8 May 1970.
175 *Irish Independent*, 24 July 1970 and *Irish Press*, 15 December 1972.
176 *Irish Press*, 15 August 1970 and *Irish Independent*, 18 August 1970.
177 *Irish Examiner*, 10 August 1970.
178 'Dáil Éireann Debate – Tuesday, 19 May 1970. Vol. 246. No. 10. Ceisteanna – Questions. Oral Answers. – School Physical Training.' Retrieved from <https://www.oireachtas.ie/en/debates/debate/dail/1970-05-19/17/> [Accessed 2 November 2020].

The Foundation of COSAC (An Comhairle Sport agus Caitheamh Aimsire)

In January 1971, Michael O'Kennedy announced the establishment of a National Council for Sport and Physical Recreation or COSAC.[179] Twenty-one members were nominated for the Council with their appointments to last initially for two years. The Council's functions were to give advice to the Parliamentary Secretary on matters such as the co-ordinating of physical and recreational activities with a view to full national participation; to give advice on financing sporting and recreation schemes; a national policy for standards; the maximum utilisation of facilities and requirements for the future; assistance of community development of physical recreation and 'any other matters relating to sport and physical recreation activities'.[180] Tony Daly was named as secretary to the Council while Captain McDonough was also to assist the new body when requested. O'Kennedy stated that the council would act as a 'national watchdog' in sporting matters and that it would 'help to improve co-operation between governing bodies of sport, stimulate high level coaching, broaden the range of physical recreation activities and improve the national standard of athletic endeavour'.[181] However, he also noted that the Council would not be 'the panacea for all their ills' and that members of local communities would need to co-operate. He also expected graduates of the new college to be 'a potent force' in carrying out the recommendations of the council and that physical education in schools would be 'a prime concern'. He felt that amongst the reasons for establishing the Council were the change in lifestyle in the 1970s, as standards of living were increasing, while social barriers were being broken down, and people had more leisure time, increased mobility and living pressures. Integration into the European Economic Community

---

179   *Evening Herald*, 23 January 1971 and *Irish Independent*, 28 January 1971.
180   *Evening Herald*, 23 January 1971.
181   Ibid.

would also bring challenges and Irish industry and education needed to be prepared to meet this.[182]

O'Kennedy went on to state that a full programme in PE was taking place in schools where the facilities were present.[183] Members of the Council included Edith Hudson, the principal of Ling College, two delegates based in Northern Ireland, Jim McKeever and Olympian Maeve Kyle, and others who were experienced in the world of sport including athletes, teachers and organisers.[184] The Council was expected to meet on a monthly basis with sub-committees to be formed and reports compiled.[185] O'Kennedy also stated that the people appointed had not been selected as representatives of particular sporting bodies but were chosen 'because of their achievements and interest in sport and recreation in the broadest sense'.[186] However, as Diarmaid Ferriter has stated, infighting 'was an intrinsic part of the Irish sporting infrastructure' and even the selection of COSAC members was not immune to this.[187]

The 1971 Primary School Curriculum

By March 1967, there were 10,000 fully qualified national school teachers in the Republic of Ireland, with 6,500 of these female.[188] Overall, there were 490,168 national school pupils in 4,847 schools, with a total of 14,469 teachers employed.[189] 756 were one-teacher schools while 2,407 were two-teacher.[190] By June of that year, PE was still optional in primary

182   Ibid.
183   Ibid.
184   *Sunday Independent*, 24 January 1971 and *Belfast Telegraph*, 25 January 1971.
185   *Sunday Independent*, 24 January 1971.
186   *Irish Examiner*, 25 January 1971.
187   Diarmaid Ferriter, *Ambiguous Republic: Ireland in the 1970s* [Paperback edition] (London: Profile Books, 2013), 315–16.
188   *Irish Farmers' Journal*, 25 March 1967.
189   *Irish Independent*, 8 April 1967.
190   Ibid.

schools but was 'taught through the medium of major recreational games and athletics'.[191] Through their teacher-training college courses, national school teachers were 'qualified to implement such a programme'. It was also noted that 'in larger schools, and in some of the smaller ones', the curriculum was 'usually widened to include other aspects of physical education such as gymnastics, minor games, dancing and swimming'.[192] The following month, the *Irish Independent* stated that 'some schools had already in operation a sound basic programme of PE' but 'others however, provided very little, mainly because the teachers in these schools were not equipped with either the facilities or the basic training'.[193] The development of the subject was proposed as part of a wider expansion of the primary school curriculum in 1968 along with social and environmental studies and arts and crafts.[194] By that stage, there was a growing awareness of the need to modernise certain aspects of the curriculum, and communications with PE administrators in other countries were a help in discussing the best way to update the Irish system. In 1968, the Department of Education began the draft of a new primary school curriculum with submissions from a number of educational bodies considered.[195] This appears to have generally well received by principals and teachers, unlike the previous proposals of committees undertaking reports on physical education. In 1969, one school principal writing to the *Limerick Leader* noted that

> The draft of the new curriculum for primary schools gives a special section to physical education and has made us aware that its educational value resides not alone in those effects which concern the development of the body, but that it has moral and mental effects as well. We welcome its inclusion as an essential part of the curriculum.[196]

In May and October 1971 respectively, the first and second parts of the new curriculum were introduced. Some schools had piloted parts of it over the

---

191   Ibid., 2 June 1967.
192   Ibid.
193   Ibid., 6 July 1967.
194   Walsh, *The Politics of Expansion*, 253.
195   *Irish Examiner*, 24 November 1971.
196   *Limerick Leader*, 28 June 1969.

previous year while in November teachers were given a full school day to discuss it.[197] It was intended that the teachers and children would be given more freedom within the curriculum with more emphasis placed on the child learning by undertaking activities rather than through the didactic approach.[198] The 1971 *Primary School Curriculum Teacher's Handbook* (part 2) stated that 'the traditional approach to Physical Education was to instruct the children as a class in a limited range of functional skills'.[199] However, the new curriculum was intended to take into account 'the modern approach' which allowed 'each child to develop, working at his own particular rate, according to his own ability and aptitude'.[200] It was noted that 'how a child learns is just as important as what he learns; nowadays, emphasis has moved from class instruction to child activity and personal involvement'.[201] It was also stated that 'this presupposes an environment which encourages experiment and stimulates mental response. There are few areas of work in the curriculum which stimulus and environment are more important than in Physical Education.'[202] While infant classes learned 'largely through play', those in senior classes experienced the PE curriculum through 'isolated skills' which were 'combined in fluent sequences'.[203]

Under the new curriculum, 'internal organised games' were included as a recommended part of the new syllabus.[204] Courses were held to enable teachers to come to terms with the new content, with 200 primary school teachers attending Carlow College for this purpose in July 1972.[205] PE courses for primary school teachers also took place in areas such as Tullow, County Offaly the following year.[206] In March 1973, as Mary Immaculate

197 *Irish Examiner*, 24 November 1971.
198 Ibid.
199 *Primary School Curriculum: Teacher's Handbook Part 2* (Dublin: Government of Ireland, 1971), 289.
200 Ibid.
201 Ibid.
202 Ibid.
203 Ibid.
204 *Evening Herald*, 15 December 1971.
205 *Nationalist and Leinster Times*, 21 and 28 July 1972.
206 Ibid., 2 February 1973.

College in Limerick celebrated its 75th anniversary, the PE itinerary for
students there included gymnastics, movement, games, swimming, health
education and national dance with two PE lecturers, Sylvia Lee-Doyle and
Noreen Lynch, employed there.[207]

The Opening of the NCPE

In January 1971 it was reported that the NCPE would be opened in
Limerick the following year.[208] It was to be co-educational with a four-
year course in place which would lead to 'a degree-type qualification'.[209]
This would mean that, in theory, males who aspired to be physical education teachers would no longer have to go to Britain or the United
States of America to qualify in the subject. In October 1971, one reporter described the establishment of the NCPE as 'one of the major developments in Irish sport for many years'.[210] It was to be situated on the
same campus as the National Institute for Higher Education [NIHE].[211]
Speaking to the *Sunday Independent*, Michael O'Kennedy stated that the
college would eventually produce around 100 physical education teachers
every year, while he also hoped that 'post-primary schools of around the
400 pupil mark' would be given physical education equipment.[212] Having
visited PE establishments in Britain, France and Germany to view facilities, the Department's 'consultants' decided to include 'a top-class swimming pool, gymnasium, track athletics, tennis courts and playing pitches'
with 'all the modern aids' included.[213]

207   *Limerick Leader*, 24 March 1973.
208   *Evening Herald*, 23 January 1971.
209   *Sunday Independent*, 17 January 1971.
210   Ibid., 10 October 1971.
211   Ibid., and *Irish Press*, 2 October 1971.
212   *Sunday Independent*, 10 October 1971.
213   Ibid.

While the NIHE in Limerick was to offer programmes in applied science, electronics, European studies, secretarial science and business studies, the NCPE there was to be an adjoining part of the institute.[214] O'Kennedy noted in February 1972 that school managers had responded positively to inquiries from the National Council for Sport and Physical Recreation as well as the National Youth Council and were eager to provide facilities.[215] He also stated that a COSAC survey of provincial facilities had been undertaken and that regional recreational councils had been nominated with a view to his appointment of members.[216] Others felt that more needed to be done, with Dr Hugh Byrne of Fine Gael expressing the view that the £100,000 which had been allocated for the development of sport had not been properly distributed as those responsible for this were civil servants who 'had not shown that they had any qualifications for sport'.[217] He also felt this figure was inadequate, with at least £500,000 needed, and recommended that a Ministry of Sport, Recreation and Environment be established in line with developments in other European countries.[218] In April 1972 it was announced by O'Kennedy that sports grants to the value of £126,000 would be allocated 'to supplement the normal income of national organisations' to allow a more extensive range of coaching courses to be undertaken, and to provide essential equipment and to improve administration.[219] £55,000 of this was to be given to sports' organisations, while about £2,000 was allocated to community centres and the rest to 'various non-sporting youth organisations'.[220] The Department of Education also announced plans that sports centres would become part of community schools.[221] Post-primary schools were also entitled to apply for grants to the value of £800 for physical education equipment.[222] Initiatives were also

214   *Irish Press*, 25 January and 18 February 1972.
215   Ibid., 25 February 1972.
216   Ibid.
217   *Irish Examiner*, 2 March 1972.
218   Ibid. and *Irish Independent*, 2 March 1972.
219   *Irish Press*, 8 April 1972.
220   Ibid., 22 July 1972.
221   Ibid., 12 April 1972.
222   Ibid., 22 July 1972.

undertaken to raise awareness of the need to maintain an adequate standard of health. 'Fitness for All Week', organised by COSAC, was held in July 1972, with a special conference on planning for recreation held in Dublin.[223] The initial development of the NCPE was hampered by building problems. By March 1972 'virtually no work' had been done on the Limerick site and the opening of the new physical education college would have to be delayed from September 1972 until January 1973.[224] This had repercussions for Irish students of PE at Strawberry Hill as they were supposed to transfer to Limerick in September, while Department of Education plans to send those at Sion Hill and Ling College (who would also be taking up the course at Limerick), to London for three months were opposed by their principals.[225] Sixty male PE students from Ireland, based in Strawberry Hill, each received funding 'to the tune of £1000 per year' while there were thirty-six first year students at St Raphael's and Ling, whom, as noted, could apply for a much lower sum.[226]

As stated above, students undertaking the new PE course at the NCPE were required to complete four years for the graduate award.[227] Candidates needed to have 'the usual qualifications for university entry, plus physical aptitudes and a wide interest in sport' according to O'Kennedy.[228] They also had to pass a number of 'rigorous tests and examinations'. There was huge interest amongst students in the new course, as 850 boys and 650 girls were said to have applied in 1972.[229] In addition, forty-eight students from St Raphael's, Ling College and St Mary's College Strawberry Hill were to join the first year students.[230] When fully operational, the NCPE was to have an enrolment of 400 undergraduate students.[231]

223   *Sunday Independent*, 2 July 1972 and *Irish Press*, 4 July 1972.
224   *Irish Independent*, 10 March 1972.
225   Ibid.
226   Ibid.
227   *Sunday Independent*, 25 June 1972.
228   *Waterford News and Star*, 8 December 1972.
229   Ibid.
230   Ibid.
231   *Irish Press*, 13 April 1973.

Facilities included those expected of a top-class venue for studying PE. The first phase of building consisted of completing a sports hall, dance and movement studio and gymnasium, and was scheduled for completion by January 1973.[232] The second phase, which was to be finished by September 1973, was to include a thirty-three and one-third metres swimming pool, along with a sauna, diving pit, handball alleys, lecture theatre, tutorial rooms, social areas and administrative offices.[233] Outdoor facilities included a 400 metre athletic track, basketball and tennis courts, a floodlit all-weather play area and twelve acres of playing fields while a boating wharf was also to be provided on the Shannon.[234]

In January 1973 former Dublin Gaelic footballer Jim Tunney became the third Parliamentary Secretary to the Minister for Education with a responsibility for sport, leisure and physical recreation, following Michael O'Kennedy's appointment as Minister for Transport and Power.[235] However, by the middle of March John Bruton had taken over Tunney's role.[236] At the beginning of 1973 the facilities for students at the NCPE were still not finished.[237] The enrolment of students was a phased development as the venue was not ready. Following a request from the Department of Education, the Tralee VEC agreed that the recently developed Technical College at Clash be made available for the seventy-six students undertaking the degree in physical education, which began on 22 January 1973.[238] Students were chosen through three criteria, which were academic qualifications, physical talent and fitness, and personality.[239] Candidates also needed to pass an oral Irish test and the Leaving Certificate with honours in at least two subjects and to be at least seventeen years old on 30 June in their year of initial admission.[240]

232   *Waterford News and Star*, 8 December 1972.
233   Ibid.
234   Ibid.
235   *Irish Press*, 10 January 1973.
236   Ibid., 23 March 1973.
237   *Irish Examiner*, 3 January 1973.
238   Ibid., and *The Kerryman*, 7 April 1973.
239   *Irish Examiner*, 7 June 1973.
240   *Evening Herald*, 3 August 1973.

Specialist lecturers were made available while the course was based in Kerry while the Physical Education students themselves were booked into the Mount Brandon Hotel.[241] Despite discontent from other hotel owners that the students were all centred in one hotel, newspaper reports also indicate that it created a sense of well-being amongst the students and some were genuinely disappointed at having to leave Tralee in April 1973, with one student commenting that the scattered nature of their new digs in Limerick was not something they wanted.[242] At the end of the month, a letter written on behalf of the first year PE students was published in the local press, in which the people of Tralee were thanked for their hospitality and kindness and 'the wonderful start' it had given the students in undertaking the course.[243]

Although it was clear that being located temporarily in Tralee had helped to create a strong sense of camaraderie, the students also had to work hard on the course, with classes beginning every morning at 9 a.m., while three nights a week there were lectures to attend and games on Saturdays.[244] In addition, swimming took place at the local hotel pool on Monday and Friday afternoons, and although there were initially thirty-six of the students who could not swim, by the beginning of April most of them were comfortable in the water.[245] Dr Paul Robinson, a Derbyshire-born man who was in charge of the group, stated that 'they must know all about movement and the workings of the body, and not only must they know the principles of movement and the skills of the various exercises, they must be able to teach them as well'.[246] The students' timetable was 'more or less evenly divided between practical and theoretical subjects', with basketball, camogie, dance, Gaelic football, gymnastics, hockey, hurling, rugby and swimming all included.[247]

241 *Irish Independent*, 24 January 1973 and *The Kerryman*, 27 January 1973.
242 *The Kerryman*, 3 February and 7 April 1973.
243 Ibid., 28 April 1973.
244 Ibid., 7 April 1973.
245 Ibid.
246 Ibid.
247 Ibid.

In May 1973, 'the first major phase' of the development of the NCPE had, according to a spokesman on behalf of the college authorities, been completed, and facilities were ready for the start of the summer term.[248] However, by the beginning of the following month it was evident that the students were unhappy with facilities.[249] Despite being encouraged to continue by Acting Director, Dr John Kane, it soon became clear that the 130 first and second year students were unwilling to do this, and they went on strike in June 1973 by refusing to go to lectures and instead held a discussion of general college conditions there.[250] They also sought clarification about their course content, and were assured by the Secretary of the Department of Education, Seán O'Connor, that 'a fully worked-out curriculum' would be available to them by September 1973.[251] Brendan Lillis, the president of the Students' Union at the NCPE, stated that reassurances had been given to the four-member delegation which travelled to Dublin to meet O'Connor that new gymnasium equipment would be purchased, and that the Department of Education would review the question of National Council of Education Awards degree or diploma recognition.[252] It was also announced later that year that the NCPE would merge with the NIHE in Limerick.[253]

In January 1973, the Union of Students in Ireland had challenged a move by the Minister for Education Pádraig Faulkner (1969–73), to discontinue awarding the same level of grants to twelve students who had begun studying PE in London with a view to moving to Limerick once the NCPE courses had begun.[254] This development came about as the Minister deemed the level of grants required to live in London was greater than that required in Limerick and the level of higher education funding in Ireland needed to be matched.[255] In October of that year, it was also reported that the

248   *Irish Examiner*, 2 May 1973.
249   Ibid., 2 June 1973.
250   Ibid., 7 June 1973, *Evening Herald*, 13 June 1973 and *Irish Independent*, 16 June 1973.
251   *Irish Independent*, 16 June 1973.
252   Ibid.
253   *Irish Examiner*, 3 November 1973.
254   *Irish Press*, 9 January 1973.
255   Ibid.

Registration Council would not recognise the qualifications of a number of Irish students who had undertaken a degree from London University which had a special emphasis on PE and recreation.[256]

As noted, the scholarship scheme had been established by then Parliamentary Secretary to the Department of Education with a special responsibility for physical education, Robert Molloy, in 1969, with a view to providing physical education teachers in Irish schools. The students had firstly attended St Mary's College at Strawberry Hill where they completed a diploma after three years there. They then had the option of doing another year at St Mary's or going to London University to complete a B.Ed. degree, depending on the results they achieved.[257] Six students qualified with a degree from London University but the Registration Council in Ireland, after vetting their degrees, 'decided that the London B.Ed. degree was not equivalent to a degree plus teaching qualifications'.[258] This was despite the fact that the Department of Education had funded their studies in London, with £4,000 being paid per student, and that assistant principal officer in the Department, Tony Daly stated that the matter would be cleared up.[259] However, issues between students and college administrators remained into the mid-1970s, and ensured that the early years of the new college were not smooth.

Conclusion

In 1969, an updated ICHPER report highlighted a number of changes introduced late in that decade.[260] These included a growth in the number of schools employing graduates of St Raphael's Training College and

---

256 *Sunday Independent*, 7 October 1973.
257 Ibid.
258 Ibid.
259 Ibid.
260 *Physical Education in the School Curriculum. ICHPER International Questionnaire Report Part 1, 1967–1968 Revision* (Washington, DC: ICHPER, 1969), 42.

progress 'in the teaching of educational gymnastics and movement educa-tion'.[261] The building of school gymnasia and efforts to obtain equipment were also noted while second level school building plans had to include a gymnasium or they would not be granted government funding.[262] The decision of the Government to focus on establishing PE more fully in Irish schools reflected wider concerns about educational developments in other parts of Europe. It also mirrored to some extent modernised Irish educational policies in that decade which saw second and third level edu-cation becoming more accessible, and the increased prosperity in Irish society in the 1960s meant that more funds were available to assist the subject's development. While teacher training in PE had been available at primary level, and courses for second level female PE trainee teachers were already operational in Dublin, a co-educational PE college for second level teachers was badly needed to ensure that male students did not have to continue to emigrate to undertake PE courses in England, and to allow females with aspirations of teaching PE to also gain full teaching degrees and recognised qualifications in a government-funded institution. In add-ition, by 1973 it appears it was the policy of the Department of Education not to provide special equipment grants to schools which did not have a qualified PE teacher, such as the Presentation Convent in Cashel, County Tipperary, which must also have impacted on the subject's development to some extent.[263]

A crucial element in PE's growth in the Republic of Ireland was of course the appointment of Captain McDonough as PE inspector in the early 1960s, but this needed to be supported by the appointment of Robert Molloy as parliamentary secretary to the Minister of Education with a special responsibility for physical education in 1969 for real progress to be made. The PEAI's foundation also helped in bringing PE teachers together and its spread meant that meetings could also be held in regional areas to

261 Ibid.
262 Ibid.
263 'Dáil Éireann Debate – Tuesday, 12 June 1973. Vol. 266. No. 2. Ceisteanna – Questions. Oral Answers. – Special Equipment Grants.' Retrieved from <https://www.oireachtas.ie/en/debates/debate/dail/1973-06-12/26/> [Accessed 4 Nov-ember 2020].

discuss aspects of the subject's development. The foundation of COSAC in 1971 was also important in raising awareness of the value of physical fitness and sport, while the revamping of the primary school curriculum that year meant that its status took on more importance in national schools. Despite this, problems remained, and by the middle of the decade the Irish government continued to make excuses to underfund sport, with Ferriter noting that 'the money being spent on sports promotion and support was paltry'.[264] The opening of the NCPE did not go according to plan and was delayed, and the status of the qualifications available continued to be debated. However, much progress had been made and the bedrock of modern structures for regular PE in schools had been laid down. Chapter 9 assesses developments in the subject's status in Northern Ireland in the period from 1973 until 2000.

264   Ferriter, *Ambiguous Republic: Ireland in the 1970s*, 316.

A Difficult Period: PE in Northern Ireland, 1973–2000

Introduction

This chapter assesses the development of PE in Northern Ireland's schools in the period from 1973 to 2000, and examines the impact of the Troubles on this mainly through the use of teacher interviews. Despite the introduction of a co-educational PE course in Belfast in the early 1970s, by the middle part of that decade there was an over-supply of new PE teachers with the result that additional degree courses were created. These allowed more flexibility in providing qualifications for physical exercise-related careers.[1] Attitudes towards PE's status remained slow to change within some schools and issues with facilities remained by the 1990s, and in some areas a noted reduction in teachers' involvement in the provision of extra-curricular activities echoed the decline of school sport in England by this time.[2] The impact of the introduction of the new national curriculum in 1991, which saw PE becoming a compulsory subject for 5 to 16 year olds, was an important development in cementing its status.[3] One survey undertaken in the latter part of that decade highlighted that the subject was highly valued by teachers and school management of post-primary schools.[4] By this point, PE had been much more widely accepted as a

---

1   PRONI. D4327/4/8. *Ulster Polytechnic. Annual Report 1978–1979* (Belfast: Ulster Polytechnic, 1979), 17.

2   *Belfast Telegraph*, 9 August 1990.

3   Ibid., 27 February 1992.

4   *Department of Education (Northern Ireland). Report on Physical Education in Secondary Schools. Inspected 1998–99* (Belfast: The Education and Training Inspectorate, 2000), 1.

curricular subject, although more specific planning and assessment was recommended.[5] In this way, it had become more valued within Northern Ireland's schools by the late twentieth century, and this was best exemplified in its introduction as an 'A' Level examination subject in a number of schools by the late 1990s.[6] Despite some integration of schools and cross-community involvement, tensions remained by the end of the century, but the Good Friday Agreement of April 1998 offered the opportunity to move on from the violent sectarian conflict that had blighted the region for almost thirty years.[7]

The Development of Teacher Training Courses in PE

By 1973, the training of specialist teachers in PE, domestic science and art was 'almost entirely concentrated in the Ulster College' which had by then introduced a B.Ed. course.[8] At that time, twenty-nine students were enrolled in the three-year Diploma in PE teaching course and fourteen in the four-year course in PE.[9] Ed Saunders had replaced Oonagh Pim in August 1972 as Director of Studies in the School of Physical Education.[10] Not the first British resident to migrate to Northern Ireland to take up a position in a PE-related post, Saunders and his wife, Christine, were Scottish and moved to Belfast with their infant son, Rob, who later went on to play rugby for Ireland and captain the team.[11] In addition, his parents

---

5   Ibid., 13.
6   *Belfast Telegraph*, 29 September 1997.
7   Bartlett, *Ireland: A History*, 566.
8   DENI, *Government of Northern Ireland. Education in Northern Ireland in 1973. Being the Report of the Ministry of Education for Northern Ireland for the Year Ended 31 December 1973* (Belfast: H.M. Stationery Office, 1974), 15.
9   Ibid.
10   PRONI. D4327/4/2. *Ulster College. The Northern Ireland Polytechnic. Annual Report to 31 August 1973* (Belfast, 1973), 5 and *Belfast Telegraph*, 1 January 1973.
11   *Irish Independent*, 15 January 1991.

both had first class degrees in PE and Mrs Saunders later took up a position as senior lecturer at what was to become known as the University of Ulster, Jordanstown.[12]

During 1972–3 the work of the Education Faculty at the Ulster College had been expanded to include, along with the Teacher's Diploma in PE, a number of other education courses.[13] In addition, the School of Physical Education had 'also designed a recreation option in the Diploma of Management Studies'.[14] In 1973, thirty-six students graduated in the Teacher's Diploma in PE course, with an increase in resources said to have been beneficial.[15] However, PE jobs were in short supply in Northern Ireland in 1974, with one graduate from Holywood claiming in a letter to the press in August of that year that of thirty-seven in their course, only thirteen had been able to obtain teaching positions.[16] It was stated that 'this situation did not suddenly occur out of the blue this year, but has gradually been getting worse over the past five years; some former students have never been able to obtain a teaching appointment'.[17] The PE graduate questioned why the Department of Education of Northern Ireland was allowing the Northern Ireland Polytechnic to raise the PE course intake from forty to fifty-five during the 1974–5 academic year and added that more increases were also planned for the coming years.[18] It was also noted that the first B.Ed. degree students would be graduating in 1977 along with those who were undertaking the new Diploma in PE course, thereby increasing the numbers with PE qualifications.[19]

The PE graduate called for the Ulster College to reduce the number of students undertaking their course, while it was also felt that the number of staff a school could have should be increased. In addition, they suggested that primary schools be allowed to employ PE teachers 'instead of allowing

12   *Sunday Independent*, 20 January 1991.
13   *Ulster College. The Northern Ireland Polytechnic. Annual Report to 31 August 1973*, 11.
14   Ibid.
15   Ibid.
16   *Belfast Telegraph*, 26 August 1974.
17   Ibid.
18   Ibid.
19   Ibid.

their facilities to be unused because the staff are uninterested'.[20] In conclusion, it was stated by the writer that 'if anyone is contemplating going to the Polytechnic, I would say think twice; this situation is not unique to physical education'.[21] Although the comments on PE were naturally refuted later in the same newspaper, by a correspondent writing under a pen name, it was also stated that those with qualifications in Domestic Science too faced the prospect of unemployment.[22]

The issue gained more traction a few weeks later as the story made the headlines on the front page of the *Belfast Telegraph*. PE graduates were also finding it difficult to get work because of their lack of previous teaching positions. One PE graduate from Bangor felt that schools were mainly selecting those with experience, and instead had taken up a post with the Department of Education as a civil servant, where she was responsible for registering teachers properly.[23] This had its own issues as newly qualified teachers in the subject who had to take up temporary employment outside of schools could not get to complete their probationary year and become fully qualified.[24] The reporter stated that the graduates wanted 'to see a new approach to physical education in schools' and the same girl who was interviewed claimed that 'for too long it has been regarded as a time-filler, especially in grammar schools'.[25] She also felt that 'in the primary schools, too, PE is given practically no place at all. Teachers with no training in PE take children for a while each week. They give them a bat and a ball and that's it'.[26] Along with these criticisms, both she and another female graduate felt that the Department of Education should expand PE within schools.[27]

Despite the allegations that the Ulster College was increasing its intake of PE students yearly, the college denied this in a statement, and added that the number recruited was actually smaller than the previous year.[28] While

20   Ibid.
21   Ibid.
22   Ibid., 11 September 1974.
23   Ibid., 30 August 1974.
24   Ibid.
25   Ibid.
26   Ibid.
27   Ibid.
28   Ibid.

it was admitted that the numbers took into account male as well as female students and an honours degree in addition to the diploma course, they added that 'the demands for places greatly exceeded the number the college could offer'.[29] The Northern Ireland Polytechnic's statement reflected the view that figures admitted were based on DENI estimates and that this was a matter for that body to comment upon, although the Department gave no immediate response.[30]

Additional educational-related courses were developed with, at least partially, a view to allowing those interested in teaching PE to have a wider range of options and additional qualifications. In 1973–4 the Northern Ireland Polytechnic staff also started to develop the PE elements of 'a proposed part-time in-service Bachelor of Education Degree and Degree with honours course' while they also 'began tentatively planning possible Leisure Studies options for courses in Business Administration and Tourism'.[31] Following a one-day PE curriculum conference, a report entitled *The Curriculum of Physical Education in Secondary Schools* was published. This was stated to be the first in a number of publications recording the outcomes of major conferences hosted by the School of Physical Education. An in-service workshop, held over three half days, was focused on structuring courses for the Certificate of Secondary Education Awards.[32] Despite this progress, at the start of summer 1974 examinations and work were 'seriously disrupted' by the Unionist-organised Ulster Workers' Council Strike, which mainly centred on the proposals of the Sunningdale Agreement, with building work on the college also delayed.[33]

It was noted in the Ulster College's annual report for 1974–5 that a focus was placed by staff on improvements to the integration of theory and practice parts of their degree and diploma courses.[34] The School of

29   Ibid.
30   Ibid.
31   PRONI. D4327/4/3. *Ulster College. The Northern Ireland Polytechnic. Annual Report to 31 August 1974* (Belfast, 1974), 18.
32   Ibid., 19.
33   Ibid., 2.
34   PRONI. D4327/4/4. *Ulster College. The Northern Ireland Polytechnic. Annual Report 1974–1975* (Belfast: Ulster College, 1975),16.

Physical Education also organised conferences and workshops 'for teachers interested in the development of a new Certificate in Education in Physical Education'.[35] By the latter part of the decade some efforts to lessen the number of students undertaking courses were evident, but the intake remained relatively high on PE courses. In February 1976 over fifty students at Ulster College began the new in-service B.Ed. degree which had been approved by the Council for National Academic Awards. Main studies were focused in PE, art or mathematics.[36] This began despite 'drastic changes in government policies reducing the number of initial teacher places for student teachers'.[37]

In 1977 the institution's annual report noted that 'despite the national policy of reduction in student intakes to teacher training the year was an interesting one' with an increase shown in the provision of in-service courses for teachers.[38] Facilities at the college were also improved. While the new playing fields were not ready for use, the final phase of building the sports complex had been finished with swimming, diving and hydrotherapy pools completed along with changing rooms. Along with students of PE and physiotherapy, the sports centre had been used by polytechnic clubs, while a number of national competitions such as the Northern Ireland Netball Shield Finals had been held there.[39]

During the 1978–9 college year, the B.Ed. course run by the School of Physical Education 'was replaced by a new structure leading to a B.A. Degree with Honours in Sports Studies and a Certificate in Education'.[40] This was said to provide 'an additional career outlet' while it enabled students to defer their career choices, with options such as teaching or working in the field of leisure and recreation, 'for at least two years'.[41] In the summer

---

35   Ibid.
36   PRONI. D4327/4/5. *Ulster College. The Northern Ireland Polytechnic. Annual Report 1975–1976* (Belfast: Ulster College, 1976), 14.
37   Ibid.
38   PRONI. D4327/4/6. *Ulster College. The Northern Ireland Polytechnic. Annual Report 1976–1977* (Belfast: Ulster College, 1977), 14.
39   Ibid., 28.
40   PRONI. D4327/4/8. *Ulster Polytechnic. Annual Report 1978–1979* (Belfast: Ulster College, 1979), 17.
41   Ibid.

of 1980, the first year of a BA Honours Degree in Sports Studies was completed by students at Ulster Polytechnic.[42] In addition, seven people participated in the part-time B.Ed. in-service course in PE, with all passing.[43] In 1982, the first intake of BA Sports Studies students qualified from Ulster Polytechnic, with career choices such as recreation management and sports administration and practice available.[44]

In April 1983, the DENI announced that 'from 1983/84, provision for training secondary teachers in commercial studies and craft design and technology' would be located at the colleges of education while training in PE, art, home economics and music would be given 'in the first instance at the Ulster Polytechnic' and afterwards would 'be subsumed within the new university institution', which was the new University of Ulster at Jordanstown.[45] The final year of the Ulster Polytechnic, 1983–4, saw the deaths of three students when a bomb exploded in a lecture room, illustrating how classroom teaching was not exempt from the ongoing conflict.[46] With the opening of the new University of Ulster imminent, and the merging of this with the Ulster Polytechnic, it was noted in the annual report of the latter that recreation and sport was 'on a firm footing' at the Jordanstown campus.[47] As Bardon has stated, 'access to higher education was greatly improved, particularly for mature students, and the amalgamation of the Ulster Polytechnic and the New University to form the University of Ulster in 1984 banished the last trace of bad taste lingering since the Lockwood Report'.[48] He also notes that 'by far the largest integrated sector was further education – which had been bringing Protestants and Catholics unobtrusively together since 1947 – and when the three

---

42   PRONI. D4327/4/9. *Ulster Polytechnic. Annual Report 1979/80* (Belfast: Ulster College, 1980), 17 and 54.
43   Ibid., 54.
44   PRONI. D4327/4/11. *Ulster Polytechnic. Annual Report 1981–82* (Belfast: Ulster College, 1982), 17.
45   *Ulster Herald*, 30 April 1983.
46   PRONI. D4327/4/13. *Ulster Polytechnic. Annual Report 1983–1984* (Belfast: Ulster College, 1984), 3.
47   Ibid., 32.
48   Bardon, *A History of Ulster*, 802.

Belfast colleges (College of Business Studies, College of Technology and Rupert Stanley College) were amalgamated in 1991 as the Belfast Institute of Further and Higher Education, it was the biggest of its kind in the United Kingdom'.[49] By February 1985, Queen's University was offering a two-year part-time diploma in Physical Education as part of their Diploma in the Advanced Study of Education specialist options for teachers.[50]

Instruction in the teaching of PE was also increased in more peripheral areas in Northern Ireland in the late 1970s and 1980s. In March 1979, the aforementioned Billy Ingram, who had progressed to become a Physical Education lecturer at what had by then become known as the Ulster Polytechnic, visited Strabane in West Tyrone to help establish swimming training courses for teachers.[51] In February 1980 another PE course for primary school teachers was held in Strabane over a six-week period with PE staff from the Ulster College in Belfast giving instruction.[52] The Faculty of Education also provided other in-service courses at other regional centres including Enniskillen in County Fermanagh.[53] In addition, an Institute of Coaching was established in conjunction with the Sports Council at Ulster Polytechnic.[54] This was said to be 'an independent unit whose objectives' were 'the improvement of coaching and coaching qualifications' and it was hoped that it would have 'an important influence on sport and recreation' in Northern Ireland.[55] In April 1983 the Strabane Teachers' Centre announced details of another PE course to be held there in the summer, under the instruction of Hilary O'Neill and the Ulster Polytechnic's PE staff, and it was also intended to involve local school classes.[56] By November 1987, a pilot scheme for teaching PE was being developed in the Western Board area in conjunction with the Northern Ireland Council for Educational Development.[57] By that stage, a much

49   Ibid., and *Belfast Telegraph*, 30 January 1991.
50   *Belfast Telegraph*, 7 February 1985.
51   *Ulster Herald*, 31 March 1979.
52   *Strabane Chronicle*, 19 January 1980.
53   *Ulster Polytechnic. Annual Report 1979–1980*, 18.
54   Ibid.
55   Ibid.
56   *Strabane Chronicle*, 2 April 1983 and 14 May 1983.
57   *Fermanagh Herald*, 28 November 1987.

wider choice of sports-related courses was being offered and attempts had been made to bring courses to more peripheral areas.

PE in Northern Ireland's Schools, 1973–2000

In April 1973 it was announced that a new sports council would be set up in Northern Ireland with the power 'to establish sports centres and make cash grants to voluntary organisations'.[58] It would also give advice to the Ministry of Education and other organisations in relation to physical recreation and sport.[59] The new Council was developed to unite the 'advisory role of the Youth and Sports Council' with 'the active promotion of sport carried on by the Central Council for Physical Recreation'.[60] A Northern Ireland Youth Committee was also to be established, while District Councils were required 'to secure the adequate provision for a broad spectrum of activities-recreational, social, physical and cultural'.[61]

Despite these developments, the provision of facilities was not always forthcoming. In December 1975, it was announced that due to cuts by the Education and Library Board, the hiring of extra halls for PE classes would be reduced in accordance with a new budget as part of a number of changes within educational funding.[62] In September 1976 the Northern Ireland Sport-For-All week took place, with Sports Minister Ray Carter announcing that £15,000 would be available for sportspeople there.[63] The money was allocated by the Department of Education, with Minister Carter noting 'the alarming physical drop-out which occurs when formal school instruction ceases'.[64] According to the chairman of the Northern Ireland

58   *Belfast Telegraph*, 4 April 1973.
59   Ibid.
60   Ibid.
61   Ibid.
62   Ibid., 2 December 1975.
63   Ibid., 13 September 1976.
64   Ibid.

Sports Council, Don Shearer, the event was organised by that organisation to encourage the general public to participate more widely in sport while Minister Carter expressed hopes that sport could help play a stabilising role in the Troubles.[65] In June 1977, the Northern Ireland Sports Council highlighted in their planning guide *Community Indoor Provision* that there were sixty-four sites in Northern Ireland which were 'identified as inadequate to meet the needs of the people'.[66] It was also noted that more swimming pools and indoor centres were required with a Northern Ireland Centre which included a fifty-metre pool recommended along with recreation centres at district level suggested.[67] As shown elsewhere, the hopes of sporting administrators that sport might act as a uniting force within Northern Ireland were not always realised. As Sugden and Bairner have highlighted, the provision of additional leisure centres in Belfast during the Troubles did little to lessen sectarian divisions.[68]

In June 1980, the position of the Northern Ireland Sports Council was to be amended as the Government felt that the Council's work was 'being duplicated to a great extent by district councils throughout Northern Ireland and sporting bodies' and there were concerns about the finance involved in running the Council.[69] Jack Allen, the Chairman of the former Sports Council of Northern Ireland, agreed to take up the position of head of the new organisation.[70] The Sports Council of Northern Ireland's work was to be taken on 'by a specific branch within the Department of Education'.[71] However, following public pressure, the Northern Ireland Sports Council was allowed to continue, with its headquarters, the House of Sport, a £360,000 building on the Malone Road overlooking the Queen's University playing fields, completed in 1981.[72]

65   Ibid.
66   Ibid., 27 June 1977.
67   Ibid.
68   Sugden and Bairner, *Sport, Sectarianism and Society*, 111–24.
69   *Belfast Telegraph*, 16 June 1980.
70   Ibid., 26 June 1980.
71   Ibid.
72   Ibid., 8 December 1982.

Sugden and Bairner have stated that the DENI was 'effectively, in all but name ... the Ministry of Sport, Leisure and Culture' by the middle of the 1970s following the implementation of direct rule from Westminster in 1972.[73] The DENI's *Primary Education Teachers' Guide* of 1974 highlighted that 'a programme of physical education should provide opportunities for experience of a wide range of activities rather than concentrate on the acquisition of a few specific skills'.[74] Efforts were made to raise awareness of the value of PE in line with developments in Britain. In November 1977 the Belfast Education and Library Board launched a scheme 'to discover and acknowledge senior pupils who have rendered special service to their schools and fellow pupils in and through the field of physical education'.[75] The scheme was arranged in support of the Queen's Silver Jubilee Appeal, and was organised by the Physical Education Association of Great Britain and Northern Ireland. It was sponsored by the National Westminster Bank and was also being run in England, Scotland and Wales.[76] In June 1978 fifteen students from Northern Ireland were chosen by the Physical Education Association as nominees.[77] The following month, six winners from this group received the awards for 'distinction in sport' at a ceremony in London following interviews.[78] However, this type of event appears to have only taken place intermittently.

In February 1981, the results of a report by DENI inspectors on 130 primary schools in Northern Ireland highlighted that progress was good, but there was room for improvement.[79] In particular, it was stated that curriculum planning was absent in many schools, particularly 'in aesthetic studies' such as music, art and craft and for PE.[80] The report recommended that members of staff be allocated responsibility for certain subjects, and

---

73   Sugden and Bairner, *Sport, Sectarianism and Society*, 97.
74   DENI. *Department of Education for Northern Ireland. Primary Education Teachers' Guide* (Belfast: H.M. Stationery Office, 1974), 96.
75   *Belfast Telegraph*, 16 November 1977.
76   Ibid.
77   Ibid., 27 June 1978.
78   Ibid., 20 July 1978.
79   Ibid., 26 February 1981.
80   Ibid.

'more exploratory work, in which the child learns through self-discovery' needed to take place.[81] It was also noted that 'in many schools there is too much emphasis on mental skills at the expense of social skills and awareness and half the schools do not place appropriate emphasis on physical development of the children'.[82] Physical Education remained unstructured as a school subject in some areas of Northern Ireland, with one PE teacher from a peripheral area stating of his days as a school pupil in the late 1970s and early 1980s that 'I can't recall it being scheduled, at a specific time every week … [the teacher] just took us out when he fancied taking us out [at primary school]. I don't think anything was scheduled. In the secondary school, again, there was no soccer, only Gaelic.'[83]

Amongst the issues listed as being detrimental to the survival of small rural schools in the press in Northern Ireland in February 1983 were that these schools were 'unlikely to have the variety of expertise needed for subjects like music, drama, physical education, domestic science and sports'.[84] In 1983, pupils at Magheraknock Primary School in County Antrim only received PE in the summer months because of a lack of indoor space, although they did receive swimming lessons in a pool in Lisburn.[85] In June 1983, the release of the results of a study conducted by the West Belfast branch of the INTO illustrated that in one school in the area, only 40 per cent of the pupils received PE due to a building project being shelved because of 'serious cuts in provision as a result of lower budgets'.[86]

Some schools had no problems with PE facilities. Princess Gardens School at Finaghy, Belfast, 'an interdenominational voluntary Grammar school with preparatory department on site' was home to 500 boarders in 1983.[87] It was noted that 'a wide range of extra-curricular activities are enjoyed and the many successes in Physical Education reflect maximum

81   Ibid.
82   Ibid.
83   Interview with Northern Ireland second level PE teacher number two, 18 September 2019.
84   *Belfast Telegraph*, 21 February 1983.
85   Ibid., 12 May 1983.
86   Ibid., 1 June 1983.
87   Ibid., 16 June 1983.

utilisation of the school's beautiful 37 acre woodland, including all weather hockey pitches, facilities for field and track athletics, tennis, badminton and gymnastics' while golf, squash, swimming and horse riding were also undertaken there.[88]

While some other schools such as Methodist College had top-class facilities and highly competitive teams, such as the girls' rowing side, pictured in Figure 34, the mixed nature of the facilities available in Northern Ireland's primary and second level schools reflected wider trends in the United Kingdom. In December 1983 the results of a report on seventy-two secondary schools, commissioned by British Minister for Education, Nicholas Scott, illustrated that some were 'seriously sub-standard' and in need of replacement.[89] It was stated that 'one matter of particular concern is the inadequacy of facilities for physical education, both indoor and outdoor, in a large number of secondary schools'.[90]

By the middle of the 1980s a wider variety of sports was being proposed within primary schools guidelines. *The Northern Ireland Council for Educational Development Physical Education Guidelines for Primary Schools*

Figure 34. Methodist College girls' rowing team, 1982. Courtesy of Laura McKinney.

88 Ibid.
89 Ibid., 9 December 1983.
90 Ibid.

(1986) recommended that 'a well-structured and balanced programme' would include educational gymnastics, dance, games, athletics, swimming and outdoor activities.[91] Facilities and resources remained a concern as it was noted that 'many small schools and indeed some larger schools have specific problems related to a lack of indoor and outdoor space'.[92] The use of local facilities such as halls was recommended along with cooperation with other schools and giving 'more time to physical education in good weather'. It was advised that 'the use of the local environment for activities such as rambling or fishing' be considered, illustrating the ad hoc nature of official views on the subject.[93] The provision of facilities continued to be problematic in some schools across Northern Ireland in the latter stages of the 1980s. The results of an inspection of a primary school in Brookeborough, County Fermanagh, undertaken in 1987 revealed that 'lack of resources and equipment limited the provision of sufficient scope in music and physical education'.[94] In January 1990, DENI Inspectors noted that the indoor facilities for PE at Envaugh Primary School, a rural school in Drumquin, County Tyrone, were 'unsatisfactory', although they also stated that 'the school was a good one, where the teachers worked hard and provided a varied and stimulating curriculum'.[95] It would appear that many teachers could only work with what they had in their schools, and their capacity to teach PE was often determined by what was available in the schools.

Seán McGourty's 1986 study of the PE curriculum in 'boys and mixed post-primary schools from the five education and library board areas in Northern Ireland', based on data received from 103 of the 202 schools in question, is important in assessing the state of PE in Northern Ireland in second level schools at that time in comparison with those in mainland

---

91   *The Northern Ireland Council for Educational Development Physical Education Guidelines for Primary Schools* (Belfast: Northern Ireland Council for Educational Development, 1986), 2.
92   Ibid., 8.
93   Ibid.
94   *Fermanagh Herald*, 12 November 1988.
95   *Ulster Herald*, 27 January 1990.

Britain.[96] He found that 'schools in Northern Ireland received less time for physical education than schools in England and Wales and secondary schools had more time for physical education than grammar schools'.[97] He also noted that 'the time given to Physical Education on the timetable was decided by the headteacher, or the headteacher in consultation with the vice-principal(s) or heads of department'.[98]

Pupils' preparation for PE classes was shown to be time-consuming. Students 'using off-site facilities for physical education' utilised up to 26 per cent of their allocated PE time in travelling and preparation for the subject.[99] McGourty also highlighted that 'on-site school facilities for cross-country and athletics were considered to be no more than adequate' while over 78 per cent of schools' PE facilities were located away from the school.[100] More than 93 per cent of schools who responded, however, 'maintained a compulsory programme in the first three years'.[101]

The Decline of School Sport in Britain in the 1980s

As Holt and Mason have stated, 'school sport bucked the trend towards rising participation in the 1980s as industrial disputes led teachers to withdraw the goodwill upon which extra-curricular sport depended'.[102] Prime Minister John Major (1990–7), has stated that the 1984–5 industrial dispute and subsequent educational reforms were a contributing factor in the decline of sport within schools.[103] His own party did little

---

96   McGourty, 'The Boys' Physical Education Curriculum in Secondary Schools in Northern Ireland', 109. These Education and Library Board areas were listed as Belfast, Western, North Eastern, South Eastern and Southern.

97   Ibid., ii.

98   Ibid., ii–iii.

99   Ibid., iii.

100   Ibid., 200–1.

101   Ibid., 201.

102   Holt and Mason, *Sport in Britain 1945–2000*, 17.

103   Ibid., 155.

to stem this issue. The Conservative government-backed sale of 5000 schools' playing fields from 1987 to 1995 was also detrimental while Holt and Mason suggest that 'the fall in male recruits may also have played a part in the decline of sports in schools'.[104] There was also the issue of comprehensive education, 'which did not make sport a priority' and 'some radical teachers didn't like it at all, complaining that traditional games were sexist and aggressively competitive'.[105]

There is strong evidence to back up these two authors' claims regarding the decline of school sports in Britain. In November 1986, Kevin Mitchell, the chairman of the British Central Council of Physical Recreation lamented the lessening in school sports at a conference in London, noting that PE in Britain's schools previously had been 'the envy of the world'.[106] He felt that this deterioration was caused by the two-year industrial action taken by teachers, which, although finished, had left many teachers reluctant to continue with coaching sport in their own time in schools.[107] He was also of the opinion that the idea that competition was 'undesirable', and that children should be shielded from it, had taken hold. Not everyone agreed with this view. In contrast, Jenny Bacon, the undersecretary to the Department of Education and Science responsible for School Sports, was of the view that individual sports were more beneficial than team games.[108] Some inspectors' reports highlighted that schools were giving as much time to PE as they had done ten years earlier and the subject was compulsory for children aged between 11 and 16 in the majority of schools.[109] However, in January 1990, the results of a survey on eight schools in the Brighton and Hove area carried out by the CCPR illustrated that there was a decline in the numbers of PE teachers while those not specialised in the subject were growing less reluctant to give up their time to help in organising school sport.[110]

104   Ibid.
105   Ibid., 17.
106   *Belfast Telegraph*, 27 November 1986.
107   Ibid.
108   Ibid.
109   Ibid.
110   Ibid., 11 January 1990.

Holt and Mason have also noted the negative results of a number of surveys carried out in that decade, one of which illustrated marked declines by 1990 in weekend and lunch-time or after-school sport in over 1500 British schools.[111] A comparison of two surveys of PE time given to 9 and 10 year olds showed a drop in the provision of 'two hours or more of PE per week' from 42 per cent in 1994 to 21 per cent in 1999.[112] One survey of facilities undertaken by the National Association of Head Teachers undertaken in 1999 illustrated that there were no swimming pools, gymnasia or tennis courts in 94 per cent of primary schools and 172 had no playground.[113] A survey undertaken of teenage school pupils by St Luke's College, Exeter illustrated that 'most were uninterested in sport or physical exercise and a large proportion were already overweight'.[114] In June 1991 a committee, chaired by Conservative MP Malcolm Thornton, submitted a report to the government which 'demanded sport be properly financed and made an essential part of the school curriculum, taken seriously by national policy-makers, local education authorities, governing bodies and teachers alike'.[115] They had gathered evidence from over fifty organisations, 'including a delegation of sports stars led by footballer Garth Crooks and swimmer Sharron Davies'.[116] However, it is not clear if this had any major bearing on educational policies towards school sports in Britain in this decade.

Attitudes towards the provision of PE in some schools in Northern Ireland continued to be negative despite the progress made in previous decades regarding teacher-training courses for males and females. In March 1988, the results of one study undertaken by two lecturers at Stranmillis College, based on twenty-two small schools in Northern Ireland and nine in Scotland revealed that principals in the Northern Ireland schools did not regard PE, music, art or science 'as a top priority' and more emphasis was placed on 'intellectual development'.[117] There is also evidence of a reluctance

111   Holt and Mason, *Sport in Britain 1945–2000*, 17.
112   Ibid.
113   Ibid., 152.
114   Ibid.
115   *Belfast Telegraph*, 20 June 1991.
116   Ibid.
117   Ibid., 28 March 1988.

to take on extra-curricular sport in some schools in Northern Ireland. In August 1990, it was reported that academic pressures were affecting sport in some schools there, with Wallace High School, 'a noted Ulster hockey nursery', having to reduce its commitment to the game as the teachers who had been involved could 'no longer spare the time required'.[118] However, one PE teacher interviewed felt that the Industrial Action in the 1980s had been a positive development, as it led to more games and matches being organised during school time, with games' afternoons becoming more common on Mondays.[119] He added that it was mainly grammar schools who continued to host Saturday morning games, as teachers there were getting paid for their additional work, which differed to the situation in secondary schools.[120]

Some schools still struggled to provide PE within the school classroom curriculum, however. An inspectors' report published in January 1989 on Gibson Primary School, Omagh, illustrated that, while generally positive, 'the allocation of time for physical education classes was insufficient with all children only having at least one time table physical education lesson a week'.[121] One report undertaken by Queen's University in 1990 illustrated that girls in Northern Ireland 'were not getting enough exercise to maintain their fitness into adulthood' and it was also noted that boys, who were 'generally more active', could do better.[122] Having started teaching in the 1990s, one PE teacher interviewed felt that some other teachers did not take PE seriously. He stated that 'well I think there was a bad attitude towards PE normally, there was a stigma attached to PE at one time. What was the saying – "if you can't teach, teach PE".[123]

118   Ibid., 9 August 1990.
119   Interview with Northern Ireland second level PE teacher number five, 4 October 2019.
120   Ibid.
121   *Ulster Herald*, 7 January 1989.
122   *Belfast Telegraph*, 9 August 1990.
123   Interview with Northern Ireland second level PE teacher number two, 18 September 2019.

PE in the 1991 National Curriculum

Amendments within the curriculum did, however, help to strengthen PE's position within many schools. In 1988, the Education Reform Act stipulated that a new curriculum would be implemented into schools in Northern Ireland, England and Scotland.[124] PE became compulsory in primary schools for primary one and first form secondary students in Northern Ireland from September 1991 'after a separate programme of study was drawn up by a Government working party'.[125] This was overseen by Jim McKeever, the head of practical studies at St Mary's College of Education in Belfast, with the findings released in September 1990. These focused on 'what should be taught and what pupils might be expected to achieve, at different ages in physical education'.[126] The findings of the party highlighted previous issues outlined in other reports. They noted that 'some' primary schools in Northern Ireland had 'unhygienic and inadequate facilities for physical education' and 'a large number' of small rural schools had no provision for the playing of sports indoors.[127] The provision of swimming and water safety lessons was also found to be inadequate. It was also stated that 'in the past, academically higher attaining pupils often have less access to PE than others'.[128] The report noted that 'provision for PE in primary schools is varied, while in secondary schools, the PE programme is often disrupted for a number of weeks when indoor facilities are used for exams, functions or events'.[129] The group also reported that with secondary schools beginning 'to operate their own budgets' in April 1990, schools which used external leisure facilities would need to review their budgets and curricular policies so

---

124 Mary Catherine Wooley, 'Experiencing the History National Curriculum 1991–2011: Voices of Veteran Teachers' in *History of Education*, vol. 48, no. 2 (2019), 212–32, 212.

125 *Belfast Telegraph*, 27 February 1992.

126 Ibid., 17 August 1990 and 12 September 1990.

127 Ibid., 12 September 1990.

128 Ibid.

129 Ibid.

that 'all pupils participate in a "broad, balanced and progressive" pro-gramme of PE'.[130]

Late in 1991, the results of a different survey on PE in post-primary schools in Northern Ireland prior to the introduction of the new curric-ulum in September of that year were released, and these reflected the above findings to a large extent. These were based on the responses of '267 heads of Physical Education departments' which had been supplied through a questionnaire circulated by the Northern Ireland Council for Educational Research [NICER], with funding given by the SCNI.[131] It was also noted that 'the survey took a deliberately "broad brush" approach, aiming to obtain an overall picture of physical education and games as taught in Northern Ireland post-primary schools in the term before the introduc-tion of the new programmes of study'.[132] Facilities for PE were assessed with 65 per cent of the Heads of Departments [HODS] identifying 'at least one new or additional sports facility which they would need for the implementation of the Northern Ireland PE curriculum' while 32 per cent named at least two new sports facilities they would require.[133] It was also stated that 'such requests came disproportionately often from grammar schools, especially from Catholic grammar schools, and from large rather than small schools'.[134] The report also highlighted that 'it therefore appears that one of the less fortunate consequences of being attractive to parents in an "open enrolment" situation can be the extreme pressure on limited space for physical education'.[135] It was also noted that 'athletics and tennis were the activities most often singled out as requiring improved facilities for the implementation of the Northern Ireland curriculum. Among the requests recurring in the questionnaires were for changing rooms, storage, transport and facilities for teaching dance.'[136]

---

130   Ibid.
131   *Physical Education and Games in Post-Primary Schools: Findings from a Survey of Northern Ireland Schools Immediately before the Introduction of the New Curriculum* (Belfast: Northern Ireland Council for Educational Research, 1991), ii and 1.
132   Ibid., 1.
133   Ibid., 80.
134   Ibid.
135   Ibid.
136   Ibid.

The implementation of the new curriculum reflected wider trends in England and Scotland, as noted above. In January 1991, British Sports Minister Robert Atkins confirmed that PE was to become mandatory for school pupils in Britain aged between 5 and 16, while the government sought more ways to encourage children to become more active in sport.[137] However, the proposed introduction of the new PE curriculum raised concerns, particularly in regard to the provision of swimming. In March 1991, the Northern Ireland Curriculum Council stated that all secondary school pupils should have compulsory swimming.[138] Despite this, there were doubts expressed by post-primary school principals that they would not be able to offer swimming 'within the cash provided for them to operate their own budgets' and that the price of utilising leisure centres would be increased.[139] There were also fears amongst primary governors and heads that the proposals were unrealistic and could not be delivered. Worries about specialist support, costs, resources and time were all noted by the Council, and as a result they made 'one significant change' to the working party's original plan, in that swimming implementation strategies would differ from school to school.[140] The Council also held a number of conferences with a focus on allowing 14 to 16 year olds more flexibility in relation to the school curriculum.[141] Following some confusion over the matter in the press, in June 1991, the Principal Information Officer of the Department of Education, Robert Burnett, attempted to clarify notions that some schools would not have compulsory swimming by stating that it was indeed compulsory for pupils aged between 8 and 14.[142]

In June 1991, it was noted in the press that Northern Ireland teachers would be spending their summer holidays in part preparing for the introduction of compulsory physical education, along with mandatory history and geography, for primary and first form pupils in September 1991.[143]

---

137 *Irish Independent*, 16 January 1991.
138 *Belfast Telegraph*, 12 March 1991.
139 Ibid.
140 Ibid.
141 Ibid.
142 Ibid., 4 June 1991.
143 Ibid., 28 June 1991.

Compulsory English, maths and science had been introduced the previous year.[144] In February 1992, the results of a study undertaken by the
Central Council of Physical Education and the National Association of
Head Teachers illustrated that 56 per cent of 3,000 primary schools in
Northern Ireland, Wales and England were unable to deliver the new PE
curriculum.[145] It was noted that schools in Northern Ireland were 'a year
ahead of the mainland on PE' and 'a separate working group there' had 'built
on the framework outlined' for pupils.[146] The survey, which was undertaken between October and December 1991, showed that 40 per cent of
all schools 'had no PE budget' while in 51 per cent of the schools, financial
help for the subject's provision had come from parents.[147] It was also noted
that 86 per cent of all school heads requested in-service physical education
training for their staff.[148] They also wanted to see 'a number of remedial
measures including an emergency summer programme of training courses
for teachers'. Walter Bleakley, who was a working party member and lecturer
in pre-service education at the University of Ulster, felt that PE situation
in Northern Ireland's primary schools was 'broadly similar to that on the
mainland'.[149] He noted that he was aware of only one school, Strandtown,
which had a specialist in PE and this was 'a luxury'.[150] He added that 'most
others will be appointing maths and English and other specialists a long
way before they can afford it for PE' and that the Government needed to
re-assess funding for PE, especially in terms of in-service training.[151]

In February 1993, the SCNI launched their strategy for 'Sport for
Young People' which aimed to help them 'to have a range of opportunities
to take part in quality sport'.[152] Some efforts were also made to encourage
awareness of the value of PE and its position in the New Curriculum

144   Ibid., 2 September 1991.
145   Ibid., 27 February 1992.
146   Ibid.
147   Ibid.
148   Ibid.
149   Ibid.
150   Ibid.
151   Ibid.
152   Ibid., 9 March 1999.

through the provision of resources for teachers and pupils. In July 1993 the confectionery company Mars sent 'special packs' to Northern Ireland's secondary schools with a view to 'helping them deliver the new common curriculum on physical education'.[153] In December 1993 the South Eastern Board launched a PE resource pack, which included a video, to assist teacher training in the subject, with the video available free to all primary schools in the area.[154]

The Northern Ireland Physical Activity Strategy 1996–2002

In 1996, the new curriculum was reduced as teachers were of the view that it contained too much content.[155] Following the publication of the *Northern Ireland Physical Activity Strategy 1996–2002* in March 1996, an action plan was agreed upon by the Northern Ireland Physical Activity Strategy Implementation Group and around seventy organisations including the DENI.[156] One of the recommendations of the action plan was that another survey of PE be undertaken, with inspections later taking place in thirty-seven post-primary schools between the autumn of 1998 and the summer of 1999.[157] Amongst the findings highlighted, it was noted that 'in most of the schools included in the survey, the teachers and members of senior management value highly the contribution of PE to the curriculum'.[158] Relationships between teachers and pupils were

153 Ibid., 2 July 1993.
154 *Belfast Telegraph*, 6 December 1993.
155 *Curriculum Review, Summary of Proposal for the Revised Primary Curriculum and Its Assessment Arrangements* (Belfast, 2002), 5. Retrieved from <http://www.nicurriculum.org.uk/docs/background/curriculum_review/primsubt.pdf> [Accessed 19 July 2020].
156 *Department of Education (Northern Ireland). Report on Physical Education in Secondary Schools. Inspected 1998–99* (Belfast: The Education and Training Inspectorate, 2000), 1.
157 Ibid.
158 Ibid.

described as 'good and often excellent' while 'in most lessons' the students were motivated and enthusiastic, and were said to respond well when the classes were enjoyable and challenging and when teachers set and expected 'high standards of behaviour'.[159] Planning was 'satisfactory or better in a majority of schools', it was said to be 'poor' in the rest, while the heads of department were noted as the most significant influence on the quality of PE provided. However, 'only a minority of the schools visited' gave two hours per week to the subject and it was noted that 'for the majority of schools, the allocation is inadequate to cover fully the programme on study'.[160] It was also highlighted that while there were discrepancies in the quality of extra-curricular activities, these were 'generally satisfactory' and 'just under a third of the schools visited' had 'poor indoor and out-door facilities for PE and in a fifth of the schools' outdoor facilities were 'poor'.[161]

The report recommended that pupils be given enough time for PE per week, and in a way that satisfactory progress could be made in 'all areas of the programme' while more specific planning to highlight lesson outcomes was also suggested.[162] Assessment information gathered from pupils' work was to be utilised more effectively while it was also suggested that a wider range of teaching approaches be used for those 'who show little proficiency in PE'.[163] More support for teachers was needed in gymnastics and dance, while greater consistency was needed in providing support for non-specialist teachers' professional development in their assistance with extra-curricular and curricular programmes.[164] Other recommendations included that wider extra-curricular programmes be developed through community-based organisations and the Youth Sport initiative, and that pupils be made more fully aware of the importance of a healthy lifestyle.[165]

159   Ibid.
160   Ibid., 2.
161   Ibid.
162   Ibid., 13.
163   Ibid.
164   Ibid.
165   Ibid.

An additional report, *Improving Physical Education in Post-Primary Schools* (2001), 'based on inspections of and visits to physical education departments in post-primary schools in Northern Ireland during the period 1996–2000' brought a number of similar insights in terms of strengths, weaknesses and recommendations.[166] In particular, it was stated that 'the accommodation and resources for PE are good or better in around two-thirds of post-primary schools' but it was noted that there were variations in what was offered as extra-curricular activities.[167] There were 'marked differences' between what was offered in secondary and grammar schools, in rural and urban schools, and to boys and girls.[168] In addition, it was noted that 'the quality of teaching in PE provided by non-specialist teachers is generally poor and sometimes satisfactory'.[169] It was also stated that 'in many grammar schools, there is an over-dependence on non-specialist teachers with little expertise in the activities they are deployed to teach'.[170] This led to the specific recommendation 'to introduce in grammar schools, a more consistent approach to the professional development of non-specialist teachers who assist with PE and extra-curricular programmes'.[171]

By the late 1990s progress had been made in a number of areas. In November 1996 the SCNI combined with the DENI 'for the promotion of Physical Education and sport during and after school'.[172] Some primary schools also benefited from the Superschools initiative, with Donaghdee primary school pupils in County Down being coached by British gymnastics star Hayley Price and Glenn Wilkinson, a Gladiators contender.[173] This movement had been established to help schools in the United Kingdom raise funds for resources as well as to improve pupils' fitness levels.[174] Belfast

166 *Department of Education (Northern Ireland) Improving Physical Education in Post-Primary Schools* (Belfast: The Education and Training Inspectorate, 2001), 1–3.
167 Ibid., 2.
168 Ibid.
169 Ibid.
170 Ibid., 2–3.
171 Ibid., 3.
172 *Belfast Telegraph*, 26 November 1996.
173 Ibid., 29 September 1997.
174 Ibid.

Education and Library Board [BELB] advisor Seán McElhatton felt that 'sports awareness for children had been considerably enhanced by greater partnerships between the boards and the Sports Council of Northern Ireland'.[175] He noted that 'every education board has a youth sport programme supported by the Council which promotes after-school activities' with the BELB having nineteen post-primary schools who ran these in conjunction with the Youth Sports Programme.[176]

Within the Northern Ireland curriculum, primary pupils were required to be given two 30 minute physical education sessions per week, with post-primary schools undertaking a minimum of two weekly sessions, especially in the 11 to 14 age group. The subject was also a requirement between the ages of 14 and 18, although time reductions were more common.[177] Despite this progress, McElhatton felt that there were still misconceptions that PE was based on games only, and stated that dance, swimming and gymnastics were also part of the curriculum.[178] One research officer with the SCNI noted in 1997 that 80 per cent of children 'were involved in sport to some extent' and that they were no less physically active than they had been in 1995, although he felt that they were not being given enough choice within physical education in schools in terms of what sports they wanted to do.[179] There were also complaints from some teachers of the subject that not enough time was being given to it 'because of the pressures of the timetable'.[180] A similar situation was said to exist in England, with concerns raised by the SCNI there that at least two hours of exercise a week was needed by pupils while at school. Parental worries about safety also meant that fewer children were walking to school.[181] One PE Head felt there was still not enough time given to PE, however, as 'while the Department outlined the subjects to be taught, they left it to the individual schools to

175   Ibid.
176   Ibid.
177   Ibid.
178   Ibid.
179   Ibid.
180   Ibid.
181   Ibid.

allocate the amount of time to be given'.[182] He also noted that in his own school, which was located in Belfast, the time given to fourth-sixth year students dropped from eighty in their first-third years to sixty minutes.[183]

Cross-Community Relations and PE

Opinions varied on the difficulties of teaching PE during the Troubles. One former PE teacher recalled that he did not think travelling to play matches was a difficulty for his school in Belfast during the conflict:

> I mean obviously you know with the Troubles, you would have known to play at certain times, so we never played after school, we had to play during school time, because of where you were going, and we did go into areas which were dodgy enough. They would have come up into our area as well, you soon got used to it, and just went with it, and if you had any difficulty about where you were playing you just went to a neutral venue, it wasn't too bad that way.[184]

One PE teacher stated that on his teaching practice, he had to 'climb over the barricades past the boys in the masks to get down in to teach PE' in 'one of the really bad areas'.[185] One other interviewee noted that while checkpoints and searches were commonplace, 'there was no sense that schoolkids on a bus were targets'.[186] Playing at opponents' school grounds could sometimes be difficult, as one PE teacher who was on the staff of a secondary school in a nationalist area stated:

---

182 Ibid. In 1995 the Sports Council had been split for grassroots and elite purposes with Sport England catering for the former and UK Sport for the latter. See Carter, *Medicine, Sport and the Body*, 34.

183 *Belfast Telegraph*, 29 Sept. 1997.

184 Interview with Northern Ireland second level PE teacher number ten, 16 November 2019.

185 Interview with Northern Ireland second level PE teacher number eight, 31 October 2019.

186 Interview with Northern Ireland second level PE teacher number one, 12 September 2019.

In Gaelic games there weren't any problems but in soccer, it was tough because we were one of the few Catholic schools who were involved in the soccer. And we became very, very successful at it and we had numerous instances where buses would have been stoned, or where we went to play a school match a crowd gathered. A 'posse' as we would have called it. It was quite difficult and there were a number of incidents that had to be investigated and the police had to be involved. But we never stepped back I suppose we're part of that movement at that time that said 'we're entitled to play here like everybody else and nobody's gonna stop us.'[187]

While most schools' rugby teams were Protestant, and Gaelic games' teams generally Catholic, soccer teams could come from both religious denominations. The arrangement of venues for competitive fixtures did not please every school involved at times. In 1974, St Colman's of Strabane refused to travel to Belfast for their Irish Schools' Cup Final versus Ashfield, claiming that the game should be played at a more neutral venue, with the result that the city team were awarded the trophy.[188] Similarly, basketball brought teachers and pupils from opposite sides of the community together through competition, although one former PE teacher felt that they 'knew where to avoid' when going to matches and generally remained on friendly terms with other teachers.[189] He felt that some school teams of the same religion were more likely to start fighting during matches than those from opposing religious backgrounds.[190]

A number of teachers felt that life during the Troubles became 'normal' and they learned to adapt to the situation and were generally able to get on with their teaching despite what was going on around them.[191] Despite this, the organisation of cross-community schools matches was clearly affected, with one PE teacher recalling that as the Troubles worsened in the 1970s, arranging matches became 'stressful' and 'it got to a stage where you

187 Interview with Northern Ireland second level PE teacher number three, 26 September 2019.
188 Curran, *Irish Soccer Migrants*, 84.
189 Interview with Northern Ireland second level PE teacher number nine, 13 November 2019.
190 Ibid.
191 Interview with Northern Ireland second level PE teacher number one, 12 September 2019 and Interview with Northern Ireland second level PE teacher number three, 26 September 2019.

couldn't actually go to some schools'.[192] He recalled that Protestant and Catholic basketball teams had to be segregated into two different groups based on religion with the winners of each playing in the final. He claimed that his school's bus had been stoned and they 'had to be smuggled out of school once'. This 'led to very insular sport', he felt.[193] Provincial towns were also affected, with school buses being taken over and burned in some areas, which, as one PE teacher stated, had led to serious restrictions on travel to matches.[194]

The positioning of the British Army near some schools was an unwanted distraction for some PE teachers. One interviewee who taught in a nationalist area felt that the presence of the British Army made it more difficult to conducted PE lessons:

> Well it's something that I would say when I look back on it now, as hard to believe that I lived through the Troubles. I was probably child of the Troubles in the sense and grew up with it but we, in a sense, accepted it for the thing as it was. Somebody like yourself, say coming in, landing yourself in the middle of it, would say 'what the hell am I doing here?' But our school actually had an army camp just across the street and there were numerous clashes between our boys and the army because the army, it seemed for some reason, wanted to take their patrols at the time we had break. They wanted to take their patrols out at the time we had lunch. And they wanted to take their patrol at the time school finished. And there were numerous skirmishes. But I suppose I'm quite proud of the fact we would have had very, very few boys who were hugely involved in the Troubles. We tried to point them in other directions [but] there was a number of boys who went to school that were shot dead.[195]

The presence of the army and the police impacted on both unionist and nationalist communities in terms of PE, however, with one former PE teacher from a provincial town noting that the swimming pool used by

192 Interview with Northern Ireland second level PE teacher number five, 4 October 2019.
193 Ibid.
194 Interview with Northern Ireland second level PE teacher number eight, 31 October 2019.
195 Interview with Northern Ireland second level PE teacher number three, 26 September 2019.

his school was blown up by the IRA as it was also used for the training of Royal Ulster Constabulary [RUC] recruits.[196]

The Education Reform Order was fundamental to the introduction of a 'statutory curriculum' in Northern Ireland in 1991.[197] As Bardon has stated, 'the preparations for the introduction of the national curriculum from 1989 onwards provided a unique opportunity to bridge the gulf dividing Protestant and Catholic schools: henceforth, all pupils during the compulsory years of schooling would be following the same programmes of study'.[198] Cross-cultural themes were to be implemented within the curriculum with two aspects of these, 'cultural heritage and education for mutual understanding', exclusive to Northern Ireland's schools.[199] This 'included encouragement of joint work between schools of both main traditions, the study of cultural traditions within the pupils' locality, region and further afield, and the extent to which the heritage was shared' with a view to students' having a knowledge of the origins of the ongoing conflict and both British and Irish history.[200] These proposals were later implemented into the 1989 Northern Ireland Education Reform Order.[201]

However, attitudes towards alternative cultures have been slow to change in some areas. As one interviewee recalled of this move:

> they brought it in then, with these new subject specifications in 1989, these things – it was 'education for mutual understanding' – it was one of the themes and our principal explained it to us and my good friend who took the soccer teams in the school stood up and said 'they're bringing in this new theme; mutual understanding'. He said 'we're doing that already' and the principal said, 'well, what do you mean?' He said 'when we play the [Protestant] boys – they know we're going to kick them and we know they're going to kick us!'[202]

196 Interview with Northern Ireland second level PE teacher number one, 12 September 2019.

197 *Curriculum Review, Summary of Proposal for the Revised Primary Curriculum and Its Assessment Arrangements*, 5.

198 Bardon, *A History of Ulster*, 801.

199 Ibid.

200 Ibid.

201 Ibid.

202 Interview with Northern Ireland second level PE teacher number three, 26 September 2019.

He added that, more recently, with the falling numbers in school attendances, some Catholic and Protestant schools had no option but to
work together to provide teacher expertise for pupils undertaking certain subjects or risk school closures.[203] The loss of numbers could impact
on PE's place within a school's curriculum in some areas. In May 1985,
Willie Anderson, the Irish rugby international, lost his job as head of
PE at Rainey Endowed School in Magherafelt due to a decrease in pupil
numbers.[204]

In 1991, Lagan College, which welcomed pupils of all religions as
pupils and had been without a proper building structure since it was established in 1981, was officially opened and by 1992, 'there were sixteen schools
educating Protestants and Catholics together in roughly even numbers,
but they accounted for a mere one per cent of pupils in the region'.[205] The
Catholic Church was adamant that Catholic pupils should receive their
education in Catholic schools, while hostility to integration also came from
the Democratic Unionist Party.[206] Some unionists and clergy were open to
integrated education and 'Protestant schools-most of them fully funded by
the state-regarded themselves as being open to young people of all beliefs'.[207]
In addition, 'several prestigious grammar schools did, indeed, attract significant numbers of Catholics; it was undeniable, however, that they and
the great majority of state schools retained a distinctly Protestant ethos'.[208]

The 1991 NICER PE report provides a useful assessment of the distinctions in codes offered in both Catholic and Protestant schools at that
time.[209] The report highlighted that 'the activities offered to pupils as part
of their Curricular Physical Education [CPE] course was found to vary

203   Ibid.
204   *Evening Herald*, 21 May 1985.
205   Bardon, *A History of Ulster*, 800–1.
206   Ibid., 801.
207   Ibid.
208   Ibid.
209   For a further discussion of pupil participation in sport in Northern Ireland's
       schools in the late twentieth century see also Karen Trew, John Kremer, Anthony
       M. Gallagher, Deirdre Scully and Shaun Ogle, 'Young People's Participation in
       Sport in Northern Ireland' in *International Review for the Sociology of Sport*, vol. 32,
       no. 4 (1997), 419–31.

with the age and sex of the young people, whether they were enrolled in a grammar or secondary school and whether the school was Catholic or Protestant in its affiliation'.[210] It was noted that 'during the years of compulsory education', athletics, basketball and soccer were the three games that appeared most frequently on boys' CPE syllabuses, although Gaelic football was taught in nearly all the boys' Catholic schools' and hurling 'in over half' of these.[211] These codes were not on the syllabus of any Protestant school in the responses received.[212] Cricket (see Figure 35), rugby and athletics were 'the three most frequently offered activities in boys' Protestant grammar schools', while rugby, hockey and cricket were only occasionally offered in Catholic schools. It was noted that 'perhaps partly because of the more generous time-allocation, the Protestant grammar schools offered their boys a wider range of CPE activities than other grammar schools'.[213]

Figure 35.   The Royal Belfast Academical Institution cricket first team XI, 1976.
Courtesy of Sharon Casement.

210   *Physical Education and Games in Post-Primary Schools*, 74.
211   Ibid., 75.
212   Ibid.
213   Ibid.

Netball, athletics and rounders were noted as the three games appearing most frequently on girls' CPE syllabuses in compulsory education, but differences in the CPE subjects offered in Catholic and Protestant girls' schools were 'rather less pronounced' than in the boys' schools.[214] Camogie, which was offered in 'over half the girls' Catholic secondary schools and about a quarter of the girls' Catholic grammar schools, was not taught in any Protestant school'.[215] Although hockey was also offered in Catholic girls' schools, it was played more frequently in Protestant schools, while 'by Years 11–12 girls in Protestant grammar schools enjoyed a wider range of CPE activities … than those elsewhere, while those in Catholic grammar schools, who had the lowest time allocation for Physical Education, had a notably limited range'.[216]

The report also illustrated that 'most boys' grammar schools, especially in the Protestant sector, offered their pupils a considerable variety of CPE activities in sixth form.'[217] Naturally, 'Gaelic football continued to be very popular, though only in the Catholic sector, while in the Protestant sector, rugby and cricket maintained their high level of availability and hockey its moderate level'.[218] With the success of the Ulster Rugby team in January 1999 in winning the European Cup, interest in the sport was said to have grown in some schools.[219] In particular, St Patrick's Academy Dungannon had been playing rugby since 1995 after 'several cross-community trips to Garryowen' with the local Royal School.[220] They had then started training at Dungannon Rugby Club and took part in joint training session with Drumglass High School, a nearby secondary school. St Patrick's Academy physical education headmaster Fintan Colgan also stated that they were introducing an under fourteen team as a result of the increased interest following Ulster's victory in the final.[221] By the 1990s, a number of traditional

---

214 Ibid.
215 Ibid.
216 Ibid.
217 Ibid., 76.
218 Ibid.
219 *Belfast Telegraph*, 20 February 1999.
220 Ibid.
221 Ibid.

rugby-playing schools had also taken on soccer, with the Royal Belfast Academical Institution (see Figure 36) taking up the sport through PE teacher Paul McKinstry in the late 1970s.[222]

Despite this shift in some areas, many schools clung to what they knew best. By the late 1990s, some schools still prioritised expertise in a particular code in making their physical education appointments.[223] Belfast High School, a voluntary grammar school on the Shore Road, advertised a vacant physical education teacher position in the school in April 1997, with the notice highlighting that the 'ability to coach rugby football' was 'essential'.[224] The traditional ethos of many schools remained a vital part of their identity. Similarly an advertisement for a PE teacher at Campbell College in May 1999 stipulated that 'the ability to make a major contribution to the college's strong sporting tradition' was also 'essential' for prospective candidates.[225]

Figure 36. The Royal Belfast Academical Institution soccer first team XI, 1996–7. Courtesy of Sharon Casement.

222   Curran, *Irish Soccer Migrants*, 98.
223   *Belfast Telegraph*, 11 April 1997.
224   Ibid.
225   Ibid., 4 May 1999.

PE as an Examination Subject in Northern Ireland

One teacher interviewed felt that PE had taken on 'a new character' in terms of how it was viewed through its gaining of an examination status while the subject's compulsory status from September 1991 onwards was also a positive step in lessening stereotypical attitudes about the nature of its place within the curriculum.[226] By the late 1990s PE had become more firmly established as an examination subject at GCSE and 'A' Level within Northern Ireland's schools. This development had its origins in the 1970s. Denis O'Boyle has written that 'in Northern Ireland the year 1974 marked the initial period that led to the development of examinations in physical education'.[227] Two Belfast schools, Orangefield Boys' School and Lisnasharragh Secondary school, 'had prepared schemes and submitted to the Northern Ireland CSE Examination Board'. Those at Orangefield had done so because there was 'a demand for the introduction of theoretical aspects into the physical education programme and a demand from the students for a greater choice and depth of involvement in activities'.[228] At Lisnasharragh, it was felt that examinations in the subject would lead to greater development in the content of the PE programme and help raise the numbers of PE staff there and also would see 'an increase in the provision of the means to satisfy many of the needs and interests of the pupils'.[229]

PE examinations had been initiated as 'an unofficial pilot scheme' in Birmingham in the latter half of the 1950s and despite some opposition to these from the Secondary School Examinations' Council in 1963, by 1981 a survey illustrated that they were becoming 'well established and appeared to be increasing in demand'.[230] Malcolm Tozer has written that in England, 'several independent schools from the 1970s promoted classroom studies in

---

226   Interview with Northern Ireland second level PE teacher number five, 4 October 2019.
227   O'Boyle, 'Examinations in Physical Education: An Irish Perspective', 181.
228   Ibid.
229   Ibid.
230   Ibid., 179–80.

physical education as part of integrated science, general studies or health-related programmes' and these had an impact on the subject's development as a GCSE and 'A' Level examination subject.[231] O'Boyle has also noted that 'in 1975 the Schools Examination Council in Northern Ireland recommended that physical education be added to the list of subjects accepted for examination at CSE level'.[232] One PE teacher noted, of this initial system in the 1970s that in his school, when interviewed that

> we did a lot of CSE PE, which is where you wrote your own sort of course … it was just CSE, for our school, we would have done a camping section, where you had to go on out and put a tent up and all that sort of stuff, it went great. And then what happened was the CSE then was stopped and obviously it's GCSE PE now.[233]

By the latter part of the decade support for PE as an examination subject had grown, as one survey undertaken in 1978 found that around three-fifths of PE teachers in Northern Ireland were in favour of this.[234] Despite the positive sentiments in the 1970s, progress was slow in this regard, and, as one former PE teacher noted, grammar schools have been more inclined to offer 'A' Level PE than secondary schools.[235] In addition, the subject began to take up more time as classroom theory was also needed and required more planning from PE teachers, while the additional attention given to it at times drew negative comments from other teachers.[236] Some schools had initially been reluctant to take it on as they were unsure of its nature, as one former PE teacher noted:

> It took quite a while in Northern Ireland to catch on because grammar schools were very reticent about this subject and would it stand the test of being accepted as an 'A' level. I think it was only when a girl in England was accepted into Oxford with one of her 'A' levels in physical education that the grammar schools started to look

---

231   Tozer, *Edward Thring's Theory, Practice and Legacy*, 326.
232   O'Boyle, 'Examinations in Physical Education', 181.
233   Interview with Northern Ireland second level PE teacher Number ten, 16 November 2019.
234   O'Boyle, 'Examinations in Physical Education', 181.
235   Interview with Northern Ireland second level PE teacher number five, 4 October 2019.
236   Ibid.

at it and say 'some of our kids are talented here, it's a subject they can do well at.' In Newry, there are two main grammar schools for the boys, there's Abbey and St Colman's, and they are constantly in conflict over the pupils that they can attract. So when one school introduced 'A' level physical education and their numbers increased, it wasn't very long before the other school said 'well we have to catch up here' and so they introduced 'A' level physical education as well to attract pupils back again. [237]

In 1986, O'Boyle estimated that only less than 10 per cent of Northern Ireland's second level schools were 'participating in examinations in the subject' and noted that 'there also existed a dissatisfaction with the ability of the students who have opted for the course' despite the opportunities given to teachers and students to gain experience of second level examinations in PE.[238] In 1989–90, physical education was amongst four subjects available as Advanced Supplementary (AS) subjects which had been 'introduced to broaden the sixth-form curriculum', although it appears that the numbers taking these subjects were quite small.[239]

As Tozer states, by the 1990s, 'courses directed at these examinations became popular and many physical education teachers now devoted all their time to their specialist subject, whether in the sports centre or in the classroom'.[240] Assessment of Curriculum Physical Education held an important place in the majority of schools by the early 1990s, but examinations were not held everywhere. The 1991 NICER report noted that assessment in PE was undertaken in 97 per cent of schools with teachers' observations 'by far the commonest method', utilised in 95 per cent of the schools.[241] However, written tests were used by only 7 per cent of those who responded.[242] In addition, 'though none of the schools was as yet engaged on an "A" Level course in Physical Education, nearly a quarter of the respondents (66 HODS) were already entering pupils for a GCSE examination in the subject, the number of entrants in schools ranging from 2

237 Interview with Northern Ireland second level PE teacher Number three, 26 September 2019.
238 O'Boyle, 'Examinations in Physical Education', 181–2.
239 *Belfast Telegraph*, 9 April 1990.
240 Tozer, *Edward Thring's Theory, Practice and Legacy*, 326.
241 *Physical Education and Games in Post-Primary Schools*, 77.
242 Ibid.

to 38'.[243] In June 1994 it was announced that PE would be available to take as part of 'a new "modular GCSE course"'.[244]

By the late 1990s, PE had become more commonly available as an 'A' Level subject in schools in Northern Ireland. One PE teacher recalled when interviewed that

> It was a wee bit of practical and a lot of theory, which is a bigger step from GCSE PE which I had, it's a really big jump, you know, from that to 'A' Level. Because they want different things, for example, in PE it's all about the circulatory system and all that kind of thing. They don't delve too much into the heart [at GCSE level] -a wee bit like, you go into greater depth for the heart and stuff in 'A' Level PE.[245]

In September 1997, PE was said to be 'the fasting growing GCSE subject in Northern Ireland'.[246] 1,610 pupils at ninety-one schools in Northern Ireland took the GCSE physical education examination that year, which was a vast increase from the 759 who sat it in 1991.[247] Fifteen schools were said to be providing 'A' Level physical education 'through mainland boards'. One Belfast-based PE Head stated that this was a reflection of modern society and a greater awareness of the advantages of benefits and there was also 'a unity of purpose amongst various bodies'.[248] He also noted that grammar schools were taking it 'much more seriously as an examination subject' and in 1996, there had been 1,500 applications for the fifty places on the University of Ulster sports science course as jobs in leisure management and sport became more sought after.[249] However, not every school carried the subject at 'A' Level, with one current PE teacher of the opinion that in his school, GCSE PE was provided, but it made more sense for pupils to do a BTEC sports course as it was perceived to

243   Ibid., 77–8.
244   *Belfast Telegraph*, 29 June 1994.
245   Interview with Northern Ireland second level PE teacher number two, 18 September 2019.
246   *Belfast Telegraph*, 29 September 1997.
247   Ibid.
248   Ibid.
249   Ibid.

be easier for them and more suited to their ability.[250] One PE teacher admitted he felt nervous about its implementation as an examination subject there in the 1990s, but noted that it was now more fully accepted and he expected the new Irish Leaving Certificate examination to follow the same pattern.[251] All the Northern Ireland PE teachers interviewed for this study felt that this was a positive move, although one teacher felt that it also needed to be fun. She believed while it was valuable for university points, it also needed to retain this aspect of its nature.[252]

Conclusion

The status of PE rose significantly in Northern Ireland's schools in the period from 1973 until 2000 despite the difficulties in organising lessons in some areas with the dangers of the Troubles. The development of co-educational courses for teaching qualifications in the early 1970s was important in offering a local base for both males and females interested in teaching PE. Despite the scarcity of jobs by the middle of the decade, the expansion of sports-related courses allowed those interested in teaching sports more options. This was at times linked to the lack of a specialised PE position in many schools, and in some cases a decline in pupil numbers meant the loss of the designated PE teacher. There is some evidence that the decrease of school sport in England in the 1980s was reflected in some educational institutions of Northern Ireland such as Wallace High School. Despite the implementation of a New Curriculum in September 1991, resources for PE remained inadequate in some areas, both in an indoor and outdoor capacity. The provision of indoor space for physical

---

250 Interview with Northern Ireland second level PE teacher number seven, 8 October 2019.
251 Interview with Northern Ireland second level PE teacher number nine, 13 November 2019.
252 Interview with Northern Ireland second level PE teacher number six, 8 October 2019.

education remained an issue for some schools such as Millburn Primary School in Coleraine in May 1994.[253] Resources continued to be a problem in some areas, with one Derry-based school principal lamenting the lack of outdoor facilities for PE at his high school in Carnhill in November 1997.[254] The provision of these continued to be awkward for primary and secondary schools, and sentiments regarding the subject in smaller schools were in many ways reflective of those much earlier in the century as attention remained focused on the provision of what were viewed as more academic lessons. However, with the subject taking on a compulsory nature in 1991, it could no longer be ignored, although the amount of attention given to it depended in many ways on what a school could afford. Much progress had been made however, particularly in regard to the requirements of the new National Curriculum.

Despite some interest in the implementation of PE as an examination subject in the 1970s, by the mid-1980s the majority of schools were still reluctant to offer this option to their pupils. However, by the end of the following decade it was more commonly available as a choice in schools, while the number of sport related courses on offer as university degrees had grown substantially since the early 1970s. Religious divides meant that the provision of school sports was generally run on traditional lines, although, as seen in the case of rugby in Dungannon, this was not always clear cut. In June 2000, the Northern Ireland Sports Council was reconstituted, with the Strategy for the Development of Sport, launched by the former Sports Council in 1997, said to have 'laid a strong foundation on which to build for the future'.[255] The Good Friday Agreement of the following year offered fresh hope of a wider societal reconciliation, even if this was only temporary and the St Andrew's Agreement of 2006 was necessary to move political developments along.[256] Chapter 10 examines the development of PE in primary schools in the Republic of Ireland between 1974 and 2000.

253 *Belfast Telegraph*, 2 July 1994.
254 Ibid., 29 November 1997.
255 *Ulster Herald*, 15 June 2000.
256 Bartlett, *Ireland: A History*, 575–9.

Struggling Along: PE in the Republic of Ireland's Primary Schools, 1974–2000

Introduction

This chapter begins by examining the impact of the revised curriculum of 1971 on PE in the Republic of Ireland's primary schools. As Coolahan has written, 'guidelines and approaches were suggested but teachers were encouraged to adapt the programme to suit the needs and educational environment of the district in which the school was situated'.[1] In assessing the views of a number of interviewees who taught at that time and also initial reactions to the implementation of the new PE syllabus in studies undertaken in the 1970s, this chapter illustrates how the provision of regular, timetabled PE remained difficult as many schools lacked the resources, and in some cases the expertise, to adhere to this rigorously. A number of initial national surveys undertaken reflected badly on the Irish education system in terms of PE time and resources. Along with music and art and crafts, PE was the subject which gave teachers most difficulty.[2] In April 1987, new Minister for Youth and Sport, Frank Fahey, announced that one of his aims would be to increase the significance of PE in primary and post-primary schools.[3] However, this remained a difficult task as other subjects remained prioritised. In the latter decade of the twentieth century the amount of time allocated to PE in Irish schools was still inadequate in comparison with some of Europe's other nations and the provision of facilities remained an issue in teachers' ability to conduct

1   Coolahan, *Towards the Era of Lifelong Learning*, 123.
2   Ibid., 124.
3   *Irish Press*, 14 April 1987.

classes in the subject. There were also concerns that the amount of time allocated to PE in teacher-training colleges remained insufficient towards the end of the 1990s. Changes were underway however and the primary school curriculum was revised in 1999 and the inclusion of a new PE syllabus, albeit with what was still a relatively small time allocation per week, was an important step in cementing its teaching within schools.

Physical Education and the Revised Curriculum in Primary Schools

With the implementation of the Revised Curriculum in 1971, PE in Irish primary schools was officially given an increased status, but this was not a straightforward process and was not always reflected in the classroom. A number of teachers who were active in schools at that time stated that they received no Department notification surrounding Captain McDonough's appointment in the previous decade and his related work.[4] A PE teacher who spent most of his career in a school in a small town noted that in relation to the revised curriculum's introduction, 'I can vaguely remember a teachers' meeting called by the Department to discuss the new curriculum and PE was discussed. And after that, you know, nobody-no teachers [in my school] had any interest in it anyhow.'[5]

It was highlighted in the 1971 *Primary School Curriculum Teacher's Handbook* (part 1) that along with improvements in methods for group-teaching and curriculum integration, in newly built schools, provisions such as floor space, lighting, heating and new furniture had improved through modern design.[6] It was also stated that 'substantial reductions'

---

4   Interview with primary school teacher number seven, 3 July 2019; interview with
      primary school teacher number eight, 23 July 2019 and interview with primary
      school teacher number nine, 24 July 2019.
5   Interview with primary school teacher number 25 July 2019.
6   *Primary School Curriculum: Teacher's Handbook Part 1* (Dublin: Government of
      Ireland, 1971), 16.

had 'been made in the pupil/teacher ratio', but in many schools facilities stayed as they were and this impacted on how physical education could be taught.[7] One PE teacher interviewed recalled that in the school in which she was employed, which was in a rural area, there was little change as its implementation was largely dependent on facilities. She stated that 'there was nothing for it only out in the school yard if the weather was suitable, if it wasn't suitable, you just didn't do it … so it was just mostly ignored in the country schools anyway, it was probably taught in the bigger schools, all right'.[8] PE's implementation at that time was often down to a teacher's personal interest, as one teacher recalled:

> When I started primary teaching in 1971, I started off in [names school], there were no facilities there, there was just a yard. But in fairness to the principal in that school he was very much into athletics, so he developed sort of a circuit within the yard, where you had actually running around the school building and you had a long-jump pitch and you had a high-jump and there was emphasis on that sort of athletics. But only because he had an interest, there wouldn't have been any. So it was down to the individual teacher or principal in any particular school.[9]

The interviewees also all noted a lack of pressure to implement the subject in their daily teaching. As one teacher recalled of his teaching in the late twentieth century, 'anything they [the Department of Education] were serious about, there would be pressure brought to do it, and that never happened with PE'.[10]

These views regarding the subject's peripheral position in the curriculum were reflected in contemporary surveys. A survey carried out by the INTO and published in 1974, described as 'the first serious attempt' to evaluate the new curriculum, revealed that out of 7,677 questionnaires returned, 4,884 INTO members or 64.6 per cent stated that they taught PE, but only 2,492 or 34.2 per cent felt that they were teaching it satisfactorily.[11] The INTO concluded that the PE curriculum was 'an up to date

7   Ibid.
8   Interview with primary school teacher number seven, 3 July 2019.
9   Interview with primary school teacher number eight, 23 July 2019.
10   Interview with primary school teacher number nine, 24 July 2019.
11   *INTO Primary School Curriculum Survey* (Dublin: INTO, 1974), 17 and 23.

enlightened programme based upon principles accepted in many developed countries'.[12] Despite this, they felt that it would be 'impossible, however, to carry out the programme in many schools because of inadequate indoor space, unsuitable playing grounds and lack of equipment'.[13]

This continued throughout that decade. Issues were also noted by Michael Anthony Cotter in his study of PE in Irish primary schools in 1978.[14] In particular, he identified that facilities 'were inadequate' and that the training of teachers in the subject was 'unsatisfactory'. He also stated that PE was 'not highly rated in relation to other subjects' and that the curriculum for it was 'unrealistic in its aspirations'.[15]

In 1974 the B.Ed. university degree for teachers was inaugurated, with St Patrick's College Drumcondra, Mary Immaculate, Limerick and Our Lady of Mercy, Carysfort gaining recognition as National University of Ireland colleges.[16] Smaller primary teaching colleges became affiliated with Trinity College Dublin, although the Church of Ireland College had already held this association.[17] Cotter's study also sheds light on the state of PE in the primary teacher-training colleges at that time. His work highlighted that the subject was 'largely optional in the largest colleges of education' and that students could graduate 'having had little contact' with it.[18] Despite this, Cotter stated that there were 'qualified Physical Education staff' within the Departments of Education in all the Colleges of Education while the PE section of the Department of Education itself had four PE staff by 1978.[19] Opinions on the value of the training received were mixed, however. Fifty per cent of all teachers who took part in the study 'felt that their training was of little help in the schools situation'.[20] Figures for those undertaking

12   Ibid.
13   Ibid., 24.
14   Cotter, 'An Investigation into the Teaching of Physical Education in National Schools', 184.
15   Ibid.
16   Coolahan, *Irish Education: History and Structure*, 228.
17   Ibid.
18   Cotter, 'An Investigation into the Teaching of Physical Education in National Schools', 185–6.
19   Ibid., 12.
20   Ibid.

additional training on teaching the subject were low. Although only 15 per cent undertook in-service courses on the subject, they felt that the training received at these was beneficial.[21]

Teachers' attitudes to the subject remained slow to evolve. Cotter also found that 'relative to the other curricular areas, Physical Education is not highly rated by national teachers. Instead it tends to be equated with the pre-1970 optional subjects.'[22] He also noticed differences between how male and female teachers viewed the teaching of the subject.[23] He added that 'the Physical Education curriculum is not designed for the vast majority of national schools'. He also stated that the study revealed that teaching the subject was more common amongst young teachers, while swimming was generally neglected.[24] Cotter concluded his findings by stating that 'the divergence between what is happening in these schools and what the Department of Education would wish to occur, as expressed in the New Curriculum, is significant.'[25]

School facilities remained a primary concern in that decade, according to one teacher interviewed for this book. Now retired, he began teaching in the early 1970s and recalled that the school he taught in late in that decade 'had a gravel-surfaced school yard, where it was actually dangerous to even run. And there was no way you could have PE lessons in those days.'[26] He added that 'the first priority was to get a decent surface on the school yard, a tarmacadam yard, and then we developed other little things but it wasn't until the end of the last century that there was funding for PE equipment.'[27] John P. Wilson, the Minister for Education from 1977–81, stated in 1979 that he aimed to develop yard surfaces and provide basic equipment for 'older schools'.[28] Primary schools could also include in their building plans

21 Ibid.
22 Ibid., 187.
23 Ibid.
24 Ibid., 187–8.
25 Ibid., 188.
26 Interview with primary school teacher number eight, 23 July 2019.
27 Ibid.
28 'Dáil Éireann Debate – Wednesday, 21 Feb 1979, Vol. 311. No. 10. Ceisteanna – Questions. Oral Answers. – Physical Education in Schools.' Retrieved from <https://www.oireachtas.ie/en/debates/debate/dail/1979-02-21/25/> [Accessed 2 November 2020].

'paved play spaces, ball courts and, except in the case of smaller schools, general purpose rooms'.[29] The treatment of PE in some primary schools contrasted to that in second level. One current primary school teacher who grew up in the 1970s noted a distinct difference in the provision of PE in her primary and second level education:

> In relation to my childhood experiences of physical education in primary school during the '70s, I had no experience whatsoever of PE, I do not remember ever being brought outside to take part in any PE lessons. Both primary schools I attended had quite small yard space and there was never a PE lesson whatsoever, in either of those schools. In relation to my teenage experiences I went to a vocational schools and there was plenty of opportunity for PE there. We did basketball, badminton, rounders, so we were well enough catered for at secondary school level.[30]

The 1980s

A number of surveys completed early in the following decade demonstrate that by then there were still concerns about the subject's teaching at primary school level. In December 1981, the results of a survey undertaken by graduates of St Patrick's College of 1961 revealed that a scarcity of in-service training for teachers was their biggest issue, while 'large classes and inadequate provision for physical education' were also amongst their chief concerns.[31] Issues with resources reflected wider problems with facilities within schools. In April 1982, what was described as 'the biggest ever survey of our [national] schools', conducted by the INTO, revealed that most of them did not have 'basic necessities such as a telephone, a typewriter, a filing cabinet, a movie projector or even a separate principal's room'.[32] It was also revealed that only one-third of schools had a hall, while

---

29   'Dáil Éireann Debate – Wednesday, 8 Mar 1978. Vol. 304. No. 7. Ceisteanna – Questions. Oral Answers. – Primary Schools.' Retrieved from <https://www.oireachtas.ie/en/debates/debate/dail/1978-03-08/8/> [Accessed 4 November 2020].
30   Interview with primary school teacher number six, 3 July 2019.
31   *Irish Independent*, 16 December 1981.
32   *Sunday Independent*, 4 April 1982.

slightly over 60 per cent had no access to playing fields.[33] The survey concluded that national schools were 'badly served in terms of equipment and resources and that small schools are the worst hit', with just over 21 per cent having 'basic equipment for physical education'.[34]

Some initiatives towards improving teacher training in PE were driven by teachers themselves. In June 1982, a survey undertaken by Cospóir (the name given to the National Sports Council at that point) member and school principal, Noel Keating, found that most teachers who took part in this 'felt that they were inadequately trained to teach physical education in the schools'.[35] With the assistance of 'national governing bodies of sporting organisations, the Department of Education, Health Education Bureau and College Staff' he developed a 160 hour course 'to fill the vacuum in training'.[36] It was initially run at the Teachers' Centre in Drumcondra with twenty-two teachers from the Dublin area completing it, but it was not compulsory and does not appear to have been an annual event.[37]

By the summer of 1984 there were 3,500 national schools in the Republic of Ireland with 555,000 pupils enrolled.[38] Occasionally, government-backed efforts were made to raise awareness of the importance of sport and physical fitness but a lot of this was aimed at teachers taking the initiative themselves. In May 1984, the National Dairy Council published a booklet for a 'Sports for All' day for primary schools, with primary and Physical Education Inspectors from the Department of Education involved in its compilation.[39] The actual event, held on 8 May, was organised by Cospóir, with a view to increasing primary school pupils' awareness of sport. It was to 'be regarded as a normal school day' with teachers encouraged to plan sports-related activities.[40] Minister for Education, Gemma Hussey (1982–6) also noted the organisation by Cospóir of 'seminars and other promotional activities' for PE which could be attended by pupils and teachers and which she felt

33   Ibid.
34   Ibid.
35   *Irish Independent*, 30 June 1982.
36   Ibid.
37   Ibid.
38   *Irish Examiner*, 2 May 1984.
39   Ibid.
40   Ibid.

influenced the subject's promotion.[41] In October 1984 she launched a PE course, 'Ceol agus Gluaiseacht' (Music and Movement) which consisted of a tape and illustrated book.[42] This development was said to be reflective of the growing numbers of all-Irish primary schools, but again it illustrated how primary school teachers generally had to act independently in teaching PE.[43]

Primary schools' funding for PE equipment was part of more general assistance from the Department of Education. In May 1986, Minister for Education Patrick Mark Cooney (1986–7) outlined his policy towards PE equipment for national schools, stating that

> Capital grants for national school accommodation would cover the provision of a ballcourt together with nets and posts, and for gymnastic mats, balancing benches, bar box and climbing units where a general purposes area is available. Current or capitation grants to these schools would be expected to meet in some measure the cost of a variety of small items such as balls, ropes, hoops and bats.[44]

However, funding of school PE resources continued to be a problem by the latter years of the decade. By then, Fine Gael politician and former PE teacher and ex-Kerry Gaelic footballer Jimmy Deenihan was of the view that Ireland was becoming 'a video society', with PE's neglect in schools 'farcical' given grants from the National Lottery, which had its initial draw in 1987, were being allocated for other non-school related sports facilities.[45] He raised this matter in the Dáil in November 1988 and stated that

> Physical education in our national schools is almost non-existent at the moment. Most teachers go through their training with just 20 hours of training in physical education. In

41 'Dáil Éireann Debate – Thursday, 28 Jun 1984. Vol. 352. No. 5.' <https://www.oireachtas.ie/en/debates/debate/dail/1984-06-28/218/> [Accessed 4 November 2020].

42 *Irish Press*, 5 October 1984.

43 Ibid.

44 'Dáil Éireann Debate – Tuesday, 20 May 1986. Vol. 366. No. 8. Written Answers. – Physical Education Equipment.' Retrieved from <https://www.oireachtas.ie/en/debates/debate/dail/1986-05-20/131/> [Accessed 3 November 2020].

45 *Irish Independent*, 12 October 1988.

our secondary schools 60 per cent of students at senior level are not now doing physical education. That is a national scandal. Here we are providing facilities and looking for results in the Olympics, yet we are not providing the basic training and education for these people. Instead of running around the country and trying to be popular and providing facilities everywhere, why do we not start at the kernel of our problem, why do we not start in the schools and ensure that there is a proper physical education curriculum implemented? If we are serious about putting sport on the agenda we should start there.[46]

By this point, INTO representatives' attitudes towards PE's development contrasted greatly with the first half of the twentieth century. In December 1988, the INTO told an international OECD team, which was investigating Irish education, that primary schools in Ireland were 'seriously under-funded compared to other countries'.[47] The INTO also noted that 60 per cent of schools 'did not have appropriate indoor facilities and less than a third had appropriate equipment', while 'annual grants were needed to replace and maintain equipment'.[48] It was also stated that 'lack of accommodation and equipment inhibited the teaching of PE in primary schools'.[49]

In theory, monitoring of the subject appeared to be well catered for by the Department of Education, but this masked the actual situation. In February 1989, Minister for Education Mary O'Rourke (1987–91) noted, when questioned by Deputy Deenihan in the Dáil, that at primary school level, there were seventy-five inspectors who were responsible 'for inspecting physical education in schools as part of general inspection and six inspectors who have responsibility for conducting PE courses and for the development of PE programmes'.[50] Later that year, when questioned about the

46   'Dáil Éireann Debate – Tuesday, 8 Nov 1988. Vol. 383, No. 8. Private Members' Business. – National Lottery (Amendment) Bill, 1988: Second Stage.' Retrieved from <https://www.oireachtas.ie/en/debates/debate/dail/1988-11-08/21/> [Accessed 2 November 2020].

47   *Irish Independent*, 19 December 1988.

48   Ibid.

49   Ibid.

50   'Dáil Debates – Wednesday 15 February 1989, vol. 387, no. 2. Written Answers – Physical Education.' Retrieved from <https://www.oireachtas.ie/ga/debates/debate/dail/1989-02-15/95/> [Accessed 30 October 2020].

place of PE on the school timetable, she stated that 'it is the responsibility of the principal teacher, in consultation with school staff to outline a plan of work for the school as a whole and ensure that each area of the curriculum is adequately dealt with in all classes'.[51] This was not always satisfactory, however. One current primary school teacher who grew up in rural Ireland in the late 1980s illustrated the ad hoc system which existed in her school at the time:

> I went to a small three-teacher country school, and I don't really remember PE much as a small child, except lots of running, and then when we got into the middle and senior classes … the girls all kind of played rounders, the boys played football- and I vaguely remember in 5th and 6th class the principal bought a unihoc set, and we did a bit of unihoc, which seemed quite advanced for the time. But mostly it was rounders, and we had a school team-you know, PE was rounders. We'd no hall or anything like that – it was out in the fields – if it was raining you didn't do it.[52]

Physical Education in Irish Primary Schools in the Early 1990s

Attention given to the subject remained inadequate and again, this drew attention from some international visitors. In January 1990, All-Blacks hooker Warren Gatland, while coaching in Connacht, noted that in New Zealand, children as young as five were being exposed to ball-skills in rugby training at school, with each child having their own ball.[53] Gatland felt that in Ireland, schools rugby was 'much inferior to New Zealand schools rugby' because there were 'not enough periods at school devoted to physical education'.[54] In March 1990, the results of a survey undertaken

51 'Dáil Éireann Debate – Tuesday, 14 Nov 1989. Vol. 393. No. 1. Written Answers. – Physical Education Programmes.' Retrieved from <https://www.oireachtas.ie/en/debates/debate/dail/1989-11-14/235/?highlight> [accessed 3 November 2020].
52 Interview with primary school teacher number one, 14 June 2019.
53 *Irish Independent*, 27 January 1990.
54 Ibid.

by Jimmy Deenihan on PE, on the basis of 1,456 Irish schools' replies, illustrated that 'one in three primary schools' had no indoor PE facilities
and that schoolyards had to be utilised.[55] He claimed that there was 'a
crisis in physical education' and stated that 80 per cent of schools felt that
equipment and facilities were 'totally inadequate'.[56] In addition, it was
noted that 60 per cent of schools wanted to see an annual grant given to
'the provision and renewal of equipment'.[57] Deenihan added that 'many
children were experiencing very little' PE.[58] Two-thirds of the teachers
surveyed did not feel they were properly prepared in college to teach the
subject while the average time given to teaching it each week varied from
ten minutes to one hour. He stated that extra time given to the subject
did not impair academic performance and was actually shown to improve
this. Deenihan also felt that large classes and a lack of space, along with
fears regarding insurance claims were to blame for the state of the subject
in Ireland.[59] He called on Minister O'Rourke and her Department to address the issue and requested that 'a working party of partners in education' be established to amend the situation as children were being denied
'a basic right enunciated in the U[nited] N[ations] Charter of Physical
Education and Sport'.[60]

The poor state of PE in Irish schools continued to be raised by journalists in the press. Support for its improvement came from the aforementioned
Seán Diffley, who was employed by the *Irish Independent* at that point
and who was of the opinion that the situation was 'a scandalous neglect'.[61]
Many schools had to deal with a lack of shower and changing facilities
for pupils, while one teacher stating at that time that PE was not taught
in infant classes in their school from October to April because it was too
cold.[62] Like other reporters before him, Diffley felt that Ireland's general

55   *Evening Herald*, 20 March 1990.
56   Ibid.
57   Ibid.
58   Ibid.
59   *Irish Examiner*, 21 March 1990.
60   Ibid., and *Evening Herald*, 20 March 1990.
61   *Irish Independent*, 21 April 1990.
62   Ibid.

lack of international sporting success could be linked to the inadequate PE system and he added that 'the Stephen Roches, Seán Kellys and Eamon Coughlans are simply happy accidents. They owe us no gratitude at all.'[63]

Some improvements were made to the provision of facilities in primary schools, but there was no major overhaul of the system. That same year, the Department of Education announced that grants for small items of PE equipment, including balls, hoolahoops and skipping ropes would be available through Cospóir following the approval of this move by Minister of State at the Department of Education, Frank Fahey.[64] One- and three-teacher schools were to receive grants during 1990 with two-teacher schools to receive them the following year, and district inspectors were to advise schools regarding what could be purchased.[65] Some other action was taken in the early part of the decade. In February 1991 the Primary Curriculum Review Body recommended that primary school teachers receive more in-service teaching in PE, while they also suggested more provision of specially qualified PE teachers and for more time to be allocated to the subject in training colleges.[66] INTO president, John White, supported these recommendations and called on the government to supply the resources which were necessary.[67] It was estimated that around 1,000 schools in the country were 'small, between one and five-teacher schools with no facilities'.[68]

Issues regarding gender and the teaching of certain games in schools were also noted at that time. In March 1991, the INTO's Equality Committee condemned the results of a survey which illustrated that 95 per cent of space in national newspapers' sports' sections was given to coverage of 'male sports'.[69] The committee was said to be drawing up aims to tackle gender bias, 'including a major revision of the physical education curriculum and a working party to address poor media portrayal of women in sport'.[70]

---

63   Ibid.
64   Department of Education Files. *Department of Education Circular. Scheme of Grants towards the Provision of Physical Education Equipment*, Cir. 87/90.
65   Ibid.
66   *Evening Herald*, 8 February 1991.
67   Ibid.
68   Ibid.
69   *Irish Press*, 6 March 1991.
70   Ibid.

They also intended to circulate a newsletter focused on gender equality within the media, school teachers and the Department of Education. The committee highlighted sections within the curriculum which apparently illustrated gender bias, including one which stated that 'girls tend to choose light delicate movements and retain longer a love of fantasy, whereas boys generally move with strength and tend to be more realistic'.[71] The INTO urged the Department of Education to 'issue a circular promoting equal participation in sport in primary schools' and 'called for Government funding for sport and access to clubs to be based on the principle of equality of access and opportunity for women and men'.[72] They also stated that all PE-related material in primary schools needed to feature girls as well as boys, and they wanted to see in-service training given to teachers to help them promote equal opportunities in sport.[73] Along with their 'Fair-Play' action plan, they wanted a major revision of the PE curriculum to ensure that both boys and girls were encouraged to take part in sports and games which were traditionally strongly associated with one sex rather than the other.[74] Therefore boys were to be urged to take up dance classes, skipping, rounders and netball while girls were to participate in rugby, soccer and Gaelic football.[75] The following month in the Dáil, Minister O'Rourke stated that the PE handbook for schools was being revised to eliminate any sexism, following a recommendation from the Primary Curriculum Review Body.[76] Jimmy Deenihan remained unimpressed by the lack of wider action and stated that in any case, PE in primary schools was 'a total shambles'.[77]

The INTO were also critical of the government's general failure to fully address the plight of PE. In August 1991, INTO general secretary-designate Senator Joe O'Toole felt that Minister O'Rourke was not taking

71   Ibid.
72   *Irish Independent*, 6 March 1991.
73   Ibid.
74   Ibid.
75   Ibid.
76   'Dáil Éireann Debate – Wednesday, 13 Mar 1991. Vol. 406. No. 4. Ceisteanna – Questions. Oral Answers. – Handbook on Physical Education.' Retrieved from <https://www.oireachtas.ie/en/debates/debate/dail/1991-03-13/25/> [Accessed 2 November 2020].
77   Ibid.

enough responsibility for the subject's failings and that the Department of Education needed to take greater action rather than look at the role of colleges in the problem.[78] He felt that schools' PE problems were also due to the fact that there was a scarcity of general purpose rooms in schools, with over 1,500 of the 3,000 national schools still requiring these.[79]

Jimmy Deenihan also continued with his efforts to improve the status of PE in the early years to the decade. At the end of January 1992, he organised a one-day conference on PE, health and lifestyle, which was held at the Burlington Hotel in Dublin.[80] Deenihan, the spokesman for Youth and Sport for Fine Gael, claimed at that time that his surveys on PE in schools illustrated that 80 per cent 'had either inadequate or no physical education facilities'.[81] It was noted at the PE symposium that Irish schools still lagged behind their European counterparts in terms of the amount of time allocated to PE. Swedish schoolchildren received six hours of PE each week, while in France five hours were given and three in Germany.[82] In Sweden, swimming lessons were compulsory for all 8 year olds while outdoor activities such as orienteering and winter sports were also given much attention. In France, by the end of mandatory schooling at 16, each student was expected to swim 500 meters in an outdoor setting while in Germany, 'centrally controlled sports competitions' were prominent.[83] In England and Wales, there were also opportunities for adventure activities.[84] In addition, in Canada and Australia, 'quality daily physical education' was available to school pupils.[85]

---

78   *Irish Press*, 20 August 1991.
79   Ibid.
80   *Irish Examiner*, 22 January 1992.
81   Ibid.
82   *Irish Press*, 12 March 1992.
83   See also Geoff Hare, *Football in France: A Cultural History* (Oxford/New York: Berg, 2003), 92. Hare states that in France, a test in sport and PE became compulsory as part of the school-leaving examination, the baccalauréat, in the 1950s, while after 1984 this test became worth 8 per cent of the full result. In addition, this was doubled after 1992 as 'an incentive for youth participation in sport and physical education.'
84   *Irish Press*, 12 March 1992.
85   Ibid.

Small-scale initiatives continued to be favoured by the government in order to raise awareness of physical fitness amongst schoolchildren. In April 1992, Irish Minister for Sport Liam Aylward launched a project entitled 'The Irish Mini-Sport Movement' to encourage Irish schoolchildren to become fitter.[86] In particular, a chart sponsored by Calvita, a well-known Irish cheese for children, was to be made available within all primary schools, with an emphasis placed on exercise to music, and the development of skills rather than competitiveness.[87] The Minister stated that 'children must achieve certain skills, attitudes and physical attributes before 11 if they were to lead normal lives'.[88]

The Green Paper on Education, released in April 1992, also saw some encouragement of raising health awareness in schools. It included recommendations that a PE programme be developed to incorporate younger classes in primary classes, with linkage 'to education on hygiene and nutrition, a systematic health screening programme linked to support and advice for families of young people in need, and sex education, appropriate to all levels of pupils, also beginning in the early stages of primary education'.[89] It also recommended that thirty minutes be given to PE daily.[90] In addition, the former National Sports Council, Cospóir, was to be re-established 'to advise on all aspects of sport' while 'a network of sports and leisure development officers' was to be set up through VECs.[91]

These initiatives were hardly ground-breaking and the consensus remained that more should be done. At the end of September 1992, in an article published in the *Irish Independent*, Jimmy Deenihan again highlighted the poor state of PE in Irish schools, which he linked to Ireland having 'one of the highest death rates from cardiac-related diseases in Europe'.[92] This was 'four times higher than that of France, three times higher than Spain, and twice that of Italy and Belgium'.[93] He added that 'there was scant reference

---

86   *Irish Independent*, 8 April 1992.
87   Ibid.
88   Ibid.
89   Ibid., 21 April 1992.
90   *Irish Press*, 26 June 1992.
91   Ibid.
92   *Irish Independent*, 30 September 1992.
93   Ibid.

given to physical education in the recent *Green Paper on Education*' and 'there is no effort to provide a balance between the "physical" and the "intellectual" development of our young people'.[94]

Despite these comparisons, PE in European schools was not perfect, but more time was still being allocated to the subject in a number of countries. In December 1992, delegates from twenty-one countries expressed concerns at a conference in Strasbourg that PE and sport were being reduced in schools across Europe as a result of 'budget restrictions, reform of school structures and competition from other disciplines'.[95] Three to four hours of PE per week was the European average, but it was also stated that poorer families were unable to send their children to sports clubs and private athletic events.[96]

Surveys continued to highlight the inadequate state of PE in Irish schools, but only one appears to have taken the views of parents on PE into account. A survey completed by the Federation of Catholic Primary Schools Parents' Councils that year, which involved over 130 primary schools, highlighted that parents felt that 'all primary schools children should have the services of qualified physical education instructors as some teachers were not interested in PE as a subject while some were not physically fit to take a class'.[97] A National Parents Council for education had been established in 1985 and 'gave overdue recognition to the role of parents in the school system'.[98] In general, however, there was no major push by parents to see that PE was improved in Irish primary schools at this time as it appears other issues were prioritised, although many parents were involved in school teams in a voluntary capacity.[99]

Throughout the 1990s, the provision of PE in Irish schools continued to rank poorly in comparison with those in Europe and this was regularly highlighted. At the National Physical Education Conference in Waterford in October 1993, Ger Murphy, the Irish Physical Education Association's

94   Ibid.
95   Ibid., 30 December 1992.
96   Ibid.
97   Ibid.
98   Coolahan, *Towards the Era of Lifelong Learning*, 170.
99   Interview with primary school teacher number fourteen, 26 July 2019.

president, stated that 'the European Physical Education Association had identified Ireland as making the poorest provision for PE' while she added that Ireland was 'the only country in the EC which does not have statutory entitlement for all children to PE'.[100] It was also noted that in a study conducted of eighteen European countries, Ireland was 'the only one with an allocation of less than two hours PE a week at second level'.[101] It was announced in the press that the European Physical Education Association was scheduled 'to hold its next annual conference in Ireland to highlight the situation and put pressure on the Department of Education to give greater recognition to PE'.[102] In many ways, the idea that a PE conference being held in Dublin would force the Irish government to take action was not a new development, and echoed the situation in the late 1960s.

Moving towards Another Revised Curriculum and Increased Funding

The allocation of funding towards the GAA also highlighted inadequacies within government policies towards PE in all Irish schools. In February 1994, one writer to the *Irish Press* questioned the government's decision to give the GAA £5 million to assist the re-development of Croke Park and highlighting the failure to provide sports halls in some areas, he stated that 'one must wonder what the priorities of this Government are in relation to sport'.[103] This is not to say that the GAA were informally expected to organise schools' sport. Nor did it show that the GAA key administrators were overly pleased with their organisation's role in educational institutions. In fact, this was perceived to be inadequate by those at the highest levels of the national body. At the GAA's Annual Congress in April 1994, both outgoing president, Peter Quinn, and his

100 *Irish Independent*, 4 October 1993.
101 Ibid.
102 Ibid.
103 *Irish Press*, 3 February 1994.

successor, Jack Boothman, were critical of structures for Gaelic games in schools and colleges.[104] Quinn was of the view that 'many schools, especially in the colleges sector, adamantly refused to allow participation in GAA competitions, while some institutions actively discouraged involvement in GAA activities outside the school'.[105] By the late 1970s, Cumann na mBunscoil, which promotes the GAA in primary schools, was operational.[106] Therefore, while the GAA had certainly been able to gain a foothold in many Irish schools, with the presence of numerous GAA members within school staff, and the organisation of parish and school leagues (see Figure 37) and coaching passionately undertaken in many areas, there were some schools which they could not penetrate.[107]

The Department of Education undertook initiatives to ensure teachers were at least aware of what could be done in a PE lesson by supplying packs which included lesson plans. In June 1996, Brian O'Shea, the Minister of State at the Department of Health, launched a resource pack for primary school teachers for PE lessons.[108] Entitled *Action for Life*, it was supported by the Departments of Health and Education, the Electricity Supply Board and the Irish Heart Foundation.[109] It had been prepared by a team specialising in the promotion of health and exercise and was initially piloted in twelve schools in Galway. It was viewed as 'a resource to reverse the present trend towards inactivity' with the aim of motivating young people to become more active and healthy.[110]

Later that month more concrete action was taken when details of the proposed new curriculum for primary schools were announced, with PE one of twelve subjects listed.[111] The new curriculum had been recommended in an earlier review by Minister O'Rourke.[112] There were also wider

---

104   *Irish Press*, 11 April 1994.
105   Ibid.
106   *Evening Herald*, 2 October 1979.
107   Interview with Secondary School PE teacher number three, 26 August 2019.
108   *Irish Farmers' Journal*, 8 June 1996.
109   Ibid.
110   Ibid.
111   *Irish Examiner*, 2 July 1996.
112   McManus, *Irish Education: The Ministerial Legacy, 1919–99*, 270.

Figure 37.   Brackey National School 1984 Donegal Gaelic football county finalists and
south-west divisional champions. Courtesy of John McConnell.

changes within the monitoring of Irish sport that summer. In July of that
year, the Irish Sports Council was re-established, with a reduction from
twenty-three members, which had been the norm in Cospóir, to fifteen,
which hinted at a more modern outlook towards the Republic of Ireland's
sporting infrastructure.[113]

At this point, the promise of the early 1970s had not been fulfilled.
In August 1996, the results of an international study carried out by the
European Union of Physical Education Associations illustrated that Irish
primary pupils were at the bottom of a European PE league in terms of time
given to PE, with those in France, Luxembourg, Portugal and Switzerland
receiving three hours a week on average compared to one hour in Irish

113   *Irish Independent*, 10 July 1996.

primary schools.[114] Conditions for teaching PE remained less developed in smaller schools in the 1990s, particularly in rural areas. One primary school teacher who began teaching in the city before moving to a peripheral area at that time noted a huge difference:

> Once I moved out into the country, where there was no hall, it's a different story, then it's very awkward. I remember one time we had a load of mats – we were doing gymnastics, and then where do you store them, because there was no hall, and they were stuck in the turf-shed, things like that. So there were practical difficulties at a logistical level, there definitely were.[115]

Despite this, schools in the city could naturally also vary in terms of resources and facilities available, particularly in disadvantaged areas, with two Dublin-born teachers noting this in recalling their primary level PE in the late twentieth century.[116]

In September 1999, the launch of the new primary school curriculum brought its 'first major overhaul' since 1971.[117] It was 'designed to make school more fun for children as well as making it more productive' through more child-centred teaching approaches.[118] PE was set to become 'more wide ranging' with adventure and outdoor activities included in the new curriculum while Social, Personal and Health Education was formally introduced.[119] Six strands, including athletics, dance, gymnastics, games, outdoor activities and aquatics were to form the new PE curriculum.[120] In addition, schools were 'encouraged to provide activities equally suitable for girls and boys' with a balance between competitive and non-competitive activities recommended.[121] Coolahan has described the 1999 Curriculum as a 'landmark' development which contained 'a balance of knowledge, concepts and

---

114   Ibid., 6 August 1996.
115   Interview with primary school teacher number eleven, 25 July 2019.
116   Interview with primary school teacher number three, 22 June 2019 and interview with primary school teacher number four, 26 June 2019.
117   *Irish Examiner*, 10 September 1999.
118   Ibid.
119   Ibid.
120   *Evening Herald*, 9 September 1999.
121   Ibid.

skills' and emphasised different methods of learning and more assessment with literary and numeracy featuring heavily in the programme.[122]

In March 2000, new Minister for Education and Science, Dr Michael Woods (2000–2), announced that £2 million would be available for PE in primary schools, with a new scheme to give each primary school the opportunity annually to 'pay coaches and sports mentors and to buy equipment'.[123] He also unveiled plans to appoint a national sports coordinator at primary school level, as well as using radio as a medium to tackle disadvantage within education. In addition, he promised to give support to multi-denominational schools which were 'educationally viable' and to appoint a director for co-ordinating 'measures aimed at tackling educational disadvantage'.[124] Minister Woods stated that he wanted to give children the opportunity to engage in sport 'from a young age' and while agreeing that they could gain skills from new technology, felt that there needed to be a balance so that they would not become 'couch potatoes'.[125] Schools in disadvantaged areas were to receive grants of £1,000 each for coaching while other primary schools would receive £500 each for the same purpose, beginning in September 2000.[126]

This came as part of a wider sporting development and was linked to a more affluent Irish society with the rise of the 'Celtic Tiger' at the turn of the century.[127] Minister for Tourism, Sport and Recreation (1997–2002), Dr Jim McDaid, announced in March 2000 that every county in the Republic of Ireland would get £200,000 for developing sports facilities so that the distribution of grants between counties would be more balanced, as this had not been the case in the past.[128] Dr McDaid had been a talented soccer player at University College Galway and had been appointed to the governmental role, a new position, in 1997.[129] Despite this welcome initiative,

122   Coolahan, *Towards the Era of Lifelong Learning*, 207–8.
123   *Irish Independent*, 4 March 2000.
124   Ibid.
125   Ibid.
126   Ibid. and *Evening Herald*, 11 August 2000.
127   Bartlett, *Ireland: A History*, 537–40.
128   *Evening Herald*, 4 March 2000.
129   Ibid., 7 May 2006.

dissatisfaction remained. In May 2000, the results of an INTO survey into PE facilities in schools were described by the organisation's general secretary, Senator Joe O'Toole, as 'quite appalling'.[130] He stated that 'primary schools should have access to adequate and appropriate PE equipment in order to fully implement the physical education programme' and because this was not the case, he added that most schools could only hold PE lessons when the weather was suitable.[131] The survey revealed that 54 per cent of all primary schools had no general purpose room, while 78 per cent said they could not run the programme fully due to 'inadequate space'. In addition, it was found that 67 per cent of schools needed 'either additional or replacement PE equipment'.[132]

Senator O'Toole continued his criticism of the government's attitude to PE later that year. In November 2000, he stated at the National PE Conference in Galway that the Minister for Education Woods' 'miserable level' of funding for PE, which he calculated to work out at '£3.25 per pupil per year', was 'another smokescreen'.[133] He also called for a School of Excellence to be founded for young athletes at the new national stadium, which was in the pipeline at that time (but was never built).[134] While PE's status had improved greatly in Irish primary school classrooms through its place in the 1999 Revised Curriculum by the early twenty-first century, there was still a long way to go in terms of the provision of facilities to support what had become a mandatory subject within the school timetable.

The time allocated to the training of primary school physical education in colleges remained low in the late twentieth century, with students at Mary Immaculate College receiving only forty-five minutes per week in first year, the same amount per fortnight in second year and none in their third year in 1991.[135] It was noted in the Dáil that the situation was 'equally

---

130   *Irish Independent*, 26 May 2000.
131   Ibid.
132   Ibid.
133   *Irish Independent*, 13 November 2000.
134   Ibid.
135   'Dáil Éireann Debate – Thursday, 13 Jun 1991. Vol. 409. No. 8. Ceisteanna – Questions. Oral Answers. – PE in National Schools.' Retrieved from <https://www.oireachtas. ie/en/debates/debate/dail/1991-06-13/18/> [Accessed 3 November 2020].

bad in the Church of Ireland Training College and St Patrick's College, Drumcondra'.[136] By 1997 St Patrick's College still relied on one full-time PE lecturer 'and a number of part-time teachers' in the provision of the student training PE course there.[137] The majority of late twentieth century primary school teacher graduates interviewed for this book were positive about their college studies in PE. However, one female principal, who attended a small training college, stated that she felt-ill equipped to teach it after a bad experience on her PE course and as soon as she had taken up the position as head of her school, she sought outside help with the subject from the local council.[138] In addition, a number of secondary school teachers interviewed felt that more needed to be done to develop primary schools' PE as many teenagers lacked a firm grounding in the subject on reaching post-primary education.[139]

Conclusion

The Department of Education planned to improve PE's status in Irish primary schools with the introduction of a new curriculum in 1971. While the subject was a peripheral element within teacher-training college courses since the early 1900s, and remained so throughout the twentieth century, the in-service training of already qualified teachers was inconsistent throughout Ireland and the subject retained a lowly status in many schools, particularly those that could be termed 'smaller' buildings where space and resources were limited. This can be most clearly seen in comparisons with European nations, although some may argue that the amount of time given was often not necessarily reflected in the quality

---

136 Ibid.
137 'Dáil Éireann Debate – Tuesday, 18 Feb 1997. Vol. 475. No. 1. Written Answers – Teacher Appointments.' <https://www.oireachtas.ie/en/debates/debate/dail/1997-02-18/186/> [Accessed 2 November 2020].
138 Interview with primary school teacher number two, 15 June 2019.
139 Interview with secondary school PE teacher number one, 26 July 2019 and number three, 26 August 2019.

offered. Teaching of the subject was not something that was prioritised by visiting inspectors, and 'PE' often consisted of play during the school break or only took place during good weather in schools where there were no indoor facilities. In addition, as Coolahan has stated, 'the large number of pupils in many classes, in the early years after 1971 at least, was a great obstacle to teachers trying to implement child-centred approaches'.[140] By the late 1980s, a rise in insurance claims against teachers accused of being negligent during PE lessons or at other times in the schoolyard meant that the idea of children playing informally during school hours had to be revised as insurance issues became more acute and school playtime and related supervision became more formalised. In November 1988, it was noted in the press that in some primary schools children were not allowed to play games because the schools could not afford to pay insurance to cover accidents.[141] In many schools, running or ball games during break time are now simply not permitted.

Government intervention towards the implementation of PE in national schools remained basic until the end of the 1990s when another revised curriculum was launched. PE was named as one of twelve subjects on the curriculum, with one hour designated per week.[142] Numerous enthusiastic teachers had, however, made it a central part of their classroom ethos and in doing so enlivened the lives of pupils through the organisation of school leagues and parish competitions and by integrating sport into informal conversations with pupils and as part of the integration of other subjects. However, many of those interviewed for this study alluded to the fact that during inspections, there had been no pressure to teach it and no inquiries about its regularity within schools. Criticism of the system of inspection was highlighted in a report undertaken by Dr Clive Hopes in 1991, and in an OECD report that same year, with the result that the need to improve this was recognised in the Green Paper of 1992 and in the White Paper of 1995.[143] The Education Act of 1998 gave the inspectorate 'a strategic and focused role' as opposed to 'the previous multitasked and

---

140   Coolahan, *Towards the Era of Lifelong Learning*, 124.
141   *Irish Independent*, 19 November 1988.
142   *Irish Examiner*, 10 September 1999.
143   Coolahan, *Towards the Era of Lifelong Learning*, 288–92.

diversified' position.[144] Despite this, monitoring of PE remains inconsistent, with one current primary school teacher noting when interviewed that he had not yet had an inspection in the subject in his ten years of teaching.[145] Chapter 11 discusses how PE developed in the late twentieth century in post-primary schools, illustrating that many of the issues at primary level such as the provision of facilities and acceptance of the subject amongst staff were reflected at second level and continued to also cast a shadow over the progressive developments of the late 1960s and early 1970s.

144   Ibid., 293.
145   Interview with primary school teacher number five, 28 June 2019.

Unfulfilled Expectations: PE in Second Level Schools in the Republic of Ireland, 1974–2000

Introduction

Although Captain Michael McDonough heralded 'a new era in physical education' in Ireland early in 1974, problems also remained in second level schools.[1] This was particularly the case in the development of PE halls and the provision of equipment, as wider economic concerns saw the temporary suspension of the building of sports halls in the mid-1970s, and the issue of space to teach the subject properly remained throughout the later twentieth century in many schools. Despite the opening of the NCPE in 1973, placement of qualified second level PE teachers within the workforce remained difficult in some areas and at times the general state of the economy was an indicator of the ability of schools to take on PE teachers as employees.[2] In turn, the number of places allocated to trainee PE teachers in the Limerick course was not always consistent and sometimes mirrored the job opportunities deemed to be available. By the 1980s there was a growing awareness within Irish society of the need to keep fit, and a number of organisations such as the PEAI helped raise public knowledge of the state of the subject in Irish schools through the organisation of conferences and related publicity in the national media.[3] Politician Jimmy Deenihan was particularly relentless in raising attention in the Dáil to the inadequate structure of PE at both primary and second level, and also conducted a number of second level school surveys

1   *Irish Examiner*, 23 February 1974.
2   Ibid., 23 April 1984.
3   *Evening Herald*, 2 May 1987 and *Irish Examiner*, 10 October 1988.

with which he provided evidence of this neglect.[4] Despite his efforts, Irish second level schools also continued to lag behind many of those in Europe and this was highlighted on a number of occasions in the 1990s.[5] Following fruitless discussions in the 1980s, governmental plans to give the subject Leaving Certificate examination status were revived in the late 1990s as Ireland began to increase in modernity with the Celtic Tiger.[6] This chapter also illustrates that the provision of PE as an examination subject proved to be an overly optimistic venture at that time, and it was not until late in the second decade of the twenty-first century that steps towards fulfilling this promise were taken. Examinations were scheduled for 2020, although the general Leaving Certificate structure was later adapted due to the COVID-19 Pandemic.[7]

Developing Physical Education in Second Level Schools

Despite the progress of the late 1960s and early 1970s, the provision of equipment for PE remained a source of frustration for many teachers. One post-primary school in Meath was informed in January 1974 that despite initial approval from the Department of Education to improve PE facilities, 'a heavy backlog' of applications for these meant that this would be 'carried out only on a phased basis over a number of years . . . because of demands generally on the funds for educational building'.[8] In some towns with a number of second level schools, such as Raphoe in County Donegal, the Department of Education refused to sanction the building of separate gymnasia and instead encouraged that one would be shared.[9] Issues with the provision of facilities were also noted by VECs

4   *Irish Press*, 11 June 1991.
5   See, for example, *Irish Independent*, 26 August 1997.
6   *Evening Herald*, 18 February 1997.
7   'Leaving Certificate Physical Education 2020' Retrieved from <https://www.examinations.ie/?l=en&mc=ex&sc=pe> [Accessed 30 October 2020].
8   *Meath Chronicle*, 26 January 1974.
9   *Donegal Democrat*, 22 February 1974.

in Carlow, Cork, Mayo and Galway in the spring of 1974.[10] The appointment of PE teachers remained a problem in some areas. In February 1974 at a meeting of the Carlow VEC, it was stated that 'physical education teachers were needed by all the schools but there was no provision for them'.[11] One reporter felt that there was not enough continuity in the specialised government position that John Bruton had charge of, with Robert Molloy, Michael O'Kennedy and Jim Tunney all moving on from it in recent years. He was also of the opinion that the Irish government did not realise 'that like most civilised countries' PE was 'part of our society and our education'.[12] However, the state of the Irish economy often meant that the subject suffered in terms of funding and resources allocated for its growth.

In January 1977, a £1 million Department of Education 'shock cut-back' meant that plans to build sports halls in post-primary schools were to be postponed 'for a number of years', with 'essential general classroom and special subject accommodation' to be given financial priority.[13] This move meant that 'a three year programme of providing sports halls in community schools and regional technical colleges' was halted with only one-third of the scheme finished.[14] In 1976 ten sports halls, costing approximately £60,000 each, had been provided and there were plans in place to provide a similar number in 1977 and 1978, but the programme was 'delayed indefinitely'.[15] This meant that schools such as Cabinteely Community School had to face late withdrawals of proposed funding for related facilities.[16] It was noted at the PEAI's conference in September 1977 that 'one of the most disappointing features with regard to the development of physical education in Ireland has been the continued development of new schools without any gymnasia', particularly in Donegal and Monaghan.[17]

10 *Nationalist and Leinster Times*, 12 April 1974, *Southern Star*, 2 March 1974, *Connaught Telegraph*, 28 March 1974 and *Connacht Tribune*, 29 March 1974.
11 *Nationalist and Leinster Times*, 8 March 1974.
12 *Irish Independent*, 24 April 1974.
13 *Evening Herald*, 26 January 1977.
14 Ibid.
15 Ibid.
16 *Irish Independent*, 14 April 1977.
17 *Irish Examiner*, 3 October 1977.

Interest remained high in PE teaching as an occupation despite qualified teachers' frustrations. By February 1976 there were at least 2,000 applicants for fifty places at the NCPE, with the previous year's successful
applicants all having four honours in the Leaving Certificate, despite
the basic requirement being two honours in the national examination,
illustrating the growing competition for places on the course.[18] One PE
teacher interviewed felt that this had allowed non-sports people to take
up offers although they might have not been genuinely been interested in
it.[19] However, candidates had to undergo tests in 'suitability', including an
oral knowledge of the Irish language as a Ceard Teastas remained necessary.[20] The four-year course in Limerick had 'a near 100 per cent guarantee
of jobs in schools afterwards' and was 'one of the most popular in the
country' according to one school counsellor.[21] It led to 'a teaching degree
with specialist qualifications in physical education and one other area of
the school curriculum', which meant that students also chose an elective
subject.[22] They could pick English Studies, Irish Studies, Science Studies
or Social and Environmental Studies.[23]

In 1975 the NCPE became incorporated into Thomond College of
Education.[24] Student protest continued intermittently into the late 1970s,
with some scholars unhappy with the status of their PE degree. In November
1977 Student Union president, Kieran McFadden, protested about what he
felt was the mistreatment of the college through a public act at the graduation ceremony, at which 132 students were conferred.[25] He was unhappy
that the National University of Ireland [NUI] was conferring PE students
with B.Ed. degrees although 'graduates had demanded that Bachelor of

18   *Irish Independent*, 7 February 1976.
19   Interview with Secondary School PE teacher number four, 24 August 2019.
20   *Irish Independent*, 7 February 1976 and Coolahan, *Irish Education: History and Structure*, 240.
21   *Irish Independent*, 7 February 1976.
22   Ibid., 2 January 1976.
23   Ibid.
24   John Walsh, *Higher Education in Ireland: Politics, Policy and Power-A History of Higher Education in the Irish State* (London: Palgrave Macmillan, 2018), 280.
25   *Irish Independent*, 11 November 1977.

Arts degrees should be conferred by the National Council for Education Awards [NCEA]'.[26] He highlighted this by taking off his academic gown and hood at the ceremony, and gave them to the vice-chancellor of the NUI, Dr Donal McCarthy and also refused to shake hands with him.[27] The move, which was backed by the Union of Students in Ireland, was condemned by the Director of Thomond, James Christian, who apologised and stated that he did not condone this. McFadden later stated that 'the major problem that many graduates of PE had was the lack of a real State commitment to the development of sport and recreation'.[28] He also noted that they had been led to believe they would receive a B.A. degree when they started the course and as they sat their exams. A week after the ceremony, it was announced that the link with the NUI would be ended and the NCEA would be restored with its degree-awarding powers.[29] [30]

Disruptions at the college appear to have affected the success rates of students, with thirty-two out of eighty-three students said to have failed their final PE exams in 1977.[31] The following year, the graduation ceremony was delayed by three months after an examinations pay dispute which was resolved following Labour Court talks.[32] Naturally, this led to another student protest at the graduation ceremony, with thirty-eight graduates walking out as they felt they had missed out on job opportunities because of the delay in conferral.[33] However, not every student got involved in politics within the college, with one PE teacher who studied there at the time stating that he felt the facilities were 'fantastic' and he was happy enough just to get on with the course, with PE lecturer Dave Weldrick said to be ahead of his time in using video analysis to assess college teams'

26 Ibid. See in particular, Fleming, *The University of Limerick*, 92–102 for a full discussion of this dispute.
27 *Irish Independent*, 11 November 1977.
28 Ibid.
29 *Irish Press*, 11 November 1977.
30 Fleming, *The University of Limerick*, 97.
31 *Sunday Independent*, 4 December 1977.
32 *Irish Independent*, 6 September 1978.
33 *Irish Examiner*, 30 September 1978.

sports performance.[34] Similarly, one fellow PE teacher felt that the quality of teaching was top class, stating that

> we had some excellent lecturers there - Dave Weldrick, we'd a P. J. Smith who was involved in rugby and very good at athletics too, we had a man called Robson, who could walk about [in the lecture] and talk to you at the same time, was excellent at gymnastics. We'd Joanne Wilkinson, a great swimming coach, Cathal Vekins, who was outdoor pursuits, canoeing, hill-walking and stuff, so we had good quality people there I have to say when I started off at the PE college in Limerick.[35]

By January 1978, over half of Ireland's post-primary schools had unsuitable facilities according to a survey undertaken on PE by a 1977 Thomond College graduate, Andrew Kavanagh.[36] He had surveyed 468 schools, which was 57 per cent of the total number of second level schools. Fifty-six per cent of these schools had a physical education teacher when the statistics were gathered, but only 45 per cent of those employed as physical education teachers 'had training of two years or more'.[37] In addition, while all community schools examined had PE teachers, 82 per cent of girls' secondary schools had them while only 44 per cent of boys' secondary schools did so. Seventy-eight per cent of comprehensive schools employed PE teachers while 39 per cent of vocational schools surveyed had them. It was also noted that 'much of time-tabled physical activity classes' were under the supervision of 'academic' teachers.[38] While the Department of Education advised that post-primary schools students should get four forty-five minute PE lessons per week, the survey illustrated that 'most schools' fell 'far short of this area'.[39]

The Association of Secondary Teachers [of] Ireland [ASTI] had passed a resolution at their 1977 conference deploring the neglect of the subject 'in very many schools' and set up a sub-committee to investigate how many PE teachers were employed in post-primary schools.[40] They also demanded

---

34   Interview with secondary school PE teacher number four, 29 August 2019.
35   Interview with secondary school PE teacher number two, 24 August 2019.
36   *Irish Examiner*, 11 January 1978.
37   Ibid.
38   Ibid.
39   Ibid.
40   Ibid., 29 April 1978.

that the Department of Education 'set a target date' for having 'at least one qualified PE teacher on the staff of each school'.[41] A survey undertaken comparing the rates of PE teachers in secondary schools in 1974 and 1977 illustrated that there had been an increase in intake by seventy-five by December of the latter year, but in schools with an enrolment of under 300, restrictions on quota and a scarcity of facilities were said to have been the reasons why PE was not as commonly available.[42] The ASTI, while acknowledging difficulties such as quotas, facilities, class contact time, marketability and availability of teachers into consideration, recommended that a target date of 1988 be set for having one PE teacher in each secondary school.[43] This indicates how far off they thought the position was in terms of being fully accepted.

In September 1978, the results of another survey on post-primary schools completed by Mike Sleap, a lecturer at Thomond College, confirmed the above findings.[44] He highlighted that only 56 per cent of secondary schools employed a qualified PE teacher, while the time given to the subject was less than that recommended by the Department of Education and that fewer than half of the schools had gymnasium and just over half owned a playing field.[45] He also noted that 'a relatively high proportion of secondary girls' schools' had PE teachers but 'the most striking feature of the survey' was said to be 'the dearth of PE specialists in vocational and secondary boys' schools'.[46] Sleap's work, based on replies in questionnaires from 548 schools (out of 817), illustrated that the pupil-teacher ratio or quota system was one of the main obstacles to the employment of PE teachers, as 'if a staff member were to leave, a PE teacher could not be employed without some reduction of content in other areas of the curriculum'.[47] In addition, 'the lack of suitable facilities' was identified as the second major hindrance, with 35 per cent of schools which did not have

41   Ibid.
42   Ibid.
43   Ibid.
44   Ibid., 23 September 1978.
45   Ibid., 23 June 1976 and 23 September 1978.
46   Ibid., 23 September 1978.
47   Ibid.

a PE teacher stating that this was a factor in their failure to employ one.[48] Sleap also reported that due to examination pressures in final school years, 'the overwhelming majority' of second level students had no time for PE in their Leaving Certificate year, and that the time given to PE in Ireland was much lower than that in secondary schools in England and Wales.[49]

The lack of facilities and the position of PE in some schools also meant that some Thomond PE graduates began to focus solely on the academic subject they had taken along with PE.[50] These included Arthur Twomey, a graduate of Thomond and PRO of the PEAI at the beginning of 1978. While PE was said to be increasing in popularity, 'a large number of the smaller schools' were still operating with no PE teachers or facilities for the subject.[51] Twomey noted that 'you will still find a school where a PE teacher is supposed to take a class out into a field on a freezing winter morning and give them proper instruction', while he added that 'an essential feature must be the provision of indoor areas together with gymnasia and changing rooms'.[52] He also stated that the PEAI would continue to press for these, and that it would 'have to become a compulsory post-primary subject'.[53]

Further Funding Issues

At the end of the decade, it looked as though funding would improve. In February 1979, the Taoiseach, Jack Lynch, stated at the Texaco Sports Awards that the government was going to increase its sports funding by 200 per cent on the previous year, but that they 'could not be totally responsible for aid to sport'.[54] He called on 'the private sector' to

---

48   Ibid.
49   Ibid.
50   Ibid., 29 April 1978.
51   Ibid.
52   Ibid.
53   Ibid.
54   Ibid., 9 February 1979.

provide funds to the Olympic Council of Ireland for the 1980 Moscow Olympics.[55] In addition, Minister for Education, John P. Wilson, stated that there would be a £3.9 million boost for education, which meant that the programme for providing PE facilities in community, secondary and vocational schools was to recommence.[56] In April, Minister for State, Jim Tunney, announced that £2.6 million would be given by the government in grants for sport for that year.[57] Despite this, there was criticism in the national press that too much money was being spent on 'a massive advertising campaign' for the National Sports Council with one writer claiming that 'on paper, Cospóir is a nice idea-but it shows little evidence that the Government is in touch with the realities of sport or physical education in this country.'[58] It was noted that the Olympic Council was to get only £60,000, while 'the governing bodies of sports such as basketball, athletics, juvenile GAA, tennis and hockey' were to receive just £27,100 between them, and 'fringe organisations' including the Irish Wildlife Conservancy also had to share this.[59]

Within the distribution of funding, secondary schools were deemed to be in a lesser position than those in the vocational and community category. In September 1979, the general secretary of the Secretariat of Secondary Schools, Brother Declan Duffy, wrote to Minister Wilson, to inform him that the Joint Managerial Body [JMB] had 'expressed deep disquiet at the allocation of recent grants for Physical Education Halls in post-primary schools.'[60] Brother Duffy added that it appeared, following enquiries at the Department of Education, that 'all of these grants had been given to Community and Vocational schools' and that 'the Voluntary Sector had already shown its interest in Physical Education halls by building them at great sacrifice before Department grants became available.'[61] The

55   Ibid.
56   *Irish Press*, 9 February 1979.
57   Ibid., 20 April 1979.
58   Ibid.
59   Ibid.
60   Secretariat of Secondary Schools Archives. Joint Managerial Body files. Letter from Brother Declan Duffy to John P. Wilson, 5 September 1979.
61   Ibid.

Voluntary Sector, which had 'large schools in many centres of population growth throughout the country' had applied for newly announced grants but had received 'a most unsatisfactory response from the Department of Education' and there had been 'a disquieting evasiveness' in how their queries were processed.[62] He requested information on the criteria for obtaining the grants and a list of schools which had obtained them. In addition, he wanted assurance from the Department of Education that applications from the voluntary sector would be 'considered promptly and equitably'.[63] In response, the Minister's secretary arranged a meeting between senior officials of the Department of Education and Brother Duffy and other representatives of the JMB to discuss these concerns.[64]

The meeting took place at the Department of Education on 5 October 1979.[65] The Department of Education's scheme for providing PE halls was outlined by a representative, Tom Gillen, who noted that grants for the provision of halls had been part of the 1964 grants scheme. He stated that 'the community schools which were comparatively big schools and which were begun in the seventies got halls'. In addition, 'following the recession of 1975 to '76 the building of all halls stopped'. Although the Minister for Education was eager to continue providing PE halls, 'the problem was lack of finance' and with 'limited funds', classrooms and laboratories were prioritised.[66] In February 1979 the provision of PE halls for secondary, community and vocational schools was begun again, with school size given as one of the criteria, but this was not the only determining factor. It was noted that vocational and community schools had 'a strong community aspect' which was 'not so obvious in the case of the secondary schools'.[67]

62   Ibid.
63   Ibid.
64   Secretariat of Secondary Schools Archives. Joint Managerial Body files. Letter from Secretary to the Minister of Education, P. Heffernan, to Brother Declan Duffy, 26 September 1979.
65   Secretariat of Secondary Schools Archives. Joint Managerial Body files. Report of Meeting in the Department of Education re P. E. Halls, 5 October 1979, 1.
66   Ibid.
67   Ibid.

Given the pressure from communities for the halls to be more widely used, the Department of Education considered that 'a PE hall is too big an asset to be limited to school use only'. While they stated that it was a 'firm intention' that secondary schools would get PE halls, no grants had been given to them at that point.[68] Following discussion of the use of PE halls by communities, it was decided that the JMB would give the Department of Education 'a suggested list of criteria and with comments on the equitable distribution of grants for PE halls'. The Department's Building Unit would then advise the Minister on the recommendations of the JMB. The Department clarified that there were no specified conditions on community and vocational schools that had received grants, but they could assume the halls would be used by the wider community, which was not the case with secondary schools.[69] Some schools simply raised funds themselves. St Brendan's College Killarney, a 'famed [Gaelic] football nursery' was said to have raised funds for facilities through its past pupils, with 'a first class gymnasium' opened by the Bishop of Kerry in September 1979.[70]

Application was no guarantee of funding success in any case and government policies towards funding often shifted depending on the economy. In December 1979 the Minister of Education announced that 117 schools had applied for PE halls by the beginning of the month, and that thirteen community and vocational schools would get them.[71] He blamed the backlog on the previous government's suspension of the plan in 1975.[72] However, in February 1980, Minister Wilson indicated that there would be 'major cutbacks' in the provision of post-primary school PE halls as there was 'a huge backlog' and the government needed to slow down in their provision of resources.[73] This came only a year after he had promised that funding would again be available.[74] This announcement followed the global crisis brought on by an increase in the price of oil. Minister Wilson's

---

68   Ibid.
69   Ibid.
70   *Irish Examiner*, 1 September 1979.
71   *Irish Independent*, 14 December 1979.
72   Ibid.
73   *Evening Herald*, 16 February 1980.
74   *Irish Press*, 9 February 1979.

decision to slow the development of PE halls coincided with Taoiseach
Charles Haughey's national broadcast in which he 'patiently explained to
the Irish people the dire state of the Irish economy and sternly enjoined
on all the absolute need for belt-tightening and stringent retrenchment'.[75]
As Bartlett has stated, 'he was living like a prince at the time', highlighting
the inequalities which persisted within Irish society by the late twentieth
century.[76]

Increasing Involvement in PE

An important development in the late 1970s was the foundation of
the Association of Special Physical Education at Thomond College in
September 1979, with an aim 'to unite all professional Physical Education
teachers' involved with children with disabilities in Ireland.[77] The new
association intended to meet with the PEAI at their annual conference,
which was scheduled for Ballina the following month.[78] The president
of the organisation, Gerard Kennedy, was based in St Vincent's Centre
on the Navan Road, Dublin, while vice-president, Helen McCarthy, was
employed at St Vincent's Special School, Lisnagry, Limerick.[79] Their first
activity was the National Walk Day on 7 October.[80]

    Like in the primary sector, there were those who felt that team success
in schools was being prioritised at the expense of individual pupils. At the
PEAI's annual conference, held in Kilkenny at the Halloween weekend in
1980, it was noted that many teachers were being put under pressure at job
interviews to take on the management of school teams 'often outside of
school hours' and that too much emphasis was placed on winning trophies

---

75   Bartlett, *Ireland: A History*, 510.
76   Ibid.
77   *Irish Independent*, 26 September 1979.
78   Ibid.
79   Ibid.
80   Ibid.

for the school.[81] Association president, Pat Staunton, stated that while they accepted that extra-curricular activity was needed, 'it should not be such that it becomes a burden or that it means that the needs of some pupils are being neglected'.[82] In addition, it was felt by some present that 'undue time is often spent coaching the most gifted sports pupils in school while those needing the most time and attention are largely neglected'.[83]

As Carter has written, 'the popular health consciousness that pervaded Western culture in the 1970s was accompanied by a fitness boom'.[84] By August 1983 a revolution in fitness was said to be engulfing Irish society, with one Irish Management Institute specialist of the opinion that the lack of stability caused by the recession was a factor in inspiring people to take more control of their health.[85] Some government-backed initiatives were undertaken at that time. Cospóir published a number of exercise charts as part of a campaign to get women more involved in sport in August 1983.[86] In September 1983, Assistant Chief Inspector of the Department of Education, Denis Healy, launched a new scheme backed by the *Irish Press* and Yoplait, the yoghurt brand, which aimed to award sports equipment to the value of £500 each month to schools where pupils had performed outstanding achievements in sport, with judges seeking evidence of activity which resulted in more awareness and participation in sport.[87] With the development of the National Basketball League in the late twentieth century, interest in basketball coaching in schools also grew, with over 300 secondary school teachers taking part in a training course in the sport at Presentation Convent, Croshaven, County Cork in October 1983.[88] School competitions remained an important part of the ethos of many schools, and the growth of GAA's provincial and All-Ireland Vocational Schools' championships since the early 1960s allowed talented pupils to play for

81   *Irish Independent*, 3 November 1980.
82   Ibid.
83   *Irish Examiner*, 4 November 1980.
84   Carter, *Medicine, Sport and the Body*, 30.
85   *Sunday Independent*, 14 August 1983.
86   *Irish Independent*, 18 August 1983.
87   *Irish Press*, 21 September 1983 and 1 March 1984.
88   *Irish Independent*, 21 September 1983 and *Irish Examiner*, 26 October 1983.

Figure 38. The Donegal Vocational Schools' team which won the Ulster and All-Ireland Vocational Schools' championship in 1984. Courtesy of John McConnell.

their counties in Gaelic football (see Figure 38) and hurling in addition to non-school related intercounty representation.[89]

Efforts to Change the PE Syllabus

The Department of Education organised the National Conference on Physical Education and Sport which was launched in October 1984 by former Taoiseach, Jack Lynch, with over 200 PE teachers in attendance.[90] It was noted that 'the main topic of conversation was the likelihood that, following the Draft Document on Physical Education, PE might become an accepted second level examination subject.'[91] The following year, other

89   *Kerryman*, 11 March 1961.
90   *Irish Independent*, 8 October 1984.
91   Ibid.

initiatives to improve the status of PE were mentioned. In April 1985, the Department of Education announced that a Revised Syllabus in Physical Education would be introduced in post-primary schools at the beginning of the 1985–6 school year.[92] It was intended that pupils, having undertaken the primary school course in Physical Education, would begin Stage 1 of the new syllabus, which would consist of a 'Basic Introductory Course' over two years, while Stage 2 would take place in the third year and be made up of 'Specialisation'. Stage 3, to be completed over years four and five, would consist of 'Options' and a 'Leadership Project'.[93]

O'Boyle's study of 795 correspondents mainly involved in second level education, published in 1986, examined their views on the state of the subject in regard to the possibility of it becoming a Leaving Certificate examination subject.[94] He found that there was 'a great diversity in facilities for the teaching of physical education throughout Ireland from the excellent to the very poor'.[95] It was felt that if PE was to become an examination subject, resources would be needed 'to ensure standardisation of facilities to meet the syllabus requirements', although the Department of Education had already made it 'compulsory for all new schools to have provision for physical education in their construction'.[96] Most of those involved in the study felt that the Department was not doing enough to support the subject's development, with the fact it was not a compulsory subject, and the unsatisfactory nature of facilities, cited as evidence to back up this view.[97] The vast majority of O'Boyle's participants, which included PE teachers and student teachers of the subject, felt that its status would be raised if it was made an examination subject.[98]

However, and somewhat contradictorily, he found that 62 per cent of PE teachers were opposed to it becoming a Leaving Certificate examination

92   Department of Education Files. *Department of Education Circular. Revised Syllabus in Physical Education*, Cir. 29/85.
93   Ibid., 2.
94   O'Boyle, 'Examinations in Physical Education', 183.
95   Ibid.
96   Ibid.
97   Ibid., 183–4.
98   Ibid., 184.

subject, but 'the majority of all other participants' were in favour of such a move.[99] O'Boyle's research also revealed that many PE teachers felt that as well as increasing its status, examinations would offer those good at PE the chance to get a mark in it. It would also become more standardised in terms of facilities and content of the course, would increase the spread of knowledge in PE theory and would give direction to students and teachers.[100] However, they also felt that there would be disadvantages in having PE as an examination subject, namely that 'it would restrict the teaching of the subject', it would put more stress and pressure on pupils and that 'it would become an elitist subject'.[101] O'Boyle concluded by noting that PE in Ireland had 'just entered a new stage in its development' in that 'the Curriculum and Examinations Board had recommended that it become a "core subject" and that it be assessed in second-level schools'.[102] He added 'that the case for examinations in physical education is as yet not fully proven' and that there was 'a lack of consensus among physical educationists in this issue'.[103]

Insurance Issues and Inequalities

Insurance claims also impacted on second level school policies and on teachers' attitudes to what was safe to teach and led to the teaching of PE and schoolyard games taking on a more formalised structure. In May 1984, in what appears to be an unprecedented case involving an Irish school, a teenage student from a secondary school in Waterford lost her case in the High Court after she took action having been hit by a shot-putt during a sports event in 1980.[104] One 1986 survey of 123 Second level schools conducted by Dr Tony Watson, a sports injuries specialist at Thomond

99   Ibid., 185.
100   Ibid.
101   Ibid.
102   Ibid., 187.
103   Ibid.
104   *Irish Independent*, 18 May 1984 and *Irish Press*, 18 and 19 May 1984.

College, found a higher level of serious injury in Irish schools than in those in the USA and Europe, with better facilities offered as the main reason for this as 'other countries had far greater safety precautions and a higher level of fitness [amongst pupils] than those in Ireland'.[105] In April 1987 the PEAI, alarmed at the growing number of court cases against PE teachers, announced it was to set up 'a panel of experts trained to draw up reports and give evidence on behalf of teachers accused of negligence'.[106] They were concerned about the rise in these cases particularly when numerous PE activities 'had no safety standards laid down'.[107] A spokesman for the PEAI, Kieran McFadden, who evidently had maintained his previous efforts to strengthen the subject's status at university level, noted that PE teachers were forced to 'teach defensively' and that this was having a negative impact when he felt that a sense of adventure was necessary in teaching.[108] In August 1988, the Minister for Education issued a circular to chief executive officers of VECs regarding accidents during PE classes.[109] Vocational school authorities were reminded to take sufficient precautions to ensure pupils' safety, and to ensure that the equipment was up to standard and that pupils wore proper footwear in school gyms.[110] The results of a survey undertaken by the Irish Red Cross and released in February 1990, highlighted that 'thousands' of schoolchildren were being injured in schools in Ireland each year with claims said to be 'rising at an alarming rate' while parents were said to 'have become more compensation conscious'.[111] However, Louis Kelly, the PEAI's Education Officer, stated that in schools where PE was being taught, the number of accidents was declining, as they were placing more emphasis on safety, and a booklet on safety and insurance was being compiled.[112] While PE

105   *Irish Press*, 8 July 1986 and *Irish Independent*, 3 October 1986.
106   *Evening Herald*, 6 April 1987.
107   Ibid.
108   Ibid.
109   *Department of Education Files. Department of Education Circular. Accidents during Physical Education classes*, Cir. 55/88. 17 August 1988.
110   Ibid.
111   *Evening Herald*, 28 February 1990.
112   Ibid.

was said to be the class to be removed first in the case of cut-backs, Kelly also felt that supervision by those fully qualified to teach the subject was 'essential'.[113]

PE Teaching Positions in Second Level Schools

A lack of PE jobs was evident by the mid-1980s in line with the wider recession that gripped Irish society in that decade, with emigration rampant. As Enda Delaney has stated, 'mass emigration became a feature of life in the 1980s, the so called "new wave" of Irish emigration'.[114] In April 1984, it was stated by Dr Ken Hill of Thomond College that less than 50 per cent of Irish schools had a permanent PE teacher.[115] He also believed that 'in the present economic situation, where there are cut-backs on staffing within secondary schools the examined subjects tend to have priority in terms of employment for teachers' and that 'physical education seems to be put on the long finger'.[116] He also noted that of fifty PE students who had graduated in 1983, 'only six students received full incremental PE posts in the country' and 'the remainder either took up temporary appointments or got jobs outside of teaching. Others got work in health studios or sought higher qualifications in the United States or elsewhere.'[117] He expressed concerns that Thomond PE graduates' employment prospects did 'not seem to be that healthy' although they also had a second teaching subject.[118] Later that month, Teachers' Union of Ireland president Harry Kavanagh stated that unemployment levels of graduate teachers lay between 2,000 and 3,000.[119]

---

113   Ibid.
114   Enda Delaney, *Irish Emigration Since 1921* (Dundalk: Dundalgan Press, 2002), 7.
115   *Irish Examiner*, 20 April 1984.
116   Ibid.
117   Ibid.
118   Ibid.
119   *Irish Independent*, 25 April 1984.

In June 1985, it was reported that places on the PE course at Thomond College would be made available to overseas students following a decision by the Board of Governors, while all graduates since 1973 were said to have gained full-time or part-time jobs.[120] Irish students who failed to gain a place in the course and wanted to pursue a career teaching PE had to look outside the country, with the University of Ulster generally keeping 2 per cent of its places on the PE course there for students from the Republic of Ireland, and in 1985 fifteen Irish students enrolled on the postgraduate PE course at Strawberry Hill in London.[121] Despite the seemingly improved curricular regulations, the reality was that many schools in Ireland still did not have the facilities or resources for a varied PE curriculum, or in some cases, any kind of PE.[122]

Notwithstanding the scarcity of jobs in the subject, a career in PE continued to be of interest to many school-leavers. In August 1985, the PE course at Thomond was said to be 'the most sought-after place' in third level courses, with more than 900 people applying that year.[123] By May 1987 the PEAI reported there were over 800 full-time PE teachers in the Republic of Ireland, while its president, Patrick Duffy, stated that PE was taught formally in 80 per cent of Irish schools although the time allocated to it could range from forty minutes to three hours per week.[124] In order to emphasise the significance of PE in schools, the PEAI launched a two-day exhibition, sponsored by Kellogg's, which took place in the Shelbourne Hotel in Dublin early in May 1987. This was said to be 'loosely modelled on the Aer Lingus Young Scientists exhibition'.[125] More than 280 projects from schools around the country were displayed with the awards presented by Minister of State for Youth and Sport, Frank Fahey.[126] However, over 20 per cent of schools were deemed ineligible to take part as they had no qualified PE teacher, with Duffy stating that 'at a time when litigation is

120   Ibid., 19 June 1985.
121   Ibid.
122   *Evening Herald*, 22 October 1985.
123   *Irish Independent*, 26 August 1985.
124   *Evening Herald*, 2 May 1987.
125   Ibid.
126   *Irish Press*, 4 May 1987.

so common, schools cannot stand over letting people who do not know what they are doing supervise games and PE'. He also felt that 'much of the sporting activity in education' was 'haphazard' and left 'a great deal to be desired'.[127] Only 25 per cent of Irish adults exercised regularly and the PEAI hoped that this figure would improve with proper physical education in schools leading to pupils to take more responsibility for their own fitness.[128]

In the late 1980s the situation regarding PE's position actually appeared to be worsening. In December 1987, the results of an ASTI survey illustrated that with cut-backs, in some schools, the subject was being 'downgraded and even dropped in some cases'.[129] In March 1988 the ASTI expressed fears that with increasing numbers of teachers seeking early retirement, 'areas like remedial teaching, modern languages, art and physical education' were 'distinctly under threat'.[130] That same month, PEAI vice-president, Pat Flanaghan, stated that PE 'was being whittled away at second level'.[131] It was reported that due to an emphasis on gaining good examination marks, 'many schools' were 'falling far short of the minimum hours laid down for physical education' and that 'too many school managers consider it a low status subject'.[132] They were also 'diverting trained teachers into academic work', according to Flanaghan.[133]

In June 1988, the National Council for Curriculum and Assessment [NCCA] founded a Physical Education Working Party, the intention of which was 'to review the role of PE in the school curriculum (with particular reference to the post-primary curriculum) and to advise the Council on issues requiring policy consideration'.[134] This was not well received by the president of the PEAI, however. In November of that year, Patrick Duffy

---

127   Ibid.
128   Ibid.
129   *Irish Independent*, 21 December 1987.
130   Ibid., 8 March 1988.
131   *Evening Herald*, 17 March 1988.
132   Ibid.
133   Ibid.
134   Secretariat of Secondary Schools Archives. Joint Managerial Body files. Letter from NCCA Chief Executive Albert Ó Ceallaigh to Brother Declan Duffy, 27 February 1989.

accused the NACA of appointing 'an exclusive, non-representative, non-specialist working party on Physical Education'. In particular, Duffy called for the Physical Education Working Party to be 're-formulated' before his organisation would correspond with them.[135] As highlighted earlier, disharmony was a continuous issue within Irish sporting organisations, and in their relations with other associational bodies.

Progress in developing the subject continued to be hindered by the state of the Irish economy with other issues prioritised. At the PEAI's annual conference in October 1988 in Tralee, it was stated by Minister Fahey that 66 per cent of post-primary schools had no PE teachers, but with cut-backs in education finance, it was not easy to remedy this.[136] He also stated that despite the cut-backs, he wanted to see PE and sport gain a greater role in schools, and noted that the PEAI was to receive £23,000 for a number of chosen projects from the National Lottery, while it was also intended to appoint a coaching director as well as a field officer for the Sport for All programme.[137] Later that month, at the Dublin Millennium Sports Conference in Bolton Street, the minister promised that he would discuss the situation with 'those involved in sport' having stated that the Department of Education was to blame 'for much of' Ireland's poor results in the Olympics in Seoul.[138] He admitted it had been 'grossly negligent' in its attitude to PE, which was 'an also-ran' in the curriculum and that the athletic situation would have been worse only for individual teachers who were training young athletes.[139] Minister for Education, Mary O'Rourke, later denied that the Minister of State had made these statements and highlighted instead that the Department of Education had actually increased funding for a 'mini-sport movement', appointed a full-time development officer to offer assistance to teachers as well as providing funding to the PEAI for the first time.[140]

135   *Irish Press*, 6 December 1988.
136   *Irish Examiner*, 10 October 1988.
137   Ibid.
138   *Evening Herald*, 28 October 1988.
139   Ibid.
140   'Dáil Éireann Debate – Thursday, 8 Dec 1988. Vol. 385. No. 4. Written Answers. – Physical Education.' Retrieved from <https://www.oireachtas.ie/en/debates/debate/dail/1988-12-08/42/> [Accessed 2 November 2020].

This denial came following comments by President of the PEAI, Patrick Duffy, who felt that many advances made in the 1960s and 1970s were reversed in a 'frenzy of fiscal butchery'.[141] He added that in some schools PE was being 'squeezed out of the Leaving Cert. Cycle' while 'in most European countries' the subject received 1.5 hours per week, but in Ireland it was 'less than half of that'.[142] Duffy, a lecturer at Thomond College, highlighted Ireland's lack of success at the Seoul Olympics and stated that 'politicians and civil servants started a PE programme but never finished it', referring to the initiatives undertaken in the late 1960s and early 1970s.[143]

One 1988 report by a Department of Education inspector illustrated Irish pupils were 'the least fit in Europe' and that nearly half of Leaving Certificate students had no PE.[144] Around 40 per cent of second level schools offered one class in the subject per week, while 'only one-in-eight schools' offered two periods per week.[145] Another study highlighted that two-thirds of inspectors felt that the standard at primary level was unsatisfactory, with indoor and other facilities lacking. In response to this, PEAI president Patrick Duffy stated that 'provision was inadequate at primary level, improved in the first three years of post-primary and then dropped off again in senior classes'.[146] He also felt that PE was especially needed in Leaving Certificate years because of the stress.[147] Head of the Physical Education Department at Thomond, Dr Ken Hill, claimed in relation to the Physical Education syllabus, the Department of Education had not fully implemented their 'clearly stated policy in the most recent Rules and Programmes for Secondary Schools'.[148]

---

141   *Irish Independent*, 10 October 1988.
142   *Irish Examiner*, 10 October 1988.
143   Ibid.
144   *Irish Independent*, 12 October 1988.
145   Ibid.
146   Ibid.
147   Ibid.
148   *Irish Independent*, 3 November 1988.

New Initiatives and More Criticism

By the late 1980s, vocational, community and comprehensive schools were expected to pay for equipment through annual budgets granted for overall costs while 'privately owned and managed' secondary schools had to pay for it themselves although schools participating in the Free Education scheme could apply for special grants.[149] In May 1989 Minister Fahey announced details of a new scheme for health and fitness in schools, which was entitled 'Action for Life'.[150] A pilot programme was to be launched in a number of secondary schools in Dublin in September 1989, with programme Co-Director Ann Hope stating that the emphasis would be placed on educating pupils to eat more healthily and get more exercise. It was sponsored by Yoplait and run in conjunction with the Health Promotion Unit in the Department of Health and Cospóir.[151] It was intended to introduce the programme in all secondary schools in September 1990 and in primary schools by 1992.[152] The scheme was said to contain work schemes, lesson plans, teacher and student manuals and audio visual aids, which would provide 'a much needed resource and teaching aid for Physical Education teachers'.[153] However, like many of those encouraged at primary school level, it was also said to be 'very much person centred and not dependent on facilities or the school curriculum'.[154]

The report of the NCCA's Working Party on Physical Education was released in October 1989, with recommendations that the subject become compulsory in second level schools, while the provision of time allocation, teacher allocation, facilities and equipment were all in need of

---

149   'Dáil Éireann Debate – Tuesday, 20 May 1986. Vol. 366. No. 8. Written Answers. – Physical Education Equipment.' Retrieved from <https://www.oireachtas.ie/en/debates/debate/dail/1986-05-20/131/> [Accessed 3 November 2020].

150   *Evening Herald*, 23 May 1989.

151   *Irish Independent*, 24 May 1989.

152   Ibid.

153   *Irish Farmers' Journal*, 24 June 1989.

154   *Evening Herald*, 11 July 1989.

improvement.[155] It argued that PE was 'in a precarious decline due to the undersupply of personnel and facilities' and the time given to it, and the provision of facilities, compared 'vary badly with E[uropean] C[ommunity] norms'.[156] Although two-thirds of schools at post primary level had PE teachers and most Junior Cycle students were offered classes in the subject each week, 60 per cent of Leaving Certificate students did not take any PE classes.[157] While there was a shortage of PE teachers for the Junior Cycle, it suggested that a minimum of 200 hours be given to PE at Junior Certificate level over three years, and that a Steering Committee be established to compile and monitor 'a development strategy' for the subject at primary and second level.[158] In addition, it recommended that assessment of PE be developed, but it was unable to produce a recommendation for a national certificate in PE as this was a matter of debate.[159] It expected that, through these recommendations, PE would be established 'on a sound footing' in Irish schools by the middle of the 1990s.[160] In December 1989, Minister Fahey announced that sixty-nine sports organisations would share a record in £1,399,879 in sports funding, with some organisations including the PEAI also benefiting through the creation of jobs.[161]

By the end of the decade, interest amongst school-leavers in the PE course at Limerick was deteriorating, and the demand for places in 1988 had lessened from 1367 applications to 867.[162] Arthur Dunne, the chairperson of the Institute of Guidance Counsellors, stated that 'this was most likely because of the decline in jobs for Physical Education teachers'.[163] By March 1990, it was noted in the press that 'in the absence of teaching posts, graduates of the Physical Education Degree courses in Thomond College are beginning to widen their horizons. Thomond College and the

155   *Irish Independent*, 6 October 1989.
156   Ibid.
157   Ibid.
158   Ibid.
159   Ibid.
160   Ibid.
161   *Irish Press*, 15 December 1989.
162   *Irish Independent*, 8 February 1989.
163   Ibid.

University of Limerick provide a course in Recreation Management for Business Studies/Physical Education graduates.'[164] In addition, Waterford Regional Technical College provided 'a very popular National Diploma in Recreation and Leisure' while Strawberry Hill College of Education in London, Loughborough University and the University of Ulster continued to receive Irish students.[165] In May 1990, Dr Ken Hill stated that the rate of PE graduates at Thomond College had dropped from fifty in 1984–5 to twenty-five in 1990 because of the lack of jobs available.[166]

In February 1991 there were further calls to make PE a Leaving Certificate examination subject. It was noted by the aforementioned Arthur Twomey, then a Cork-based PE teacher, that only 50 per cent of secondary schools in Kerry, Limerick, Waterford and Tipperary provided PE in the Leaving Certificate year, with exam subjects prioritised by school principals.[167] Twomey had drawn on Department of Education statistics from 1985–9, which highlighted that most schools in these areas which did provide the subject for Leaving Certificate students offered only thirty-five to forty minutes per week, despite Department of Education regulations stating that between one and a half and two hours should be allocated per week.[168] This was said to reflect a recent Cospóir study, which showed that Irish students were generally less fit than those in the rest of Europe.[169]

Attempts to rectify gender bias were also undertaken at second level. A report by the PEAI entitled *Girls and Boys Come Out To Play*, made public in February 1991, followed investigations of 'sex role stereotyping' within PE and schools' sport in second level schools.[170] It was based on a survey undertaken of eighty-six PE teachers and over 2,000 senior cycle second level school students between the ages of 15 and 19 in 170 schools.[171] The report found that activities were 'sharply classified on the basis of

164   *Irish Press*, 6 March 1990.
165   Ibid.
166   *Sunday Independent*, 27 May 1990.
167   *Irish Examiner*, 1 February 1991.
168   Ibid.
169   Ibid.
170   *Irish Independent*, 13 February 1991.
171   Ibid.

gender' and 'males had more positive and involvement-orientated views
of themselves than females and the teachers in the sample reinforced these
perceptions'.[172] The study also showed that 'sporting role models as portrayed in the media added to the cycle of male dominance in sport and
physical activity'.[173] It was also noted that 'girls displayed an alarming tendency to be unhappy about important aspects of their bodies' and 'the
fact that up to one-third were unhappy with their weight and shape' was
'a strong reflection of modern media messages'.[174] The authors also claimed
that the results 'reinforced the stereotypical images with team games and
aggressive-type activities more associated with boys while girls were more
strongly associated with rhythmic-type activities'.[175] While half the girls
said they were unhappy with their physiques, only one-fifth of boys were,
and the report, said to be 'the first study of its kind', called for 'a national
policy relating to school sport to tackle the question of gender bias in the
provision of time and facilities available for boys and girls'.[176]

In June 1991, the results of another Jimmy Deenihan-led survey, which
was based upon questionnaires sent to 794 post-primary schools, were
released.[177] Although it appears that only 492 replied, Deenihan found
that only 2 per cent were happy with the Department of Education's PE
programme, and that 42 per cent of schools had no PE.[178] In addition,
nearly 30 per cent of pupils had no PE teacher, with Deenihan stating
that 'the emphasis in the senior cycle' was 'almost exclusively on points'.
He concluded that almost 40 per cent of Leaving Certificate pupils had
no PE and felt that 'the social, emotional and physical development of
the students' was 'almost totally neglected' and that PE was 'becoming
marginalised' in post-primary schools.[179] It was also noted that the time
allocated to PE decreased every year in second level schools.[180] Overall, in

172   Ibid.
173   Ibid.
174   Ibid.
175   Ibid.
176   Ibid.
177   *Irish Press*, 11 June 1991.
178   Ibid. and *Evening Herald*, 14 June 1991.
179   *Irish Press*, 11 June 1991.
180   *Evening Herald*, 14 June 1991.

first year pupils spent fifty-five minutes per week on PE, while by fifth year this figure had dropped to thirty-four.[181] 135 schools were without indoor PE facilities while thirty-eight had no outdoor facilities for the subject. Twenty-five had no PE facilities of any sort.[182] The previous year, Minister O'Rourke stated that the building of PE halls in second level schools was 'dependent on the availability of capital resources' and the Department of Education's 'other commitments and priorities'.[183] The lack of provision for sports halls could have a huge impact on a secondary school student's PE as opposed to games, as one current primary school teacher recalled of her second level education:

> I was really poorly serviced at second level, because my secondary school had not long opened, and they didn't actually have a PE hall, so we literally had no PE curriculum timetabled PE in second level at all, so the only sense of physical activity or sport we got was in an extra-curricular capacity and they did provide things like tennis, GAA football, soccer, basketball, but aside from that I actually had zero experience of physical education in second level, so it was really disappointing.[184]

Criticisms of government policies on PE continued into the summer of 1991. In July 1991, ASTI president Senator Joe Costello criticised the Department of Education's decision to reduce spending on school sports centre building, stating that PE was 'an integral part of the curriculum and all weather facilities are required to ensure that adequate participation levels are achieved'.[185] He added that 'the size of classes in Ireland is the largest in the EC and our per capita spending on education is the lowest. We have the poorest participation rate in physical education, largely because of the lack of gymnasia and sports centres in many of our schools.'[186] In August 1991, Liam Dugdale, the head of Physical Education and Sports

---

181 Ibid.
182 Ibid.
183 'Dáil Éireann Debate – Tuesday, 6 February 1990. Vol. 395. No. 3. Written Answers. – Clane, Kildare, School Facilities.' Retrieved from <https://www.oireachtas.ie/en/debates/debate/dail/1990-02-06/144/> [Accessed 4 November 2020].
184 Interview with primary school teacher number fifteen, 29 July 2019.
185 *Irish Independent*, 20 July 1991.
186 Ibid.

Science at the University of Limerick, claimed that many Irish children were 'physically illiterate' on entering second level school 'because of the lack of a consistent and comprehensive physical education programme in primary schools'.[187] He was speaking at a press conference which was held to discuss the forthcoming ICHPER Congress in Limerick that month, and 'called on the Government to implement a policy whereby all children have the opportunity to take part in physical education under the direction of a qualified PE person'.[188] In welcoming delegates to the Congress, Limerick Mayor Alderman Joe Kemmy also stated that the Government needed to take more action in regard to the provision of PE, and claimed that 'all too often PE and recreational courses are re-garded as the Cinderella subjects of the school curriculum'.[189] Minister for Education, Mary O'Rourke, while speaking at the Congress, 'called for a complete review of sports and recreation facilities' in Irish schools and stated that 'a significant part of the Green Paper on the whole future of Irish education' which was to be published that autumn, would 'be devoted to physical education, sports and education'.[190] She also felt that more pre-service training was needed for teachers and that schools' and colleges' facilities should be made available to the public, and praised the thirty-eight VECs which had been prominent in encouraging sport.[191] As shown above in the previous chapter, the Green Paper's coverage of sport was less than she had promised.

Replying to these comments at the Congress, which was attended by more than 400 delegates from thirty countries, PEAI President John Halbert stated that it was the organisation's view that more was needed in terms of teaching PE, and that specialist PE teachers along with a well-designed' PE syllabus was 'the only solution to the problems which exist in that area'.[192] He felt that PE provision in primary schools was 'wholly unsat-isfactory' while the subject was 'under constant attack' in the timetables of

187 *Irish Examiner*, 7 August 1991.
188 Ibid.
189 Ibid., 13 August 1991.
190 *Irish Press*, 14 August 1991.
191 *Irish Independent*, 14 August 1991.
192 Ibid., and *Irish Press*, 15 August 1991.

many second level schools.[193] He added in a newspaper article that Ireland was twenty-five years behind 'developed countries in this sphere' and that the gap would widen 'unless urgent positive action is taken'.[194] In particular, Halbert wanted more action taken on NCCA reports and he also wanted to see 'a central body' set up 'to co-ordinate the expenditure of available funds to ensure that they reach those most in need'.[195] In addition, it was revealed by Thomond College graduates Mary O'Sullivan and Larry McCarthy at the Congress that only 46 per cent of the Irish adult population took part in sport and leisure.[196] They felt that this was due to factors including 'lack of education, lack of resources, lack of encouragement to become involved, lack of non-competitive sports opportunities' while 'too much orientation towards team sports' was also listed as a reason.[197]

By January 1992, 'the former Thomond College of Education courses in teacher training' had been 'fully integrated into the University of Limerick' with 'the interview, and the oral Irish test which formed part of their selection processes' being discontinued.[198] The degrees available for those who finished the programmes were now 'a Bachelor of Arts (in Education) for PE students, a Bachelor of Science (Education) replaced what had been the General and Rural Science course while a Bachelor of Technology course replaced what was the Wood and Building Technology or the Metal and Engineering Technology programmes.'[199]

In June 1992, it was announced that the Departments of Health and Education were to join forces with school authorities 'in a major initiative to foster health promotion in primary and second level schools', entitled the 'Health-Promoting School Project'.[200] The programme, which involved consultation with parents, intended to focus on the promotion of a healthy lifestyle, health screening, sexuality education and 'a physical education

---

193   *Irish Press*, 15 August 1991 and *Irish Examiner*, 15 August 1991.
194   *Irish Independent*, 15 August 1991.
195   Ibid.
196   Ibid.
197   Ibid.
198   *Irish Independent*, 16 January 1992.
199   Ibid.
200   *Irish Independent*, 26 June 1992.

programme from the early stages of primary school that would be linked to education on hygiene and diet'.[201] It was approved by the EC and was to begin as a pilot programme in twelve schools that year.[202] Swimming was another sport which continually received less attention in Irish schools than it merited. In August 1992 Jim Higgins, Fine Gael's Education Spokesman, called for more focus on water safety and awareness in schools' PE programmes following the release of National Safety Council figures, which illustrated that the rate of accidental drownings in Ireland was three times greater than that in Britain.[203]

The attitudes of some parents towards PE at times illustrated a complete lack of interest, with 'the concerns or desires of some parents to have an alternative provided to physical education classes' raised in the Dáil in October 1994.[204] In September 1996, ASTI president, John Mulcahy, stated that parents who sent their children to 'costly second level colleges' in order to gain high Leaving Certificate grades were 'denying them a proper education' as PE was being ignored, while there was also 'a worrying shortage of qualified PE teachers' and facilities for the subject were inadequate. He also claimed that more teachers were now unwilling to stay on after school to coach sports, due to parental and pupil pressure to obtain high grades. He called on the Minister for Education, Niamh Bhreathnach (1993–7), 'to take steps to prevent the total disappearance of sport in secondary schools'.[205] In some ways, this development reflected trends in Northern Ireland and England.

The provision of PE halls remained inadequate with only thirteen out of twenty-four post-primary schools in Donegal having these in 1993 and Minister Bhreathnach stated that further developments were to be determined by the easing of pressure 'on available resources for urgent

201   Ibid.
202   Ibid.
203   Ibid., 8 August 1992.
204   'Dáil Éireann Debate – Tuesday, 11 Oct 1994. vol. 445, no. 6. Written Answers – Physical Education.' Retrieved from <https://www.oireachtas.ie/en/debates/debate/dail/1994-10-11/351/> [Accessed 2 November 2020].
205   *Irish Independent*, 8 August 1992.

classroom accommodation'.[206] By the mid-1990s, it still was the policy of the government to 'allocate an annual block budget' to each VEC to covering general costs rather than allocating specific amounts to develop physical education.[207] Physical Education halls were provided in secondary schools on a 'phased basis' but numbers remained low, with two sanctioned by the Department of Education in 1995 and ten in 1996.[208] When questioned about the provision of PE facilities at a school in Palmerstown in January 1996, the Minister replied to say that it could 'only be considered in the context of the capital available for post-primary building purposes generally'.[209] This was 'because of the huge demand for additional classroom accommodation in schools throughout the country'.[210]

Revising the PE Syllabus

In January 1997, Fianna Fáil launched their sports policy discussion document, *Taking the lead-a policy for Sport and Leisure*, which proposed a new Department of Tourism and Sport, a new national sports body and the building of a fifty-metre swimming pool.[211] It was also proposed that more PE teachers be appointed in schools. Fianna Fáil's spokesman on

---

206   'Dáil Éireann Debate – Wednesday, 3 Nov 1993 Vol. 435. No. 4. Written Answers. – Donegal Schools' Facilities.' Retrieved from <https://www.oireachtas.ie/en/debates/debate/dail/1993-11-03/68/> [Accessed 4 November 2020].

207   'Dáil Éireann Debate – Thursday, 16 Feb 1995. vol. 449 no. 3. Written Answers – Promotion of Physical Education.' Retrieved from <https://www.oireachtas.ie/en/debates/debate/dail/1995-02-16/66/> [Accessed 2 November 2020].

208   'Dáil Éireann Debate – Wednesday, 7 May 1997. Vol. 478 No. 7. Written Answers – Sports Capital Programme.' Retrieved from <https://www.oireachtas.ie/en/debates/debate/dail/1997-05-07/173/> [Accessed 4 November 2020].

209   'Dáil Éireann Debate – Tuesday, 23 Jan 1996.Vol. 460. No. 3. Written Answers. – Physical Education Facilities.' Retrieved from <https://www.oireachtas.ie/en/debates/debate/dail/1996-01-23/235/> [Accessed 4 November 2020].

210   Ibid.

211   *Irish Examiner*, 14 January 1997 and *Irish Independent*, 13 September 1997.

sport, Liam Aylward, stated that the Government was not giving sport and leisure enough attention, and one of the party's central proposals was 'that sport should be given a direct vote at cabinet'.[212] In February 1997, Minister of State at the Department of Education and the Environment with special responsibility for Youth and Sport, Bernard Allen, launched 'a major sports strategy plan' which, along with recommendations that Ireland get a national stadium, suggested that PE become a Leaving Certificate subject.[213] Known as *Targeting Sporting Change in Ireland*, it also recommended the appointment of two national sports officers to help with the coordination of sport for youths.[214]

Another European survey exposed the state of PE in Irish schools as the century drew to a close. In August 1997, a survey of twenty-five European countries undertaken by the European Physical Education Authority (EUPEA) revealed that Ireland was lagging behind twenty-one other European nations in the teaching of PE.[215] Research undertaken examined the amount of weekly time given to the subject in primary and post-primary schools, with a focus on 6 to 12 year olds, 13 to 16 year olds and 17 to 18 year olds.[216] Ireland was at the bottom of the league in each of these age groups. This led to calls from PE teachers for a revision of the secondary level syllabus and a new curriculum at primary level. Post-primary schools in Ireland were said to allocate just over one hour per week to the subject, while three times that much was given to it in schools in Austria, France, Germany, Norway, Portugal, Spain, Switzerland and the Netherlands.[217] Ireland's results at junior cycle level were, according to the PEAI, 'alarming'. With only forty-five minutes given to PE at the 13 to 16 age group, Ireland was again at the bottom of the league in comparison 'to most other European countries which have at least two hours per week'.[218] At senior cycle, Irish schools averaged only twenty minutes

---

212   Ibid., 14 January 1997.
213   *Evening Herald*, 18 February 1997.
214   Ibid., and *Irish Independent*, 13 September 1997.
215   *Irish Independent*, 26 August 1997.
216   Ibid.
217   Ibid.
218   Ibid.

per week while some countries such as Belgium allocated as much as two and a half hours per week.[219]

The PEAI called on Minister for Education Micheál Martin (1997–2000) to take immediate action and to implement the Irish Sports Council's recommendations which had been set down in the National Sports Strategy document. As noted, this report posited that PE should be a subject at Leaving Certificate level. PEAI president, John Michael Porter, stated that 'the present syllabus was only a draft one in 1984, but somehow managed to become the core syllabus' and was 'totally irrelevant to practicing teachers'.[220]

In September 1997, it was announced that the Department of Education would make PE a Leaving Certificate subject within two years, having 'arranged for the National Council for Curriculum Assessment to begin drawing up the necessary syllabus'.[221] Most of the 369,000 students in second level education were expected to choose the option. The Minister of Education had met with the chairman of the Sports Council, John Treacy, as well as with Departmental Inspectors.[222] Minister Martin, however, defended the time allocated by stating that in the Dáil that

> The data for the different countries are difficult to compare because of varying interpretations of what constitutes physical education in schools. In a number of European countries physical education and sport education are synonymous. The data supplied for Ireland excluded time allocated to sport-games in our schools which can be significant in many cases.[223]

In mid-January 1998, the move to give the subject examination status received further acknowledgement with the Junior Certificate also

---

219   Ibid.
220   *Irish Examiner*, 28 August 1997.
221   Ibid., 30 September 1997.
222   Ibid., Physical Education had been introduced as part of a leisure studies module in the Leaving Certificate Applied programme at this point. See 'Dáil Éireann debate, Tuesday 7 Oct. 1997. vol. 481, no. 1. Written Answers' Retrieved from <https://www.oireachtas.ie/en/debates/debate/dail/1997-10-07/221/> [Accessed 2 November 2020].
223   'Dáil Éireann Debate – Thursday 16 Oct. 1997. Vol. 481, Number 6. Written Answers – Physical Education.' Retrieved from <https://www.oireachtas.ie/en/debates/debate/dail/1997-10-16/86/> [Accessed 2 November 2020].

included when Minister Martin 'proposed making sport a formal Leaving and Junior Cert subject' with points awarded', with a view to this move coming into place in 'the 1999/2000 Leaving Cert year at the earliest.[224] This followed discussions with Minister for Tourism, Sports and Recreation, Dr Jim McDaid, However, it had to be endorsed by the NCCA, and 'the teaching unions, while hailing the proposal as exciting and in line with recommendations tabled over recent years, expressed reservations'.[225] In particular, the ASTI stated that 'if the move was to be made "drastic improvements" would have to be carried out on sports facilities in schools'.[226] They were also said to be 'concerned with the exam procedures for the subject and called on the Minister to ensure that every school, regardless of whether it offered sport as an exam subject, provides physical education'.[227] In addition, the spokesman for the National Post Primary Parents' Council, Seán Mitchell, 'expressed concern about the inclusion of sport as an exam subject' particularly 'when many schools don't even have basic PE facilities'.[228] He stated that 'the first priority should be to provide all students with adequate facilities so that they can go through some sort of physical exercise routine'.[229] It appears that the NCCA had recommended in 1997 that PE 'be tried out on a pilot basis in the Leaving Certificate in a number of schools, on an optional basis'.[230] The NCCA, in reviewing the Junior Cycle, had 'decided not to categorise sports as a core subject because it felt the subject couldn't be made mandatory while so many schools lacked facilities'.[231]

Despite these concerns, hope remained that it would reach examination status. In January 1999, Minister Martin stated that PE would be a Leaving Certificate subject by 2001.[232] In May 1999, a draft report of

224   *Irish Independent*, 17 January 1998.
225   Ibid.
226   Ibid.
227   Ibid.
228   Ibid.
229   Ibid.
230   Ibid.
231   Ibid.
232   *Irish Examiner*, 16 January 1999.

the Points Commission highlighted that a number of areas, including PE 'should be given some form of recognition at the end of the Senior Cycle'.[233] In October 1999, the recommendations of a briefing document compiled by the NCCA proposed that a new PE course Leaving Certificate examination would consist of a 40 per cent written exam, with 40 per cent allocated for a practical exam and 10 per cent for a project and 10 per cent on movement analysis.[234] The document stated that it was 'envisaged that such students will have opportunities similar to those afforded to the committed artist, musician or woodworker'.[235] Minister Martin intended the course to be available by September 2001 as an optional school exam subject.[236] It was noted that second level schools were obliged to provide PE facilities, but many final year Leaving Certificate students were said to drop the subject.[237] One national newspaper described this as 'an admirable proposal' but 'ambitious' and noted that the NCCA's chief executive foresaw 'difficulties in arranging for assessment'.[238]

Issues relating to facilities remained by the beginning of the new millennium. In January 2000, while speaking as guest of honour at St Mary's CBS annual awards ceremony in Youghal, Minister Martin stated that the three secondary schools in the area, Coláiste Eoin, Loreto and St Mary's CBS would have to amalgamate in order to gain funding for sports facilities.[239] He outlined his policy on PE when he noted that sport in schools had previously been neglected and that while 'almost every school' had 'some form of physical education on the curriculum', its importance had not received enough attention from the Government.[240] He added that 'we intend to give it new status through a new Leaving Cert. programme' and that his Department hoped 'to give future students the opportunity to study physical education on the curriculum and sit formal exams-in

233   *Irish Independent*, 11 May 1999.
234   Ibid., 1 October 1999.
235   Ibid.
236   Ibid.
237   Ibid.
238   Ibid.
239   *Irish Examiner*, 11 January 2000.
240   Ibid.

other words to give them the same opportunities as students who excel, say, in art or music'.[241]

In March 2000, the NCCA 'recommended that a two-year physical education course be included on the curriculum just like music' and proposed that three hours a week be given to teaching PE.[242] It also suggested that 'water sports, athletics, dance, gymnastics and games should be included with both a theory paper and an assessment of the student's own games abilities'.[243] Despite the obvious need for outdoor and indoor PE facilities, 15 per cent of second level schools in the Republic of Ireland had no PE halls, however.[244] The NCCA insisted that the PE syllabus should only be delivered by those who specialised in the subject, although not every PE teacher had a third level qualification in it.[245] A draft of the syllabus was circulated to school managers and teacher unions, with the Department of Education stating that the development of this plan was only at 'a preliminary stage'.[246] In May 2000 the PEAI advertised their hosting of Consultation Workshops in PE, which included presentations on the new PE syllabus in second level schools, at various venues around the country, and all PE teachers were invited.[247] In June 2000, TD Mary Coughlan stated in the Dáil that 'up to 60pc of children drop out of physical education classes in school'.[248] In addition, she noted that second level pupils were still dropping out of PE 'due to increased pressure to excel' in other subjects.[249]

In October 2000, it was stated in the national press that the NCCA expected that PE would 'be introduced as Leaving Certificate exam subject' from September 2001, with the first exams scheduled for 2003.[250] However,

241   Ibid.
242   *Evening Herald*, 6 March 2000.
243   Ibid.
244   Ibid.
245   Ibid.
246   Ibid.
247   *Irish Examiner*, 10 May 2000.
248   *Irish Independent*, 30 June 2000.
249   Ibid.
250   *Irish Independent*, 3 October 2000.

schools needed to have 'a sports hall, a grass pitch and hard-court areas and access to a swimming pool'.[251] Unsurprisingly, these proposals were not realised at that time, and the downturn in the Global Economy by 2008 further hindered aspirations that PE would receive a higher status in Irish schools as 'the Republic of Ireland had moved into the greatest recession the country had seen since the Great Famine'.[252] In 2011, one North Dublin second level school, Trinity Comprehensive, in Ballymun (see Figures 39 and 40), took the initiative in introducing GSCE examinations in physical education through PE teacher Paddy O'Reilly, with schools in Ashbourne, Dundalk and Mullingar following this move.[253] As the economy improved, in 2014, Sports Minster Leo Varadkar stated that he wanted to see PE become a Leaving Certificate examination subject.[254] In 2017 plans were unveiled to pilot this idea in some schools, although the outcome of this initiative remains to be seen at the time of writing.[255]

A number of PE teachers interviewed expressed mixed views on this with three expressing reservations about the funding required to run the exam course in the subject in Irish schools.[256] One teacher in particular, who taught in a disadvantaged school, felt that at least €30,000 would be required to set it up in his school and said it would be some time before it would happen where he taught.[257] A retired PE teacher who was interviewed felt that the subject should maintain its non-examination status as he felt its value lay in giving students the opportunity to relax and enjoy sport.[258] Another teacher who was also retired was generally in favour of its inclusion as an examination subject as it allowed students who were good

---

251   Ibid.
252   Bartlett, *Ireland: A History*, 552.
253   *Evening Herald*, 20 December 2012.
254   *Irish Independent*, 12 April 2014.
255   'Curriculum and Syllabus: Phase 1 Physical Education in Senior Cycle' Retrieved from <https://www.education.ie/en/Schools-Colleges/Information/ Curriculum-and-Syllabus/leaving-certificate-physical-education.html> [Accessed 25 March 2018].
256   Interview with Secondary School PE teachers number one, 26 July 2019, number five, 9 September 2019 and number eight, 9 October 2019.
257   Interview with Secondary School PE teacher number eight, 9 October 2019.
258   Interview with Secondary School PE teacher number two, 24 August 2019.

Figure 39. A gymnastics display at Trinity Comprehensive, Ballymun, 1994. Courtesy of Paddy O'Reilly.

Figure 40. Sports day at Trinity Comprehensive, Ballymun, 1996. Courtesy of Paddy O'Reilly.

at sport to get points for college, but he hoped that it would not become too academic and was also interested to see how the facilities and course content would be laid out.[259] Similarly, one current PE teacher expressed doubts about how it had been prepared and felt that teachers did not have enough time to adapt to the course content.[260] However, one other existing PE teacher was of the view that it was a 'brilliant' move and that it should not be left as a non-examination subject any longer as this would only delay the development of the subject even further.[261]

Conclusion

At post-primary level, facilities also remained an issue throughout the period covered in this chapter. The provision of government funding was generally affected by the wider state of the economy and on occasions, funding was postponed or staggered. While the supply of PE teachers improved after the opening of a specialised college for PE in Limerick in 1973, not every school could employ a specialised PE teacher and reductions in numbers at times affected this position. As shown here, while PE teaching was generally a much sought-after college course until the late 1980s, at times the number of places available were insufficient to meet demand as this was offset with the number of jobs available in schools, which were not always guaranteed. PE's status as a school subject remained low from the point of view of various governments despite talk of making it an examination subject in the mid-1980s, and again in the late 1990s there were promises that this would be prioritised. However, it was not until late in the second decade of the twenty-first century that this plan came to fruition, and even then it is not available as an examination subject in every second level school. By 2000, two hours per week were

259   Interview with Secondary school PE teacher number four, 29 August 2019.
260   Interview with Secondary school PE teacher number 1, 26 July 2019.
261   Interview with Secondary school PE teacher number seven, 3 October 2019.

recommended in the programme for secondary schools.[262] However, almost remarkably, some second level schools have only recently begun to take on teachers to instruct in PE.[263] Issues with jobs still remain, with PE positions said to be difficult to obtain in Irish schools in the second decade of the twenty-first century.[264]

Inspections of physical education remained limited at post-primary level, with only four inspectors covering the entire Republic of Ireland by the end of the 1980s.[265] Two retired second level PE teachers interviewed who had both taught over a thirty year period beginning in the late 1970s both stated that they had both only received one inspection in this time, illustrating the subject's perceived place within the curriculum.[266] Attempts to raise attention to the subject's plight had been made by the PEAI and teachers unions such as the INTO, TUI, ASTI and Secretariat of Secondary Schools. In the national and local press, journalists with a related interest such as Seán Diffley were important in raising issues about facilities and resources, but these were often ignored or deflected by those in the government. An exception was Jimmy Deenihan, who regularly articulated his dissatisfaction in the early 1990s. Deenihan was motivated by his own background in sport, but there were other politicians who had been involved in the GAA, and in other sporting organisations, who prioritised other matters. It was not until the late twentieth century that parental involvement within schools became more pronounced, and this lack of demand for regular PE was also probably a factor in its failure to

262 'Dáil Éireann Debate – Tuesday, 8 Feb 2000. vol. 513, no. 6. Written Answers – Physical Education Facilities.' Retrieved from <https://www.oireachtas.ie/en/debates/debate/dail/2000-02-08/34/> [Accessed 2 November 2020].

263 Interview with Secondary School PE teacher number three, 26 August 2019.

264 Ibid., and interview with Secondary School PE teacher number five, 9 September 2019.

265 'Dáil Debates– Wednesday 15 February 1989, vol. 387, no. 2. Written Answers – Physical Education.' Retrieved from <https://www.oireachtas.ie/ga/debates/debate/dail/1989-02-15/95/> [Accessed 30 October 2020].

266 Interview with Secondary School PE teacher number two, 24 August 2019 and Interview with Secondary school PE teacher number four, 29 August 2019.

develop as a serious subject. By the beginning of the twenty-first century, however, much progress had been made, and the Celtic Tiger of the late 1990s and early 2000s was helpful not only in the increased modernisation of Ireland but in the provision of greater wealth for distribution within Irish sport.

Conclusion

This study is based upon three key themes. Firstly, it has illustrated that the Irish government neglected to take significant action to establish a structure for compulsory PE at both primary and secondary school level from the mid-1920s until the early 1960s. This came despite consistent criticism from journalists and sporting organisations. Wider changes in Irish education in the 1960s were driven by developments abroad and increased communications with international organisations were helpful in raising awareness of standards in schools elsewhere, although government knowledge of PE in other countries had been available since the early years of the Irish Free State. The decision to appoint a PE Inspector, Captain Michael McDonough, was key to developing the subject but there was only so much he could do on his own. The foundation of the PEAI in 1967 was also helpful although this organisation lacked the clout, despite being given government grants to assist with in-service and administration, to secure significant funding for the subject's development throughout the Republic of Ireland's schools.[1] It was not until the late 1980s that the Department of Education first gave the PEAI financial assistance for developing the subject in post-primary schools.[2] In addition, not every PE teacher became a member with only 350 'out of a possible 800' enrolled in 1994.[3] In the late 1960s the promotion of sport, through wider government funding, began to gain

---

1   See, for example, *Physical Education Association of Ireland Annual Report 1993/1994* (Limerick: Physical Education Association of Ireland, 1994), 11 and *Physical Education Association of Ireland Annual Report 1996/1997* (Limerick: Physical Education Association of Ireland, 1997), 18.

2   'Dáil Éireann Debate – Thursday, 8 Dec 1988. Vol. 385 No. 4. Written Answers. – Physical Education.' Retrieved from <https://www.oireachtas.ie/en/debates/debate/dail/1988-12-08/42/> [Accessed 4 November 2020].

3   *Physical Education Association of Ireland Annual Report 1993/1994*, 11.

traction in Ireland, and the employment of Robert Molloy in an associated governmental role was an important step. This move had been a
long time in coming and there were a number of false starts. This state of
affairs unfortunately continued after initial enthusiasm had worn off by
the mid-1970s and the ever-precarious condition of the Irish economy
meant that funding projects such as school PE halls were often postponed or simply ignored. As Thomas Walsh has stated, 'the neglect of
planning and providing for the implementation of educational policy
in Ireland has been a recurring theme throughout the last century'.[4]

Under the system of education in pre-partition Ireland, influence generally came from Britain, but by the second decade of the twentieth century
Irish games were also beginning to establish a place in Irish schools, although
it must be noted that many Intermediate schools did not discriminate in
their choice of sport. Although physical drill was not compulsory at that
level, inspectors' reports in 1910 indicate that games and physical exercise
were generally well catered for in boys, girls and mixed schools, although
facilities and levels of organisation varied. With the partition of Ireland in
1921 the systems of education in Northern Ireland and the Irish Free State
differed. The reduction of physical drill's status as a compulsory subject in
primary schools in Independent Ireland in the mid-1920s did not bring
about much fuss at the time. Indeed it may not have been well taught in
many Irish schools by that time as facilities and resources were poor in many
areas. However, decreasing the status of the subject meant that in many
schools the physical needs of pupils were given no attention at all. While
raising the status of the subject was contemplated by the Department of
Education, particularly on the eve of the Emergency, ministers could not
take decisive action and excuses for not doing so were regularly found as
divisions in attitudes existed. Despite recognition of the view that Ireland
should have its own system of PE, they failed to come up with something
that had its origins in Irish culture, unlike in Germany and Scandinavia. In
failing to do so, the PE system in Irish schools often borrowed from games
and methods utilised in other nations (including England) and apart from

4   Walsh, 'The Revised Programme of Instruction, 1900–1922', 141.

the inclusion of Gaelic games and Irish dancing, and attempts to teach it through Irish, lacked any real national identity.

In particular, the issue of promoting the Irish language, and the view amongst many primary school teachers that the curriculum was overloaded, meant that PE was not given the attention it received in many European countries throughout the twentieth century. Traditional notions about physical fitness were commonplace and linked to work on the land despite repeated calls from medical officials that more needed to be done in schools to improve the physical condition and postural awareness of children. In addition, many Irish schoolchildren missed out on the fun that came with taking part regularly in physical exercise together, while teachers often failed to develop the rapport with pupils that could be found through games. As one former PE teacher noted, 'the social side of PE is unbelievable, it's something you can't teach in the classroom'.[5]

A reluctance to develop a physical training college for male and female students, and the government's failure to build on the Ling institution and later, St Raphael's College at Sion Hill, meant that male physical training teachers generally had to look abroad for specialised training in the subject until the building of the NCPE in the early 1970s. With the high points requirement and limited number of places available there – there were just thirty-five places available for school-leavers on the PE training course at the University of Limerick in 1998 – Irish students still continued to migrate to Britain to gain qualifications in teaching PE.[6] However, by the early twenty-first century, other Irish universities had begun to offer degrees in the subject, although movement to British universities to gain qualifications continues.[7] A number of those migrants interviewed felt that

---

5   Interview with secondary school PE teacher number four, 29 August 2019.
6   'Dáil Éireann Debate – Tuesday, 12 May 1998 Vol. 490. No. 7. Written Answers. – Physical Education Places.' Retrieved from <https://www.oireachtas.ie/en/debates/debate/dail/1998-05-12/35/> [Accessed 2 November 2020] and interview with secondary school PE teacher number one, 26 July 2019.
7   Interview with secondary school PE teachers number five, 9 September 2019, number six, 17 September 2019 and number eight, 9 October 2019.

the British system of teaching PE was a lot more structured and advanced and linked this to students' examinations in the subject.[8]

While the involvement of army instructors in teaching drill in schools was important in Irish schools, this was often dependent on instructors gaining permission from their superiors to do so, and as shown in the case of Sergeant Kavanagh, by the 1950s the Department of Defence were not overly concerned with assisting in facilitating the subject in schools. Attempts to promote the Sokol system in the 1930s did not result in any nationwide scheme being implemented, despite sporadic efforts around the country, although its influence continued on in some schools by the post-war years. By the middle of the twentieth century, stipulations that PE teachers needed to have certification in Irish was a hindrance to many who were unable to pass the required language test despite them having a genuine interest in the subject and a talent for its teaching. Krüger and Hofmann have stated that after the Second World War, 'the link between military and civil physical education became weaker. Instead, high perform-ance and elite sport developed as worldwide societal phenomena.'[9] This was not the case in Ireland as various Irish governments paid little attention to calls to develop the nation's athletes. Notwithstanding the decline in military involvement in the late twentieth century with the development of a more formal structure in Limerick, notions that the Irish Army could somehow assist with PE in schools remained, with the matter discussed in the Dáil as late as 2010.[10]

The Irish Government's neglect of the provision of compulsory PE in Irish schools for most of the twentieth century reflected its wider attitudes to the development of sport. As Diarmaid Ferriter has stated, by the late

---

8   Interview with secondary school teacher number one, 26 July 2019; secondary school teacher number eight, 9 October 2019 and number nine, 22 October 2019.

9   Krüger and Hofmann, 'The Development of Physical-Education Institutions in Europe: A Short Introduction', 738–9.

10   'Joint Committee on Justice, Equality, Defence and Women's Rights Debate – Wednesday, 13 Jan 2010. Role of Defence Forces in Promoting Physical Fitness: Discussion.' Retrieved from <https://www.oireachtas.ie/en/debates/debate/joint_committee_on_justice_equality_defence_and_womens_rights/2010-01-13/2/> [Accessed 30 October 2020].

1970s, there was still 'the absence of a centralised policy, with government departments operating independently of each other'.[11] One PE teacher interviewed summed up his view of the general policy when he stated that 'they didn't seem to have a huge interest in it until it came to a stage where fitness and everything became so important … obesity and everything like that … I think early on they didn't really have much interest in it, they just looked at it as a kind of an add-on'.[12] Some politicians did attempt to push for improvements to PE's status. From the late 1980s onwards, Jimmy Deenihan, like General Mulcahy in the 1920s, was the politician who remained most vociferous in calling for changes to schools' PE. While Deenihan had a successful sports career himself, albeit at an amateur level, many talented athletes who had aspirations of a professional career in sport were generally forced to go abroad and opportunities to combine the development of a professional sporting career and education at third level for them usually meant seeking scholarships.

As Tom Hunt has shown, Irish athletes have been migrating to the USA to participate in these since the late 1940s, with Jimmy Reardon the first Irish athletic scholarship awardee to move there when he took up a position at Villanova in 1949.[13] Despite this international pathway, success was not guaranteed, and Ireland's level of success in the Olympic Games was regularly lamented in the national press after each four-year spell. Post-Games' 'post-mortems' carried out by journalists consistently highlighted the lack of development of a proper schools structure for Ireland's best athletes and a scarcity of facilities and funding.[14] Journalist Karl MacGinty, writing in the aftermath of the 2000 Sydney Olympics, felt that 'all of Ireland's Olympic medals in athletics since the war … must be credited, in part at least, to the US collegiate system'.[15]

In addition, it was stated that 'literally tens of thousands of Irish people are denied the opportunity to discover their sporting potential, never mind achieve it, by the chronic lack of facilities, personnel and resources

---

11   Ferriter, *Ambiguous Republic*, 316.
12   Interview with secondary school PE teacher number four, 29 August 2019.
13   Tom Hunt, *The Little Book of Irish Athletics* (Dublin: The History Press, 2017), 139.
14   See, for example, *Irish Independent*, 7 October 2000.
15   Ibid.

which persists in Irish sport'.[16] The writer also felt that the decline of religious teachers in Irish schools had been detrimental to the development of sport within education, and noted that although 'social and financial pressures' were making it 'increasingly difficult for lay teachers to volunteer for extra-curricular activities, there has been precious little effort to provide professional, qualified physical educationalists in their place'.[17] These were very reasonable comments, although in the past twenty years the use of external coaches in schools has become more commonplace. Additionally, the early twenty-first century has seen more recognition given to PE within the primary and second level curricula. University access for a wider cohort of students has also improved, with PE courses in more geographically accessible areas for students throughout the country, although some aspiring primary school teachers have still had to migrate to gain teaching qualifications with proficiency in the Irish language a requirement for their teacher-training entry in the Republic of Ireland.[18] Many primary schools also remain preoccupied with a focus on teaching the core daily subjects of English, Irish and mathematics, and this still impacts on PE time.[19]

Secondly, this book has highlighted that while PE was not compulsory in the Republic of Ireland's schools for most of the twentieth century, it would be incorrect to assume that it was completely ignored or that it was solely left to the military. Many schools took the initiative themselves and had regular timetables in place for physical training. Games were organised and school competitions developed, with school pride an important factor in stimulating rivalries such as those seen in rugby competitions north and south of the border. This may have come at a cost to those less suited to team sports or less prolific on the sports field as in some cases an overwhelming emphasis was placed upon developing school teams. External organisations also played their part in some schools' sports programmes, with the GAA eager to closely guard their sporting and social position in

16 Ibid.
17 Ibid.
18 Interview with primary school teacher twelve and primary school teacher thirteen, 26 July 2019.
19 Interview with primary school teachers number six, 3 July 2019 and number fourteen, 26 July 2019.

many parishes. The input of religious organisations was also important in fostering PE, particularly the Christian Brothers, although as noted above, this religious input declined greatly with a reduction of the Catholic Church's influence within Irish society following the exposure of historic scandals in the late twentieth century.[20] Despite their assistance, a lack of resources, facilities and space were often detrimental to its teaching being implemented in many areas. This still continues today. One PE teacher interviewed stated that he had recently written to a government minister about getting a sports hall for his school, but was told it would be 2040 before any definitive action could be taken.[21]

While there was perhaps a tendency on the part of various governments to rely on the GAA to organise school sports, as shown in this book, at times GAA officials complained that their efforts were not fully supported within schools at a local and national level. Not every school welcomed their advances, but some other sports administrators suffered worse treatment in trying to establish their games, with soccer being practically outlawed in many schools as a result of societal pressure related to the GAA's 'ban' on foreign games which was not lifted until 1971, and related attempts to Gaelicise Ireland following partition in 1921.[22] It was not until the Jack Charlton era (1986–96) that many schools began to look more favourably in allowing association football to be formally played within their school yards and fields.[23] By the late twentieth century, at least one midland Irish county had a soccer league for its primary schools, but this development was generally the exception rather than the norm in rural areas.[24] The organisation of the Community Games, firstly at a regional level in 1968,

20   Bartlett, *A History of Ireland*, 533–7.
21   Interview with secondary school PE teacher number three, 26 August 2019.
22   See Conor Curran, 'It Has Almost Been an Underground Movement'. The Development of Grassroots Football in Regional Ireland: The Case of County Donegal, 1971–1996' in Jürgen Mittag, Kristian Naglo and Dilwyn Porter (eds), Special Issue of *Moving the Social: Journal of Social History and the History of Social Movements. Small Worlds: Football at the Grassroots in Europe*, vol. 61 (2019), 33–60.
23   Curran, *Irish Soccer Migrants*, 95–9.
24   Interview with secondary school PE teacher number nine, 22 October 2019.

and nationally by the early 1970s, was also helpful in the development of sport for children.[25]

While the changes in attitudes to PE in the late 1960s and early 1970s offered much promise, in some ways they echoed government plans to implement Sokol in the late 1930s in Irish schools in that there was no clear plan regarding how to implement the subject on a consistent basis, and to make sure it was regularly taught. In theory, curriculum changes were laid down, but in practice, many schools could not adopt these, and in looking to the government for support, they were often forced to take matters into their own hands in organising structured PE themselves. Speaking in relation to the subject in rural areas in the Dáil in 1977, Minister for Education John P. Wilson stated that 'the compass of physical education is very wide and teachers are free to choose the activities which best suit their pupils and local circumstances.'[26] At times the only help received was departmental circulars or resource packs containing lesson plans, and changes in governments also affected the importance given to the subject. Major developments within PE in the Republic of Ireland generally took place in eras of increased prosperity, and when there was more money available to put plans into operation, with the late 1960s and late 1990s evidence of this. Irish politics generally lacked a group who were forceful enough to instigate real change in governmental attitudes towards PE in Irish schools for much of the twentieth century.

Unlike in France and Germany, for example, both the Republic of Ireland and Northern Ireland, and mainland Britain, gave preponderance to sport over PE within schools. In Northern Ireland, the official PE system after 1922 naturally mirrored that in mainland Britain, while many Catholic schools, in looking to events south of the border, became more trenchant in their attitudes towards Gaelicisation. Funding from Britain was certainly helpful in putting PE on a firmer footing in Northern Ireland, although there were many similarities with Independent Ireland in that it was often haphazard and numerous schools there did not have the resources or staff

---

25   *Nenagh Guardian*, 8 August 1970 and *Meath Chronicle*, 6 March 1971.
26   'Dáil Éireann Debate – Wednesday, 30 Nov. 1977. vol. 302 no. 3. Written Answers – Physical Education.' Retrieved from <https://www.oireachtas.ie/en/debates/debate/dail/1977-11-30/68/> [Accessed 2 November 2020].

to fulfil the needs of their pupils. In particular, the impact of the Troubles after 1968 in Northern Ireland affected the teaching of PE to some degree, although teachers in nationalist and unionist leaning schools generally dealt with this as best they could.

Aside from the experiences of the Troubles, developments in physical training in schools in Northern Ireland were therefore naturally reflective of those in Britain to some extent, but like in the Republic of Ireland, it was not until the 1970s that both males and females were given the opportunity to study the subject together in a national institution for second level school trainee teachers there. Attitudes towards PE were slow to change despite the efforts of Oonagh Pim to draw attention to the specialised nature of the subject and to raise standards of professionalism at the UCPE. While the Stormont government portrayed an image of PE as a well-established subject in the Ministry of Education's official publications, the comparative standards of the subject and related issues with facilities were exposed by the Wolfenden Report in 1960. Some fee-paying schools such as Campbell College had well-cemented traditions of games and exercise by then, but in less affluent institutions facilities were often limited. Again, however, it is important to state that many pupils did receive adequate PE and team games were an important part of the identity of pupils and schools themselves, particularly in a country where education was generally divided on religious lines. The role of schools in producing star athletes of an international standard was also shown to be restricted. High ranking Olympic placements have also been limited, although success has been enjoyed by Thelma Hopkins and Lady Mary Peters, both of whom were born in England, and a number of non-track and field athletes such as boxers and rowers.[27]

Thirdly, PE's progress in the Republic of Ireland was dependent on the perceived need to follow international trends, yet it ultimately remained reliant on the work of individuals in many ways. While government policies towards the subject in the Republic of Ireland remained basic in ensuring the provision of forms of physical exercise in schools for much of the twentieth century, by the late 1960s it could no longer be ignored, particularly

27   *Belfast Telegraph*, 7 July 2020.

in light of OECD reports on inequalities within education and the need to improve the Irish economy.[28] The Republic of Ireland had begun to modernise under Seán Lemass in the late 1950s as it was clear that the policy of Gaelicisation and isolationism favoured by Eamon de Valera and others was not a success.[29] The huge numbers of emigrants leaving the country in the 1950s were testimony to that and it was evident that something needed to be done to bring Ireland up to speed with developments in a number of more advanced European countries.[30] Despite this, PE returned to its usual status within government ideology after the enthusiasm of the late 1960s.

Improvements in the educational sector in this decade were in many ways later significant in helping the Irish economy through the provision of third level technological colleges. This has been linked to the success of the Celtic Tiger of the late 1990s/early 2000s. Developing a 'well educated, "high-tech" labour force' was one reason why multinational companies looking for a suitable venue in Europe chose Ireland.[31] However, developing sports science courses remained slow until the early 2000s as these were generally not seen as being of significant relevance to the Irish economy and professional sport in Ireland remains underdeveloped. Following Captain Michael McDonough's vital work in the late 1960s, there is less evidence that the Department of Education continued to push to develop PE despite his postgraduate study of the subject in 1980, his work within the Department of Education as physical education inspector, and his role as chief technical advisor to the Irish Sports Council in the later twentieth century.[32] After the early 1970s, it is apparent that it was mainly left to enthusiastic individuals to lobby for the subject's greater importance within the curriculum at both primary and second level, and only one paper on physical education was produced by the Department in that decade.[33] While the work of individuals in developing Irish sport

28   Walsh 'History of Education in Ireland', 56.
29   Bartlett, *Ireland: A History*, 493.
30   Ibid., 482–3.
31   Ibid., 538–9.
32   *Evening Press*, 20 April 1985 and *Sligo Champion*, 17 December 2003.
33   O'Donoghue, 'The Policy of the State', 171.

has been well assessed elsewhere, it similarly cannot be ignored in the case of PE.[34] Many of those with an interest in the subject were talented sports men and women who were denied the opportunity to earn a living playing professionally in Ireland by the underdeveloped structures for sport which have existed. While they may not have all been successful in raising attention to the subject's neglect, they did much to keep it in the public eye and this book has sought to identify these men and women through examining their contributions in the newspapers and at meetings and conferences. Although the efforts of General Richard Mulcahy and Jimmy Deenihan must be commended, they lacked the support to ensure their pleas received significant attention. Similarly, the work of females involved in physical education, such as Kathleen O'Rourke, was hindered by a lack of government assistance.

Despite the modernised thinking of Lemass, he was adamant that sports organisations would have to look after themselves and failed, like numerous other Taoisigh, to provide for the development of Irish sport. It was not until the Celtic Tiger of the late 1990s and early 2000s that sport and PE in Irish schools began to gain more attention from governments in terms of the funding allocated. This temporary increased prosperity brought a change in attitudes to the treatment of PE in Irish schools, although issues clearly remain in terms of the time allocated to the subject and the implementation of an examination in the subject has not yet become widespread for all students. However, there is hope that this will develop smoothly with the successful example of the development of 'A' Level PE in many of Northern Ireland's schools. Whether or not the subject will ever become specialised for teachers in Ireland's primary schools, as in the case in England and in the USA and a number of other nations, remains to be seen.[35]

With the lack of significance given to the subject by the Irish government for much of the twentieth century, teachers' facilitation of children running freely around school playgrounds during extended breaks on warm summer afternoons were often necessary given the lack of covered outdoor facilities and resources for what little timetabled PE was allowed.[36] These

34 See, for example, Curran, *The Development of Sport in Donegal 1880–1935*.
35 Interview with secondary school PE teacher number nine, 22 October 2019.
36 Interview with primary school teacher number five, 28 June 2019.

are now a thing of the past in most schools, and issues with insurance have created concerns for schools and teachers. One PE teacher interviewed was of the view that there was now 'a culture of claims' which meant that he was highly reluctant to teach elements of the subject such as archery or javelin throwing.[37] A number of teachers interviewed noted how increased awareness of body image has made many students reluctant to take part in PE lessons, particularly in their later teenage years.[38] One PE teacher felt that more emphasis needs to be placed by the government on diet within the home rather than relying on PE classes to alleviate obesity.[39] On a more positive note, the introduction in 2009 of an Active School Flag award for schools and an 'Active Schools Week' each year has been an important step, according to one primary school teacher interviewed.[40]

Unfortunately, in the twentieth century, the perceived lack of academic value associated with sport overshadowed PE's treatment in many areas in Ireland. However, with a wider selection of opportunities for Ireland's youth to balance academic qualifications with sport, and the development of more sports science and performance-related degrees, those aspiring to develop a career in a sports-related field, or combine their own sports career with other related work, can look forward to the future with greater optimism.[41] PE still remains on the periphery of the curriculum in primary and second level schools, however, and some teachers have noted how other staff members have not treated the subject with the importance or respect

---

37   Interview with secondary school PE teacher number ten, 23 October 2019.
38   Interview with secondary school PE teachers number seven, 3 October 2019; number eight, 9 October 2019; number nine, 22 October 2019 and number ten, 23 October 2019.
39   Interview with secondary school PE teacher number ten, 23 October 2019.
40   Interview with primary school teacher number thirteen, 26 July 2019.
41   See, for example, Tom O'Connor, 'From Schoolboy Teams to College Dreams: Player Progression on the League of Ireland Elite Underage Pathway – An Early Look at the First Structured Approach to Elite Adult Football in the League of Ireland' in Conor Curran and Dilwyn Porter (eds), Sport and Education in Ireland, Special issue of *Sport in Society*, vol. 23, no. 8 (2020), 1337–53.

it deserves, while inspectors' interest in and knowledge of the subject was also questioned by interviewees.[42] However, much progress has been made despite all the challenges of the twentieth century and the future looks promising for Irish pupils in PE classes, and for those striving to increase its importance within the education system.

42 Interview with secondary school PE teachers number one, 26 July 2019, number nine, 22 October 2019 and number ten, 23 October 2019.

Bibliography

Primary Sources

British Newspaper Archives

'The British Newspaper Archive' Available at <https://www.britishnewspaperarchive.co.uk/>
Coleraine Chronicle
Dublin Daily Express
Dublin Evening Mail
Dundalk Examiner and Louth Advertiser
Enniscorthy Guardian
Irish Daily Independent
Londonderry Standard
Mid-Ulster Mail
Munster Express
Nationalist and Leinster Times
North Down Herald and County Down Independent
Northern Constitution
Northern Whig
Portadown News
Sport
The Cork Examiner
The Daily Express
The Irish News and Belfast Morning News
The Liberator
The National Teacher and Irish Educational Journal
The New Ross Standard
The Standard
Tyrone Constitution
Tyrone Courier
Weekly Irish Times

Department of Defence Files, Military Archives, Cathal Brugha Barracks, Rathmines

2/32357. Physical Training. Promotion of Physical Training in the Army. Proposal to Employ a Continental (P.T.) Expert. Information Regarding P.T. in Foreign Countries. Secretary of the Minister of Defence to the Secretary of the Minister of Finance, 8 November 1933.

2/41656. Physical Training. Sokol Drill. Particulars of Exercises etc. Application by Newry Christian Brothers Schools. Captain Seán O'Neill to Brother P. W. Newell, 6 June 1935.

2/92315. Instruction. P.T. Schools and Colleges, Dublin Area. Commandant M. Gray, Operations Officer, Eastern Command, to Chief Staff Officer, 17 April 1945.

2/92315. Instruction. P.T. Schools and Colleges, Dublin Area. Letter from Diarmaid Ó Tuama to the Secretary of the Minister for Defence, 21 August 1945.

2/92315. Instruction. P.T. Schools and Colleges, Dublin Area. Letter from the Secretary of the Department of Defence to Diarmuid Ó Tuama, 7 September 1945.

2/92315. Instruction. P.T. Schools and Colleges, Dublin Area. Letter from Secretary A. J. Hyland to Reverend Brother Lewis, 1 December 1948.

2/92315. Instruction. P.T. Schools and Colleges, Dublin Area. Letter from Command Operations Officer D. A. Kelly to Chief Staff Officer, Department of Defence, 26 August 1946.

2/92315. Instruction. P.T. Schools and Colleges, Dublin Area. Letter from M. Ó Corráin to the Secretary of the Minister of Defence, 23 January 1952.

2/92315. Instruction. P.T. Schools and Colleges, Dublin Area. Letter from R. Q. O'Driscoll to the Secretary of the Department of Defence, 28 January 1952.

2/92315. Instruction. P.T. Schools and Colleges, Dublin Area. Letter from Private Secretary J. Boland to Brother T. N. MacDonnchadha, Headmaster, St Fintan's High School, 23 February 1952.

2/92315. Instruction. P.T. Schools and Colleges, Dublin Area. 1948-Memorandum. February 1955.

2/92315. Instruction. P.T. Schools and Colleges, Dublin Area. Letter from Secretary M. P. Healy to the Reverend Superior, St Fintan's High School, 8 February 1955.

2/92315. Instruction. P.T. Schools and Colleges, Dublin Area. Letter from Reverend Killian Kehoe to Minister for Defence, General Seán Mac Eoin, 9 February 1955.

2/92315. Instruction. P.T. Schools and Colleges, Dublin Area. Leathan Miontuairisce, Deputy Adjutant Gray, 15 February 1955.

2/92315. Instruction. P.T. Schools and Colleges, Dublin Area. Letter from Secretary M. P. Healy to the Reverend Superior, St Fintan's High School, April 1955.

2/92315. Instruction. P.T. Schools and Colleges, Dublin Area. Lawler to Secretary M. P. Healy, June 1955.

2/92315. Instruction. P.T. Schools and Colleges, Dublin Area. Letter from Lieutenant Colonel Harpur to the Director of Training, Army Headquarters, 1 August 1956.

2/92315. Instruction. P.T. Schools and Colleges, Dublin Area. Letter from the Secretary of the Department of Defence to the Secretary of the Department of Finance, 19 November 1956.

2/92315. Instruction. P.T. Schools and Colleges, Dublin Area. Department of Defence Secretary to Fr Piaras Ó h-Uiginn, 29 September 1960.

2/92315. Instruction. P.T. Schools and Colleges, Dublin Area. Department of Defence Secretary to D. S. Pringle, 3 October 1960.

Department of Education and Skills Archives, Cornamaddy, Westmeath

An Roinn Oideachais, Oideachais Náisiúnta. Notes for Teachers: Physical Training (Dublin, The Stationery Office, 1933).

Department of Education Circular, Revised Notes on Physical Training 1933. Cir. 4/33. (1933).

Department of Education Circular, Irish Qualifications Required in the Case of Part-Time Teachers of Choral Singing and of Physical Training. Cir. 6/52. (1952).

Department of Education. Report of the Council of Education as Presented to the Minister of Education. (1) The Function of the Primary School (2) The Curriculum to Be Pursued in the Primary School from the Infant Age Up to 12 Years of Age (Dublin: The Stationery Office, 1954).

Department of Education Report for 1958–59 (Dublin: The Stationery Office, 1960).

Department of Education Report for 1962–63 (Dublin: The Stationery Office, 1964).

Department of Education Circular. Summer Course in Physical Education, Cir. 12/66. (1966).

Department of Education Archives. Department of Education Circular, Summer Courses on Physical Education. Cir. 19/68. (1968).

Department of Education Circular. Revised Syllabus in Physical Education, Cir. 29/85. (1985).

Department of Education Circular. Accidents during Physical Education classes, Cir. 55/88. 17 August 1988.

Department of Education Circular. Scheme of Grants towards the Provision of Physical Education Equipment, Cir. 87/90. (1990).

Investment in Education. Report of the Survey Team Appointed by the Minister for Education in October, 1962 (Dublin: The Stationery Office, 1965).

Investment in Education. Annexes and Appendices to the Report of the Survey Team Appointed by the Minister for Education in October, 1962 (Dublin: The Stationery Office, 1965).

Primary School Curriculum: Teacher's Handbook Part 1 (Dublin: Government of Ireland, 1971).

Primary School Curriculum: Teacher's Handbook Part 2 (Dublin: Government of Ireland, 1971).

Report of the Department of Education 1929–30 (Dublin: The Stationery Office, 1930).

Report of the Department of Education for 1931–32 (Dublin: The Stationery Office, 1933).

Report of the Department of Education for 1932–33 (Dublin: The Stationery Office, 1934).

Report of the Department of Education 1933–34 (Dublin: The Stationery Office, 1935).

Report of the Department of Education 1934–35 (Dublin: The Stationery Office, 1936).

Report of the Department of Education 1940–41 (Dublin: The Stationery Office, 1942).

Report of the Department of Education 1943–44 (Dublin: The Stationery Office, 1945).

Report of the Department of Education 1944–45 (Dublin: The Stationery Office, 1946).

Department of Education (Northern Ireland), Belfast

Department of Education for Northern Ireland. Primary Education Teachers' Guide (Belfast: H.M. Stationery Office, 1974).

Department of Education (Northern Ireland). Report on Physical Education in Secondary Schools. Inspected 1998–99 (Belfast: The Education and Training Inspectorate, 2000).

Department of Education (Northern Ireland) Improving Physical Education in Post-Primary Schools (Belfast: The Education and Training Inspectorate, 2001).

Government of Northern Ireland. Education in Northern Ireland in 1973. Being the Report of the Ministry of Education for Northern Ireland for the Year Ended 31 December 1973 (Belfast: H.M. Stationery Office, 1974).

Physical Education and Games in Post-Primary Schools: Findings from a Survey of Northern Ireland Schools Immediately before the Introduction of the New Curriculum (Belfast: Northern Ireland Council for Educational Research, 1991).

Primary Education in Northern Ireland: Report of Advisory Council for Education (Belfast: Her Majesty's Stationery Office, 1968).

The Curriculum of Secondary Schools: Report of Working Party (Belfast: Her Majesty's Stationery Office, 1967).

The Northern Ireland Council for Educational Development Physical Education Guidelines for Primary Schools (Belfast: Northern Ireland Council for Educational Development, 1986).
Ulster Yearbook 1983 (Belfast: General Register Office, 1983).

Football Association of Ireland Archives, University College Dublin

P137/24. Junior Committee Minutes, 24 February 1938.
P137/29 Junior Emergency Committee Minutes, 2 September 1943.
P137/17. Coaching and Development Committee Meeting, 30 July 1976.

Gaelic Athletic Association Archives, Croke Park, Dublin

Gaelic Athletic Association Dublin Schools League Minute Book 1917–1920.
Gaelic Athletic Association/CC/01/03 (1925–1929). Central Council Meeting Minutes, 26 May 1928.
Gaelic Athletic Association/CC/01/03 (1925–1929). Central Council Meeting Minutes, 30 June 1928.
Gaelic Athletic Association/CC/01/03 (1925–1929). Central Council Meeting Minutes, 19 January 1929.
Gaelic Athletic Association/CC/01/04 (1929–1932). Secretary's Report for the Year Ended 31 December 1931.
Gaelic Athletic Association/CC/01/04 (1929–1932). Central Council Meeting Minutes, 24 September 1932.
Gaelic Athletic Association/CC/01/06 (1934–1938). Secretary's Report for Year Ended 31 December 1936.
Gaelic Athletic Association/CC/01/06 (1934–1938). Annual Congress Report for Leinster, 17 April 1938.

Irish National Teachers' Organisation

A Plan for Education. Issued by the Irish National Teachers' Organisation (Dublin: INTO, 1947).
INTO Primary School Curriculum Survey (Dublin: INTO, 1974).

Irish Newspaper Archives

Irish Newspaper Archives' Available at <https://www.irishnewsarchive.com/>
An Claidheamh Soluis
Anglo-Celt
Ballina Herald
Belfast Newsletter
Belfast Telegraph
Connacht Sentinel
Connacht Tribune
Connaught Telegraph
Derry Journal
Donegal Democrat
Donegal News
Drogheda Argus and Leinster Journal
Drogheda Independent
Evening Herald
Fermanagh Herald
Freeman's Journal
Irish Examiner
Irish Farmers' Journal
Irish Independent
Irish Press
Irish Times
Kerry Champion
Kerry Weekly Reporter
Kerryman
Kilkenny People
Leinster Leader
Limerick Leader
Meath Chronicle
Munster Express
Nationalist and Leinster Times
Sligo Champion
Southern Star
Strabane Chronicle
Sunday Independent
Tuam Herald
Ulster Herald

Waterford News and Star
Western People
Westmeath Examiner
Westmeath Independent
Wicklow People

Joint Managerial Body, Secretariat of Secondary Schools Archives, Dublin

Joint Managerial Body files. Letter from Brother Declan Duffy to John P. Wilson, 5 September 1979.

Letter from Secretary to the Minister of Education, P. Heffernan, to Brother Declan Duffy, 26 September 1979.

Joint Managerial Body files. Report of Meeting in the Department of Education re P. E. Halls, 5 October 1979.

Joint Managerial Body files. Letter from NCCA Chief Executive Albert Ó Ceallaigh to Brother Declan Duffy, 27 February 1989.

National Archives of Ireland, Bishop Street, Dublin

ED/12/12848. National Programme Conference Decisions 1925–1926. Meeting of 17 November 1925.

ED/12/12848. National Programme Conference, Minutes of Meetings on the 17, 18, 19, 20, 24, 25 and 26 November 1925.

ED/12/ 22858. Gymnastics and Physical Training in Primary Schools and Training Colleges. Letter from Seosamh O'Neill to H. Errickson, Swedish Consul, September 1929.

ED/12/22858. Gymnastics and Physical Training in Primary Schools and Training Colleges. Syllabus in Physical Training for Students in the Colleges for the Training of National School Teachers. (1929).

ED/12/31032. Revised Notes for Teachers' Drill. Physical Training in National Schools, Preparatory Colleges and in Training Colleges. Professors of Drill. (1932).

ED/12/31032. 'Revised Notes for Teachers' Drill. Physical Training in National Schools, Preparatory Colleges and in Training Colleges. Memo of 9.9.32 of Chief Inspector.'

ED/12/31032. Revised Notes for Teachers' Drill. Physical Training in National Schools. Instruction in Drill in the Preparatory Colleges. 15 June 1932.

TAOIS/S11053. Physical Education. The Report of the Committee. 1938.

TAOIS/S11053. Report of the Committee appointed by the Government to Examine the Question of the Promotion of the Revival of Athletics. 1939.

TAOIS/S11053. Parliamentary Secretary Seán Moylan to the Minister for Industry and Commerce, Seán Lemass, Memorandum 26 January 1939.

TAOIS/S11053. Minute from P. Ó Murchadha, Private Secretary, Department of Industry and Commerce, to the Parliamentary Secretary for the Minister of Industry and Commerce, Seán Moylan, 15 March 1940.

TAOIS/S11053. Letter from Secretary to the Minister for Lands to the Secretary to the Department of the Taoiseach, 5 April 1940.

TAOIS/S11053. Secretary for the Minister of Education to the Secretary of the Taoiseach, 9 January 1943.

TAOIS/S11053. Proposals for Promoting the Revival of Athletics and General Physical Training. Report of the Inter-departmental Committee. 18 June 1943.

TAOIS/S11053. Letter from Private Secretary of the Minister for Education to the Private Secretary of the Taoiseach, 6 December 1943.

TAOIS/S11053. Cabinet Committee on Economic Planning. Extract from Minutes of Meeting Held on 20 December, 1943. Revival of Athletics.

TAOIS/S11053. Private Secretary for the Minister for Defence to the Private Secretary of the Taoiseach, 15 January 1944.

TAOIS/S11053. Revival of Athletics and Physical Training. Department of the Taoiseach, 17 January 1944.

TAOIS/S11053. Cabinet Committee on Economic Planning. Revival of Athletics. Minutes from Meeting Held on 21 February 1944. 29 February 1944.

National Library of Ireland, Kildare Street, Dublin

Board of Education, *The Syllabus of Physical Exercises for Schools. 1909* [Third Edition] (London: His Majesty's Stationery Office, 1911).

Circular to Inspectors. Revised Programme-New System of Inspection (Dublin: Office of National Education), 28 November 1901.

Commission on Manual and Practical Instruction in Primary Schools under the Board of National Education in Ireland. Final Report of Commissioners (Dublin: Alexander Thom, 1898).

Football Sports Weekly (1925–8).

ICHPER Questionnaire Report. Part II. 1967–1968 Revision. Teacher Training for Physical Education (Washington, DC: ICHPER, 1968).

Intermediate Education Board for Ireland. Reports of Inspectors 1909–10. From No. 1 to No. 81. Volume I (Dublin: Intermediate Education Board for Ireland, 1910).

Intermediate Education Board for Ireland. Reports of Inspectors 1909–10. From No. 82 to No. 168. Volume II (Dublin: Intermediate Education Board for Ireland, 1910).

Intermediate Education Board for Ireland. Reports of Inspectors 1909–10. From No. 201 to 332. Volume III (Dublin: Intermediate Education Board for Ireland, 1910).

Intermediate Education Board for Ireland. Reports of Inspectors 1909–10. From No. 401 to 436 Volume IV (Dublin: Intermediate Education Board for Ireland, 1910).

The Irish Teachers' Journal (1900–4).

The Irish School Weekly (1904–12).

Physical Education Association of Ireland Annual Report 1993/1994 (Limerick: Physical Education Association of Ireland, 1994).

Physical Education Association of Ireland Annual Report 1996/1997 (Limerick: Physical Education Association of Ireland, 1997).

Report of Mr F.H. Dale, His Majesty's Inspector of Schools, Board of Education, on Primary Education in Ireland (Dublin: Alexander Thom, 1904).

Report of Mr F.H. Dale and Mr T.A. Stephens on Intermediate Education (Ireland) (Dublin: Alexander Thom, 1905).

Starkie, W. J. M., *The History of Irish Primary and Secondary Education during the Last Decade: An Inaugural Address Delivered on Monday 3rd July 1911 on the Occasion of the Inauguration of University Extension Lectures in the Queen's University, Belfast* (Belfast: Queen's University, 1911).

The Sixty-Eighth Report of the Commissioners of National Education in Ireland. Year 1901 (Dublin: Alexander Thom, 1902).

The Seventieth Report of the Commissioners of National Education in Ireland. Year 1903 (Dublin: Alexander Thom, 1905).

The Seventy-First Report of the Commissioners of National Education in Ireland. Year 1904 (Dublin: Alexander Thom, 1905).

The Seventy-Second Report of the Commissioners of National Education in Ireland. School Year 1905–6 (Dublin: Alexander Thom, 1906).

The Seventy-Seventh Report of the Commissioners of National Education in Ireland. Year 1910–11 (Dublin: Alexander Thom, 1911).

The Seventy-Eighth Report of the Commissioners of National Education in Ireland. Year 1911–12 (Dublin: Alexander Thom, 1912).

The Eighty-Second Report of the Commissioners of National Education in Ireland. School Year 1915–16 (Dublin: His Majesty's Stationery Office, 1917).

The Eighty-Third Report of the Commissioners of National Education in Ireland. School Year 1916–17 (Dublin: His Majesty's Stationery Office, 1918).

The Eighty-Fourth Report of the Commissioners of National Education in Ireland. School Year 1917–18 (Dublin: His Majesty's Stationery Office, 1919).

The Eighty-Fifth Report of the Commissioners of National Education in Ireland. School Year 1918–19 (Dublin: His Majesty's Stationery Office, 1920).

Thom's Official Directory of the United Kingdom of Great Britain and Ireland: For the Year 1911 (Dublin: Alexander Thom and Co., 1911).

Vice-Regal Committee of Inquiry into Primary Education (Ireland) 1913. Appendix to the Second Report of the Committee. Minutes of Evidence 15th April-22nd May 1913. With Appendices (London: Alexander Thom, 1913).

Vice-Regal Committee of Inquiry into Primary Education (Ireland) 1913. Appendix to the Third Report of the Committee. Minutes of Evidence 26th June–17th September 1913. with Appendices (London: Alexander Thom, 1913).

Public Record Office of Northern Ireland, Titanic Boulevard, Belfast

Belfast College of Technology Files

BCT/7/5/3. Government of Northern Ireland Reports of the Ministry of Education. Report of the Ministry of Education for the Year 1925–6 (Belfast: H.M. Stationary Office, 1926).

BCT/7/5/3. Government of Northern Ireland Reports of the Ministry of Education. Report of the Ministry of Education for the Year 1926–7 (Belfast: H.M. Stationary Office, 1927).

BCT/7/5/3. Government of Northern Ireland Reports of the Ministry of Education. Report of the Ministry of Education for the Year 1927–8 (Belfast: H.M. Stationary Office, 1928).

BCT/7/5/3. Government of Northern Ireland Reports of the Ministry of Education. Report of the Ministry of Education for the Year 1928–9 (Belfast: H.M. Stationary Office, 1929).

BCT/7/5/3. Government of Northern Ireland Reports of the Ministry of Education. Report of the Ministry of Education for the Year 1929–30 (Belfast: H.M. Stationary Office, 1930).

BCT/7/5/3. Government of Northern Ireland Reports of the Ministry of Education. Report of the Ministry of Education for the Year 1935–6 (Belfast: H.M. Stationary Office, 1936).

BCT/7/5/3. Government of Northern Ireland Reports of the Ministry of Education. Report of the Ministry of Education for the Year 1936–7 (Belfast: H.M. Stationary Office, 1937).

BCT/7/5/3. Government of Northern Ireland Reports of the Ministry of Education. Report of the Ministry of Education for the Year 1937–8 (Belfast: H.M. Stationary Office, 1938).

BCT/7/5/5. Government of Northern Ireland Reports of the Ministry of Education. Report of the Ministry of Education for the Year 1948–9 (Belfast: H.M. Stationary Office, 1949).

Cabinet Secretariat Records

CAB/9/D/57/1. Physical Education 1930–1935. Letter from CH Blackmore to the Under Secretary of State, 27 May 1930.

CAB/9/D/57/1. Physical Education 1930–1935. Letter from W. A. Houston to the Secretary to the Cabinet, 7 June 1935.

CAB/9/D/72. Physical Recreation and Training 1937–43. Physical Training and Recreation Meeting, 9 April 1937.

Irish Football Association Archives

IFA Council Minutes, D4196/2/4, 24 November 1925.

Ministry of Education

ED/13/1/1490. Physical Training. Recognition of Diplomas, Vocational Courses 1928–1932. Letter from Irene M. Marsh to the Secretary of the Ministry of Education, 12 October 1925.

ED/13/1/1490. Physical Training. Recognition of Diplomas, Vocational Courses 1928–1932. Letter from W. A. Houston to Mr Smyth, 12 November 1925.

ED/13/1/1490. Physical Training. Recognition of Diplomas, Vocational Courses. Letter from the Secretary of the Ministry of Education to Miss P. McAlinney, 14 March 1936.

ED/13/1/2081. Physical Training Organisers Appointment 1943–1946. Letters from J. Stuart Hawnt to the Secretary of the Ministry of Education, 21 July 1943, 12, 27 and 29 February and 21 December 1944 and 27 February 1945.

ED/13/1/2081. Physical Training Organisers Appointment 1943–1946. Belfast Education Authority. Appointment of Organiser of Physical Training (Woman). Conditions of Appointment. Undated.

ED/13/1/2162. 1946–1947. Larkfield Training College. Bangor Summer School of PE. Second Summer School of Physical Education Booklet.

ED/13/1/2166. Larkfield Training College. Short Courses in Physical Education for Men and Women Students. Letter from Assistant Secretary to the Minister of Education to R. Groves, 22 March 1948.

ED/13/1/2166. Letter from Assistant Secretary to the Minister for Education to A. E. Lewis, 22 March 1948.

ED/13/1/2166. Letter from Assistant Secretary to the Minister of Education to R. Groves, 6 August 1948.

ED/13/1/2166. Letter from Assistant Secretary to the Minister of Education to the Secretary of the Church of Ireland Young Men's Society, 21 October 1949.

ED/13/1/2166. Larkfield Training College. Short Courses in Physical Education for Men and Women Students. L. B. Dickinson to Major Pomeroy, 23 March 1948.

ED/13/1/2292. Physical Education and Physical Training 1945–1948. Secretary for Ministry of Education of Northern Ireland to Secretary for Minister for Finance, 28 March 1947.

ED/13/1/2293. Proposed Establishment of Physical Education College 1947–1954. Memo on Proposed Physical Education College, 12 December 1949.

ED/13/1/2456. Teachers' Courses: One Term (Ten Week) Course for Physical Education (25 September to 2 December 1950). Ministry of Education for Northern Ireland. Qualification of Teachers for Appointment to Intermediate Schools. One Term Courses. Circular G. 1950/16.

ED/14C/385. 1922–27 St Mary's Girls National School. Newcastle. Inspection of PT. Extracts from general report dated 15th September 1926, by Mr John D. MacManus, Inspector to St Mary's Girls' Public Elementary School, County Down. Roll Number 15,306. Postal Address Newcastle. Efficiency of the instruction, and ratings assigned to teachers.

ED/14C/385. 1922–27 St Mary's Girls National School. Newcastle. Inspection of PT. Letter from William J. Nolan to the Secretary of the Minister of Education, 22 January 1927.

ED/14C/385. 1922–27 St Mary's Girls National School. Newcastle. Inspection of PT. Letter from the Assistant Secretary to the Minister of Education to W. J. Nolan, 3 February 1927.

ED/ Scheme of Physical Recreation and Training, 26 November 1937.

ED/ Rhona E. Jackson. Confidential Report on Ling Physical Training College, 24 Upper Mount Street, Dublin. 1942.

ED/13/1/2680. Recognition of Certain Courses for Teaching Purposes. Men with Service in HM Forces as Specialists in Physical Training. Letter from L. B. Dickinson to Major S. J. Parker, 12 February 1945.

ED/13/1/2337. Grammar Schools: Qualifications Required for Recognition of Teachers-Special Examination for Teachers' Qualifications in Physical

Education, 1951. Letter from Harry McClure to Rhona E. Jackson, 23 March 1946.

ED/13/1/2292. Physical Education and Physical Training 1945–1948. Secretary for Ministry of Education of Northern Ireland to Secretary for Minister for Finance, 28 March 1947.

ED/13/1/2292. Physical Education and Physical Training 1945–1948. Ministry of Education for Northern Ireland. Physical Education Scholarships, 1947. Secretary to Ministry of Education of Northern Ireland, Circular to Secondary School Teachers, 15 April 1947.

ED/13/1/2166. Larkfield Training College. Short Courses in Physical Education for Men and Women Students. Secretary to the Minister of Education to A. J. Kissock, 30 January 1948.

ED/13/1/2293. Proposed Establishment of Physical Education College 1947–1954. Memo on Proposed Physical Education College, 12 December 1949.

ED/13/1/2293. Proposed Establishment of Physical Education College 1947–1954. Letter from Minister of Education to Minister of Finance, 27 February 1950.

ED/13/1/2337. Letter from R. S. Brownell, Secretary for the Minister of Education, to Mr. Glen. Qualifications of Teachers. Physical Education, 24 May 1950.

ED/13/1/2337. Grammar Schools: Qualifications Required for Recognition of Teachers-Special Examination for Teachers' Qualifications in Physical Education, 1951. Special Examination for Teacher's Qualification in Physical Education, 1951, List of Candidates.

ED 25/1/1 9125. Ministry of Education Northern Ireland. Report of the Ministry of Education 1922–23 (Belfast: H.M. Stationary Office, 1923).

ED/25/31. Government of Northern Ireland Reports of the Ministry of Education. Report of the Ministry of Education for the Year 1952–3 (Belfast: H.M. Stationary Office, 1953).

ED/25/32. Government of Northern Ireland Reports of the Ministry of Education. *Report of the Ministry of Education for the Year 1953–4* (Belfast: H.M. Stationary Office, 1954).

ED/25/36. Government of Northern Ireland Reports of the Ministry of Education. Report of the Ministry of Education for the Year 1957–8 (Belfast: H.M. Stationary Office, 1958).

ED/25/37. Government of Northern Ireland Reports of the Ministry of Education. *Report of the Ministry of Education for the Year 1958–59* (Belfast: H.M. Stationary Office, 1959).

ED/25/42. Government of Northern Ireland Reports of the Ministry of Education. *Education in Northern Ireland in 1964* (Belfast: H.M. Stationary Office, 1965).

ED/13/1/1247. Training of Semi-Specialists: Fourth Year Course in Physical Education (Women) at Ulster College of Physical Education 1956–57 and

Proposed 1957–58. R. S. Brownell to Chief Education Officers and Principals of All Recognised Schools. Training Scholarships for a One-Year Course in Physical Education for Women Teachers, 1956–57. Ulster College of Physical Education. 19 January 1956.

ED/13/1/2716A. Formal Opening of the Ulster College of Physical Education. Opening of the College and Presentation of Diplomas by Her Excellency the Lady Wakehurst. Thursday, 26 June 1956, at 2.30 p.m.

ED/25/38. Government of Northern Ireland Reports of the Ministry of Education. *Report of the Ministry of Education for the Year 1959–60* (Belfast: H.M. Stationary Office, 1960).

Ministry of Finance

FIN/18/7/254. Physical Training and Recreation. Physical Training and Recreation Facilities in Northern Ireland. July 1937.

University of Ulster Papers

D4327/4/2. Ulster College. *The Northern Ireland Polytechnic. Annual Report to 31 August 1972* (Belfast: Ulster College, 1972).

D4327/4/2. Ulster College. *The Northern Ireland Polytechnic. Annual Report to 31 August 1973* (Belfast: Ulster College, 1973).

D4327/4/3. Ulster College. *The Northern Ireland Polytechnic. Annual Report to 31 August 1974* (Belfast: Ulster College, 1974).

D4327/4/4. Ulster College. *The Northern Ireland Polytechnic. Annual Report 1974–1975* (Belfast: Ulster College, 1975).

D4327/4/5. Ulster College. *The Northern Ireland Polytechnic. Annual Report 1975–1976* (Belfast: Ulster College, 1976).

D4327/4/6. Ulster College. *The Northern Ireland Polytechnic. Annual Report 1976–1977* (Belfast: Ulster College, 1977).

D4327/4/8. *Ulster Polytechnic. Annual Report 1978–1979* (Belfast: Ulster Polytechnic, 1979).

D4327/4/9. *Ulster Polytechnic. Annual Report 1979/80* (Belfast: Ulster Polytechnic, 1980).

D4327/4/11. *Ulster Polytechnic. Annual Report 1981–82* (Belfast: Ulster Polytechnic, 1982).

D4327/4/12. *Ulster Polytechnic. Annual Report 1982–83* (Belfast: Ulster Polytechnic, 1983).

D4327/4/13. *Ulster Polytechnic. Annual Report 1983–1984* (Belfast: Ulster Polytechnic, 1984).

Local Authorities' Files

LAI/3AL/6/3. *Government of Northern Ireland. Ministry of Education. Youth Committee. Report for the Period June 1952 to June 1955* (Belfast: Her Majesty's Stationery Office, 1955).
LAI/3AL/6/3. *Government of Northern Ireland. Ministry of Education. Youth Committee. Report for the Period October 1955 to October 1958* (Belfast: Her Majesty's Stationery Office, 1958).
LAI/3AL/6/3. *Government of Northern Ireland. Ministry of Education. Youth and Sports Council. Report for the Period 1965 to 1968.* (Belfast: Her Majesty's Stationery Office, 1968)

HM Stationary Office, Belfast Files

So/1B/883. *Government of Northern Ireland Reports of the Ministry of Education. Report of the Ministry of Education for the Year 1947–48* (Belfast: H.M. Stationary Office, 1949).
SO/1A/542. *Government of Northern Ireland Reports of the Ministry of Education. Education in Northern Ireland in 1969* (Belfast: H.M. Stationary Office, 1970).
SO/1A/573. *Government of Northern Ireland Reports of the Ministry of Education. Education in Northern Ireland in 1971* (Belfast: H.M. Stationary Office, 1972).

Private Papers of Joan Burnett-Knight

Application for Physical Education Advisor (Woman) 1947.
Recommendation for Miss J. L. Burnett-Knight by Sergeant H. Priestley, Director of the British Families Education Service, Dusseldorf, 11 February 1956.

Teacher Interviews

Republic of Ireland primary school teachers

Interview with primary school teacher number one, 14 June 2019.
Interview with primary school teacher number two, 15 June 2019.
Interview with primary school teacher number three, 22 June 2019.

Interview with primary school teacher number four, 26 June 2019.
Interview with primary school teacher number five, 28 June 2019.
Interview with primary school teacher number six, 3 July 2020.
Interview with primary school teacher number seven, 3 July 2019.
Interview with primary school teacher number eight, 23 July 2019.
Interview with primary school teacher number nine, 24 July 2019.
Interview with primary school teacher number ten, 25 July 2019.
Interview with primary school teacher number eleven, 25 July 2019.
Interview with primary school teacher number twelve, 26 July 2019.
Interview with primary school teacher number thirteen, 26 July 2019.
Interview with primary school teacher number fourteen, 26 July 2019.
Interview with primary school teacher number fifteen, 29 July 2019.

Republic of Ireland secondary school PE teachers

Interview with secondary school PE teacher number one, 26 July 2019.
Interview with secondary school PE teacher number two, 24 August 2019.
Interview with secondary school PE teacher number three, 26 August 2019.
Interview with secondary school PE teacher number four, 29 August 2019.
Interview with secondary school PE teacher number five, 9 September 2019.
Interview with secondary school PE teacher number six, 17 September 2019.
Interview with secondary school PE teacher number seven, 3 October 2019.
Interview with secondary school PE teacher number eight, 9 October 2019.
Interview with secondary school PE teacher number nine, 22 October 2019.
Interview with secondary school PE teacher number ten, 23 October 2019.

Northern Ireland second level school PE teachers

Interview with Northern Ireland second level PE teacher number one, 12 September. 2019.
Interview with Northern Ireland second level PE teacher number two, 18 September 2019.
Interview with Northern Ireland second level PE teacher number three, 26 September 2019.
Interview with Northern Ireland second level PE teacher number three, 26 September 2019.
Interview with Northern Ireland second level PE teacher number four, 26 September 2019.

Interview with Northern Ireland second level PE teacher number five, 4 October 2019.

Interview with Northern Ireland second level PE teacher number six, 8 October 2019.

Interview with Northern Ireland second level PE teacher number seven, 8 October 2019.

Interview with Northern Ireland second level PE teacher number eight, 31 October 2019.

Interview with Northern Ireland second level PE teacher number nine, 13 November 2020.

Interview with Northern Ireland second level PE teacher number ten, 16 November 2019.

Secondary Sources

Books, chapters and articles

Akenson, Donald Harman, *Education and Enmity: The Control of Schooling in Northern Ireland 1920–1950* (New York: David & Charles (Holdings) Limited, Newton Abbot/Barnes& Noble Books, 1973).

Akenson, Donald Harman, *A Mirror to Kathleen's Face: Education in Independent Ireland 1922–1960* (Montreal and London: McGill-Queen's University Press, 1975).

Bailey, Steve and Vamplew, Wray, *100 Years of Physical Education 1899–1999* (Warwick: Warwick Printing, 1999).

Bardon, Jonathan, *A History of Ulster* [New Updated Version] (Belfast: The Blackstaff Press, 2005).

Bartlett, Thomas, *Ireland: A History* (Cambridge: Cambridge University Press, 2010).

Bonde, Hans, *Gymnastics and Politics. Nils Bukh and Male Aesthetics* (Gylling: Narayana Press, 2006).

Bowers, Matthew T. and Hunt, Thomas M., 'The President's Council on Physical Fitness and the Systematisation of Children's Play in America' in *International Journal of the History of Sport*, vol. 28, no. 11 (2011), 1496–1511.

Bracken, Pat, *The Growth and Development of Sport in County Tipperary 1840–1880* (Cork: Cork University Press, 2018).

Browne, Terence, *Ireland: A Social and Cultural History 1922–2002* (London: Harper Perennial, 2004).

Carter, Neil, *Medicine, Sport and the Body: A Historical Perspective* [Paperback Edition] (London and New York: Bloomsbury Academic, 2014).

Chivers, Harry, 'St Joseph's Training College' in Seán McGettigan (ed.), *Ulster Games Annual 1966* (Belfast: Howard Publications, 1966), 33–4.

Clenet, Julien, 'Sport in Nineteenth Century Dublin Schools.' Paper given at Sport and Education in Ireland and Britain Conference, Public Record Office of Northern Ireland, Belfast, 27 September 2019.

Comerford, R. V., *Ireland: Inventing the Nation* (London: Hodder Arnold, 2003).

'College Reports' in S. O'Hagan (ed.), *Ulster College of Physical Education Jordanstown* (Belfast: Ulster College of Physical Education, 1957), 34–8.

Coolahan, John, *Irish Education: History and Structure* (Dublin: Institute of Public Administration, 1981).

Coolahan, John, *Towards the Era of Lifelong Learning: A History of Irish Education 1800–2016* (Dublin: Institute of Public Administration, 2017).

Cronin, Mike, 'Trinity Mysteries': Responding to a Chaotic Reading of Irish History' in *International Journal of the History of Sport*, vol. 28, no. 18 (2011), 2753–60.

Cronin, Mike, *Sport: A Very Short Introduction* (Oxford: Oxford University Press, 2014).

Cronin, Mike and Higgins, Roisín, *Places We Play: Ireland's Sporting Heritage* (Cork: Collins Press, 2011).

Curran, Conor, 'The Social Background of Ireland's Pre-World War I Association Football Clubs, Players and Administrators: The Case of South and West Ulster' in *International Journal of the History of Sport*, vol. 33, no. 16 (2016), 1982–2005.

Curran, Conor, *Sport in Donegal: A History* (Dublin: The History Press Ireland, 2010).

Curran, Conor, *The Development of Sport in Donegal 1880–1935* (Cork: Cork University Press, 2015).

Curran, Conor, *Irish Soccer Migrants: A Social and Cultural History* (Cork: Cork University Press, 2017).

Curran, Conor, 'The Implementation of Physical Education in Primary Schools in the Irish Free State, 1922–1932.' Sport and Education in Ireland: History, Policy and Contemporary Issues Conference, Trinity College Dublin, 2018.

Curran, Conor, ' "The Present Deplorably Low Standard-Perhaps the Lowest in Western Europe-Is Due, in the Main, to the Shortage of Trained Teachers": The Supply of Physical Education Teachers in Northern Ireland, 1922–1954.' Economic and Social History Society of Ireland Annual Conference, Queen's University, Belfast, 2018.

Curran, Conor, 'The Development of Physical Education in Northern Ireland, 1922–1954.' PRONI Lunchtime Guest Lecture, 2019.

Curran, Conor, 'Physical Education in Ireland, 1922–1973.' Trinity College Dublin Contemporary Irish History Seminar, 2019.

Curran, Conor, 'The Sokol System of Physical Training in Irish Schools in the 1930s.' ESAI Conference 2019, Radisson Hotel Sligo.

Curran, Conor, '"It Has Almost Been an Underground Movement". The Development of Grassroots Football in Regional Ireland: The Case of County Donegal, 1971–1996" in Jürgen Mittag, Kristian Naglo and Dilwyn Porter (eds), Special Issue of *Moving the Social: Journal of Social History and the History of Social Movements. Small Worlds: Football at the Grassroots in Europe*, vol. 61 (2019), 33–60.

Curran, Conor, 'Physical Education in Ireland and Europe on the Eve of the Second World War.' ISHPES Congress 2019, University of Madrid.

Curran, Conor, 'Physical Drill in Irish Free State Schools and the National Programme Conference, 1925–6.' BSSH Conference, 2019, Hope University Liverpool.

Curran, Conor, 'The Career of Joan Burnett Knight, Female PE organiser for Northern Ireland, 1944–51.' Sport and Education in Ireland and Britain Conference, PRONI, 2019.

Curran, Conor, 'The Development of Physical Education in Northern Ireland, 1922–1953 and the Role of Joan Burnett-Knight' in Conor Curran and Dilwyn Porter (eds), Sport and Education in Ireland: Special edition of *Sport in Society*, vol. 23, no. 8 (2020), 1299–319.

Curran, Conor, 'The Irish Government and Physical Education in Primary Schools, 1922–37 in *Irish Historical Studies*, vol. 45, no. 167 (May 2021), 43–60.

Delaney, Enda, *Irish Emigration Since 1921* (Dundalk: Dundalgan Press, 2002).

Dixon, J. G., McIntosh, P. C., Munrow, A. D., and Willets, R. F., (eds), *Landmarks in the History of Physical Education* (London: Routledge, 1957).

Farragher, Seán P., *Blackrock College 1860–1995* (Dublin: Paraclete Press, 1995).

Farren, Seán, *The Politics of Irish Education 1920–65* (Belfast: The Institute of Irish Studies, 1995).

Farren, Seán, 'Denominationally Integrated Education in Northern Ireland-Panacea or Civil Right' in *Paedagogica Historica: International Journal of the History of Education*, vol. 35, sup 1 (1999), 353–68.

Farren, Seán, Clarke, Linda and O'Doherty, Theresa, *Teacher Preparation in Northern Ireland: History, Policy and Future Directions* (Bingley: Emerald, 2019).

Ferriter, Diarmaid, *The Transformation of Ireland 1900–2000* (London: Profile Books, 2004).

Ferriter, Diarmaid, *Ambiguous Republic: Ireland in the 1970s* [Paperback edition] (London: Profile Books, 2013).

Finn, Gerry T., 'Trinity Mysteries: University, Elite Schooling and Sport in Ireland' in *International Journal of the History of Sport*, vol. 27, no. 13 (2010), 2255–87.

Fitzpatrick, David, 'Militarism in Ireland, 1900–1922' in Bartlett, Thomas and Jeffery, Keith (eds), *A Military History of Ireland* (Cambridge: Cambridge University Press, 1996), 379–406.

Fleming, David A., *The University of Limerick: A History* (Dublin: Four Courts Press, 2012).

Fleming, N. C., 'Education since the Late Eighteenth Century' in Liam Kennedy and Philip Ollerenshaw (eds), *Ulster since 1600: Politics, Economy and Society* (Oxford: Oxford University Press, 2013), 211–27.

Fletcher, Sheila, *Women First: The Female Tradition in English Physical Education 1880–1980* (London; Dover, NY: Athlone Press, 1984).

Garnham, Neal, *Association Football and Society in Pre-partition Ireland* (Belfast: Ulster Historical Foundation, 2004).

Gems, Gerald, Borish, Linda J. and Pfister, Gertrud, *Sport in American History: From Colonization to Globalization* (Champaign: Human Kinetics, 2008).

Goldblatt, David, *The Games: A Global History of the Olympics* [Revised edition] (London: Pan Macmillan, 2018).

Guttmann, Allen, *Sports: The First Five Millennia* (Amherst and Boston: University of Massachusetts Press, 2000).

Hare, Geoff, *Football in France: A Cultural History* (Oxford/New York: Berg, 2003).

Harford, Judith and O'Donoghue, Tom, 'Exploring the Experience of Secondary-School Education in Ireland Prior to 1967' in James Kelly and Susan Hegarty (eds), *Schools and Schooling, 1650–2000: New Perspectives on the History of Education* (Dublin: Four Courts Press, 2017), 159–77.

Heffernan, Conor, 'Fitness and Fun that's Not Just for Mum: The Women's League of Health and Beauty in 1930s Ireland' in *Women's History Review*, vol. 28, no. 7 (2019), 1017–38.

Heffernan, Conor, 'The Irish Sandow School: Physical Culture Competitions in fin-de-siècle Ireland' in *Irish Studies Review*, Brian Griffin and John Strachan (eds) Special Edition: 'Sport in Ireland from the 1880s to the 1920s' vol. 27, no. 3 (2019), 402–21.

Heffernan, Conor and Curran, Conor, 'Much Ado about Nothing? The Problems of Irish Physical Education, 1820–1920' in *Sporting Traditions*, vol. 37, no. 1 (May 2020), 65–86.

Heffernan, Conor, 'Marching Forwards or Backwards? Physical Education and the Army in Early Twentieth Century Ireland' in Curran and Porter (eds), Sport and Education in Ireland: Special edition of *Sport in Society*, vol. 23, no. 8 (2020), 1280–98.

Heggie, Vanessa, *A History of British Sports Medicine* (Manchester: Manchester University Press, 2011).

Henry, Miles and Burn, Ian, *Portora. The School on the Hill: A Quatercentenary History* (Enniskillen: The Royal School Portora, 2008).

Hickey, Colm, 'The Evolution of Athleticism in Elite Irish Schools 1878–1914. Beyond the Finn/Cronin Debate' in *International Journal of the History of Sport*, vol. 30, no. 12 (2013), 1394–417.

Holt, Richard, *Sport and Society in Modern France* (London and Basingstoke: The MacMillan Press Ltd., 1981).

Holt, Richard, *Sport and the British: A Modern History* (Oxford: Oxford University Press, 1989).

Holt, Richard and Mason, Tony, *Sport in Britain 1945–2000* (Oxford: Blackwell Publishers, 2000).

Holt, Richard, 'Ireland and the Birth of Modern Sport' in Mike Cronin, William Murphy and Paul Rouse (eds), *The Gaelic Athletic Association 1884–2009* (Dublin: Irish Academic Press, 2009), 33–45.

Hunt, Tom, *Sport and Society in Victorian Ireland: The Case of Westmeath* (Cork: Cork University Press, 2007).

Hunt, Tom, 'The National Athletic Association of Ireland and Irish Athletics, 1922–1937: Steps on the Road to Athletic Isolation' in *Sport and Society*, vol. 19, no. 1 (2016), 130–46.

Hunt, Tom, *The Little Book of Irish Athletics* (Dublin: The History Press, 2017).

Jefferys, Kevin, 'The Thatcher Governments and the British Sports Council, 1979–1990' in *Sport in History*, vol. 36, no. 1 (2016), 73–97.

Kelly, James (ed.), *St Patrick's College Drumcondra: A History* (Dublin: Four Courts Press, 2006).

Kelly, Susan, 'Education of Tubercular Children in Northern Ireland, 1921 to 1955' in *Social History of Medicine*, vol. 24, no. 2 (2010), 407–25.

Kelly, James and Hegarty, Susan (eds), *Schools and Schooling, 1650–2000: New Perspectives on the History of Education* (Dublin: Four Courts Press, 2017).

Krüger, Michael and Hofmann, Annette R., 'The Development of Physical-Education Institutions in Europe: A Short Introduction' in *International Journal of the History of Sport*, vol. 32, no. 6 (2015), 737–9.

Lawton, Denis and Gordon, Peter, *A History of Western Educational Ideas* (London: Routledge, 2002).

MacConaill, Seán (ed.), *Idir Pheil agus Pobal: A History of the GAA in the Parish of Ardara* (Ardara: Black Lion Books, 2004).

Mangan, J. A., *Athleticism in the Victorian and Edwardian Public School* (Cambridge: Cambridge University Press, 1981).

Mangan, J. A., *Manliness and Morality: Middle-class Masculinity in Britain and America 1800–1940* (Manchester: Palgrave Macmillan, 1987).

McAnallen, Dónal, Mossey, Peter and Moore, Stephen, 'The "Temporary Diaspora" at Play: The Development of Gaelic Games in British Universities' in *Sport and Society*, vol. 10. no. 3 (2007), 402–24.

McAnallen, Dónal, *The Cups that Cheered: A History of the Sigerson, Fitzgibbon and Higher Education Gaelic games* (Cork: Collins Press, 2012).

McAnallen, Dónal, 'Partition, Sport and Education in Ireland, 1921–72.' Paper given at Paper given at Sport and Education in Ireland and Britain Conference, Public Record Office of Northern Ireland, Belfast, 27 September 2019.

McElligott, Richard, '"Boys Indifferent to the Manly Sports of Their Race" Nationalism and Children's Sport in Ireland, 1880–1920' in Brian Griffin and John Strachan (eds), Special edition of *Irish Studies Review*, 'Sport in Ireland from the 1880s to the 1920s', vol. 27, no. 3 (2019), 344–61.

McGrath, Michael, *The Catholic Church and Catholic Schools in Northern Ireland* (Dublin: Irish Academic Press, 2000).

McIntosh, P. C., *Physical Education in England since 1800* (London: G. Bell and Sons. Ltd, 1952).

McIntosh, P. C., 'Games and Gymnastics for Two Nations in One' in J. G. Dixon, P. C. McIntosh, A. D. Munrow and R. F. Willetts (eds), *Landmarks in the History of Physical Education* (London: Routledge, 1957) [2007 edition].

McManus, Antonia, *Irish Education: The Ministerial Legacy, 1919–99* (Dublin: The History Press Ireland, 2014).

Milne, Ida, *Stacking the Coffins: Influenza, War and Revolution in Ireland, 1918–19* (Manchester: Manchester University Press, 2018).

Moore, Cormac, *Birth of the Border: The Impact of Partition in Ireland* (Kildare: Merrion Press, 2019).

Murphy, Frances and McEvoy, Eileen, 'Listening to the Voices of Teachers: Primary Physical Education in Ireland' in Curran and Porter (eds), Sport and Education in Ireland: Special edition of *Sport in Society*, vol. 23, no. 8 (2020), 1320–36.

Murphy, J. J., 'Physical Culture Plans: A Plea for a National Principle' in *The Catholic Bulletin*, vol. XXIV, no. 7 (1934), 577–84.

Nic Congáil, Ríona, '"Looking on for Centuries from the Sideline": Gaelic Feminism and the Rise of Camogie' in *Éire-Ireland*, vol. 48, no. 1 & 2 (2013), 168–90.

O'Boyle, Denis, 'Examinations in Physical Education: An Irish Perspective' in *Irish Educational Studies*, vol. 6, no. 2 (1986), 176–91.

Ó Buachalla, Séamus, *Education Policy in Twentieth Century Ireland* (Dublin: Wolfhound Press, 1988).

O'Callaghan, John, *Plassey's Gaels: A History of the GAA at NIHE, NCPE, Thomond College and the University of Limerick, 1972–2012* (Cork: The Collins Press, 2013).

O'Callaghan, Liam, *Rugby in Munster: A Social and Cultural History* (Cork: Cork University Press, 2011).

O'Connor, Tom, 'From Schoolboy Teams to College Dreams: Player Progression on the League of Ireland Elite Underage Pathway – An Early Look at the First Structured Approach to Elite Adult Football in the League of Ireland' in Curran and Porter (eds), Sport and Education in Ireland, Special issue of *Sport in Society*, 1337–53.

O'Donoghue, Thomas A., 'The Attempt by the Department of Defence to Introduce the Sokol System of Physical Education into Irish Schools in the 1930s' in *Irish Educational Studies*, vol. 5, no. 2 (1985), 329–42.

O'Donoghue, Thomas A., 'Sport, Recreation and Physical Education: The Evolution of a National Policy of Regeneration in Éire, 1926–48' in *The International Journal of the History of Sport*, vol. 3, no. 2 (1986), 216–33.

O'Donoghue, Thomas A., 'The Dáil Commission on Secondary Education 1921–1922' in *Oideas*, 34 (Autumn, 1989), 61–74.

O'Donoghue, Thomas A., Judith Harford, Judith and O'Doherty, Theresa, *Teacher Preparation in Ireland: History, Policy and Future Directions* (Bingley: Emerald Publishing, 2017).

O'Keeffe, Declan, 'All the Other Boots and Legs Ran After': The Long Life and Slow Death of '*Gravel*' Football. Paper given at Sport and Education in Ireland and Britain Conference, Public Record Office of Northern Ireland, Belfast, 27 September 2019.

O'Neill, Ciaran, 'Literacy and Education' in Eugenio Biagini and Mary E. Daly (eds), *The Cambridge Social History of Modern Ireland* (Cambridge: Cambridge University Press, 2017), 244–60.

Pim, O. M. 'Third International Congress in Physical Education and Sports for Girls and Women' in S. O'Hagan (ed.), *Ulster College of Physical Education Jordanstown* (Belfast: Ulster College of Physical Education, 1957), 6–7.

Raftery, Deirdre and Delaney, Catriona, '"Un-Irish and un-Catholic": Sports, Physical Education and Girls' Schooling' in *Irish Studies Review*, vol. 27 (2019), 325–43.

Rouse, Paul, *Sport and Ireland: A History* (Oxford: Oxford University Press, 2015).

Sleap, Mike, 'A Survey of Physical Education in Irish Post-Primary Schools' in *The Irish Journal of Education*, vol. xii, no. 2 (1978), 107–18.

Smith, W. D., *Stretching Their Bodies: A History of Physical Education* (London: David and Charles, 1974).

Sugden, John and Bairner, Alan, *Sport, Sectarianism and Society in a Divided Ireland* (London: Leicester University Press, 1993).

Tarakçıoğlu, Sait, 'A Failed Project in Turkey's Sports History: The Law on Physical Education of 1938' in *International Journal of the History of Sport*, vol. 31, no. 14 (2014), 1807–19.

Tozer, Malcolm, *Edward Thring's Theory, Practice and Legacy: Physical Education in Britain since 1800* (Cambridge: Cambridge Scholars Publishing, 2019).

Trew, Karen, Kremer, John, Gallagher, Anthony M., Scully, Deirdre and Ogle, Shaun, 'Young People's Participation in Sport in Northern Ireland' in *International Review for the Sociology of Sport*, vol. 32, no. 4 (1997), 419–31.

Vertinsky, Patricia, 'Re-examining *Women First*: Rewriting the History of the "End of an Era"' in David Kirk and Patricia Vertinsky (eds), *The Female Tradition in Physical Education: Women First Revisited* (London: Routledge, 2016), 1–20.

Walsh, Brendan, 'History of Education in Ireland' in Brendan Walsh (ed.), *Education Studies in Ireland: The Key Disciplines* (Dublin: Gill & Macmillan, 2011), 34–71.

Walsh, John, *The Politics of Expansion: The Transformation of Educational Policy in the Republic of Ireland, 1957–72* (Manchester: Manchester University Press, 2009).

Walsh, John, 'The Transformation of Higher Education, 1945–80' in Andrew Loxley, Aidan Seery and John Walsh (eds), *Higher Education in Ireland: Practices, Policies, Possibilities* (Basingstoke: Palgrave Macmillan, 2014), 5–32.

Walsh, John, *Higher Education in Ireland: Politics, Policy and Power – A History of Higher Education in the Irish State* (London: Palgrave Macmillan, 2018).

Walsh, Thomas, 'The Revised Programme of Instruction, 1900–1922' in *Irish Educational Studies*, vol. 26, no. 2 (2007), 127–43.

Walsh, Thomas, 'Concepts of Children and Childhood from an Educational Perspective 1900–1940: Context, Curriculum and Experiences' in Ciara Boylan and Ciara Gallagher (eds), *Constructions of the Irish Child in the Independence Period* (Basingstoke: Palgrave Macmillan, 2018), 279–305.

Webb, Ida M., *The Challenge of Change in Physical Education: Chelsea College of Physical Education-Chelsea School, University of Brighton 1898–1998* (London: Falmer Press, 1999).

Welshman, John, 'Physical Education and the School Medical Service in England and Wales, 1907–1939' in *Social History of Medicine*, vol. 9, no. 1 (1996), 31–48.

Welshman, John, 'Physical Culture and Sport in Schools in England and Wales, 1900–40' in *The International Journal of the History of Sport*, vol. 15, no. 1 (1998), 54–75.

Wooley, Mary Catherine, 'Experiencing the History National Curriculum 1991–2011: Voices of Veteran Teachers' in *History of Education*, vol. 48, no. 2 (2019), 212–32.

Young, Christopher, 'Sport in West and North Europe' in Robert Edelman and Wayne Wilson (eds), *The Oxford Handbook of Sports History* (Oxford: Oxford University Press, 2017), 331–45.

Unpublished theses

Cooney, Ellen, 'The Tendency towards Physical Training in the Sokol Way' (unpublished Minor Dissertation for Degree of M.A. in Educational Science, University College Dublin, 1939).

Cotter, Michael Anthony, 'An Investigation into the Teaching of Physical Education in National Schools (Public Primary Schools) in the Republic of Ireland' (unpublished M.Ed. thesis, Trinity College Dublin, 1978).

Duffy, Patrick, 'State Policy on School Physical Education with Specific Reference to the Period 1960–1996' (unpublished Ph.D. thesis, St Patrick's College Maynooth, 1997).

Heffernan, Conor, 'Physical Culture in Ireland, 1893–1939' (unpublished Ph.D. thesis, University College Dublin, 2018).

McGourty, Seán, 'The Boys' Physical Education Curriculum in Secondary Schools in Northern Ireland' (unpublished M.A. in Education thesis, Queen's University, Belfast, 1987).

McDonough, Captain Michael, 'Physical Education and the Sports Complex in the Community School' (unpublished M.Ed. thesis, Trinity College Dublin 1980).

Moran, Joseph, 'The Role of the Military in the Development of Physical Education in Irish Schools from 1922 to 1973' (unpublished M.Science (Sports Studies) Dissertation, University College Dublin, 2013).

O'Donoghue, Thomas, 'The Policy of the State on the Promotion of Physical Education in Irish Secondary Schools 1924–73' (unpublished M.Ed. thesis, Trinity College Dublin, 1985).

Online sources

Dáil debates

Available at <https://www.oireachtas.ie>.

'Dáil Éireann Debate – Tuesday, 6 Jun 1961. Vol. 189. No. 10. Ceisteanna – Questions. Oral Answers. – Physical Training in National Schools.' Retrieved from <https://www.oireachtas.ie/en/debates/debate/dail/1961-06-06/52/> [Accessed 2 November 2020].

'Dáil Éireann Debate – Tuesday, 27 Mar 1962. Vol. 194. No. 4. Ceisteanna – Questions. Oral Answers. – School Physical Training Courses.' Retrieved from <https://www.oireachtas.ie/en/debates/debate/dail/1962-03-27/71/> [Accessed 2 November 2020].

'Dáil Éireann Debate – Tuesday, 18 May 1965. Vol. 215. No. 11. Ceisteanna – Questions. Oral Answers. – Physical Education.' Retrieved from <https://www.oireachtas.ie/en/debates/debate/dail/1965-05-18/58/> [Accessed 4 November 2020].

'Dáil Éireann Debate – Tuesday, 2 Apr 1968. Vol. 233. No. 11. Ceisteanna – Questions. Oral Answers. – Physical Education in Schools.' Retrieved from <https://www.oireachtas.ie/en/debates/debate/dail/1968-04-02/35/> [Accessed 2 November 2020].

'Dáil Éireann Debate – Thursday, 7 Nov 1968. Vol. 236. No. 14. Ceisteanna – Questions. Oral Answers. – Physical Training in Schools.' Retrieved from <https://www.oireachtas.ie/en/debates/debate/dail/1968-11-07/65/> [Accessed 2 November 2020].

'Dáil Éireann Debate – Thursday, 20 Nov 1969. Vol. 242. No. 9. Ceisteanna – Questions. Oral Answers. – Physical Training in Schools.' Retrieved from <https://www.oireachtas.ie/en/debates/debate/dail/1969-11-20/57/> [Accessed 2 November 2020].

'Dáil Éireann Debate – Tuesday, 19 May 1970. Vol. 246. No. 10. Ceisteanna – Questions. Oral Answers. – School Physical Training.' Retrieved from <https://www.oireachtas.ie/en/debates/debate/dail/1970-05-19/17/> [Accessed 2 November 2020].

'Dáil Éireann Debate – Tuesday, 12 Jun 1973. Vol. 266. No. 2. Ceisteanna – Questions. Oral Answers. – Special Equipment Grants.' Retrieved from <https://www.oireachtas.ie/en/debates/debate/dail/1973-06-12/26/> [Accessed 4 November 2020].

'Dáil Éireann Debate – Wednesday, 30 Nov. 1977. Vol. 302. No. 3. Written Answers – Physical Education.' Retrieved from <https://www.oireachtas.ie/en/debates/debate/dail/1977-11-30/68/> [Accessed 2 November 2020].

'Dáil Éireann Debate – Wednesday, 8 Mar 1978. Vol. 304. No. 7. Ceisteanna – Questions. Oral Answers. – Primary Schools.' Retrieved from <https://www.oireachtas.ie/en/debates/debate/dail/1978-03-08/8/?> [Accessed 4 November 2020].

'Dáil Éireann Debate – Wednesday, 21 Feb 1979, Vol. 311. No. 10. Ceisteanna – Questions. Oral Answers. – Physical Education in Schools.' Retrieved from <https://www.oireachtas.ie/en/debates/debate/dail/1979-02-21/25/> [Accessed 2 November 2020].

'Dáil Éireann Debate – Thursday, 28 Jun 1984. Vol. 352. No. 5.' Retrieved from <https://www.oireachtas.ie/en/debates/debate/dail/1984-06-28/218/> [Accessed 4 November 2020].

'Dáil Éireann Debate – Tuesday, 20 May 1986. Vol. 366. No. 8. Written Answers. – Physical Education Equipment.' Retrieved from <https://www.oireachtas.ie/en/debates/debate/dail/1986-05-20/131/> [Accessed 3 November 2020].

'Dáil Éireann Debate – Tuesday, 8 Nov. 1988. Vol. 383. No. 8. Private Members' Business. – National Lottery (Amendment) Bill, 1988: Second Stage.' Retrieved from <https://www.oireachtas.ie/en/debates/debate/dail/1988-11-08/21/> [Accessed 2 November 2020].

'Dáil Éireann Debate – Thursday, 8 Dec 1988. Vol. 385. No. 4. Written Answers. – Physical Education.' Retrieved from <https://www.oireachtas.ie/en/debates/debate/dail/1988-12-08/42/> [Accessed 2 November 2020].

'Dáil Debates – Wednesday 15 February 1989, Vol. 387. No. 2. Written Answers – Physical Education.' Retrieved from <https://www.oireachtas.ie/ga/debates/debate/dail/1989-02-15/95/> [Accessed 30 October 2020].

'Dáil Éireann Debate – Tuesday, 14 Nov 1989. Vol. 393. No. 1. Written Answers. – Physical Education Programmes.' Retrieved from <https://www.oireachtas.ie/en/debates/debate/dail/1989-11-14/235/?> [Accessed 3 November 2020].

'Dáil Éireann Debate – Tuesday, 6 Feb 1990. Vol. 395. No. 3. Written Answers. – Clane, Kildare, School Facilities.' Retrieved from <https://www.oireachtas.ie/en/debates/debate/dail/1990-02-06/144/> [Accessed 4 November 2020].

'Dáil Éireann Debate – Wednesday, 13 Mar 1991. Vol. 406. No. 4. Ceisteanna – Questions. Oral Answers. – Handbook on Physical Education.' Retrieved from <https://www.oireachtas.ie/en/debates/debate/dail/1991-03-13/25/> [Accessed 2 November 2020].

'Dáil Éireann Debate – Thursday, 13 Jun 1991. Vol. 409. No. 8. Ceisteanna – Questions. Oral Answers. – PE in National Schools.' Retrieved from <https://www.oireachtas.ie/en/debates/debate/dail/1991-06-13/18/> [Accessed 3 November 2020].

'Dáil Éireann Debate – Wednesday, 3 Nov 1993. Vol. 435. No. 4. Written Answers. – Donegal Schools' Facilities.' Retrieved from <https://www.oireachtas.ie/en/debates/debate/dail/1993-11-03/68/> [Accessed 4 November 2020].

'Dáil Éireann Debate – Tuesday, 11 Oct 1994. Vol. 445. No. 6. Written Answers – Physical Education.' Retrieved from <https://www.oireachtas.ie/en/debates/debate/dail/1994-10-11/351/> [Accessed 2 November 2020].

'Dáil Éireann Debate –Thursday, 16 Feb 1995. Vol. 449. No. 3. Written Answers – Promotion of Physical Education.' Retrieved from <https://www.oireachtas.ie/en/debates/debate/dail/1995-02-16/66/> [Accessed 2 November 2020].

'Dáil Éireann Debate – Tuesday, 23 Jan. 1996.Vol. 460. No. 3. Written Answers. – Physical Education Facilities.' Retrieved from <https://www.oireachtas.ie/en/debates/debate/dail/1996-01-23/235/> [Accessed 4 November 2020].

'Dáil Éireann Debate – Tuesday, 18 Feb 1997. Vol. 475. No. 1. Written Answers – Teacher Appointments.' <https://www.oireachtas.ie/en/debates/debate/dail/1997-02-18/186/> [Accessed 2 November 2020].

'Dáil Éireann Debate – Wednesday, 7 May 1997. Vol. 478. No. 7. Written Answers – Sports Capital Programme.' Retrieved from <https://www.oireachtas.ie/en/debates/debate/dail/1997-05-07/173/> [Accessed 4 November 2020].

'Dáil Éireann Debate, Tuesday 7 Oct. 1997. Vol. 481. No. 1. Written Answers.' Retrieved from <https://www.oireachtas.ie/en/debates/debate/dail/1997-10-07/221/> [Accessed 2 November 2020].

'Dáil Éireann Debate– Thursday 16 Oct. 1997. Vol. 481. No. 6. Written Answers – Physical Education.' Retrieved from <https://www.oireachtas.ie/en/debates/debate/dail/1997-10-16/86/> [Accessed 2 November 2020].

'Dáil Éireann Debate – Tuesday, 12 May 1998 Vol. 490. No. 7. Written Answers. – Physical Education Places.' Retrieved from <https://www.oireachtas.ie/en/debates/debate/dail/1998-05-12/35/> [Accessed 2 November 2020].

'Dáil Éireann Debate – Tuesday, 8 Feb 2000. Vol. 513. No. 6. Written Answers – Physical Education Facilities.' Retrieved from <https://www.oireachtas.ie/en/debates/debate/dail/2000-02-08/34/> [Accessed 2 November 2020].

'In Committee on Finance-Vote no. 45-Office of the Minister for Education (Resumed).' Dáil Éireann Debate. Vol. 29, No. 4.17 April 1929.' Retrieved from <http://oireachtasdebates.oireachtas.ie/debates%20authoring/DebatesWeb Pack.nsf/takes/dail1929041700036?opendocument&highlight=physical%20 training> [Accessed 7 December 2017].

'In Committee on Finance-Estimates for Public Services.-Vote 45-Office for the Minister for Education (Resumed)' Dáil Éireann Debate, 2 November 1932.' Retrieved from <http://oireachtasdebates.oireachtas.ie/Debates%20 Authoring/DebatesWebPack.nsf/takes/dail1932110200020?opendocument& highlight=physical%20training> [Accessed 7 December 2017].

'In Committee on Finance-Vote No. 45-Office of the Minister for Education.' Dáil Éireann Debate. Vol. 51, No. 12. 11 April 1934.' Retrieved from <http:// oireachtasdebates.oireachtas.ie/debates%20authoring/DebatesWebPack.nsf/ takes/dail1934041100023?opendocument&highlight=physical%20training> [Accessed 7 December 2017].

'In Committee on Finance.-Vote 45-Oifig an Aire Oireachais.' Dáil Éireann Debate. Vol. 80, No. 13. 6 June 1940. Retrieved from <http://oireachtasdebates. oireachtas.ie/debates%20authoring/DebatesWebPack.nsf/takes/dail 1940060600018?opendocument&highlight=physical%20training> [Accessed 7 December 2017].

'Joint Committee on Justice, Equality, Defence and Women's Rights debate - Wednesday, 13 Jan 2010. Role of Defence Forces in Promoting Physical

Fitness: Discussion.' Retrieved from <https://www.oireachtas.ie/en/debates/
debate/joint_committee_on_justice_equality_defence_and_womens_rights/
2010-01-13/2/> [Accessed 30 October 2020].

General online sources

'Blackrock College: History' Retrieved from <https://www.blackrockcollege.com/
about/history-of-blackrock> [Accessed 14 November 2018].

'Census 1961 Volume 1 – Population, Area and Valuation of Each DED and
Each Larger Unit of Area' Retrieved from <https://www.cso.ie/en/media/
csoie/census/census1961results/volume1/C 1961_VOL_1_T1.pdf> [Accessed
6 October 2020].

'Curriculum and Syllabus: Phase 1 Physical Education in Senior Cycle' Retrieved
from https://www.education.ie/en/Schools-Colleges/InformationCurriculum-
and-Syllabus/leaving-certificate-physical-education.html [Accessed 25 March
2018].

'*Curriculum Review, Summary of Proposal for the Revised Primary Curriculum and
Its Assessment Arrangements* (Belfast, 2002)' Retrieved from <http://www.
nicurriculum.org.uk/docs/background/curriculum_review/primsubt.pdf>
[Accessed 19 July 2020].

'History of St Mary's University College' Retrieved from <https://www.stmarys-
belfast.ac.uk/general/history/default.asp> [Accessed 16 November 2020].

'Leaving Certificate Physical Education 2020' Retrieved from <https://www.exam-
inations.ie/?l=en&mc=ex&sc=pe> [Accessed 30 October 2020].

'MacRory Cup: The Stats' Retrieved from <https://www.irishnews.com/sport/
gaafootball/2019/11/01/news/macrory-cup-the-stats-1748138/> [Accessed 27
October 2020].

'Malcolm Sutton. An Index of Deaths from the Conflict in Ireland' Retrieved from
<https://cain.ulster.ac.uk/sutton/book/> [Accessed 2 December 2020].

'Ministers for Education from 1921 to Date' Retrieved from <https://www.educa-
tion.ie/en/The-Department/Ministers/Ministers-for-Education-From-1921-
to-Date.html> [Accessed 14 September 2017].

'Northern Ireland's Footballing Greats: Hugh Barr' Retrieved from <http://nifoot
ball.blogspot.com/2006/07/hugh-barr.html> [Accessed 19 August 2020].

O'Keeffe, Declan, 'Clongowes Down through the Years' Retrieved from <https://
www.jesuit.ie/blog/declan-okeeffe/clongowes-down-the-years/> [Accessed 28
November 2020].

'Physical Education in the School Curriculum. ICHPER International Questionnaire Report Part 1, 1967–1968 Revision (Washington, DC: ICHPER, 1969)' Retrieved from <https://files.eric.ed.gov/fulltext/ED109125.pdf> [Accessed 28 October 2020].

Puirseil, Niamh, 'The Schoolmasters' Rebellion: Teachers, the INTO and 1916' Published in Saothar 41 (2016) Retrieved from <http://www.niamhpuirseil.ie/the-schoolmasters-rebellion-teachers-the-into-and-1916> [Accessed 23 September 2020].

'Roll of Honour: Danske Bank Ulster Schools' Cup' Retrieved from <https://www.ulsterrugby.com/rugby-in-ulster/rugby-development/schools/roll-of-honour/> [Accessed 20 June 2020].

'The Emergency 1939–1945' Retrieved from <http://www.military.ie/info-centre/defence-forces-history/the-emergency-1939-1946/> [Accessed 2 November 2017].

'The Official Home of Ulster Rugby: Roll of Honour' Retrieved from <https://www.ulsterrugby.com/rugby-in-ulster/rugby-development/schools/roll-of-honour/> [Accessed 20 October 2019].

'Ulster Schools GAA' Retrieved from <http://www.danskebankulsterschoolsgaa.com/history/> [Accessed 27 October 2020].

Van Esbeck, Edmund, 'Irish Game in Debt to Schools' Rugby' Retrieved from <https://www.independent.ie/sport/rugby/edmund-van-esbeck-irish-game-in-debt-to-schools-rugby-26014739.html> [Accessed 20 October 2019].

Index

Sport, History and Culture

This series publishes monographs, edited collections and reprints of classic studies on the history and the contemporary role of sport, primarily in Britain and Europe but including other parts of the world. The editors wish to make available the very best of recent doctoral and post-doctoral work in the subject area whilst also looking to established scholars for major new books or collections of articles.

Although the focus of the series is historical, it also embraces more contemporary interdisciplinary studies of the role of sport as a local, national and global phenomenon. The series includes both new and established areas of research into the class, age and gender dimensions of sport as well as its political and ideological aspects, including nationalism, imperialism and post-colonialism. The editors wish to encourage economic and transnational studies of sport as well as new work on ethnicity, sports literature and material culture. The series will also reflect on the significance for the writing of sports history of new cultural and theoretical debates.

Genuinely international in approach, the series also seeks to publish English translations of some of the most outstanding scholarship on the history and culture of sport in Europe, South America and beyond. The series aims to act as a focus for the historical study of sport internationally and facilitate interdisciplinary debate on the subject.

Printed by
CPI books GmbH, Leck